D0016688

SAGE LIBRARY OF EDUCATIONAL THOUGHT
AND PRACTICE

Foundations of Educational Thought

VOLUME 3
Postmodern Educational Thought (1979–1991)

Edited by
Eugene F. Provenzo, Jr.

With the assistance of
Asterie Baker Provenzo

Los Angeles • London • New Delhi • Singapore

Introduction and editorial arrangement © Eugene F. Provenzo, Jr. 2008

First published 2008

SAGE Publications Ltd
1 Oliver's Yard
55 City Road
London EC1Y 1SP

SAGE Publications Inc.
2455 Teller Road
Thousand Oaks, California 91320

SAGE Publications India Pvt Ltd
B 1/I 1, Mohan Cooperative Industrial Area
Mathura Road
New Delhi 110 044

SAGE Publications Asia-Pacific Pte Ltd
33 Pekin Street #02-01
Far East Square
Singapore 048763

Library of Congress Control Number: 2007934761

British Library Cataloguing in Publication Data

A catalogue record for this book is available from the British Library

ISBN 978-1-4129-4586-8 (set of four volumes)

Typeset by Star Compugraphics Private Limited, Delhi
Printed on paper from sustainable resources
Printed and bound in Zrinski d.d. Croatia

Contents

VOLUME 3
Postmodern Educational Thought (1979–1991)

Introduction: Postmodern (1979–1991)

Eugene F. Provenzo, Jr.

Modern education can be seen as having its roots in the late Renaissance and Early Modern period. During the mid-nineteenth century, modern education evolved into mass education with standardized curriculums, grading, degree requirements, grade classification and assignment, and public accreditation and certification. Education came to be increasingly dominated by the modern nation state, and was idealized, somewhat falsely, as primarily serving the needs of the individual and a generalized idea of progress.

Volumes 3 and 4 include writings that emerge as part of a postmodern consciousness. These works in large part rejected, or at the very least challenged, the metanarratives of modernity. Our dividing line for the volume is 1979, the year of publication of Jean Francois Lyotard's (1924–1998) seminal work *La Condition Postmoderne: Rapport Sur Le Savoir (The Postmodern Condition: A Report on Knowledge)*. According to Lyotard, the grand narratives of the modern period such as the mastery of the world through science, the possibility of absolute freedom, and the theme of progress were all challenged by the emergence of a series of micronarratives characteristic of the new era.

In the case of the Social and Cultural Foundations of Education, new writings emerge that are reflective of the postmodern reality. For example, in his 1981 article "The Day Our Children Disappear: Predictions of a Media Ecologist," Neil Postman argues that our traditional notion of childhood is disappearing as new forms of learning and culture such as television come to dominate the experience of children. Likewise, David Elkind argues in his 1997 article "The Death of Child Nature: Education in the Postmodern World" that postmodern conditions are radically redefining the family.

In addition, articles in the field begin to reflect a greater diversity of authors. Women and minorities are increasingly included, as are individuals with alternative sexual orientations. At the same time, the literature in the field increasingly challenges the idea of schools primarily benefiting the individual rather than special interest groups and the power elite.

Volume 3 begins with a selection from Gregory Bateson's *Mind and Nature* in which he challenges what we teach and connect with what we teach in the curriculum of the schools. We end Volume 4 with Vaclav Havel's 1994 article, "The Need for Transcendence in the Postmodern World." It is the only article in the four volumes that is not in chronological order. We include it at the end of this collection as a guide to addressing the realities and demands of the postmodern condition.

70

Introduction: Mind and Nature

Gregory Bateson

Plotinus the Platonist proves by means of the blossoms and leaves that from the Supreme God, whose beauty it invisible and ineffable, Providence reaches dawn to the things of earth here below. He points out that these frail and mortal objects could not be endowed with a beauty so immaculate and so exquisitely wrought, did they not issue from the Divinity which endlessly pervades with its invisible and unchanging beauty all things.

– Saint Augustine, *The City of God*

In June 1977, I thought I had the beginnings of two books. One I called *The Evolutionary Idea* and the other *Every Schoolboy Knows*.[1] The first was to be an attempt to reexamine the theories of biological evolution in the light of cybernetics and information theory. But as I began to write that book, I found it difficult to write with a real audience in mind who, I could hope, would understand the formal and therefore simple presuppositions of what I was saying. It became monstrously evident that schooling in this country and in England and, I suppose, in the entire Occident was so careful to avoid all crucial issues that I would have to write a second book to explain what seemed to me elementary ideas relevant to evolution and to almost any other biological or social thinking – to daily life and to the eating of breakfast. Official education was telling people almost nothing of the nature of all those things on the seashores and in the redwood forests, in the deserts and the plains. Even grown-up persons with children of their own cannot give a reasonable account of concepts such as entropy, sacrament, syntax, number, quantity, pattern, linear relation, name, class, relevance, energy, redundancy, force, probability, parts, whole, information, tautology, homology, mass (either Newtonian or Christian), explanation, description, rule of dimensions, logical type, metaphor, topology, and so on. What are butterflies? What are starfish? What are beauty and ugliness?

It seemed to me that the writing out of some of these very elementary ideas could be entitled, with a litle irony, "*Every Schoolboy Knows.*"

But as I sat in Lindisfarne working on these two manuscripts, sometimes adding a piece to one and sometimes a piece to the other, the two gradually

Source: Gregory Bateson, *Mind and Nature* (New York: E.P. Dutton, 1979), pp. 3–21.

came together, and the product of that coming together was what I think is called a *Platonic* view.[2] It seemed to me that in "*Schoolboy*," I was laying down very elementary ideas about *epistemology* (see Glossary), that is, about *how we can know anything*. In the pronoun *we*, I of course included the starfish and the redwood forest, the segmenting egg, and the Senate of the United States.

And in the *anything* which these creatures variously know, I included "how to grow into five-way symmetry," "how to survive a forest fire," "how to grow and still stay the same shape," "how to learn," "how to write a constitution," "how to invent and drive a car," "how to count to seven," and so on. Marvelous creatures with almost miraculous knowledges and skills.

Above all, I included "how to evolve," because it seemed to me that both evolution and learning must fit the same formal regularities or so-called laws. I was, you see, starting to use the ideas of "*Schoolboy*" to reflect, not upon our own knowing, but upon that *wider knowing* which is the glue holding together the starfishes and sea anemones and redwood forests and human committees.

My two manuscripts were becoming a single book because there is a single knowing which characterizes evolution as well as *aggregates* of humans, even though committees and nations may seem stupid to two-legged geniuses like you and me.

I was transcending that line which is sometimes supposed to enclose the human being. In other words, as I was writing, mind became, for me, a reflection of large parts and many parts of the natural world outside the thinker.

On the whole, it was not the crudest, the simplest, the most animalistic and primitive aspects of the human species that were reflected in the natural phenomena. It was, rather, the more complex, the aesthetic, the intricate, and the elegant aspects of people that reflected nature. It was not my greed, my purposiveness, my so-called "animal," so-called "instincts," and so forth that I was recognizing on the other side of that mirror, over there in "nature." Rather, I was seeing there the roots of human symmetry, beauty and ugliness, aesthetics, the human being's very aliveness and little bit of wisdom. His wisdom, his bodily grace, and even his habit of making beautiful objects are just as "animal" as his cruelty. After all, the very word "animal" means "endowed with mind or spirit (*animus*)."

Against this background, those theories of man that start from the most animalistic and maladapted psychology turn out to be improbable first premises from which to approach the psalmist's question: "Lord, What is man?"

I never could accept the first step of the Genesis story: "In the beginning the earth was without form and void." That primary *tabula rasa* would have set a formidable problem in thermodynamics for the next billion years. Perhaps the earth never was any more a *tabula rasa* than is, a human zygote – a fertilized egg.

It began to seem that the old-fashioned and still-established ideas about epistemology, especially human epistemology, were a reflection of an obsolete physics and contrasted in a curious way with the little we seem to know about living things. It was as if members of the species, man, were supposed to be totally unique and totally materialistic against the background of a living universe which was generalized (rather than unique) and spiritual (rather than materialistic).

There seems to be something like a Gresham's law of cultural evolution according to which the oversimplified ideas will always displace the sophisticated and the vulgar and hateful will always displace the beautiful. And yet the beautiful persists.

It began to seem as if organized matter – and I know nothing about unorganized matter, if there be any – in even such a simple set of relations as exists in a steam engine with a governor was wise and sophisticated compared with the picture of human spirit that orthodox materialism and a large part of orthodox religion currently drew.

The germ of these ideas had been in my mind since I was a boy. But let me start from two contexts in which these thoughts began to insist on utterance: In the 1950s, I had two teaching tasks. I was teaching psychiatric residents at a Veterans Administration mental hospital in Palo Alto and young beatniks in the California School of Fine Arts in San Francisco. I want to tell you how those two courses commenced, how I approached those two contrasting audiences. If you put these two first lectures side by side, you will see what I am trying to say.

To the psychiatrists, I presented a challenge in the shape of a small exam paper, telling them that by the end of the course they should understand the questions in it. Question I asked for brief definitions of (a) "sacrament" and (b) "entropy."

The young psychiatrists in the 1950s were, in general, unable to answer *either* question. Today, a few more could begin to talk about entropy (see Glossary). And I suppose there are still some Christians who could say what a sacrament is?

I was offering my class the core notions of 2,500 years of thought about religion and science. I felt that if they were going to be doctors (medical doctors) of the human soul, they should at least have a foot on each side of the ancient arguments. They should be familiar with the central ideas of both religion and science.

For the art students, I was more direct. It was a small group of about ten to fifteen students, and I knew that I would be walking into an atmosphere of skepticism bordering on hostility. When I entered it was clear that I was expected to be an incarnation of the devil, who would argue for the common sense of atomic warfare and pesticides. In those days (and even today?), science was believed to be "value-free" and not guided by "emotions."

I was prepared for that. I had two paper bags, and the first of these I opened, producing a freshly cooked crab, which I placed on the table. I then challenged the class somewhat as follows: "I want you to produce arguments which will convince me that this object is the remains of a living thing. You may imagine, if you will, that you are Martians and that on Mars you are familiar with living things, being indeed yourselves alive. But, of course, you have never seen crabs or lobsters. A number of objects like this, many of them fragmentary, have arrived, perhaps by meteor. You are to inspect them and arrive at the conclusion that they are the remains of living things. How would you arrive at that conclusion?"

Of course, the question set for the psychiatrists was the *same question* as that which I set for the artists: Is there a biological species of entropy?

Both questions concerned the underlying notion of a dividing line between the world of the living (where *distinctions* are drawn and *difference* can be a cause) and the world of nonliving billiard balls and galaxies (where forces and impacts are the "causes" of events). These are the two worlds that Jung (following the Gnostics) calls *creatura* (the living) and *pleroma* (the non-living).[3] I was asking: What is the difference between the physical world of pleroma, where forces and impacts provide sufficient basis of explanation, and the *creatura*, where nothing can be understood until *differences* and *distinctions* are invoked?

In my life, I have put the descriptions of sticks and stones and billiard balls and galaxies in one box, the pleroma, and have left them alone. In the other box, I put living things: crabs, people, problems of beauty, and problems of difference. The contents of the second box are the subject of this book.

I was griping recently about the shortcomings of occidental education. It was in a letter to my fellow regents of the University of California, and the following phrase crept into my letter:

> "*Break the pattern which connects the items of learning and you necessarily destroy all quality,*"

I offer you the phrase *the pattern which connects* as a synonym, another possible title for this book.

The pattern which connects. Why do schools teach almost nothing of the pattern which connects? Is it that teachers know that they carry the kiss of death which will turn to tastelessness whatever they touch and therefore they are wisely unwilling to touch or teach anything of real-life importance? Or is it that they carry the kiss of death *because* they dare not teach anything of real-life importance? What's wrong with them?

What pattern connects the crab to the lobster and the orchid to the primrose and all the four of them to me? And me to you? And all the six of us to the amoeba in one direction and to the back-ward schizophrenic in another?

I want to tell you why I have been a biologist all my life, what it is that I have been trying to study. What thoughts can I share regarding the total biological world in which we live and have our being? How is it put together?

What now must be said is difficult, appears to be quite *empty*, and is of very great and deep importance to you and to me. At this historic juncture, I believe it to be important to the survival of the whole biosphere, which you know is threatened.

What is the pattern which connects all the living creatures?

Let me go back to my crab and my class of beatniks. I was very lucky to be teaching people who were not scientists and the bias of whose minds was even antiscientific. All untrained as they were, their bias was aesthetic. I would define that word, for the moment, by saying that they were *not* like Peter Bly, the character of whom Wordsworth sang

> *A primrose by the river's brim*
> *A yellow primrose was to him;*
> *And it was nothing more.*

Rather, they would meet the primrose with *recognition* and *empathy*. By *aesthetic*, I mean responsive to *the pattern which connects*. So you see, I was lucky. Perhaps by coincidence, I faced them with what was (though I knew it not) an aesthetic question: *How are you related to this creature? What pattern connects you to it?*

By putting them on an imaginary planet, "Mars," I stripped them of all thought of lobsters, amoebas, cabbages, and so on and forced the diagnosis of life back into identification with living self: "*You* carry the bench marks, the criteria, with which you could look at the crab to find that it, too, carries the same marks." My question was much more sophisticated than I knew.

So they looked at the crab. And first of all, they came up with the observation that it is *symmetrical*; that is, the right side resembles the left.

"Very good. You mean it's *composed*, like a painting?" (No response.)

Then they observed that one claw was bigger than the other. So it was *not* symmetrical.

I suggested that if a number of these objects had come by meteor, they would find that in almost all specimens it was the same side (right or left) that carried the bigger claw. (No response. "What's Bateson getting at?")

Going back to symmetry, somebody said that "*yes, one claw is bigger than the other, but both claws are made of the same parts.*"

Ah! What a beautiful and noble statement that is, how the speaker politely flung into the trash can the idea that *size* could be of primary or profound importance and went after the *pattern which connects*. He discarded an asymmetry in size in favor of a deeper symmetry in formal relations.

Yes, indeed, the two claws are characterized (ugly word) by embodying *similar relations between parts*. Never quantities, always shapes, forms, and relations. This was, indeed, something that characterized the crab as a member of *creatura*, a living thing.

Later, it appeared that not only are the two claws built on the same "ground plan," (i.e., upon corresponding sets of relations between corresponding parts) but that these relations between corresponding parts extend down the series of the walking legs. We could recognize in every leg pieces that corresponded to the pieces in the claw.

And in your own body, of course, the same sort of thing is true. Humerus in the upper arm corresponds to femur in the thigh, and radius-ulna corresponds co tibia-fibula; the carpals in the wrist correspond to tarsals in the foot; fingers correspond to toes.

The anatomy of the crab is repetitive and rhythmical. It is, like music, repetitive with modulation. Indeed, the direction from head toward tail corresponds to a sequence in time: In embryology, the head is older than the tail, A flow of information is possible, from front to rear.

Professional biologists talk about phylogenetic *homology* (see Glossary) for that *class* of facts of which one example is the formal resemblance between my limb bones and those of a horse. Another example is the formal resemblance between the appendages of a crab and those of a lobster.

That is one class of facts. Another (somehow similar?) class of facts is what they call *serial homology*. One example is the rhythmic repetition with change from appendage to appendage down the length of the beast (crab or man); another (perhaps not quite comparable because of the difference in relation to time) would be the bilateral symmetry of the man or crab.[4]

Let me start again. The parts of a crab are connected by various patterns of bilateral symmetry, of serial homology, and so on. Let us call these patterns *within* the individual growing crab *first-order connections*. But now we look at crab and lobster and we again find connection by pattern. Call it *second-order connection*, or phylogenetic homology.

Now we look at man or horse and find that, here again, we can see symmetries and serial homologies. When we look at the two together, we find the same cross-species sharing of pattern with a difference (phylogenetic homology). And, of course, we also find the same discarding of magnitudes in favor of shapes, patterns, and relations. In other words, as this distribution of formal resemblances is spelled out, it turns out that gross anatomy exhibits three levels or logical types of descriptive propositions:

1. The parts of any member of *Creatura* are to be compared with other parts of the same individual to give first-order connections.
2. Crabs are to be compared with lobsters or men with horses to find similar relations between parts (i.e., to give second-order connections).
3. The *comparison* between crabs and lobsters is to be compared with the comparison between man and horse to provide third-order connections.

We have constructed a ladder of how to think about – about what? Oh, yes, the pattern which connects.

My central thesis can now be approached in words: The *pattern which connects is a metapattern*. It is a pattern of patterns. It is that metapattern which defines the vast generalization that, indeed, *it is patterns which connect.*

I warned some pages back that we would encounter emptiness, and indeed it is so. Mind is empty; it is no-thing. It exists only in its ideas, and these again are no-things. Only the ideas are immanent, embodied in their examples. And the examples are, again, no-things. The claw, *as an example*, is not the *Ding an sich*; it is precisely *not* the "*thing in itself.*" Rather, it is what mind makes of it, namely, an *example* of something or other.

Let me go back to the classroom of young artists.

You will recall that I had *two* paper bags. In one of them was the crab. In the other I had a beautiful large conch shell. By what token, I asked them, could they know that the spiral shell had been part of a living thing?

When she was about seven, somebody gave my daughter Cathy a cat's-eye mounted as a ring. She was wearing it, and I asked her what it was. She said it was a cat's-eye.

I said, "But what *is* it?"

"Well, I know it's not the eye of a cat. I guess it's some sort of stone."

I said, "Take it off and look at the back of it."

She did that and exclaimed, "Oh, it's got a spiral on it! It must have belonged to something alive."

Actually, these greenish disks are the opercula (lids) of a species of tropical marine snail. Soldiers brought lots of them back from the Pacific at the end of World War II.

Cathy was right in her major premise that all spirals in this world except whirlpools, galaxies, and spiral winds are, indeed, made by living things. There is an extensive literature on this subject, which some readers may be interested in looking up (the key words are *Fibonacci series* and *golden section*).

What comes out of all this is that a spiral is a figure that *retains its shape* (*i.e., its proportions*) *as it grows* in one dimension by addition at the open end. You see, there are no truly static spirals.

But the class had difficulty. They looked for all the beautiful formal characteristics that they had joyfully found in the crab. They had the idea that formal symmetry, repetition of parts, modulated repetition, and so on were what teacher wanted. But the spiral was *not* bilaterally symmetrical; it was not segmented.

They had to discover (a) that all symmetry and segmentation were somehow a result, a payoff from, the fact of growth; and (b) that growth makes its formal demands; and (c) that one of these is satisfied (in a mathematical, an ideal, sense) by spiral form.

So the conch shell carries the snail's *prochronism* – its record of how, *in its own past*, it successively solved a formal problem in pattern formation (see Glossary). It, too, proclaims its affiliation under that pattern of patterns which connects.

So far, all the examples that I have offered – the patterns which have membership in the pattern which connects, the anatomy of crab and lobster, the conch, and man and horse – have been superficially static. The examples have been the frozen shapes, results of regularized change, indeed, but themselves finally fixed, like the figures in Keats' "Ode on a Grecian Urn":

Fair youth, beneath the trees, than can'st not leave
Thy song, nor ever can those trees be bare;
Bold lover, never never canst thou kiss,
Though winning near the goal – yet do not grieve;
She cannot fade, though thou hast not thy bliss,
Forever wilt thou love, and she be fair!

We have been trained to think of patterns, with the exception of those of music, as fixed affairs. It is easier and lazier that way but, of course, all nonsense. In truth, the right way to begin to think about the pattern which connects is to think of it as *primarily* (whatever that means) a dance of inter-acting parts and only secondarily pegged down by various sorts of physical limits and by those limits which organisms characteristically impose.

There is a story which I have used before and shall use again: A man wanted to know about mind, not in nature, but in his private large computer. He asked it (no doubt in his best Fortran), "Do you compute that you will ever think like a human being?" The machine then set to work to analyze its own computational habits. Finally, the machine printed its answer on a piece of paper, as such machines do. The man ran to get the answer and found, neatly typed, the words:

THAT REMINDS ME OF A STORY

A story is a little knot or complex of that species of connectedness which we call *relevance*. In the 1960s, students were fighting for "relevance," and I would assume that any A is relevant to any B if both A and B are parts or components of the same "story."

Again we face connectedness at more than one level:

First, connection between A and B by virtue of their being components in the same story.

And then, connectedness between people in that all think in terms of stories. (For surely the computer was right. This is indeed how people think.)

Now I want to show that whatever the word *story* means in the story which I told you, the fact of thinking in terms of stories does not isolate human beings as something separate from the starfish and the sea anemones, the coconut palms and the primroses. Rather, if the world be connected, if I am at all fundamentally right in what I am saying, then *thinking in terms of stories* must be shared by all mind or minds, whether ours or those of redwood forests and sea anemones.

Context and relevance must be characteristic not only of all so-called be-havior (those stories which are projected out into "action"), but also of all those internal stories, the sequences of the building up of the sea anemone. Its embryology must be somehow made of the stuff of stories. And behind that, again, the evolutionary process through millions of generations whereby the sea anemone, like you and like me, came to be – that process, too, must be of the stuff of stories. There must be relevance in every step of phylogeny and among the steps.

Prospero says, "We are such stuff as dreams are made on," and surely he is nearly right. But I sometimes think that dreams are only fragments of that stuff. It is as if the stuff of which we are made were totally transparent and therefore imperceptible and as if the only appearances of which we can be aware are cracks and planes of fracture in that transparent matrix. Dreams and percepts and stories are perhaps cracks and irregularities in the uniform and timeless matrix. Was this what Plotinus meant by an "invisible and unchanging beauty which pervades all things?"

What is a story that it may connect the As and Bs, its parts? And is it true that the general fact that parts are connected in this way is at the very roor of what it is to be alive? I offer you the notion of *context*, of *pattern through time*.

What happens when, for example, I go to a Freudian psychoanalyst? I walk into and create something which we will call a *context* that is at least symbolically (as a piece of the world of ideas) limited and isolated by closing the door. The geography of the room and the door is used as a representation of some strange, nongeographic message.

But I come with stories – not just a supply of stories to deliver to the analyst but stories built into my very being. The patterns and sequences of childhood experience are built into me. Father did so and so; my aunt did such and such; and what they did was outside my skin. But whatever it was that I learned, my learning happened within my experiential sequence of what those important others – my aunt, my father – did.

Now I come to the analyst, this newly important other who must be viewed as a father (or perhaps an antifather) because nothing has meaning except it be seen as in some context. This viewing is called the *transference* and is a general phenomenon in human relations. It is a universal characteristic of all interaction between persons because, after all, the shape of what happened between you and me yesterday carries over to shape how we respond to each other today. And that shaping is, in principle, a *transference* from past learning.

This phenomenon of transference exemplifies the truth of the computer's perception that we think in stories. The analyst must be stretched or shrunk onto the Procrustean bed of the patient's childhood stories. But also, by referring to psychoanalysis, I have narrowed the idea of "story." I have suggested that it has something to do with *context*, a crucial concept, partly undefined and therefore to be examined.

And "context" is linked to another undefined notion called "meaning." Without context, words and actions have no meaning at all. This is true not only of human communication in words but also of all communication whatsoever, of all mental process, of all mind, including that which tells the sea anemone how to grow and the amoeba what he should do next.

I am drawing an analogy between context in the superficial and partly conscious business of personal relations and context in the much deeper, more archaic processes of embryology and homology. I am asserting that whatever the word *context* means, it is an appropriate word, the *necessary* word, in the description of all these distantly related processes.

Let us look at homology backwards. Conventionally, people prove that evolution occurred by citing cases of homology. Let me do the reverse. Let me assume that evolution occurred and go on to ask about the nature of homology. Let us ask what some organ *is* according to the light shed upon it by evolutionary theory.

What is an elephant's trunk? What is it phylogenetically? What did genetics tell it to be?

As you know, the answer is that the elephant's trunk is his "nose." (Even Kipling knew!) And I put the word "nose" in quotation marks because the trunk is being defined by an internal process of communication in growth. The trunk is a "nose" by a process of communication: it is the context of the trunk that identifies it as a nose. That which stands between two eyes and north of a mouth is a "nose," and that is that. It is the *context* that fixes the meaning, and it must surely be the receiving context that provides meaning for the genetic instructions. When I call that a "nose" and this a "hand" I am quoting – or misquoting – the developmental instructions in the growing organism, and quoting what the tissues which received the message thought the message intended.

There are people who would prefer to define noses by their "function" – that of smelling. But if you spell out those definitions, you arrive at the same place using a temporal instead of a spatial context. You attach meaning to the organ by seeing it as playing a given part in sequences of interaction between creature and environment. I call that a *temporal* context. The temporal classification cross-cuts the spatial classification of contexts. But in embryology, the first definition must always be in terms of formal relations. The fetal trunk cannot, in general, smell anything. Embryology is *formal*.

Let me illustrate this species of connection, this connecting pattern, a little further by citing a discovery of Goethe's. He was a considerable botanist who had great ability in recognizing the nontrivial (i.e., in recognizing the patterns that connect). He straightened out the vocabulary of the gross comparative anatomy of flowering plants. He discovered that a "leaf" is not satisfactorily defined as "a flat green thing" or a "stem" as "a cylindrical thing." The way to go about the definition – and undoubtedly somewhere deep in the growth processes of the plant, this is how the matter is handled – is to note that buds (i.e., baby stems) form in the angles of leaves. From that, the botanist constructs the definitions on the basis of the relations between stem, leaf, bud, angle, and so on.

"A stem is that which bears leaves."
"A leaf is that which has a bud in its angle."
"A stem is what was once a bud in that position,"

All that is – or should be – familiar. But the next step is perhaps new.

There is a parallel confusion in the teaching of language that has never been straightened out. Professional linguists nowadays may know what's what, but children in school are still taught nonsense. They are told that a "noun" is the "name of a person, place, or thing," that a "verb" is "an action word," and so on. That is, they are taught at a tender age that the way to define something is by what it supposedly *is* in itself, not by its relation to other things.

Most of us can remember being told that a noun is "the name of a person, place, or thing." And we can remember the utter boredom of parsing or analyzing sentences. Today all that should be changed. Children could be told that a noun is a word having a certain relationship to a predicate. A verb has a certain relation to a noun, its subject. And so on. Relationship could be used as basis for definition, and any child could then see that there is something wrong with the sentence "'Go' is a verb."

I remember the boredom of analyzing sentences and the boredom later, at Cambridge, of learning comparative anatomy. Both subjects, as taught, were torturously unreal. We *could* have been told something about the pattern which connects: that all communication necessitates context, that without context, there is no meaning, and that contexts confer meaning because there is classification of contexts. The teacher could have argued that growth and differentiation must be controlled by communication. The shapes of animals and plants are transforms of messages. Language is itself a form of communication. The structure of the input must somehow be reflected as structure in the output. Anatomy *must* contain an analogue of grammar because all anacomy is a transform of message material, which must be contextually shaped. And finally, *contextual shaping* is only another term for *grammar*.

So we come back to the patterns of connection and the more abstract, more general (and most empty) proposition that, indeed, there is a pattern of patterns of connection.

This book is built on the opinion that we are parts of a living world. I have placed as epigraph at the head of this chapter a passage from Saint Augustine in which the saint's epistemology is clearly stated. Today such a statement evokes nostalgia. Most of us have lost that sense of unity of biosphere and humanity which would bind and reassure us all with an affirmation of beauty. Most of us do not today believe that whatever the ups and downs of detail within our limited experience, the larger whole is primarily beautiful.

We have lost the core of Christianity. We have lost Shiva, the dancer of Hinduism whose dance at the trivial level is both creation and destruction but in whole is beauty. We have lost Abraxas, the terrible and beautiful god of both day and night in Gnosticism. We have lost totemism, the sense of parallelism between man's organization and that of the animals and plants. We have lost even the Dying God.

We are beginning to play with ideas of ecology, and although we immediately trivialize these ideas into commerce or politics, there is at least an impulse still in the human breast to unify and thereby sanctify the total natural world, of which we are.

Observe, however, that there have been, and still are, in the world many different and even contrasting epistemologies which have been alike in stressing an ultimate unity and, although this is less sure, which have also stressed the notion that ultimate unity is *aesthetic*. The uniformity of these views gives hope that perhaps the great authority of quantitative science may be insufficient to deny an ultimate unifying beauty.

I hold to the presupposition that our loss of the sense of aesthetic unity was, quite simply, an epistemological mistake. I believe that that mistake may be more serious than all the minor insanities that characterize those older epistemologies which agreed upon the fundamental unity.

A part of the story of our loss of the sense of unity has been elegantly told in Lovejoy's *Great Chain of Being*,[5] which traces the story from classical Greek philosophy to Kant and the beginnings of German idealism in the eighteenth century. This is the story of the idea that the world is/was timelessly created upon *deductive logic*. The idea is clear in the epigraph from *The City of God*. Supreme Mind, or Logos, is at the head of the deductive chain. Below that are the angels, then people, then apes, and so on down to the plants and stones. All is in deductive order and tied into that order by a premise which prefigures our second law of thermodynamics. The premise asserts that the "more perfect" can never be generated by the "less perfect."

In the history of biology, it was Lamarck[6] who inverted the great chain of being. By insisting that mind is immanent in living creatures and could determine their transformations, he escaped from the negative directional premise that the perfect must always precede the imperfect. He then proposed a theory of "transformism" (which we would call *evolution*) which started from infusoria (protozoa) and marched upward to man and woman.

The Lamarckian biosphere was still a *chain*. The unity of epistemology was retained in spite of a shift in emphasis from transcendent Logos to immanent mind.

The fifty years that followed saw the exponential rise of the Industrial Revolution, the triumph of Engineering over Mind, so that the culturally appropriate epistemology for the *Origin of Species* (1859) was an attempt to exclude mind as an explanatory principle. Tilting at a wind-mill.

There were protests much more profound than the shrieks of the Fundamentalists. Samuel Butler, Darwin's ablest critic, saw that the denial of mind as an explanatory principle was intolerable and tried to take evolutionary theory back to Lamarckism. But that would not do because of the hypothesis (shared even by Darwin) of the "inheritance of acquired characteristics." This hypothesis – that the responses of an organism to its environment could affect the genetics of the offspring – was an error.

I shall argue that this error was specifically an epistemological error in logical typing and shall offer a definition of *mind* very different from the notions vaguely held by both Darwin and Lamarck. Notably, I shall assume that thought resembles evolution in being a stochastic (see Glossary) process.

In what is offered in this book, the hierarchic structure of thought, which Bertrand Russell called *logical typing*, will take the place of the hierarchic structure of the Great Chain of Being and an attempt will be made to propose a sacred unity of the biosphere that will contain fewer epistemological errors than the versions of that sacred unity which the various religions of history have offered. What is important is that, tight or wrong, the epistemology shall be *explicit*. Equally explicit criticism will then be possible.

So the immediate task of this book is to construct a picture of how the world is joined together in its mental aspects. How do ideas, information, steps of logical or pragmatic consistency, and the like fit together? How is logic, the classical procedure for making chains of ideas, related to an outside world of things and creatures, parts and wholes? Do ideas really occur in chains, or is this lineal (see Glossary) structure imposed on them by scholars and philosophers? How is the world of logic, which eschews "circular argument," related to a world in which circular trains of causation are the rule rather than the exception?

What has to be investigated and described is a vast network or matrix of interlocking message material and abstract tautologies, premises, and exemplifications.

But, as of 1979, there is no conventional method of describing such a tangle. We do not know even where to begin.

Fifty years ago, we would have assumed that the best procedures for such a task would have been either logical or quantitative, or both. But we shall see as every schoolboy ought to know that logic is precisely unable to deal with recursive circuits without generating paradox and that quantities are precisely not the stuff of complex communicating systems.

In other words, logic and quantity turn out to be inappropriate devices for describing organisms and their interactions and internal organization. The particular nature of this inappropriateness will be exhibited in due course, but for the moment, the reader is asked to accept as true the assertion that, as of 1979, there is no conventional way of explaining or even describing the phenomena of biological organization and human interaction.

John Von Neumann pointed out thirty years ago, in his *Theory of Games*, that the behavioral sciences lack any reduced model which would do for biology and psychiatry what the Newtonian particle did for physics.

There are, however, a number of somewhat disconnected pieces of wisdom that will aid the task of this book. I shall therefore adopt the method of Little Jack Horner, pulling out plums one after the other and exhibiting them side by side to create an array from which we can go on to list some fundamental criteria of mental process.

In Chapter 2, "Every Schoolboy Knows," I shall gather for the reader some examples of what I regard as simple necessary truths – necessary first if the schoolboy is ever to learn to think and then again necessary because, as I believe, the biological world is geared to these simple propositions.

In Chapter 3 I shall operate in the same way but shall bring to the reader's attention a number of cases in which two or more information sources come together to give information of a sort different from what was in either source separately.

At present, there is no existing science whose special interest is the combining of pieces of information. But I shall argue that the evolutionary process must depend upon such double increments of information. Every evolutionary step is an addition of information to an already existing system. Because this is so, the combinations, harmonies, and discords between successive pieces and layers of information will present many problems of survival and determine many directions of change.

Chapter 4, "The Criteria of Mind," will deal with the characteristics that in fact always seem to be combined in our earthly biosphere to make mind. The remainder of the book will focus more narrowly on problems of biological evolution.

Throughout, the thesis will be that it is possible and worthwhile to *think* about many problems of order and disorder in the biological universe and that we have today a considerable supply of tools of thought which we do not use, partly because – professors and schoolboys alike – we are ignorant of many currently available insights and partly because we are unwilling to accept the necessities that follow from a clear view of the human dilemmas.

Notes

1. A favorite phrase of Lord Macaulay's. He is credited with, "Every schoolboy knows who imprisoned Montezuma, and who strangled Atahualpa."
2. Plato's most famous discovery concerned the "reality" of ideas. We commonly think that a dinner plate is "real" but that its circularity is "only an idea." But Plato noted, first, that the plate is not truly circular and, second, that the world can be perceived to contain a very large number of objects which simulate, approximate, or strive after "circularity." He therefore asserted that "circularity" is *ideal* (the adjective derived from *idea*) and that such ideal components of the universe are the real explanatory basis for its forms and structure. For him, as for William Blake and many others, that "Corporeal Universe" which our newspapers consider "real" was some sort of spin-off from the truly real, namely the forms and ideas. In the beginning was the idea.
3. C. G. Jung, *Septan Sermones ad Mortuos* (London: Stuart & Watkins, 1967).
4. In the serial case it is easy to imagine that each anterior segment may give information to the next segment which is developing immediately behind it. Such information might determine orientation, size, and even shape af the new segment. After all, the anterior is also antecedent in time and could be the quasi-logical antecedent or model for its successor. The relation between anterior and posterior would then be asymmetrical and complementary. It is conceivable and even expectable hat the symmetrical relation between right and left is doubly asymmetrical, i.e., that each has some complementary control over the development of the other. The pair would then constitute a circuit of *reciprocal* control. It is surprising that we have almost no knowledge of the vast system of communication which must surely exist to control growth and differentiation.

5. Arthur O. Lovejoy, *The Great Chain of Being: A Study of the History of an Idea* (Cambridge: Harvard University Press, 1936).
6. J.-B. Lamarck, *Philosophie Zoologique* (1809) translated as [Zoological philosophy: An exposition with regard to the natural history of animals, trans. Hugh Elliot] (New York & London: Hafner Press, 1963).

71

Social Class and the Hidden Curriculum of Work

Jean Anyon

Scholars in political economy and the sociology of knowledge have recently argued that public schools in complex industrial societies like our own make available different types of educational experience and curriculum knowledge to students in different social classes. Bowles and Gintis[1] for example, have argued that students in different social-class backgrounds are rewarded for classroom behaviors that correspond to personality traits allegedly rewarded in the different occupational strata – the working classes for docility and obedience, the managerial classes for initiative and personal assertiveness. Basil Bernstein, Pierre Bourdieu, and Michael W. Apple focusing on school knowledge, have argued that knowledge and skills leading to social power and regard (medical, legal, managerial) are made available to the advantaged social groups but are withheld from the working classes to whom a more "practical" curriculum is offered (manual skills, clerical knowledge). While there has been considerable argumentation of these points regarding education in England, France, and North America, there has been little or no attempt to investigate these ideas empirically in elementary or secondary schools and classrooms in this country.[3]

This article offers tentative empirical support (and qualification) of the above arguments by providing illustrative examples of differences in student *work* in classrooms in contrasting social class communities. The examples were gathered *as* part of an ethnographical[4] study of curricular, pedagogical, and pupil evaluation practices in five elementary schools. The article attempts a theoretical contribution as well and assesses student work in the light of a theoretical approach to social-class analysis... It will be suggested that there is a "hidden curriculum" in schoolwork that has profound implications for the theory – and consequence – of everyday activity in education....

Source: *Journal of Education*, 162(1) (1980): 67–92.

The Sample of Schools

... The social-class designation of each of the five schools will be identified, and the income, occupation, and other relevant available social characteristics of the students and their parents will be described. The first three schools are in a medium-sized city district in northern New Jersey, and the other two are in a nearby New Jersey suburb.

The first two schools I will call *working class schools*. Most of the parents have blue-collar jobs. Less than a third of the fathers are skilled, while the majority are in unskilled or semiskilled jobs. During the period of the study (1978–1979), approximately 15 percent of the fathers were unemployed. The large majority (85 percent) of the families are white. The following occupations are typical: platform, storeroom, and stockroom workers; foundry-men, pipe welders, and boilermakers; semiskilled and unskilled assembly-line operatives; gas station attendants, auto mechanics, maintenance workers, and security guards. Less than 30 percent of the women work, some part-time and some full-time, on assembly lines, in storerooms and stockrooms, as waitresses, barmaids, or sales clerks. Of the fifth-grade parents, none of the wives of the skilled workers had jobs. Approximately 15 percent of the families in each school are at or below the federal "poverty" level;[5] most of the rest of the family incomes are at or below $12,000, except some of the skilled workers whose incomes are higher. The incomes of the majority of the families in these two schools (at or below $12,000) are typical of 38.6 percent of the families in the United States.[6]

The third school is called the *middle-class school*, although because of 5 neighborhood residence patterns, the population is a mixture of several social classes. The parents' occupations can he divided into three groups: a small group of blue-collar "rich," who are skilled, well-paid workers such as printers, carpenters, plumbers, and construction workers. The second group is composed of parents in working-class and middle-class white-collar jobs: women in office jobs, technicians, supervisors in industry, and parents employed by the city (such as firemen, policemen, and several of the school's teachers). The third group is composed of occupations such as personnel directors in local firms, accountants, "middle management," and a few small capitalists (owners of shops in the area). The children of several local doctors attend this school. Most family incomes are between $13,000 and $25,000, with a few higher. This income range is typical of 38.9 percent of the families in the United States.[7]

The fourth school has a parent population that is at the upper income level of the upper middle class and is predominantly professional. This school will be called the *affluent professional school*. Typical jobs are: cardiologist, interior designer, corporate lawyer or engineer, executive in advertising or television. There are some families who are not as affluent as the majority (the family of the superintendent of the district's schools, and the one or two families in which the fathers are skilled workers). In addition, a few of the families are more affluent than the majority and can be classified in the capitalist class (a partner in a prestigious Wall Street stock brokerage firm). Approximately 90 percent of the children in this school are white. Most family incomes are between $40,000 and $80,000. This income span represents approximately 7 percent of the families in the United States.[8]

In the fifth school the majority of the families belong to the capitalist class. This school will be called the *executive elite school* because most of the fathers are top executives (for example, presidents and vice-presidents) in major United States-based multinational corporations – for example, AT&T, RCA, Citibank, American Express, U.S. Steel. A sizable group of fathers are top executives in financial firms in Wall Street. There are also a number of fathers who list their occupations as "general counsel" to a particular corporation, and these corporations are also among the large multi-nationals. Many of the mothers do volunteer work in the Junior League, Junior Fortnightly, or other service groups; some are intricately involved in town politics; and some are themselves in well-paid occupations. There are no minority children in the school. Almost all the family incomes are over $100,000 with some in the $500,000 range. The incomes in this school represent less than 1 percent, of the families in the United States.[9]

Since each of the five schools is only one instance of elementary education in a particular social class context, I will not generalize beyond the sample. However, the examples of schoolwork which follow will suggest characteristics of education in each social setting that appear to have theoretical and social significance and to be worth investigation in a larger number of schools.

The Working Class Schools

In the two working-class schools, work is following the steps of a procedure. The procedure is usually mechanical, involving rote behavior and very little decision making or choice. The teachers rarely explain why the work is being assigned, how it might connect to other assignments, or what the idea is that lies behind the procedure or gives it coherence and perhaps meaning or significance. Available textbooks are not always used, and the teachers often prepare their own dittos or put work examples on the board. Most of the rules regarding work are designations of what the children are to do; the rules are steps to follow. These steps are told to the children by the teachers and are often written on the board. The children are usually told to copy the steps as notes. These notes are to be studied. Work is often evaluated not according to whether it is right or wrong but according to whether the children followed the right steps.

The following examples illustrate these points. In math, when two-digit division was introduced, the teacher in one school gave a four-minute lecture on what the terms are called (which number is the divisor, dividend, quotient, and remainder). The children were told to copy these names in their notebooks. Then the teacher told them the steps to follow to do the problems, saying, "This is how you do them." The teacher listed the steps on the board, and they appeared several days later as a chart hung in the middle of the front wall: "Divide, Multiply, Subtract, Bring Down." The children often did examples of two-digit division. When the teacher went over the examples with them, he told them what the procedure was for each problem, rarely asking them to conceptualize or explain it themselves: "Three into twenty-two is seven; do your subtraction and one is left over." During the week that two-digit division was introduced (or at any other time), the investigator did not observe any discussion of the idea of grouping involved in division, any use of manipulables, or any attempt to relate two-digit division to any other mathematical process. Nor was there any attempt to relate the steps to an actual or possible thought process of the children. The observer did not hear the terms *dividend, quotient*, and so on, used again. The math teacher in the other working-class school followed similar procedures regarding two-digit division and at one point her class seemed confused. She said, "You're confusing yourselves. You're tensing up. Remember, when you do this, it's the same steps over and over again – and that's the way division always is." Several weeks later, after a test, a group of her children "still didn't get it," and she made no attempt to explain the concept of dividing things into groups or to give them manipulables for their own investigation. Rather, she went over the steps with them again and told them that they "needed more practice."

In other areas of math, work is also carrying out often unexplained fragmented procedures. For example, one of the teachers led the children through a series of steps to make a 1-inch grid on their paper *without* telling them that they were making a 1-inch grid or that it would be used to study scale. She said, "Take your ruler. Put it across the top. Make a mark at every number. Then move your ruler down to the bottom. No, put it across the bottom. Now make a mark on top of every number. Now draw a line from..." At this point a girl said that she had a faster way to do it and the teacher said, "No, you don't; you don't even know what I'm making yet. Do it this way or it's wrong." After they had made the lines up and down and across, the teacher told them she wanted them to make a figure by connecting some dots and to measure that, using the scale of 1 inch equals 1 mile. Then they were to cut it out. She said, "Don't cut it until I check it."

In both working-class schools, work in language arts is mechanics of punctuation (commas, periods, question marks, exclamation points), capitalization, and the four kinds of sentences. One teacher explained to me, "Simple punctuation is all they'll ever use." Regarding punctuation, either a teacher or a ditto stated the rules for where, for example, to put commas. The investigator heard no classroom discussion of the aural context of punctuation (which, of course, is what gives each mark its meaning). Nor did the investigator hear any statement or inference that placing a punctuation mark could be a decision-making process, depending, for example, on one's intended meaning. Rather, the children were told to follow the rules. Language arts did not involve creative writing. There were several writing assignments throughout the year but in each instance the children were given a ditto, and they wrote answers to questions on the sheet. For example, they wrote their "autobiography" by answering such questions as "Where were you born?" "What is your favorite animal?" on a sheet entitled "All About Me."

In one of the working-class schools, the class had a science period several times a week. On the three occasions observed, the children were not called upon to set up experiments or to give explanations for facts or concepts. Rather, on each occasion the teacher told them in his own words what the book said. The children copied the teacher's sentences from the board. Each day that preceded the day they were to do a science experiment, the teacher told them to copy the directions from the book for the procedure they would carry out the next day and to study the list at home that night. The day after each experiment, the teacher went over what they had "found" (they did the experiments as a class, and each was actually a class demonstration led by the teacher). Then the teacher wrote what they "found" on the board, and the children copied that in their notebooks. Once or twice a year there are science projects. The project is chosen and assigned by the teacher from a box of 3-by-5-inch cards. On the card the teacher has written the question to he answered, the books to use, and how much to write. Explaining the cards to the observer, the teacher said, "It tells them exactly what to do, or they couldn't do it."

Social studies in the working-class schools is also largely mechanical, rote work that was given little explanation or connection to larger contexts. In one school, for example, although there was a book available, social studies work was to copy the teacher's notes from the board. Several times a week for a period of several months the children copied these notes. The fifth grades in the district were to study United States history. The teacher used a booklet she had purchased called "The Fabulous Fifty States." Each day she put information from the booklet in outline form on the board and the children copied it. The type of information did not vary: the name of the state, its abbreviation, state capital, nickname of the state, its main products, main business, and a "Fabulous Fact" ("Idaho grew twenty-seven billion potatoes in one year. That's enough potatoes for each man, woman, and...") As the children finished copying the sentences, the teacher erased them and wrote more. Children would occasionally go to the front to pull down the wall map in order to locate the states they were copying, and the teacher did not dissuade them. But the observer never saw her refer to the map; nor did the observer ever hear her make other than perfunctory remarks concerning the information the children were copying. Occasionally the children colored in a ditto and cut it out to make a stand-up figure (representing, for example, a man roping a cow in the Southwest). These were referred to by the teacher as their social studies "projects."

Rote behavior was often called for in classroom work. When going over 15 math and language art skills sheets, for example, as the teacher asked for the answer to each problem, he fired the questions rapidly, staccato, and the scene reminded the observer of a sergeant drilling recruits: above all, the questions demanded that you stay at attention: "The next one? What do I put here?. . . Here? Give us the next." Or "How many commas in this sentence? Where do I put them . . . The next one?"

The four fifth grade teachers observed in the working-class schools attempted to control classroom time and space by making decisions without consulting the children and without explaining the basis for their decisions. The teacher's control thus often seemed capricious. Teachers, for instance, very often ignored the bells to switch classes – deciding among themselves to keep the children after the period was officially over to continue with the work or for disciplinary reasons or so they (the teachers) could stand in the hall and talk. There were no clocks in the rooms in either school, and the children often asked, "What period is this?" "When do we go to gym?" The children had no access to materials. These were handed out by teachers and closely guarded. Things in the room "belonged" to the teacher: "Bob, bring me my garbage can." The teachers continually gave the children orders. Only three times did the investigator hear a teacher in either working-class school preface a directive with an unsarcastic "please," or "let's" or "would you." Instead, the teachers said, "Shut up," "Shut your mouth," "Open your books," "Throw your gum away-if you want to rot your teeth, do it on your own time." Teachers made every effort to control the movement of the children, and often shouted, "'Why are you out of your seat??!!" If the children got permission to leave the room, they had to take a written pass with the date and time....

Middle-Class School

In the middle-class school, work is getting the right answer. If one accumulates enough right answers, one gets a good grade. One must follow the directions in order to get the right answers, but the directions often call for some figuring, some choice, some decision making. For example, the children must often figure out by themselves what the directions ask them to do and how to get the answer: what do you do first, second, and perhaps third? Answers are usually found in books or by listening to the teacher. Answers are usually words, sentences, numbers, or facts and dates; one writes them on paper, and one should be neat. Answers must be given in the right order, and one cannot make them up.

The following activities are illustrative. Math involves some choice: one may do two-digit division the long way or the short way, and there are some math problems that can be done "in your head." When the teacher explains how to do two-digit division, there is recognition that a cognitive process is involved; she gives you several ways and says, "I want to make sure you understand what you're doing-so you get it right"; and, when they go over the homework, she asks the *children* to tell how they did the problem and what answer they got.

In social studies the daily work is to read the assigned pages in the textbook and to answer the teacher's questions. The questions are almost always designed to check on whether the students have read the assignment and understood it: who did so-and-so; what happened after that; when did it happen, where, and sometimes, why did it happen? The answers are in the book and in one's understanding of the book; the teacher's hints when one doesn't know the answers are to "read it again" or to look at the picture or at the rest of the paragraph. One is to search for the answer in the "context," in what is given.

Language arts is "simple grammar, what they need for everyday life." The language arts teacher says, "They should learn to speak properly, to write business letters and thank-you letters, and to understand what nouns and verbs and simple subjects are." Here, as well, actual work is to choose the right answers, to understand what is given. The teacher often says, "Please read the next sentence and then I'll question you about it." One teacher said in some exasperation to a boy who was fooling around in class, "If you don't know the answers to the questions I ask, then you can't stay in this *class*! [pause] You *never* know the answers to the questions I ask, and it's not fair to me-and certainly not to you!"

Most lessons are based on the textbook. This does not involve a critical perspective on what is given there. For example, a critical perspective in social studies is perceived as dangerous by these teachers because it may lead to controversial topics; the parents might complain. The children, however, are often curious especially in social studies. Their questions are tolerated and usually answered perfunctorily. But after a few minutes the teacher will say, "All right, we're not going any farther. Please open your social studies workbook." While the teachers spend a lot of time explaining and expanding on what the textbooks say, there is little attempt to analyze how or why things happen, or to give thought to how pieces of a culture, or, say, a system of numbers or elements of a language fit together or can be analyzed. What has happened in the past and what exists now may not be equitable or fair, but (shrug) that is the way things are and one does not confront such matters in school. For example, in social studies after a child is called on to read a passage about the pilgrims, the teacher summarizes the paragraph and then says, "So you can see how strict they were about everything." A child asks, "Why?" "Well, because they felt that if you weren't busy you'd get into trouble." Another child asks, "Is it true that they burned women at the stake?" The teacher says, "Yes, if a woman did anything strange, they hanged them. [*sic*] What would a woman do, do you think, to make them burn them? [*sic*] See if you can come up with better answers than my other [social studies] class." Several children offer suggestions, to which the teacher nods but does not comment. Then she says, "Okay, good," and calls on the next child to read.

Work tasks do not usually request creativity. Serious attention is rarely given in school work on *how* the children develop or express their own feelings and ideas, either linguistically or in graphic form. On the occasions when creativity or self-expression is requested, it is peripheral to the main activity or it is "enriched" or "for fun." During a lesson on what similes are, for example, the teacher explains what they are, puts several on the board, gives some other examples herself, and then asks the children if they can "make some up." She calls on three children who give similes, two of which are actually in the book they have open before them. The teacher does not comment on this and then asks several others to choose similes from the list of phrases in the book. Several do so correctly, and she says, "Oh good! You're picking them out! See how good we are?" Their homework is to pick out the rest of the similes from the list.

Creativity is not often requested in social studies and science projects, either. Social studies projects, for example, are given with directions to "find information on your topic" and write it up. The children are not supposed to copy but to "put it in your own words." Although a number of the projects subsequently went beyond the teacher's direction to find information and had quite expressive covers and inside illustrations, the teacher's evaluative comments had to do with the amount of information, whether they had "copied," and if their work was neat.

The style of control of the three fifth-grade teachers observed in this school varied from somewhat easygoing to strict, but in contrast to the working-class schools, the teachers' decisions were usually based on external rules and regulations – for example, on criteria that were known or available to the children. Thus, the teachers always honor the bells for changing classes, and they usually evaluate children's work by what is in the textbooks and answer booklets.

There is little excitement in schoolwork for the children, and the assign-ments are perceived as having little to do with their interests and feelings. As one child said, what you do is "store facts up in your head like cold storage – until you need it later for a test or your job." Thus, doing well is important because there are thought to be *other* likely rewards: a good job or college.[10]

Affluent Professional School

In the affluent professional school, work is creative activity carried out inde-pendently. The students are continually asked to express and apply ideas and concepts. Work involves individual thought and expressiveness, expansion and illustration of ideas, and choice of appropriate method and material. (The class is not considered an open classroom, and the principal explained that because of the large number of discipline problems in the fifth grade this year they did not departmentalize. The teacher who agreed to take part in the study said she is "more structured this year than she usually is.) The products of work in this class are often written stories, editorials and essays, or representations of ideas in mural, graph, or craft form. The products of work should not be like anybody else's and should show individuality. They should exhibit good design, and (this is important) they must also fit empirical reality. The relatively few rules to be followed regarding work are usually criteria for, or limits on, individual activity. One's product is usually evaluated for the quality of its expression and for the appropriateness of its conception to the task. In many cases, one's own satisfaction with the product is an important criterion for its evaluation. When right answers are called for, as in commercial materials like SRA (Science Research Associates) and math, it is important that the children decide on an answer as a result of thinking about the idea involved in what they're being asked to do. Teacher's hints are to "think about it some more."

The following activities are illustrative. The class takes home a sheet requesting each child's parents to fill in the number of cars they have, the number of television sets, refrigerators, games, or rooms in the house, and so on. Each child is to figure the average number of a type of possession owned by the fifth grade. Each child must compile the "data" from all the sheets. A calculator is available in the classroom to do the mechanics of finding the average. Some children decide to send sheets to the fourth-grade families for comparison. Their work should be "verified" by a classmate before it is handed in.

Each child and his or her family has made a geoboard. The teacher asks the class to get their geoboards from the side cabinet, to take a handful of rubber bands, and then to listen to what she would like them to do. She says, "I would like you to design a figure and then find the perimeter and area. When you have it, check with your neighbor. After you've done that, please transfer it to graph paper and tomorrow I'll ask you to make up a question about it for someone. When you hand it in, please let me know whose it is and who verified it. Then I have something else for you to do that's really fun. [pause] Find the average number of chocolate chips in three cookies. I'll give you three cookies, and you'll have to *eat* your way through, I'm afraid!" Then she goes around the room and gives help, suggestions, praise, and admonitions that they are getting noisy. They work sittings or standing up at their desks, at benches in the back, or on the floor. A child hands the teacher his paper and she comments, I'm not accepting this paper. Do a better design." To another child she says, "That's fantastic! But you'll never find the area. Why don't you draw a figure inside [the big one] and subtract to get the area?"

The school district requires the fifth grade to study ancient civilization (in particular, Egypt, Athens, and Sumer). In this classroom, the emphasis is on illustrating and re-creating the culture of the people of ancient times. The following are typical activities: the children made an 8mm film on Egypt, which one of the parents edited. A girl in the class wrote the script, and the class acted it out. They put the sound on themselves. They read stories of those days. They wrote essays and stories depicting the lives of the people and the societal and occupational divisions. They chose from a list of projects, all of which involved graphical presentations of ideas: for example. "Make a mural depicting the division of labor in Egyptian society."

Each wrote and exchanged a letter in hieroglyphics with a fifth grader in another class, and they also exchanged stories they wrote in cuneiform. They made a scroll and singed the edges so it looked authentic. They each chose an occupation and made an Egyptian plaque representing that occupation, simulating the appropriate Egyptian design. They carved their design on a cylinder of wax, pressed the wax into clay, and then baked the clay. Although one girl did not choose an occupation but carved instead a series of gods and slaves, the teacher said, "That's all right, Amber, it's beautiful." As they were working the teacher said, "Don't cut into your clay until you're satisfied with your design."

Social studies also involves almost daily presentation by the children of some event from the news. The teacher's questions ask the children to expand what they say, to give more details, and to be more specific. Occasionally she adds some remarks to help them see connections between events.

The emphasis on expressing and illustrating ideas in social studies is accompanied in language arts by an emphasis on creative writing. Each child wrote a rebus story for a first grader whom they had interviewed to see what kind of story the child liked best. They wrote editorials on pending decisions by the school board and radio plays, some of which were read over the school intercom from the office and one of which was performed in the auditorium. There is no language arts textbook because, the teacher said, "The principal wants us to be creative." There is not much grammar, but there is punctuation. One morning when the observer arrived, the class was doing a punctuation ditto. The teacher later apologized for using the ditto. "It's just for review," she said. "I don't teach punctuation that way. We use their language." The ditto had three unambiguous rules for where to put commas in a sentence. As the teacher was going around to help the children with the ditto, she repeated several times, "where you put commas depends on how you say the sentence; it depends on the situation and what you want to say. Several weeks later the observer saw another punctuation activity. The teacher had printed a five-paragraph story on an oak tag and then cut it into phrases. She read the whole story to the class from the book, then passed out the phrases. The group had to decide how the phrases could best be put together again. (They arranged the phrases on the floor.) The point was not to replicate the story, although that was not irrelevant, but to "decide what you think the best way is." Punctuation marks on cardboard pieces were then handed out, and the children discussed and then decided what mark was best at each place they thought one was needed. At the end of each paragraph the teacher asked, "Are you satisfied with the way the paragraphs are now? Read it to yourself and see how it sounds." Then she read the original story again, and they compared the two.

Describing her goals in science to the investigator, the teacher said, "We use ESS (Elementary Science Study). It's very good because it gives a hands-on experience – so they can make *sense* out of it. It doesn't matter whether it [what they find] is right or wrong. I bring them together and there's value in discussing their ideas."

The products of work in this class are often highly valued by the children and the teacher. In fact, this was the only school in which the investigator was not allowed to take original pieces of the children's work for her files. If the work was small enough, however, and was on paper, the investigator could duplicate it on the copying machine in the office.

The teacher's attempt to control the class involves constant negotiation. She does not give direct orders unless she is angry because the children have been too noisy. Normally, she tries to get them to foresee the consequences of their actions and to decide accordingly. For example, lining them up to go see a play written by the sixth graders, she says, "I presume you're lined up by someone with whom you want to sit. I hope you're lined up by someone you won't get in trouble with."...

One of the few rules governing the children's movement is that no more than three children may be out of the room at once. There is a school rule that anyone can go to the library at any time to get a book. In the fifth grade I observed, they sign their name on the chalkboard and leave. There are no passes. Finally, the children have a fair amount of officially sanctioned say over what happens in the class. For example, they often negotiate what work is to be done. If the teacher wants to move on to the next subject, but the children say they are not ready, they want to work on their present projects some *more*, she very often lets them do it.

Executive Elite School

In the executive elite school, work is developing one's analytical intellectual powers. Children are continually asked to reason through a problem, to produce intellectual products that are both logically sound and of top academic quality. A primary goal of thought is to conceptualize rules by which elements may fit together in systems and then to apply these rules in solving a problem. Schoolwork helps one to achieve, to excel, to prepare for life.

The following are illustrative. The math teacher teaches area and perimeter by having the children derive formulas for each. First she helps them, through discussion at the board, to arrive at A = W X L as a formula (not *the* formula) for area. After discussing several, she says, "Can anyone make up a formula for perimeter? Can you figure that out yourselves? [pause] Knowing what we know, can we think of a formula?" She works out three children's suggestions at the board, saying to two, "Yes, that's a good one," and then asks the class if they can think of any more. No one volunteers. To prod them, she says, "If you use rules and good reasoning, you get many ways. Chris, can you think up a formula?"

She discusses two-digit division with the children as a decision-making process. Presenting a new type of problem to them, she asks, "What's the *first* decision you'd make if presented with this kind of example? What is the first thing you'd *think?* Craig?" Craig says, "To find my first partial quotient." She responds, "Yes, mat would be your first decision. How would you do that?" Craig explains, and then the teacher says, "OK, we'll see how that works for you." The class tries his way. Subsequently, she comments on the merits and shortcomings of several other children's decisions. Later, she tells the investigator that her goals in math are to develop their reasoning and mathematical thinking and that, unfortunately, "there's no time for manipulables."

While right answers are important in math, they are not "given" by the book or by the teacher but may be challenged by the children. Going over some problems in late September the teacher says, "Raise your hand if you do not agree." A child says, "I don't agree with sixty-four." The teacher responds, "OK, there's a question about sixty-four. [to class] Please check it. Owen, they're disagreeing with you. Kristen, they're checking yours." The teacher emphasized this repeatedly during September and October with statements like "Don't be afraid to say you disagree. In the last [math] class, somebody disagreed, and they were right. Before you disagree, check yours, and if you still think we're wrong, then we'll check it out." By Thanksgiving, the children did not often speak in terms of right and wrong math problems but of whether they agreed with the answer that had been given.

There are complicated math mimeos with many word problems. Whenever they go over the examples, they discuss how each child has set up the problem. The children must explain it precisely. On one occasion the teacher said, "I'm more – just as interested in *how* you set up the problem as in what answer you find. If you set up a problem in a good way, the answer is *easy* to find.

Social studies work is most often reading and discussion of concepts and independent research. There are only occasional artistic, expressive, or illustrative projects. Ancient Athens and Sumer are, rather, societies to analyze. The following questions are typical of those that guide the children's independent research. "What mistakes did Pericles make after the war?" "What mistakes did the citizens of Athens make?" "What are the elements of a civilization?" "How did Greece build an economic empire?" "Compare the way Athens chose its leaders with the way we choose ours." Occasionally the children are asked to make up sample questions for their social studies tests. On an occasion when the investigator was present, the social studies teacher rejected a child's question by saying, "That's just fact. If I asked you that question on a test, you'd complain it was just memory! Good questions ask for concepts."

In social studies – but also in reading, science, and health – the teachers initiate classroom discussions of current social issues and problems. These discussions occurred on every one of the investigator's visits, and a teacher told me, "These children's opinions are important – it's important that they learn to reason things through." The classroom discussions always struck the observer as quite realistic and analytical, dealing with concrete social issues like the following: "Why do workers strike?" "Is that right or wrong?" "Why do we have inflation, and what can be done to stop it?" "Why do companies put chemicals in food when the natural ingredients are available?" and so on. Usually the children did not have to be prodded to give their opinions. In fact, their statements and the interchanges between them struck the observer as quite sophisticated conceptually and verbally, and well-informed. Occasionally the teachers would prod with statements such as, "Even if you don't know [the answers], if you think logically about it, you can figure it out" And "I'm asking you [these] questions to help you think this through."

Language arts emphasizes language as a complex system, one that should be mastered. The children are asked to diagram sentences of complex grammatical construction, to memorize irregular verb conjugations (he lay, he has lain, and so on ...), and to use the proper participles, conjunctions, and interjections in their speech. The teacher (the same one who teaches social studies) told them, "It is not enough to get these right on tests; you must use what you learn [in grammar classes] in your written and oral work. I will grade you on that."

Most writing assignments are either research reports and essays for social studies or experiment analyses and write-ups for science. There is only an occasional story or other "creative writing" assignment. On the occasion observed by the investigator (the writing of a Halloween story), the points the teacher stressed in preparing the children to write involved the structural aspects of a story rather than the expression of feelings or other ideas. The teacher showed them a filmstrip, "The Seven Parts of a Story," and lectured them on plot development, mood setting, character development, consistency, and the use of a logical or appropriate ending. The stories they subsequently wrote were, in fact, well-structured, but many were also personal and expressive. The teacher's evaluative comments, however, did not refer to the expressiveness or artistry but were all directed toward whether they had "developed" the story well.

Language arts work also involved a large amount of practice in presentation of the self and in managing situations where the child was expected to be in charge. For example, there was a series of assignments in which each child had to be a "student teacher." The child had to plan a lesson in grammar, outlining, punctuation, or other language arts topic and explain the concept to the class. Each child was to prepare a worksheet or game and a homework assignment as well. After each presentation, the teacher and other children gave a critical appraisal of the "student teacher's" performance. Their criteria were: whether the student spoke clearly, whether the lesson was interesting, whether the student made any mistakes, and whether he or she kept control of the class. On an occasion when a child did not maintain control, the teacher said, "When you're up there, you have authority and you have to use it. I'll back you up."

The executive elite school is the only school where bells do not demarcate the periods of time. The two fifth-grade teachers were very strict about changing classes on schedule, however, as specific plans for each session had been made. The teachers attempted to keep tight control over the children during lessons, and the children were sometimes flippant, boisterous, and occasionally rude. However, the children may be brought into line by reminding them that "It is up to you." "You must control yourself," "you are responsible for your work," you must "set your own priorities." One teacher told a child, "You are the only driver of your car-and only you can regulate your speed." A new teacher complained to the observer that she had thought "these children" would have more control.

While strict attention to the lesson at hand is required, the teachers make relatively little attempt to regulate the movement of the children at other times. For example, except for the kindergartners the children in this school do not have to wait for the bell to ring in the morning; they may go to their classroom when they arrive at school. Fifth graders often came early to read, to finish work, or to catch up. After the first two months of school, the fifth-grade teachers did not line the children up to change classes or to go to gym, and so on, but, when the children were ready and quiet, they were told they could go – sometimes without the teachers. In the classroom, the children could get materials when they needed them and took what they needed from closets and from the teacher's desk. They were in charge of the office at lunchtime. During class they did not have to sign out or ask permission to leave the room; they just got up and left. Because of the pressure to get work done, however, they did not leave the room very often. The teachers were very polite to the children, and the investigator heard no sarcasm, no nasty remarks, and few direct orders. The teachers never called the children "honey" or "dear" but always called them by name. The teachers were expected to be available before school, after school, and for part of their lunchtime to provide extra help if needed.

The foregoing analysis of differences in schoolwork in contrasting social class contexts suggests the following conclusion: the "hidden curriculum" of schoolwork is tacit preparation for relating to the process of production in a particular way. Differing curricular, pedagogical, and pupil evaluation practices emphasize different cognitive and behavioral skills in each social setting and thus contribute to the development in the children of certain potential relationships to physical and symbolic capital,[11] to authority, and to the process of work. School experience, in the sample of schools discussed here, differed qualitatively by social class. These differences may not only contribute to the development in the children in each social class of certain types of economically significant relationships and not others but would thereby help to reproduce this system of relations in society. In the contribution to the reproduction of unequal social relations lies a theoretical meaning and social consequence of classroom practice.

The identification of different emphases in classrooms in a sample of contrasting social class contexts implies that further research should be conducted in a large number of schools to investigate the types of work tasks and interactions in each to see if they differ in the ways discussed here and to see if similar potential relationships are uncovered. Such research could have as a product the further elucidation of complex but not readily apparent connections between everyday activity in schools and classrooms and the unequal structure of economic relationships in which we work and live.

Notes

This essay first appeared in Journal of Education, Volume 1, in the Fall 1980 edition.

1. S. Bowles and H. Gintes, *Schooling in Capitalist America: Educational Reform and the Contradictions of Economic Life* (New York: Basic Books, 1976). [Author's note]
2. B. Bernstein, *Class, Codes and Control, Vol. 3. Towards a Theory of Educational Transmission*, 2d ed. (London: Routledge & Kegan Paul, 1977); P. Bourdieu and J. Passeron, *Reproduction in Education, Society and Culture* (Beverly Hills, Calif.: Sage, 1977); M.W. Apple, *Ideology and Curriculum* (Boston: Routledge Kegan Paul, 1979). [Author's note]
3. But see, in a related vein, M.W. Apple and N. King, "What Do Schools Teach?" *Curriculum Inquiry* 6 (1977); 341–58; R.C. Rist, *The Urban School: A Factory for Failure* (Cambridge, Mass.: MIT Press, 1973). [Author's note]
4. *ethnographical:* Based on an anthropological study of cultures or subcultures-the "cultures" in this case being the five schools being observed.
5. The U.S. Bureau of the Census defines *poverty* for a nonfarm family of four as a yearly income of $6,191 a year or less. U.S. Bureau of the Census, *Statistical Abstract of the United States: 1978* (Washington, D.C.: U.S. Government Printing Office, 1978), p. 465, table 754. [Author's note]
6. U.S. Bureau of the Census, "Money Income in 1977 of Families and Persons in the United States," *Current Population Reports* Series P-60, no. 118 (Washington, D.C.: U.S. Government Printing Office, 1978), p. 2, table A. [Author's note]
7. Ibid. [Author's note]
8. This figure is an estimate. According to the Bureau of the Census, only 2.6 percent of families in the United States have money income of $50,000 or over. U.S. Bureau of the Census, *Current Population Reports* Series P-60. For figures on income at these higher levels, see J.D. Smith and S. Franklin, "The Concentration of Personal Wealth, 1922–1969," *American Economic Review* 64 (1974): 162–67. [Author's note]
9. Smith and Franklin, "The Concentration of Personal Wealth." [Author's note]
10. A dominant feeling expressed directly and indirectly by teachers in this school, was boredom with their work. They did, however, in contrast to the working-class schools, almost always carry out lessons during class times. [Author's note]
11. *Physical and symbolic capital:* Elsewhere Anyon defines *capital* as "property that is used to produce profit, interest, or rent": she defines *symbolic capital* as the knowledge and skills that "may yield social and cultural power."

72

Curriculum as Cultural Reproduction: An Examination of Metaphor as a Carrier of Ideology

C. A. Bowers

The purpose of this article is to examine how dependent we are in the area of educational analysis and policy formation on the use of metaphorical thinking, and how metaphorical thinking serves as a carrier of historically rooted ideologies. A second purpose is to clarify the conceptual difficulties that arise when we fail to recognize the difference between the phenomenological world of everyday life and the symbolic world of metaphor. When we attempt to translate metaphorical thinking into a new educational policy and practice the problem becomes even more serious in terms of precipitating disruptions in people's lives. The attempts to translate the metaphors borrowed from industrial engineering into classroom practice and the more recent efforts to organize the administration of schools in accordance with metaphors borrowed from systems theory are two examples. The analysis of metaphor as carrier of ideology could focus on any one of several recent developments in education: the influence of technicism on educational thought and practice, the alternative-school movement (now more a study in the history of ideas), or the accountability movement. Each of these reform movements was heavily dependent on metaphorical thinking, and a critical analysis of this relationship is much needed. For our purposes, however, the curriculum as cultural reproduction theory will be used as a basis for analyzing the nature and influence of metaphor. The view of curriculum as cultural reproduction is central to the sociology of school knowledge being developed by Michael Young, Basil Bernstein, and Pierre Bourdieu. Their analysis of school knowledge has attracted widespread interest in this country and abroad. As the theory, in part, is derived from Marx's sociological model of social class and ideology it appears to be represented by some educational theorists as fitting into the category of thought that Marxassociated with scientific, distortion-free knowledge. This promise of knowledge about the

Source: *Teachers College Record*, 82(2) (1980): 267–288.

mechanisms of social repression and revolutionary change that can be generalized, because of its scientific nature, to different cultural contexts is what makes the writings on curriculum as cultural reproduction particularly attractive for an analysis of metaphorical thinking. As the work of Michael Apple represents a nice synthesis and restatement of the main ideas in the sociology of school knowledge, his work will be used as the primary source of reference.

The article will begin with a brief restatement of Michael Apple's interpretation of the theory of curriculum as cultural reproduction. This will enable us to identify both the metaphors and the theoretical context in which they are used. We shall then proceed to an analysis of the nature of metaphor and the relationship between metaphor and ideology. After this theoretical foundation is established we can then return to an analysis of the existential-cultural implications of key metaphors used by Apple and others working in the sociology of school knowledge.

What we should understand about the transmission of school knowledge, according to Apple, are the linkages between the form and content of the curriculum, the system of economic production, and the maintenance of class relationships. Apple focused on the importance of understanding these linkages when he posed the question: "What are the manifest and latent social functions of the knowledge that is taught in schools?" How do the principles of selection and organization that are used to plan, order, and evaluate that knowledge function in the cultural and economic reproduction of class relations in an advanced industrial society like our own?[1] One of Apple's purposes in raising the question in this way was to attack as indefensible and naive the view that what is taught in school is objective knowledge, and that teachers stand above the fray of political interests as nonpartisan public servants. Not only is school knowledge political; it must also be understood as part of the ideology of the dominant social class. The other purpose was to connect his analysis with Marx's idea that the mode of economic production "*determines the general character* of the social, political and spiritual processes of life." While he cautions against accepting an oversimplified interpretation of Marx's dictum that social existence determines consciousness, he nevertheless wants to keep in the foreground the primacy of economic activity in determining class relationships and the distribution of knowledge in society.

Cultural transmissions, of which school knowledge is an important part, not only are shaped by the mode of economic production, but in turn reproduce in the consciousness of people the ideas, values, and norms that maintain the relations of reproduction. Apple suggested that we think of culture in terms of the metaphor of distribution. "One can think about knowledge," he writes, "as being unevenly distributed among social and economic classes, occupational groups, different age groups, and groups of different power. Thus some groups have access to knowledge distributed to them and not distributed to others. . . . The lack of certain kinds of knowledge – where your particular group stands in the complex process of cultural preservation and distribution – is related, no doubt, to the absence in that group of certain kinds of political and economic power in society."[2] This process of distributing knowledge in a manner that maintains the patterns of unequal social relationships is, according to Apple, one of the primary functions of the school.

Utilizing Pierre Bourdieu's idea that knowledge can be understood as cultural capital, Apple argues that the schools reproduce the class divisions of a hierarchical society through its distribution of cultural capital. As Apple put it, "Schools, therefore, process both knowledge and people."[3] The linkage between the schools' distribution of cultural capital and unequal ownership and control of economic capital in the larger society can be seen in terms of who is given access to what he terms "high-status knowledge." "The constitutive or underlying social and economic rules," Apple writes,

> make it essential that subject-centered curricula be taught, that high status be given to technical knowledge. This is, in large part, due to the selective function of schooling. Though this is more complex than I can go into here, it is easier to stratify individuals according to "academiccriteria" when technical knowledge is used. This stratification or grouping is important because not all individuals are seen as having the ability to contribute to the required knowledge form (as well as partly because of the structural requirements of the division of labor, of course). Thus, the cultural content (legitimate or high-status knowledge) is used as a device or filter for economic stratification.[4]

Because of the hegemony of the dominant cultural code, what Apple would call the ideology that legitimates the unequal distribution of power, the teachers' participation in the process of economic and cultural reproduction is characterized by a sense of taken for grantedness.

This is, I think, an essentially fair restatement of Apple's interpretation of the curriculum as cultural reproduction theory. As Apple shares with a number of other theorists working within this paradigm – Madeleine MacDonald, Geoff Esland, Michael Young, Madan Sarup – the belief that a fundamental transformation of the social order is needed along the lines laid down by Marx, our purpose here is to examine some of the key metaphors used in the analysis (class, inequality, hegemony, and hierarchical social structure) as well as what we can call the background or reference-point metaphors (classless, equality, and terms that imply the elimination of hegemony, ideology, and status differences in knowledge). As the Marxist sociological model makes a distinction between scientific knowledge (which Marx's paradigm provides) and ideology (distorted thinking that reflects the hegemonic influence of capitalism), it is important to ask whether their key metaphors are free of ideological content. To put it more directly, if social and educational reform were based on their metaphors would a classless society, free of hegemony, emerge, or do the metaphors themselves serve as a carrier of a culturally and historically based mental template? Are metaphors like equality, freedom, and classless society culturally neutral images that can be adopted by any culture without coming under the influence of Western hegemony? Can they be adopted in our culture at the level of social practice and at the same time be reconciled, without an Orwellian distortion of the language, with other metaphors that we also value, like cultural pluralism? Before examining the cultural orientation embedded in the metaphors that are so fundamental to Apple's analysis and prescriptions for social change it will be necessary to clarify what metaphorical thinking is, and how metaphors serve as carriers of ideological orientations.

The problem for the Marxist educational theorist, for the advocate of "free schools," and for the technicist promoting "competency based education" is not that they use metaphors; it is that they do not understand the metaphorical nature of the "reality" they think they are reporting on. As a number of writers have observed, all thinking is metaphorical. As early as 1873, Friedrich Nietzsche described metaphor as basic to the intellectual process we use to establish truth and meaning. "The starting point," he wrote, "begins with a nerve-stimulus, first transcribed [*übertragen*] into an image [*Bild*]. First metaphor! The image again copied into a sound! Second metaphor! And each time he (the creator of language) leaps completely out of one sphere right into the midst of an entirely different one."[5] In another place he wrote, "In *our* thought, the essential feature is fitting new material into old schemas, . . . *making* equal what is new."[6] What he is describing as a fundamental impulse of man, the impulse toward the formation of metaphors, is later identified with the "will to power." This drive to name, to give meaning, to categorize, involves the use of metaphor, that is, the establishment of an identity between dissimilar things.

Ernst Cassirer made a similar observation on how our phenomenological world is transformed through language. "This differentiation and fixation of certain contents by words," he writes, "not only designates a definite intellectual quality through them, but actually endows them with such a quality, by virtue of which they are now raised above the mere immediacy of so-called sensory qualities. . . . Here lies the first beginning of that universal function of separation and association."[7] More recently, Susanne Langer described metaphor as "our most striking evidence of *abstractive seeing*. . . . Every new experience or new idea about things evokes first of all some metaphorical expression. As the idea becomes familiar, this expression 'fades' to a new literal use of the once metaphorical predicate, a more general use than it had before." She goes on to say that "if ritual is the cradle of language, metaphor is the law of its life. It is the force that makes it essentially relational, forever showing up new, abstractable *forms* in reality, forever laying down a deposit of old, abstracted concepts in an increasing treasure of general words."[8]

Nietzsche, Cassirer, and Langer, in addition to showing that metaphors are essential to the symbolic openness of both thought and language, provide important clues as to how metaphorical thinking occurs. Each of the quotations referred to thinking as a process of moving from one sphere to another, making associations and comparisons, and the expansion of meaning through relating one image to another. In order to formalize our discussion of metaphor in a manner that will enable us to understand the use of metaphors in the academic world where truth claims are made about our knowledge of society, and to understand the process to which Nietzsche, Cassirer, and Langer allude, it would be useful to draw on Richard H. Brown's analysis of the cognitive status of metaphor. His book, *A Poetic for Sociology*, makes an important contribution to understanding the nature of metaphorical thinking within the domains of the social sciences, science, and even educational policy and analysis.

Brown provides several clear descriptions of the mental process involved in the use of metaphors. "In the narrowest sense," he writes, "metaphors can be understood as an illustrative device whereby a term from one level or frame of reference is used within a different level or frame."[9] To use an example drawn from the previous discussion of curriculum, culture is to be understood as though it were capital. The metaphor of cultural capital derives its power from the expansion of meaning that comes from associating our understanding of culture with all that we know about capital, that is, capital is owned, unevenly distributed, and underlies the basis of class divisions. Dewey's view of education as growth, to take another example, involved the expansion of the meaning of education by associating it with the image of growth, which was largely derived from a biological frame of reference. Brown points out that the use of metaphor "concentrates our attention on what is patently not there in the language, but which emerges in the interplay of juxtaposed associations."[10] Examples taken from different ideological perspectives include competency based education, open classroom, and democratic centralism; each shows how meaning is expanded through this process of juxtaposed association.

In addition to the carry-over of meaning as terms are used within different frameworks, metaphors also provide the basis for both model building and theoretical thought. Brown suggests that *analogic* metaphors are basic to the theoretical thinking that characterizes the social sciences and science. Like illustrative metaphors, analogic metaphors involve taking an image or sense of meaning from one context and employing it in another in order to expand or clarify some new sense of meaning that we want to have understood. We use analogic metaphors when we think in terms of comparisons, relationships, and how something can be understood like something else. Thinking of the school as a distribution system would be an example, as is thinking of society in terms of structure and function. School and society are not understood in isolation, but in relation to other images. *Iconic* metaphors, according to Brown, provide us with an image or mental picture of what things are, rather than creating a new sense of meaning through comparison (analogic). Theories about class, power, intelligence, rely heavily on iconic metaphors. "*Root* metaphors," Brown writes, "are those sets of assumptions, usually implicit, about what sort of things make up the world, how they act, how they hang together, and usually, by implication, how they may be known."[11] Root metaphors constitute the basic frames of reference or paradigms for making sense of our world, and are the starting point for all theory building. Unlike analogic and iconic metaphors they usually exist below the level of conscious awareness. Thinking of society as an organism is an example of how a root metaphor provides a conceptual grammar that influences our way of thinking. Root metaphors are the basis of world views, ideologies, and religion. They also have a way of showing up in the conceptual underpinnings of social science theories that are supposedly free of archetypal thinking. Marx's statement, for example, that "new, higher relations of production never appear before the material conditions of their existence have matured in the womb of the old society"[12] reflects the basic root cultural metaphor that shaped the thinking of Aristotle, Saint Augustine, Comte, and Dewey. Stages of growth that reflect an inner telos, with the latter stages existing in the embryo of earlier stages, is a basic paradigmatic theme underlying the cultural grammar of all these Western thinkers.

As metaphors represent a mental construct they must, according to Brown, be consciously understood in terms of suggesting an "as if" set of possibilities. When Apple tells us to think of culture as a "distribution system," of schools as "processing people," and of "how hegemony acts to 'saturate' our very consciousness," it is important to keep in mind that he is inviting us to understand his meaning in a metaphorical sense rather than to interpret "distribution," "processing," and "saturate" in a literal sense. Serious difficulties arise when metaphors are interpreted literally. Brown noted that in "metaphors a logical or empirical absurdity stands in tension with fictive truth, yet this counter factual truth itself depends on a creative confrontation of perspectives that cannot be literalized or disengaged without destroying the insight which metaphor provides." He goes on to what seems to be the crucial point to remember about metaphors, namely that if the "consciously as if" aspect of metaphor is not retained, there is the danger that we will be used by them rather than using them.[13]

Nietzsche was also aware of the danger of interpreting metaphors in the literal sense. His view of how we transform metaphors into symbolic constructions that then act back on us is very similar to Marx's idea of how we have objectified the labor process in a manner that leaves the worker's contribution out of our thinking about commodity production. Both Nietzsche and Marx were addressing the fundamental problem of reification; Nietzsche was concerned with reification of our symbolic world, and Marx with the reification of our social relations. Metaphorical thinking becomes an example of reified thought when we cease to be aware that language involves a projection of our thought processes into the world. In the language of Berger and Pullberg, metaphors become reified "by detaching them from human intentionality and expressivity. . . . the end result . . . is that the dialectical process in its totality is lost, and is replaced by an experience and conception of mechanical causality."[14] The absurd and humanly tragic emerges when we begin to act on the metaphors as though they were to be taken in a literal sense as having an objective existence of their own. Educational programs based on the "freedom" of the student, decisions that are "data based" and the desire to eliminate the sources of "inequality" in all aspects of social and individual experience are examples of the kind of reified thinking that characterizes ideological positions prevalent in education today. In the face of a reified symbolic world – of which "freedom," "data," and "inequality" are examples – the individual loses sight of his intentionality in how such metaphors are to be interpreted and acted on in the context of everyday life. The alienation of man from the symbolic world that is constructed and externalized is in Nietzsche's sense the ultimate expression of will to power, but expressed in a manner that does not involve taking existential responsibility.

If we go back to Brown's description of metaphor as involving a term or image taken from "one level or frame of reference" and "used within a different level or frame" it is easy to make the connection between metaphor and ideology. Another way to understand "frame of reference" is to think of it in Clifford Geertz's sense of a symbolic world or model. Geertz suggests that we think of symbolic worlds as "culture patterns – religious, philosophical, aesthetic, scientific, ideological . . . [that] provide a template or blueprint for the organization of social and psychological processes."[15] These symbolic worlds can also be viewed as ideologies that serve as mental templates for making sense of the phenomenological world. Metaphors, as Brown suggests, derive their expanded meaning from the juxtaposition of these mental templates or from the use of an image taken from one mental template and used in a different context. Viewing society as an "organism" and the curriculum as cultural "reproduction" would be two examples. Put succinctly, metaphors always have an ideological basis that gives them their special symbolic power to expand meaning. When they are used, as in talking about equality or freedom, the metaphors carry or lay down, in Susanne Langer's phrase, "a deposit of old, abstracted concepts" that reflect the episteme or ideological framework from which they were borrowed. In this sense metaphors are carriers of meaning and images from one context to another. To think metaphorically means then the use of historically grounded mental frameworks; or as Nietzsche put it, fitting the new into old schemas.

Before examining the theory of curriculum as cultural reproduction as an example of ideological borrowing it is necessary to explain what is meant by a "context-free metaphor." This phrase was used by Alvin Gouldner in his analysis of how Marxist metaphors, such as socialism, proletariat, imperialism, class struggle, and so forth, could be used in a variety of contexts that reflected different forms of social development. What allows the Marxist-socialists, he asked, to use "socialism" in the context of agrarian as well as industrially advanced societies, or to interchange the term "proletariat" with "peasantry" and "people"?[16] He suggested that this process of metaphorical switching where one metaphor takes on the equivalencies of other metaphors results from the context-free nature of the metaphors. That is, the metaphors are used in a manner that separates them from the ideological framework out of which they are derived. In losing sight of the original image or sense of meaning the originating symbolic framework provides, the user can give them any meaning he wants. In being divorced from their historical roots, the metaphors can be switched without seeming to involve contradictions or the misuse of image or framework. Thus "peasant" can be used as interchangeable with "proletariat" or "working class," and, to change ideological framework as our source of examples, "freedom" can be interchanged with "natural" and "spontaneous," "competency" can be interchanged with "input and output measures." The tendency to switch metaphors reflects the user's lack of knowledge of what the images originally meant. The metaphor, thus separated from its historical and cultural context, is used as context free. The popular usage of "liberalism" and "conservatism" reflects this lack of historical awareness. As I shall develop in the following analysis, the metaphors used by Apple and others looking at the social-political function of curriculum within the Marxist paradigm are being used as context-free metaphors. Even though the metaphors are used in a context-free manner they continue to carry vestiges of the ideological frameworks from which they are taken.

The metaphors that are important to the development of Apple's analysis of curriculum include inequality, class, hegemony, high-status knowledge, and hierarchy (in all its social and cultural manifestations). Metaphors that suggest the opposite image, that is, classless society, equality, and so forth, are fundamental to his Marxist vision of a socialist society. Our purpose here is to point out how these metaphors serve as carriers of the deep-structure assumptions and categories of thought that characterized the historical mind set from which they were borrowed. This will help to clarify a point that seems to be generally ignored by Apple and other educational theorists using the Marxist paradigm, namely that metaphors like equality and classless society are not "culturally neutral terms. Marx himself understood the social-historical origins of language, but many of his followers seem to overlook this obvious yet exceedingly complex issue. If the metaphors of social liberation are culture specific, that is, reflect a particular ideological framework, how can they be used as the basis of cultural and social liberation within a different culture without involving a new form of cultural domination? After examining some of the characteristics of the cultural episteme that gave rise to the idea of equality, freedom, and a classless society, I want to raise several questions about how the metaphors used in the Marxist sociological model can be translated into a new social praxis without engaging in another form of cultural imperialism. The dialectical relation between theory and praxis requires that the implication of a new praxis based on culturally specific metaphors be given more careful consideration than has been characteristic of the work of Michael Apple, Madeleine MacDonald, Michael Young, and others working in this area. Examining characteristics of the mind set embedded in the metaphors will also help us to see some of the cultural issues that emerge when metaphors such as equality, freedom, and nonhierarchical relations are translated into social and educational policy in our own country.

The images evoked when we think of equality, a classless society, a people entering into their true consciousness free of hegemony (hegemony is the new term that is roughly equivalent to Marx's idea of ideology), are meaningful to us because, in Benjamin Lee Whorf's terms, we are party to categories of thought that are embedded in the language.[17] The language, which includes the metaphors, transmits the episteme of the culture, with the roots of this episteme going back to the earliest stages of cultural development. In terms of metaphors so prominent in Apple's analysis of curriculum, the cultural epistemology that surrounds and gives the metaphors their special meaning can be traced back to the ideology of the Enlightenment period in Western Europe. A general mapping of this episteme reveals some unique deep-structure assumptions about how to organize and think about reality. This mental template was in part fashioned by the burgeois intelligentsia in their struggle to overturn the Old Regime of church and feudal aristocracy; but fundamental characteristics can also be traced back even further to their Judeo-Christian roots. The purpose here is not to engage in a full-scale archeology of Western consciousness, but to identify those characteristics of thinking that are embedded in the metaphors we are examining.

Apple's use of metaphor within the Marxist paradigm clearly reflects the influence of the mental template characteristic of Western Enlightenment thinking. In order to see the pattern of thinking (episteme) he draws on, I shall quote several of his statements. Apple speaks of the schools' role in the "maintenance of an unequal social order," the need to adopt an advocacy model of research "if substantial progress is to be made," "the unequal social world that educators live in is represented by the reification, the commodification, of the language they use," and the "stratification of knowledge . . . [that] involves the stratification of people." The deep structure of the mental template that underlies his way of thinking, and is carried as part of the symbolic baggage of his metaphors, includes the following characteristics:

1. Linear sense of time that helps to organize events in a continuum that leads from a past into a future. This sense of linear time, which goes back to the earliest symbolic foundations of Western thought, underlies the teleology that is so fundamental to the Marxist idea of dialectical materialism where the conflict of social classes occurs within a linear patterned time frame.

2. Change is not only seen as part of a linear continuum but is progressive in nature. Thus whatever accelerates historical change, even if it involves violent revolutions, is progressive. While change and progress are inevitable, they can be greatly speeded up through the intervention of intellectuals who possess a special way of knowing and predicting what the future holds for others too burdened with cares of the present to concern themselves with the future. The fusing of the linear sense of time with the idea of progress

can be traced directly back to the Enlightenment period.[18] That progress is inevitable is implied in Apple's appeal for an advocacy approach to research; it also underlies and legitimates the intensions of his entire theoretical effort as well as those of his Marxist colleagues. That change might lead to greater bureaucratization of life (the case still has to be made that this would be a more progressive stage of social development) or that it might lead to more atavistic forms of political control is not seriously considered. Like the Marxist metaphor of praxis or Dewey's metaphor of growth, change represents progress.

3. The idea of causality is a basic aspect of the Western mind set that is part of the deep structure of Apple's analysis of the relationship between school knowledge and the "economic reproduction of class relations in an advanced industrial society." The relationships among the distribution function of school, status knowledge, and the patterns of class relations that are grounded in the mode of production are explained in terms of cause and effect. The mode of production causes, in terms of the Marxist way of thinking, a particular mode of consciousness to exist. In Apple's analysis an attempt is made to avoid simple economic determinism; this is done by arguing that the mode of consciousness legitimated in schools is causally related to the maintenance of the capitalist mode of production. An important aspect of the Western tendency to think in terms of cause and effect is the concomitant mental habit of thinking categorically, particularly in the categories of true-false, right-wrong, either-or. Marx's contribution to understanding dialectical thinking (which in his formulation retained the element of teleology) held out the promise of breaking away from this aspect of Western thinking, which is so characteristically represented in Aristolelian logic. While Marx was unable to shed much of the traditional mental template that stamps his work as the product of a particular historical and cultural period, his followers, including Apple, have been even less successful in avoiding a thought process that organizes reality into rigid categories and linear causal relationships. In the writings of Apple, as well as in those of Bowles and Gintis, socialism and capitalism are clearly organized into the rigid categories of right and wrong, truth and falsity, salvation and perdition. Even Harry Braverman, whose analysis is often brilliant, slips back into the categorical and causal pattern of thinking when he asserts that capitalism is the cause of the increasing separation of mental from manual work.[19] Why the phenomenon that Braverman investigated continues to exist in Russia, China, and other societies trying to develop their own form of socialism cannot be explained when it is categorically tied to capitalism. But then categorical thinking does not relate well to the complexity of actual experience, and thus is best left in its context-free status.

4. Abstract-theoretical thought is believed to have the power to represent more accurately the reality of individual and social experience, as well as to blueprint the progressive unfoldment of the future. This "faith" in the power

of rational thought, which can be traced directly back to Enlightenment thinkers for its most fundamental legitimation, is not only a uniquely cultural phenomenon, but is, according to Alvin Gouldner, class specific. The ideology of intellectuals, he points out, holds "that an argument must stand on its own legs, must be self-sufficient, that one must 'consider the speech and not the speaker,' that it must encompass all that is necessary, providing full presentation of the assumptions needed to produce and support the conclusion." Gouldner also points out that "the culture of critical discourse (intellectuals and theorists) is characterized by speech that is *relatively* more situation free, more context or field 'independent.' This speech culture thus values expressly legislated meanings and devalues tacit, context-limited meanings. It's ideal," he concludes, "is: 'one word, one meaning,' for everyone and forever."[20]

What he sees as a class-specific view of the power of rational thought must also be understood in terms of the fact that only intellectuals possess the cultural capital necessary to engage in this high-status activity. Apple, as well as the rest of us theorizing about education and society, cannot operate without incorporating these deep-structure assumptions into our work.

5. The view of individuals as potentially free, voluntaristic entities who will take responsibility for creating themselves when freed from societal forms of oppression. This humanistic ideal is expressed in the Marxist idea of praxis as a process of self-transcendence that occurs as man freely interacts with the natural environment; it is also at the basis of the Marxist metaphorical image of alienation. It is a view, as the Yugoslav Marxist Svetozar Stojanović pointed out, that is curiously free of any serious anthropological evidence.[21] That we are free to make choices based on what reason discloses to us (a process that seldom discloses the self-interest and will to power of intellectuals who provide the rational basis on which choice should be predicated) is part of the background metaphor of most writings that are intended to elicit action directed toward social change. The purpose in disclosing how the curriculum reproduces the relations of production is to provide a rational basis for action on the part of a free, voluntaristic individual who is expected to seek the good. An interesting aspect of this part of the Western mental template is that this view of the individual is often reified to the point where, in the abstract, the workers are seen as virtuous and exhibiting the self-transcendent qualities of free beings, while at the flesh and blood level of daily life where their conservative values and materialistic tastes are too evident to be denied they are seen as being in a false state of consciousness (in theological terms, their condition would be identified in terms of a "fallen state").

6. An anthropocentric universe where the individual is the source of decision making (not bound by tradition), the source of meaning, and the fundamental reference point used to legitimate any form of interference with the natural environment. In the tradition of the Western myth that gave

man the power to name, the environment has been seen as existing essentially for the purpose of serving human needs. The sense of mystery, sanctity, and the obligation to say no to the use of technological power or individual desire are not part of the natural attitude of the person who experiences an anthropocentric universe. This part of the Western mind set emphasizes the right to take direct action, to plan according to a rational process, and to be the ultimate source of moral authority. It is a fundamentally secular and man-centered universe.

For most of us the acquisition of this symbolic world has been a natural process, reinforced through daily conversations with significant others. It is so much a part of our taken-for-granted attitude toward everyday life that to have parts of this mental template identified, as in the previous discussion, is to feel that the identification of such truisms is an unnecessary form of subversion. My point here is not to claim that this is an exhaustive treatment of the deep structure of Western consciousness, or to make value judgments about it's being superior or inferior to the symbolic worlds of other cultural traditions. Instead, my purpose is to make the point that the use of metaphors derived from this cultural episteme also involves adopting these particular, historically grounded patterns of thinking. In the following discussion of the metaphors Apple uses as the basis for his analysis of the relationship between curriculum and social classes, I want to identify some of the issues that need to be addressed if we are going to consider seriously using a Marxist analysis as a basis for social reform. I am not taking the position that this should not be considered, but rather that we should acknowledge the epistemic roots of this analysis, and that it involves a peculiarly Western, modernizing, and secularizing frame of mind. When it is stated openly, rather than being part of the hidden cultural agenda embedded in revolutionary metaphors, some people may press Apple and his colleagues to justify the deep-structure categories of Western thought as superior in a moral sense and as a source of human fulfillment to those of other cultures.

Like Althusser's analysis of schools as being part of the "ideological state apparatus," the analysis of curriculum as a form of cultural reproduction is based on such a basic truism that one can only wonder about the excitement it has produced in certain quarters. Althusser states that "all ideological state apparatuses, whatever they are, [including schools] contribute to the same result: the reproduction of the relations of production, i.e., of capitalist relations of exploitation."[22] That social institutions reproduce the patterns of thought and economic activity of the culture they transmit is a fact of social existence in all societies; this may apply even more in Marxist societies where there is less freedom of inquiry and local influence on schools. The opposite – that schools would be designed to subvert the social order that established and maintains them – is too simpleminded to be seriously entertained. What raises this commonsense observation to the status of serious social criticism in the theories of Althusser and Apple is that their analysis is developed within the context of background metaphors that give expression to a secular vision that is very much in the tradition of what Max Weber called "emissary prophecy." This vision, or what Marx referred to as the beginning of human history, is based in part on the powerful image of equality that is to guarantee social justice and the realization of our human potential. As equality is one of several background metaphors that give Apple's analysis its appealing moral tone, I want to raise some questions about how we are to translate this metaphor into social action, and whether this can be done without establishing a new form of cultural imperialism. I also want to raise similar questions about other taken-for-granted metaphors – class, hierarchy, and hegemony – that seem so central to Apple's agenda of social reform. These questions, I believe, will disclose some unique assumptions and problems that will be difficult to reconcile with such other values as the democratic right of cultural self-determination.

The curriculum, according to Apple, must be understood as helping to reproduce the social relations of an "unequal" economic structure. This means that social and educational reform should lead to the replacement of the social conditions that create inequality; but this leaves us with problems of interpreting what "equality" should mean. Does it mean in the economic sense that everybody is to receive an equal wage, or that each will give according to ability and receive according to need? Marx himself does not provide a clear-cut explanation of how to achieve economic equality. Equality in the political sense could mean, as in Yugoslovia, that people should be involved in shaping the decisions that affect them. But politics very much depends on the linguistic competence of the participants. In a political environment where the power to define "What Is" depends on the possession of a complex and powerful language code, equality would have to mean achieving the same level of linguistic competence and performance. But as language codes vary in their ability to deal with certain phenomena – for example, the black ghetto vernacular is less powerful in defining "What Is" in the scientific domain than is the language code of university-trained experts – is equality to be attained by forcing one cultural group to adopt the more powerful language code of another? Whose language code is to be adopted as the basis for establishing linguistic equality? Can linguistic equality be reconciled with cultural pluralism or, for that matter, can it be achieved in a technocratic society where experts utilize their own language code as a means of legitimating both their knowledge and their status? If not, it would seem reasonable to expect the technological infrastructure to be dismantled in order to achieve linguistic equality. The metaphor of equality – that abstract, context-free image of the Enlightenment mind – is equally illusive when we ask how to structure the experience of people in a manner that fosters equality. Are the older members of society to deny that they have learned anything from their longer life in order to achieve the status of equality with youth? The alternative-school movement led many adults to adopt a stance that could only be described in terms of Sartre's idea of self-deception in order to be true to the ideological requirements of a society of equals. But, as many participants in the alternative-school movement discovered, this stance could not easily be maintained, and many had to acknowledge that the range and depth of their experience had to be recognized if they were not to act in bad faith. How is Apple's interpretation of equality to overcome this form of inequality, or, for that matter, the more existential aspects of inequality where we see people differing in their ability to take responsibility for their lives?

The metaphor of equality also raises some interesting questions about the structure of the family, particularly in cultures where the extended family involves a hierarchy of authority and responsibility. But within our cultural context of the nuclear family, the image of equality poses important questions about how equality is to be attained within the family unit (children are to have the same voice in all matters as parents?) as well as between families. To achieve equality in the sense of compensating for differences in family background is one thing; to achieve equality through state interference with the desire to pass on some sort of inheritance (moral as well as material) to one's children is a more problematic policy that runs counter to a basic human motivation that is expressed in a variety of cultural ways.

The image of equality was the creation of the Enlightenment mind set that fused romanticism and rationalism. While a progressive mode of thought in its era, it nevertheless lacked an awareness of the multiple realities experienced in different cultures. A basic aspect of the conceptual grammar of that period was the tendency toward theoretical abstract thought, and to treat it as culture free. Thinking about reason, freedom, equality, and fraternity in the abstract is an archetypal example of the mental template of the Enlightenment era. If we apply the abstract image of equality to the context of the multiple cultural realities that make up our world, we have to ask whose culture is to become the one that will be adopted as the basis for achieving an equal social-cultural order. The deep structure of Apple's metaphor of equality – the coding of reality into either-or categories, the preeminence given to theoretical-abstract thought over pretheoretical experience, the image of equality that is based on an image of atomistic-voluntaristic individualism, the anthropocentric universe – seems to imply the hegemony of Western cultural episteme.

The attempt to place Apple's use of context-free metaphors within the context of people's phenomenological culture is not intended to overturn the question of how to achieve social justice, a question that concerns more people than just Marxists. Attempts to attain social justice are bound to fail if they do not start with a recognition of cultural differences, and a recognition that these cultural differences cannot all be explained in terms of the same economic paradigm and in terms of metaphors that contain deep-structure assumptions that are foreign to the culture to which they are being applied. If the formula for defining social justice – an equalitarian society in terms of Apple's paradigm – ignores the cultural traditions that grounds the phenomenology of everyday life, the formula cannot be seen as a source of social justice. Questions of social justice must take account of differences in cultural context, which means that social justice cannot be reduced to a simple formula.

A second metaphor that is fundamental to Apple and the others looking at curriculum in terms of a Marxist framework is the image of social class. The cultural reproduction theory is predicated on the image of class relations involving two antagonistic social classes, the capitalists or the bourgeoisie who buy the labor of the working class or proletariat. It is a dichotomous model of class, highly abstracted, and highly metaphorical in its image of conflict between the owners of capital and those who, as the real producers, have only their labor to sell. The categorical thinking that underlies the epistemic tradition that Apple operates within includes the vision or metaphorical image of a classless society where alienation and exploitation cease to exist. The closest Apple comes to spelling out what would be involved in a society free of class antagonism is when he urges the "progressive articulation of a commitment to a social order that has as its very foundation not the accumulation of goals, profits, and credentials, but the maximization of economic, social, and educational equality." The structural relations, he goes on the say, "must be such as to equalize not merely access to but actual control of cultural, social, and especially economic institutions."[23] The equalization of power and cultural capital, as well as control over the means of production, would produce a society free of social class. As there is no empirical referent for such a society, it exists for Apple and his colleagues as a mental image or metaphor. More importantly for our purposes, this metaphor of a classless society serves as a carrier of the Western assumptions about free individuals who are essentially creative and self-transcendent, and who will introduce the reign of reason (scientific Marxism) into human relationships. Again, the deep structure underlying the metaphor raises the question of a new form of Western cultural hegemony when the metaphor of a classless society is adopted in a non-Western culture.

Within our own culture of advanced industrial social relationships there is a more fundamental question of how to relate Apple's metaphor of dichotomous classes to everyday experience. Categorical divisions formulated in the abstract (part of the mental template of Western thought) are difficult to relate to the lives of real people. Dean Ashenden, an Australian Marxist educational theorist, recently commented on the problem of taking the Marxist image of class out of its theoretical framework and applying it as the basis of empirical research into class relations. In looking for a contrasting sample of working-class and ruling-class students, he had to ask the question, "But who was working class, who ruling class?"[24] There were too many aspects of the students' phenomenological culture that could not be accounted for in terms of the Marxist categories of class. Within our culture the categorical thinking that underlies Apple's use of class makes it difficult to understand the symbolic world of social groups who do not fit into Marx's economic categories, for example, people who are identified with the middle class but who are salaried like the working class (but often at a lower level of remuneration), workers who are heavily invested both individually and in terms of their union pension funds in capitalistic enterprises, affluent intellectuals (Samuel Bowles and Paul Sweezy being two prominent examples) who identify with the idea of a working-class revolution.

The metaphor of a classless society, which includes the image of the equal distribution of cultural capital, also raises some rather intriguing questions about what is to happen to the role of the intellectual and the technological expert. Apple clearly sees himself as an example of the former. Yet in his vision of a classless society there is no room for his type of intellectual activity without the emergence of a fundamental contradiction. Historically Marxist revolutions have been guided by intellectuals, and the centralization of power and the extension of bureaucratic control in Marxist societies has extended the influence of intellectuals as a New Class.[25] Unfortunately, there has been no attempt on Apple's part to explain the contradiction between the theory of a classless society, and practice in Marxist societies. Apple's dependence on context-free metaphors serves as a gloss that fails to put the future of intellectuals in a classless society in any kind of perspective that takes account of the role they have played in pre- and postrevolutionary social development. The historical record of Marxist revolutionary movements gives a clear picture of Marxist practice; it would be useful if Apple could illuminate for us the disjuncture between Marxist theory and the historical evidence of Marxist practice, as well as when we might expect to see the "withering away" of the intellectual vanguard. It would also be useful if he would explain how a new educational praxis could be based on his metaphor of equality and classless society. Unless he can relate his metaphorical image to the world of experience we must either view his thinking as based on a form of historically grounded idealism or begin to ask questions about the hidden ritual-religious function of metaphor in Marxist theory.

Two other metaphors that are prominent in the writings of Apple and the other theorists who view curriculum as a process of cultural reproduction include hierarchy and hegemony. Both terms are used, like the other metaphors of inequality and class, in a categorical framework where their opposite image is held out as not only desirable but ideologically guaranteed if we take the correct revolutionary steps. A concern with the existence of hierarchy in the organization of school knowledge and in the decision-making process is fundamental to Michael Young's analysis of the relationship between curricula and social class; it is also a principle concern of Apple, though he defines it in terms of the metaphor of "high-status knowledge." Implicit in their image of the new society that is to be nonhierarchical is a strong strain of Western Romanticism. If capitalism can be overturned, men and women will become rational in the secular, scientific sense and cooperative in the sense of equal participation in the decision-making process. (Again, social change is equated with progress.) The background metaphor of social relationships that do not involve hierarchy has some rather challenging implications in terms of the family unit in most cultures, the organization of knowledge in both theocracies and technocracies, and at the basic level of socialization where at least one member in the process has prior knowledge and experience that is to be the basis of sharing with the person who is under-going socialization. As suggested earlier, a hierarchical structure is an implicit aspect of a technological mode of thought. Are Apple and Young proposing to abolish abstract-theoretical thought, which is a fundamental characteristic of a technological mode of consciousness, in order to eliminate all forms of hierarchical arrangements?

Hegemony is viewed as a form of control at the symbolic level, and in Apple's writings it is associated with capitalism. As a metaphor hegemony is similar to Marx's idea of ideology as false consciousness, but its users seem to imply that somehow it is a more powerful concept for understanding the con-nection between the symbolic world of everyday life (cultural capital) and the capitalistic relations of production. Apple sees the metaphor of hegemony as providing "a somewhat more flexible position which speaks of determination as a complex nexus of relationships which, in their final moment, are eco-nomically rooted, that exert pressures and set limits on cultural practice, including schools." Thus, "the cultural sphere," he continues, "is not a 'mere reflection' of economic practices. Instead, the influence, the 'reflection' or determination, is highly mediated by forms of human action." In terms of schools, hegemony is exercised through the codes that underlie the or-ganization and transmission of knowledge, and the interaction patterns within the school that are the basis of commonsense experience.[26] Apple's understanding of hegemonic culture is insightful but what I find particularly interesting is how his historically derived categories and assumptions lead him to imply that with the elimination of capitalism (another metaphor that needs more critical analysis) we will enter a new stage of human history free of hegemony.

One of his subchapter headings reads "Beyond Reproduction." His tendency to place ideas within a matrix of categories that organize reality in terms of dichotomous distinctions (capitalism-hegemony, elimination of capitalism-the elimination of hegemony) and linear progress (the next stage of social development is a more progressive one) raises important questions. If hegemony can be understood as the "organized assemblage of meanings and practices, the central, effective and dominant system of meanings, values and actions which are lived . . . the common sense interpretations"[27] we give to everyday life, the suggestion that somehow, through a scientifically dir-ected revolution, hegemony can be eliminated is too absurd to even consider. Apple's understanding of hegemony is similar in many ways to Clifford Geertz's idea of ideology as a mental template, though he goes beyond Geertz in relating mental templates to forms of economic activity. To imply, as Apple does, that the overturning of capitalism will lead to a state where we are free of hegemony is tantamount to saying that we can live without mental templates and without language systems. What Apple should say is that social change will lead to changes (or does it follow?) in our mental template, but that hegemonic culture, though modified in some way, will continue to exist. But perhaps the atavistic assumption of the Enlightenment period – that man is rational in the sense of consciously controlling both mental process and the social-physical world – has prevented Apple from testing his historically grounded metaphors against what new metaphors and theories are telling us about the symbolic nature of phenomenological culture.

A basic problem of the metaphors of the cultural reproduction theorists writing on schools and curriculum is that they have treated their key and background metaphors – inequality, class, hierarchy, and hegemony – in a literal sense where they become culture-free images that can be generalized to a variety of cultural contexts. This generalization of reified images becomes a new form of cultural imperialism when the historical-cultural epistemology out of which the metaphor is derived is ignored. In developing his theory of metaphor, Brown observes that "new metaphors, especially when elaborated into models and theories, are not merely new ways of looking at the facts, nor are they a revelation of what the facts really are." "Instead," he warns, "the metaphor in a fundamental way creates the facts and provides a definition of what the essential quality of an experience must be. And for this new reality to be entered into and comprehended – from the inside as it were – the metaphor must be taken *as if* it literally were the case."[28] This shaping of how we look at reality, what Alvin Gouldner has referred to as acquiring a set of conceptual lenses, points to the importance of understanding the genealogy of our language.

While we may think we can achieve liberation through the use of a revolutionary-sounding language, we also have to remember that it may be important to liberate ourselves from certain controls embedded in the structure and imagery of our language. This applies to the Marxist educational theorists like Apple, but also to the educational technocrat and the educational humanists who have their own set of metaphors that enable us to "see" certain aspects of experience and to not "see" what the metaphor puts out of focus. My own embeddedness in the Western mind set leads me to think that this ability to decode our phenomenological culture as a complex set of language systems, what I have elsewhere called cultural literacy, is important, but I no longer have a taken-for-granted sense of teleology that tells me that people will want to do this because they understand its rational nature, or that it will lead to progress. Nor would I necessarily recommend it in societies that do not share the cultural grammar of Western individualism and rationalism. However, in terms of the Western mind set, it seems that ecological and social events no longer give us a real choice as to whether we want to think about the possibility of cultural literacy. I know that articles should end in a nice summary fashion, and usually with an optimistic, uplifting thought. But somehow Nietzsche's observations seem appropriate to concluding my comments on metaphor, curriculum, and social change: "Man can no longer make his misery known to others by means of language; thus he cannot really express himself anymore . . . ; language has gradually become a force that drives humanity where it least wishes to go. . . . The results of this inability to communicate is that the creations of common action . . . all bear the stamp of mutual noncomprehension."[29] For Nietzsche, progress was not seen as an inevitable force that would shield us from our vanities and well-intentioned mistakes.

Notes

1. Michael W. Apple, "Ideology, Reproduction, and Educational Reform," *Comparative Education Review* 22, no. 3 (October 1978): 372.
2. Michael W. Apple, *Ideology and Curriculum* (London: Routledge & Kegan Paul, 1979), p. 16.
3. Apple, "Ideology, Reproduction, and Educational Reform," p. 376.
4. Ibid., p. 382.
5. Quoted in Jacques Derrida, *Of Grammatology* (Baltimore: Johns Hopkins University Press, 1976), p. xxii.
6. Friedrich Nietzsche, *The Will to Power* (New York: Vintage Books, 1968), p. 273.
7. Ernest Cassirer, *The Philosophy of Symbolic Form*, vol. 1 (New Haven, Conn.: Yale University Press, 1953), pp. 87–88.
8. Susanne K. Langer, *Philosophy in a New Key* (Cambridge: Harvard University Press, 1960), p. 141.
9. Richard H. Brown, *A Poetic for Sociology* (Cambridge: Cambridge University Press, 1978), p. 78.
10. Ibid., p. 88.
11. Ibid., p. 125.
12. Quoted in Brown, *A Poetic for Sociology*, p. 130.
13. Ibid., p. 84.
14. Peter Berger and Stanley Pullberg, "Reification and the Sociological Critique of Consciousness," *History and Theory* 4 (1964–1965): 207.
15. Clifford Geertz, *The Interpretation of Cultures* (New York: Basic Books, 1973), p. 216.
16. Alvin W. Gouldner, "The Metaphoricality of Marxism and the Context-Freeing Grammar of Socialism," *Theory and Society* 1, no. 4 (1974): 388.
17. Benjamin Lee Whorf, "Science and Linguistics," in *Everyman His Own Way: Readings in Cultural Anthropology*, ed. Alan Dundes (Englewood Cliffs, N.J.: Prentice Hall, 1968), pp. 324–25.

73

The Day Our Children Disappear: Predictions of a Media Ecologist

Neil Postman

I am aware that in addressing the question of the future of education, one can write either a "good news" or a "bad news" essay. Typically, a good news essay presents readers with a problem, then proceeds to solve it (more or less). Readers usually find such essays agreeable, as well they should. A good news essay gives us a sense of potency and control, and a really *good* "good news" essay shows us how to employ our imaginations in confronting professional issues. Although I have not yet seen the other essays in this special *KAPPAN*, I feel sure that most of them are of the good news type, solid and constructive.

A bad news essay, on the other hand, presents readers with a problem – and ends (more or less). Naturally, readers find such essays disagreeable, since they engender a sense of confusion and sometimes hopelessness. Still, they have their uses. They may, for example, help us understand some things that need explaining. Let me tell you, then, that while I hope my remarks will be illuminating, you must prepare yourself for an orthodox – even classical – bad news essay. I wish it could be otherwise, because I know my temperament to be more suited to optimism than to gloom and doom. But I write as a person whose academic interests go by the name of media ecology. Media ecology is the study of the effects of communications technology on culture. We study how media affect people's cognitive habits, their social relations, their political biases, and their personal values. And in this capacity I have almost nothing optimistic to write about, for, if I am to respect the evidence as I understand it, I am bound to say that the effects of modern media – especially television – have been and will probably continue to be disastrous, especially for our youth. What I intend to do here is describe in some detail one important respect in which this is the case and explain how it occurred. As is the custom in bad news essays, I shall offer no solution to this problem – mainly because I know of none.

Source: *Phi Delta Kappan*, 62 (1981): 425–433.

Before proceeding, I must express one bit of "good news" about what I shall be saying. It is to be understood that when I speak of some development as "disastrous," I mean that it is disastrous from my very limited point of view. Obviously, what appears disastrous to me may be regarded as marvelous by others. After all, I am a New Yorker, and most things appear to me disastrous. But even more to the point, what may appear disastrous at one historical moment may turn out to be marvelous in a later age. There are, in fact, many historical instances of someone's correctly predicting negative effects of a medium of communication but where, in the end, what appeared to be a disaster turned out to be a great advance.

The best example I know of concerns the great Athenian teacher, Socrates, who feared and mocked the written word, which in his time was beginning to be used for many purposes and with great frequency. But not by him. As you know, Socrates wrote no books, and had it not been for Plato and Xenophon, who did, we would know almost nothing about him. In one of his most enduring conversations, called the *Phaedrus*, Socrates gives three reasons why he does not like writing. Writing, he says, will deprive Athenians of their powerful memories, for if everything is written down there will be no need to memorize. Second, he says that writing will change the form of education. In particular, it will destroy the dialectic process, for writing forces students to follow an argument rather than participate in it. And third, Socrates warns that writing will change concepts of privacy and the meaning of public discourse; for once you write something down, you never know whose eyes will fall upon it – those for whom it is intended, perhaps, but just as likely those for whom it is not intended. Thus, for Socrates, the widespread use of writing was, and would be, a cultural disaster. In a sense it was. For all of Socrates' predictions were correct, and there is no doubt that writing undermined the oral tradition that Socrates believed to be the most suitable mode for expressing serious ideas, beautiful poetry, and authentic piety. But Socrates did not see what his student, Plato, did: that writing would create new modes of thought altogether and provide new and wonderful uses for the intellect – most especially what today we call *science*.

So without intending to suggest an unsupportable comparison, I write as a Socrates-like character, prophesying that the advent of the television age will have the direst outcome. I hope that among you there is a Plato-like character who will be able to see the television age as a blessing.

In order for me to get to the center of my argument as quickly as possible, I am going to resist the temptation to discuss some of the fairly obvious effects of television, such as its role in shortening our students' attention span, in eroding their capacity to handle linguistic and mathematical symbolism, and in causing them to become increasingly impatient with deferred gratification. The evidence for these effects exists in a variety of forms – from declining SAT scores to astronomical budgets for remedial writing classes to the everyday observations of teachers and parents. But I will not take the time to review any of the evidence for the intellectually incapacitating effects of television. Instead, I want to focus on what I regard as the most astonishing and serious effect of television. It is simply this: Television is causing the rapid decline of our concept of childhood. I choose to discuss this because I can think of nothing that is bound to have a more profound effect on our work as educators than that our children should disappear. I do not mean, of course, that they will physically disappear. I mean that the *idea* of children will disappear.

If this pronouncement, on first hearing, seems implausible, let me hasten to tell you that the idea of childhood is not very old. In fact, in the Western world the idea of childhood hardly existed prior to the 16th century. Up until that time children as young as 6 and 7 were not regarded as fundamentally different from adults. As far as historians can tell, the language of children, their dress, their games, their labor, and the legal rights were the same as those of adults. It was recognized, of course, that children tended to be smaller than adults, but this fact did not confer upon them any special status; there were certainly no special institutions for the nurturing of children. Prior to the 16th century, for example, there were no books on child rearing or, indeed, any books about women in their role as mothers. Children, to take another example, were always included in funeral processions, there being no reason anyone could think of to shield them from knowledge of death. Neither did it occur to anyone to keep a picture of a child if that child lived to grow to adulthood or had died in infancy. Nor are there any references to children's speech or jargon prior to the 17th century, after which they are found in abundance If you have ever seen 13th- or 14th-century paintings of children, you will have noticed that they are always depicted as small adults. Except for size, they are devoid of any of the physical characteristics we associate with childhood, and they are never shown on canvas alone – that is, isolated from adults. Such paintings are entirely accurate representations of the psychological and social perceptions of children prior to the 16th century. Here is how the historian J. H. Plumb puts it:

> There was no separate world of childhood. Children shared the same games with adults, the same toys, the same fairy stories. They lived their lives together, never apart. The coarse village festivals depicted by Breughel, showing men arid women besotted with drink, groping for each other with unbridled lust, have children eating and drinking with the adults. Even in the soberer pictures of wedding feasts and dances, the children are enjoying themselves alongside their elders, doing the same things.

Barbara Tuchman, in her marvelous book about the 14th century titled. *A Distant Mirror*, puts it more succinctly: "If children survived to age 7, their recognized life began, more or less as miniature adults. Childhood was already over."

Now the reasons for this are fairly complicated. For one thing, most children did *not* survive; their mortality rate was extraordinarily high, and it is not until the late 14th century that children are even mentioned in wills and testaments – an indication that adults did not expect them to be around very long. In fact, probably because of this, in some parts of Europe children were treated as neuter genders. In 14th-century Italy, for example, the sex of a child who had died was never recorded.

Certainly, adults did not have the emotional commitment to children that *we* accept as normal. Phillipe Aries, in his great book titled *Centuries of Childhood*, remarks that the prevailing view was to have several children in order to keep a few; people could not allow themselves to become too attached to something that was regarded as a probable loss. Aries quotes from a document that records a remark made by the neighbor of a distraught mother of five young children. In order to comfort the mother, the neighbor says, "Before they are old enough to bother you, you will have lost half of them, or perhaps all of them."

We must also not forget that in a feudal society children were often regarded as mere economic utilities, adults being less interested in the character and intelligence of children than in their capacity for work. But I think the most powerful reason for the absence of the idea of childhood is to be found in the communication environment of the Dark and Middle Ages. Since most people did not know how to read, or did not *need* to know how to read, a child became an adult – a fully participating adult – when he or she learned how to speak. Since all important social transactions involved face-to-face oral communication, full competence to speak and hear – which is usually achieved by age 7 – was the dividing line between infancy and adulthood. There was no intervening stage, because none was needed – until the middle of the 15th century. At that point an extraordinary event occurred that not only changed the religious, economic, and political face of Europe but also created our modern idea of childhood. I am referring, of course, to the invention of the printing press. And because in a few minutes you will, perhaps be thinking that I am claiming too much for the power of modern media, especially TV, it is worth saying now that no one had the slightest inkling in 1450 that the printing press would have such powerful effects on our society as it did. When Gutenberg announced that he could manufacture books, as he put it, "without the help of reed, stylus, or pen but by wondrous agreement, proportion, and harmony of punches and types," he did not imagine that his invention would undermine the authority of the Catholic Church. Yet less than 80 years later Martin Luther was in effect claiming that, with the Word of God on everyone's kitchen table, Christians did not require the Papacy to interpret it for them. Nor did Gutenberg have any inkling that his invention would create a new class of people: namely, children. Or more specifically, male children, for there is no doubt that boys were the first class of specialized children.

How was this accomplished? Simply by the fact that, less than a hundred years after Gutenberg's invention, European culture became a reading culture; i.e., adulthood was redefined. One could not become an adult unless he or she knew how to read. In order to experience God, one had to be able, obviously, to read the Bible, which is why Luther himself translated the Bible into German. In order to experience literature, one had to be able to read novels and personal essays, Forms of literature that were wholly created by the printing press. Our earliest novelists – for example, Richardson and Defoe – were themselves printers. Montaigne, who invented the essay, worked hand in hand with a printer, as did Thomas More when he produced what may be called our first science fiction novel – his *Utopia*. Of course, in order to learn science one not only had to know how to read but, by the beginning of the 17th century, one could read science in the vernacular – that is, in one's own language. Sir Francis Bacon's *The Advancement of Learning*, published in 1605, was the first scientific tract an Englishman could read in English. And of course one must not forget the great Dutch humanist, Erasmus, who, understanding the meaning of the printing press as well as anyone, wrote one of the first books of etiquette for the instruction of young men. He said of his book, "As Socrates brought philosophy from heaven to earth, so I have led philosophy to games and banquets." (By the way, Erasmus dedicated the book to his publisher's son, and the book includes advice and guidance on how to convert prostitutes to a moral life.)

The importance of books on etiquette should not be overlooked. As Norman Elias shows in his book titled *The Civilizing Proccss*, the sudden emergence in the 16th century of etiquette books signifies that one could no longer assume that children knew everything adults knew – in other words, the separation of childhood from adulthood was under way.

Alongside all of this, Europeans rediscovered what Plato had known about learning to read: namely, that it is best done at an early age. Since reading is, among other things, an unconscious reflex as well as an act of recognition, the habit of reading must be formed in that period when the brain is still engaged in the task of acquiring oral language. The adult who learns to read after his or her oral vocabulary is completed rarely becomes a fluent reader.

What this came to mean in the 16th century is that the young had to be separated from the rest of the community to be taught how to read – that is, to be taught how to function as an adult. This meant that they had to go to school. And going to school was the essential event in creating childhood. The printing press, in other words, created the idea of school. In fact, school classes originated to separate students according to their capacities as readers, not to separate them according to age. That came later. In any event, once all of this occurred it was inevitable that the young would be viewed as a special class of people whose minds and character were qualitatively different from those of adults. As any semanticist can tell you, once you categorize people for a particular purpose, you will soon discover many other reasons why they should be regarded as different. We began, in short, to see human development as a series of stages, with childhood as a bridge between infancy and adulthood. For the past 350 years we have been developing and refining our concept of childhood, this with particular intensity in the 18th, 19th, and 20th centuries. We have been developing and refining institutions for the nurturing of children: and we have conferred upon children a preferred status, reflected in the special ways we expect them to think, talk, dress, play, and learn.

All of this, I believe, is now coming to an end. And it is coming to an end because our communication environment has been radically altered once again – this time by electronic media, especially television. Television has a transforming power at least equal to that of the printing press and possibly as great as that of the alphabet itself. It is my contention that, with the assistance of other media such as radio, film, and records, television has the power to lead us to childhood's end.

Here is how the transformation is happening. To begin with, television presents information mostly in visual images. Although human speech is heard on TV and sometimes assumes importance, people mostly *watch* television. What they watch are rapidly changing visual images – as many as 1,200 different shots every hour. This requires very little conceptual thinking or analytic decoding. TV watching is almost wholly a matter of pattern recognition. The *symbolic form* of television does not require any special instruction or learning. In America, TV viewing begins at about the age of 18 months: by 30 months, according to studies by Daniel Anderson of the University of Massachusetts, children begin to understand and respond to TV imagery. Thus there is no need for any preparation or prerequisite training for watching TV. Television needs no analogue to the McGuffey *Reader*. And, as you must know, there is no such thing, in reality, as children's programming on TV. Everything is for everybody. So far as symbolic form is concerned, "Charlie's Angels" is as sophisticated or as simple to grasp as "Sesame Street." Unlike books, which vary greatly in syntactical and lexical complexity and which may be scaled according to the ability of the reader, TV presents information in a form that is undifferentiated in its accessibility. And that is why adults and children tend to watch the same programs. I might add, in case you are thinking that children and adults at least watch at different times, that according to Frank Mankiewicz's *Remote Control*, approximately 600,000 children watch TV between midnight and two in the morning.

To summarize: TV erases the dividing line between childhood and adulthood for two reasons: first, because it requires no instruction to grasp its form; second, because it does not segregate its audience. It communicates the same information to everyone simultaneously, regardless of age, sex, race, or level of education.

But it erases the dividing line in other ways as well. One might say that the main difference between an adult and a child is that the adult knows about certain facets of life – its mysteries, its contradictions, its violence, its tragedies – that are not considered suitable for children to know. As children move toward adulthood we reveal these secrets to them in what we believe to be a psychologically assimilable way. But television makes this arrangement quite impossible. Because television operates virtually around the clock – it would not be economically feasible for it to do otherwise – it requires a constant supply of novel and interesting information. This means that all adult secrets – social, sexual, physical, and the like – must be revealed. Television forces the entire culture to come out of the closet. In its quest for new and sensational information to hold its audience, TV must tap every existing taboo in the culture: homosexuality, incest, divorce, promiscuity, corruption, adultery, sadism. Each is now merely a theme for one or another television show. In the process each loses its role as an exclusively adult secret.

Some time ago, while watching a TV program called "The Vidal Sassoon Show," I came across the quintessential example of what I am talking about. Vidal Sassoon is a famous hairdresser whose TV show is a mixture of beauty hints, diet information, health suggestions, and popular psychology. As he came to the end of one segment of the show in which an attractive woman had demonstrated how to cook vegetables, the theme music came up and Sassoon just had time enough to say, "Don't go away. We'll be back with a marvelous new diet and, then, a quick look at incest." Now, this is more – much more – than demystification. It is even more than the revelation of secrets. It is the ultimate trivialization of culture. Television is relentless in both revealing and trivializing all things private and shameful, and therefore it undermines the moral basis of culture. The subject matter of the confessional box and the psychiatrist's office is now in the public domain. I have it on good authority that, shortly, we and our children will have the opportunity to see commercial TV's first experiments with presenting nudity, which will probably not be shocking to anyone, since TV commercials have been offering a form of soft-core pornography for years. And on the subject of commercials – the 700,000 of them that American youths will see in the first 18 years of their lives – they too contribute toward opening to youth all the secrets that once were the province of adults – everything from vagina! sprays to life insurance to the causes of marital conflict. And we must not omit the contributions of news shows, those curious entertainments that daily provide the young with vivid images of adult failure and even madness.

As a consequence of all of this, childhood innocence and specialness are impossible to sustain, which is why children have disappeared from television. Have you noticed that all the children on television shows are depicted as merely small adults, in the manner of 13th- or 14th-century paintings? Watch "The Love Boat" or any of the soap operas or family shows or situation comedies. You will see children whose language, dress, sexuality, and interests are not different from those of the adults on the same shows. Like the paintings of Breughel, the children *do* everything the adults do and are shielded from nothing.

And yet, as TV begins to render invisible the traditional concept of childhood, it would not be quite accurate to say that it immerses us in an adult world. Rather, it uses the material of the adult world as the basis for projecting a new kind of person altogether. We might call this person the adult-child. For reasons that have partly to do with TV's capacity to reach everyone, partly to do with the accessibility of its symbolic form, and partly to do with its commercial base, TV promotes as desirable many of the attitudes that we associate with childishness: for example, an obsessive need for immediate gratification, a lack of concern for consequences, an almost promiscuous preoccupation with consumption. TV seems to favor a population that consists of three age groups: on the one end, infancy; on the other, senility; and in between, a group of indeterminate age where everyone is somewhere between 20 and 30 and remains that way until dotage descends. In *A Distant Mirror*, Tuchman asks the question, Why was childishness so noticeable in medieval behavior, with its marked inability to restrain any kind of impulse? Her answer is that so large a proportion of society was in fact very young in years. Half the population was under 21; a third under 14. If we ask the same question about our own society, we must give a different answer, for about 65% of our population is over 21. We are a nation of chronological grown-ups. But TV will have none of it. It is biased toward the behavior of the child-adult.

In this connection, I want to remind you of a TV commercial that sells hand lotion. In it we are shown a mother and daughter and challenged to tell which is which. I find this to be a revealing piece of sociological evidence, for it tells us that in our culture it is considered desirable that a mother should not look older than her daughter, or that a daughter should not look younger than her mother. Whether this means that childhood is gone or adulthood is gone amounts to the same thing, for if there is no clear concept of what it means to be an adult, there can be no concept of what it means to be a child.

In any case, however you wish to phrase the transformation that is taking place, it is clear that the behavior, attitudes, desires, and even physical appearance of adults and children are becoming increasingly indistinguishable. There is now virtually no difference, for example, between adult crimes and children's crimes; in many states the punishments are becoming the same. There is also very little difference in dress. The children's clothing industry has undergone a virtual revolution within the past 10 years, so that there no longer exists what we once unambiguously recognized as children's clothing. Eleven-year-olds wear three-piece suits to birthday parties; 61-year-old men wear jeans to birthday parties. Twelve-year-old girls wear high heels; 42-year-old men wear sneakers. On the streets of New York and Chicago you can see grown women wearing little white socks and imitation Mary Janes. Indeed, among the highest-paid models in America are 12- and 13-year-old girls who are presented as adults. To take another case: Children's games, once so imaginatively rich and varied and so emphatically inappropriate for adults, are rapidly disappearing. Little League baseball and Peewee footbal, for example, are not only supervised by adults but are modeled in their organization and emotional style on big league sports. The language of children and adults has also been transformed so that, for example, the idea that there may be words that adults ought not to use in the presence of children now seems faintly ridiculous. With TV's relentless revelation of all adult secrets, language secrets are difficult to guard, and it is not inconceivable to me that in the near future we shall return to the 13th- and 14th-century situation in which no words were unfit for a youthful ear. Of course, with the assistance of modern contraceptives, the sexual appetite of both adults and children can be satisfied without serious restraint and without mature understanding of its meaning. Here TV has played an enormous role, since it not only keeps the entire population in a condition af high sexual excitement but stresses a kind of egalitarianism of sexual fulfillment: Sex is transformed from a dark and profound mystery to a product that is available to everyone – like mouthwash or underarm deodorant.

In the 2 November 1980 *New York Times Magazine*, Tuchman offered still another example of the homogenization of childhood and adulthood. She spoke of the declining concept of quality – in literature, in art, in food, in work. Her point was that, with the emergence of egalitarianism as a political and social philosophy, there has followed a diminution of the idea of excellence in all human tasks and modes of expression. The point is that adults are *supposed* to have different tastes and standards from those of children, but through the agency of television and other modern media the differences have largely disappeared. Junk food, once suited only to the undiscriminating palates and iron stomachs of the young, is now common fare for adults. Junk literature, junk music, junk conversation are shared equally by children and adults, so that it is now difficult to find adults who can clarify and articulate for youth the difference between quality and schlock.

It remains for me to mention that there has been a growing movement to recast the legal rights of children so that they are more or less the same as those of adults. The heart of this movement – which, for example, is opposed to compulsory schooling – resides in the claim that what has been thought to be a preferred status for children is instead only an oppression that keeps them from fully participating in the society.

All of this means, I think, that our culture is providing fewer reasons and opportunities for childhood. I am not so single-minded as to think that TV alone is responsible for this transformation. The decline of the family, the loss of a sense of roots (40 million Americans change residence every year), and the elimination, through technology, of any significance in adult work are other factors. But I believe that television creates a communication context which encourages the idea that childhood is neither desirable nor necessary – indeed, that we do not need children. I said earlier, in talking about childhood's end, that I did not mean the physical disappearance of the children. But in fact that, too, is happening. The birthrate in America is declining and has been for a decade, which is why schools are being closed all over the country.

This brings me to the final characteristic of TV that needs mentioning. The *idea* of children implies a vision of the future. They are the living messages we send to a time we will not see. But television cannot communicate a sense of the future or, for that matter, a sense of the past. It is a present-centered medium, a speed-of-light medium. Everything we see on television is experienced as happening *now*, which is why we must be told, in language, that a videotape we are seeing was made months before. The grammar of television has no analogue to the past and future tenses in language. Thus it amplifies the present out of all proportion and transforms the childish need for immediate gratification into a way of life. And we end up with what Christopher Lasch calls "the culture of narcissism" – no future, no children, everyone fixed at an age somewhere between 20 and 30.

Of course I cannot know what all of this means to you, but my own position, I'm sure, is clear. I believe that what I have been describing is disastrous – partly because I value the charm, curiosity, malleability, and innocence of childhood, which is what first drew me to a career in education, and partly because I believe that adults need, first, to be children before they can be grown-ups. For otherwise they remain like TV's adult-child all their lives, with no sense of belonging, no capacity for lasting relationships, no respect for limits, and no grasp of the future. But mainly I think it is disastrous because it makes problematic the future of school, which is one of the few institutions still based on the assumption that there are significant differences between children and adults and that adults therefore have something of value to teach children.

So my bad news essay comes down to these questions: In a world in which children are adults and adults children, what need is there for people like ourselves? Are the issues we are devoting our careers to solving being rendered irrelevant by the transforming power of our television culture? I devoutly hope your answers to these questions are more satisfactory than mine.

74

A Concept of Power for Education

David Nyberg

Why is power not in the education lexicon? The idea of power has lain more completely neglected in educational studies than in any other field of thought that is of fundamental social interest. Power talk is conspicuously absent from schools and from educational literature. There is no theory of power that contributes much at all to understanding education and its importance in American society. It would seem that the customs and culture of educators prohibit the mere mention of power and censor the impulse to think seriously about it. One is more likely to hear singing in a bank than serious talk of power in relation to education.

This claim may seem off the mark to readers who have seen such books as Brameld's *Education as Power*, Czartoryski's *Education for Power*, or Baldridge's *Power and Conflict in the University*, for example. Surely these titles would indicate that power *has* been studied and analyzed as a concept in education. This in fact was the view of one colleague who was rather put out with the idea that I should even presume to redefine and recast the forms of power when, as he observed, there are "dozens of books on education dealing with control, planned change, autonomy, authority, governance, management, etc." Of course this is true, but it is beside the point if these books deal with their topics without analyzing power *per se*. He went one step further to secure his point by mentioning that "there sit in my personal library at least two books that include 'power' in their titles – *Power, Presidents, and Professors*, and *Power and Conflict in the University*." This, he suggested, was proof that he was right and that my own familiarity with the literature was insufficient if I could not agree.

His reaction to my claim was not altogether unusual in its combination of stridence and confusion. One cannot know what a book is about merely by reading its title.[1] There are indeed many books and articles in educational

Source: *Teachers College Record*, 82(4) (1981): 535–551.

studies that use the word "power" – still there are none that provide a sustained analysis of the concept itself. One has to look to the various social sciences and to political philosophy for such analyses, and even then there are difficulties.

This particular colleague's reaction is characteristic of that group of educators who think that the meaning of power is obvious, well understood, and in some sense fixed into place by these "dozens of books" on change, governance, and management.

Instead of direct talk of power, however, what we hear is indirect and often euphemistic talk about authority, leadership, charisma, management, and motivation in school teaching and administration. While I would argue that these are concepts that represent different manifestations and uses of power, they are usually treated as contrasts – even contraries – to power. (One might look at R. S. Peters's chapter on authority in his *Ethics and Education* for an example of this.[2]) Thus, even though much has been written about authority, leadership, and so forth, still power per se, as the concept that is fundamental to a clear understanding of all these others, has been neglected.

Educational theory will remain incomplete and inadequate to meet requirements for a place among the social sciences as long as it is without a concept of power. I think Dorwin Cartwright was correct in his view that "it simply is not possible to deal adequately with data which are clearly social psychological without getting involved with matters of power."[3] Bertrand Russell put the matter in even more sweeping terms when he argued that "the fundamental concept in social science is Power, in the same sense in which energy is the fundamental concept in physics."[4]

Educational theory cannot endure the neglect of power – as a fundamental concept – forever. To go on thinking that education is somehow alien and superior to considerations of power, as a crucial and inherent aspect of all social relations, is wishful thinking with a dangerous consequence. It beguiles educators into abdicating any responsibility for teaching knowledge about power constructively. Tyrannous governments are of course delighted with this abdication and are most willing to reinforce it along with other forms of the compliant and self-defeating wish not to know.

The ethical-political premise of the conceptualization that follows is straightforward: In a system of governing that aspires to realize the democratic principle of a broad distribution of power to influence and control the system itself, public education is obligated to ensure a broad distribution of *knowledge about power* as a logical and political prerequisite of that principle.

If power is to be more broadly distributed in society, we must first distribute knowledge about power more broadly. To do this, we must begin to talk about the very idea of power and to discuss its essential characteristics, the various forms it takes in ordinary life, and what it might contribute to a renovation of educational ethics. This article is offered as a first step toward such a discussion.

Ambivalence about Power and Power Talk

Some ideas are intrinsically more salient than others. They spring out from the general line of conversation when they are mentioned to make a pungent impression. Power is one of these ideas. The human mind is sensitive to talk of power in a way that suggests a profound fascination with the very idea, a captivaiion charged with deep feeling and frustrated by superficial understanding.

Power talk excites attention in most circumstances; it is not a neutral subject. Why this is so can be explained by two facts. First, every child has had early and probably traumatic experience with power and powerlessness, experience that produces lifelong effects on character development and subsequent social relations, which include new power experiences. No social being can escape experience with power and powerlessness, and for this reason power should be recognized as a fundamental category of human experience. People sense the ineluctability of power in social relations and attend anxiously to its presence because they know its threats and promises will determine the course of their social relations.

The second fact to keep in mind is that power is not often openly discussed at all. Straight talk about power is something of an event, like talk of sex and death is for children whose apposite curiosity is tantalized by adult reticence.

When power does become a direct topic of conversation it is usually focused on *other people's* power, rather than one's own. Most such talk is also complaint about undeserved, misused, excessive, tyrannical, portentous, elitist, usurped, or dangerous power. This general slant on the subject tends to give the impression that power is not fit for polite conversation, that an interest in power talk must itself be suspect for some hidden motive, and that talk of power sullies the speaker and may corrupt or alarm the chary listener, much as carnal talk is reputed to have done in the Victorian parlor. In short, power is something of a difficult, indelicate topic and a dirty word.

But if power is both an unavoidable part of social life and a dirty word, it should be no surprise that the human mind is sensitive to talk of it and is fascinated with the prospect of satisfying its keen interest with an equally keen understanding.

Americans are of two minds about the very idea of power. What lies behind this ambivalence is a tangle of contradictory teachings that leave one both *wanting* and *fearing* power. To want what one fears and to fear what one wants is psychologically very stressful. It is no wonder that power is such a touchy subject.

American culture teaches the young to measure personal abilities against high standards of achievement, and to compete against each other in trying to meet these standards. Power, in the sense of aggressive, ambitious pursuit of these high standards, highly developed personal capacities, and achieved excellence or superior status is an accepted cultural norm. But power in the sense of someone else's (or some agency's) control over one's own life circumstances is feared in proportion to its concentration in the hands of a few, its extent – or the scope of its effects – and the secretness of its exercise. We teach the young, in other words, to think of power both as a personal capacity to do something ("It is within your power to do anything you set your mind to") and as a commodity that can be gathered and possessed like gold coins ("The real power in this country is in the banks and big corporations – where the money is"). Both of these views are misleading, and taken together they create a confusing and inhibiting ambivalence.

How can educational theorists help to overcome this confusion and this inhibiting ambivalence about power? How can the idea of power be reconciled with the aims of education in a democratically inclined society? The first step toward answering these important questions is to propose a conception of power that can serve as the focus for further thought. In the next section I will describe such a conception first by identifying the essential attributes of power wherever and whenever it occurs in social relations, and then by setting out the four basic forms that power takes.

The Concept of Power

Power is a broad but complex term that suggests standard examples (popes and presidents, generals and godfathers, judges and jailers) and less standard but more numerous examples (doctors and nurses, lawyers, professors, principals and teachers, executives, purchasing agents, mayors and city councils, mahatmas, movie stars, con artists, journalists, sexual partners, mothers, fathers, and sly children).

Power is a familiar part of life and it is common for people to use the word, confident of its meaning. But, like other familiar and fundamental aspects of life (the concepts that we use constantly to help explain *other* concepts and to assess behavior), it often goes unexamined until some puzzlement arises to focus attention on it. It takes an unusual mind to analyze the obvious. In his *Confessions*, Saint Augustine gave the clearest example of this in his remark about the idea of time: "What then is time? If no one asks me I know: if I wish to explain it to one that asks I know not."

That power is *a* fundamental concept in social science, if not *the* fundamental concept, I take to be a given in this analysis. I also take as a matter of fact the premise that power has not yet recovered from Machiavelli's curse (foreshadowed by Thrasymachus in the *Republic*), which banished it from the vocabulary of morality and the public thoughts of good people. Power is the pariah of twentieth-century social philosophy and educational studies, a pariah whose reconciliation with ordinary life is long overdue.

To begin with, power is inherent in social life. We cannot choose whether power shall be present as a quality of relations among people, we can only choose whether to think about it, to understand it, and thereby to improve our chances of managing it. *Whenever at least two people are related in some way relevant to at least one intended action, power is present as a facet of that relationship.* The minimum and necessary conditions of power are two people and one plan for action. This means that power is partly psychological and partly social. And it is ahvays instrumental because it exists in the mediation of events; it can be thought of only in terms of its effects.

These are the three essential attributes of power – the social, the psychological, and the instrumental – in all social relations. Each of the three needs some explanation.

The social aspect of power is best understood in terms of "relation." Every human being stands in relation to some others; no one stands entirely alone, outside of all social structures and organizations. We are related by birth, by choice, and by circumstances of environmental necessity to all sorts of individuals and groups at the same time. The idea of relation is the first principle of social life, and it has been transformed into various forms of deliberate organization of both formal and informal kinds.

It should be pointed out that "organization" includes both the traditional arrangements and customs that have developed responsively to various pressures for survival (e.g., extended families, ritualized beliefs in messiahs or witches, food taboos, etc.) and to the intentionally created superstructures of a society already self-consciously systematical (e.g., IBM, IRS, AFL-CIO, the interstate highway system, etc.). In a nation of more than 230,000,000 social beings, chaos is certain to break out frequently and irregularly – but order will recuperate, organization will recur, because power abhors a vacuum.

If we accept the proposition that power is present whenever at least two people are related through a plan for action, and if we accept the further proposition that all individuals stand in relation to (many) others, then we can begin to see that organization (both formal and informal) is conceptually bound to power. Where there is organization, there is power also; where there is power, there is also organization. If organization is inevitable in social life then it is also true that power is inevitable in social life, in all social relations. Power is present or potential as a quality of relationships not only in the court rooms, war rooms, and board rooms, but in the nursery room, kitchen, bedroom, school room, and the ubiquitous "waiting" room, too.

In order to understand power, then, one must understand how individuals are related to each other, and what the essential features of social organization are. I shall mention two of these essential features that are especially important in power theory: hierarchy and delegation.

The people in an organization are related by a formal or informal ordering. Hierarchy is a ranked ordering, a system of priorities or prescriptions for attending to assignments, and for making the assignments in the first place. Hierarchy is a principle of order that is close to the essence of governing in all of its familiar political forms, from aristocracy through democracy to communism. Hierarchy itself has become a permanent value in social life, being inherent to organization just as organization is inherent to social relations. But any given set of individuals has only temporary tenure in the established hierarchy. It is the rules and procedures through which new individuals replace the old that distinguish among political systems, not the presence or absence of hierarchy.

Individuals are vulnerable in direct relation to their visible responsibility. If they can be identified as responsible for X, and if X fails or is judged to be wrong, then the responsible individual can be held to account. This is a central but seldom appreciated virtue of hierarchical organization. It may be more clearly appreciated when contrasted with another form of government control known as bureaucracy or the "rule of an intricate system of bureaus in which no men, neither one nor the best, neither the few nor the many, can be held responsible, and which could properly be called rule by Nobody."[5]

The difference between these two conceptions of organization (hierarchy and bureaucracy) is the closeness of the individual to responsibility, the individual's capacity to act on that responsibility, and the ordered set of priorities that define responsibilities in public terms. In both *The Castle* and *The Trial* Kafka showed how bureaucratic camouflage can obliterate individuals, priorities, and the public definition of responsibility.

Understanding organization is crucial to understanding power in another way, too. When large enough and deeply enough etched in the social scheme of things, "organization is itself a mobilization of bias in preparation for action."[6] There is a sense in which organizations once created, like Pygmalion's ivory virgin, come to life and seem capable of existing on their own. This may sound like myth, but that does not mean it has no meaning.

Hierarchy is a tendency to organize for leadership in concerted action. To act in concert requires some number of individuals and separate parts for them to play, and it requires agreement as to plan. In other words, it requires both delegation and consent.

The idea of delegation, or division of labor, is the heart of hierarchy and it is close to the heart of power, too. One who has a plan *and* others who can help carry it out has power. The effectiveness of delegation depends on a group's acceptance of its leader and consent to the plan, at least as it affects individual obligations. Delegation works both *from a group* to the leader, as in electing a president who is thus delegated power to lead the electors; and *from the leader* to a group, as in a boss's giving orders to employees who must then perform their delegated labors. Both senses are governed by the same principles of division of labor and consent.

The psychological aspect of power is best understood as having two parts: intention and consent. My first proposition about the nature of power was that it required at least two people and *a plan* for action. Having a plan is having an intention plus some idea about how to realize it. Here it is important to separate power from other forms of social relations that produce influences of one kind or another. Power is the production of planned influence. (This must be kept in mind as a crucial qualifier when considering the influences of organization as the "mobilization of bias" and when imputing power to certain abstract characteristics of social structures, such as "mode of production.")

When I say that power requires a plan, and that a plan implies an intent, I do not wish to be taken as saying that *only* intended effects are to be taken into account when analyzing the nature of power. There are always unintended consequences of every planned human action, and power is no exception. My point is, rather, that power cannot be properly understood, or even clearly separated from other kinds of social activities, without specifying the plan that one person has for affecting others.[7] This requirement raises serious and difficult questions about the extent to which a person can know completely his or her own intentions (there may be several kinds or levels of intent operating at the same time), and about the difference between an intended outcome and an anticipated (but unintended) one. Consideration of these questions is necessary to the understanding of power. But such consideration is likely to remain in some regards unsatisfactory, and our understanding of power therefore incomplete, because of the complex nature of intention. Nevertheless, it is an indisputable part of power as it serves to distinguish power effects from other, nondeliberative and unintended effects – whether or not they are anticipated. (For example, a teacher may insist that students obey certain rules in her classroom while anticipating that some of them will dislike her for it and be less attentive to their lessons as a result. Such an effect is anticipated but not intended.)

Having an intention, a plan, is one part of the psychological aspect of power. The other part is consent to the plan. Every governing order is dependent on the consent of the governed. Étienne de la Boétie, a contemporary and friend of Montaigne, was the first to develop the insight that tyranny is always grounded in the general *acceptance* of tyranny. He wanted to know why so many people

> suffer under a single tyrant who has no other power than the power they give him; who is able to harm them only to the extent to which they have the willingness to bear with him; who could do them absolutely no injury unless they preferred to put up with him rather than contradict him. Surely a striking situation![8]

On the democratic side, the writers of the Declaration of Independence put the same thought in these words (my emphasis):

> We hold these truths to be self-evident: that all men are created equal; that they are endowed by their creator with certain inalienable rights; that among these are life, liberty, and the pursuit of happiness. That, to secure these rights, governments are instituted among men, *deriving their just powers from the consent of the governed*; that, whenever any form of government becomes destructive of these ends, it is the right of the people to alter or to abolish it . . .

The power of a governing order is great, but that power is grounded in majority consent that may be withdrawn, if well enough organized, at any time. In this way one can argue that the withdrawal of consent is a form of control over power. It is the power over power.

But the nature of consent is such that we often give it without thinking much about it. Like Mithridates, who trained himself to tolerate poison by taking small quantities over a long time, those who give their consent to power claimants often do so through a gradual habituation to obedience or to "adjustments." This is a kind of self-deception – this passive consent to the way things are – and is perhaps the greatest single enemy of freedom, and the tyrant's best friend. His worst enemy then would be education about the nature of power relations and the dynamics of consent and its withdrawal.

In fact this is a restatement of the ethical premise of my proposal that knowledge about power ought to be taught in the public school curriculum. One emphasis in this teaching would be on the different kinds of consent that can support claims for power. These would include acquiescence under moderate threats, compliance based on partial or slanted information, indifference due to habit or apathy, conformity to custom, and a different kind of consent – commitment through informed judgment. Consent of this last kind is the ideal to which political theorists from Locke's time on have appealed in their defense of the democratic structure of authority in government. It is an ideal more profoundly attractive in politics than any other as the basis for government. Under this principle of consent through understanding, power is delegated deliberately for temporary concentration in the hands of a few. When this contractual arrangement proves unsatisfactory to the majority of informed delegators, their consent is collectively withdrawn from their chosen representatives and invested in others. Protest may terminate authority peacefully when the protest is organized by procedures of legalized election.

Commitment through informed judgment is an educational ideal, too. It is here that the link is made between education and the concept of power. The nucleus of both is information and its control. One might look at this list of types of consent and read it as a progression in the control of information and the formation of judgment. The primary ideas that connect education and power in social relations are information, understanding, and judgment.

Power is greatest when it employs the instruments of *education*, not the instruments of force. The instruments of education are designed to help individuals move from simple acquiescence all the way to informed and critical approval of delegated authority coupled with the understanding that organized consent and its withdrawal is the ultimate source of all social power.

Now I would like to complete this discussion of the three essential attributes of power with a few words about its instrumental aspect.

Power is pragmatic. It is a term that cannot be understood separate from practical bearings. It is always found in relation, not in isolation, and its presence is measured by reference to effect and consequences. Although power is sometimes spoken of as an end in i tself, or as a personality trait, or motive, or even as some sort of metaphysical entity, it is better represented and better understood when spoken of as a means.

There is a distinction between short-term and long-term consequences, however, that limits the power any particular agent may have. The distinction is simply this: Short-term events can be pretty well controlled, but long-term events (or long-range consequences) cannot. As Berle has pointed out:

> One impact of power holding on the holder is his discovery that the power act, the direction of an event, causes surprisingly unpredictable consequences. . . . The power to cause an event has scant relation to capacity to control the feelings and opinions of men about the thing done, or assure their adhesion to a larger plan.[9]

Predictability is the guardian of power, but in the long term that leaves power unprotected against its own fickle effects. This should be a comfort to those who fear a future of stable, concentrated power monopolies.

When there is no effect, or only unintended ones that follow a planned action, there is no power involved. There is an absence of power. But the effect in question need not be overt behavior. If the plan was to produce, strengthen, or change a certain attitude, for example, and if the plan succeeded, then we can say that the one whose plan it was had power. However, if the plan backfired and produced an *unintended* attitude change, or no change, then no power can be imputed to the planner even though he may have had some other sort of influence.

The instrumental aspect of power is a reflection of its root meaning – (from *posse*) "to be able." Power is instrumental in the sense that it serves as instrument or means to a purpose that is carried out.

The Forms of Power

Now that we have an understanding of the social, psychological, and instrumental aspects of power – all three of which must be taken into account in every analysis of power in social relations – I want to sort out what I take to be the four generic classes, or forms of power. I hope it is not confusing to add this second set of distinctions to the first. It may be helpful to keep in mind that all three aspects are always present in each of the different forms, just as a motor, transmission, and wheels are present in each form of automobile.

Force

This form needs the least explanation. Everybody recognizes the use of actual or threatened physical harm as a means of forcing consent in others to do something they would otherwise not do. Force is primitive, common, and unstable. I say it is unstable because the use of force creates resistance to its further use. As Milton put it in *Paradise Lost:* "Who overcomes/by force, hath overcome but half his foe." The one who uses force, then, must be vigilant with regard to the resistance it creates, and one must apply more and more force as the resistance increases. It is not easy to do this and attend to the first place. Eventually so much of one's available resources will have to be spent on enforcement that the relationship and the plan will fail. This is to say that power that is reduced to force will eventually be lost. It is inherently inefficient and necessarily unstable.

This problem can be seen in schools where the threat of punishment is used routinely as the means for maintaining "discipline." In such schools maintaining discipline often becomes such a problem that it eventually takes up all of the teachers' and administrators' time, and they are met with counter-threats and actual physical harm themselves.

Force is clearly one form of power, but it is not the only one. I think the single biggest error educators have made with regard to power has been to *equate* it with force, to think of the two as synonymous. The error has a long history and it begins in the dialogue between Socrates and Callides in the *Gorgias*. Callicles argued that power derives from the very struggle for existence and that the strongest will win. His position was that force is justified in the struggle for survival, success in the struggle brings happiness because the victors can do as they please, and this being-able-to-do-as-you-please is what it means to have power. His philosophy of power is equated with the doctrine of force.

Socrates would have none of this and argued for an opposite philosophy that he called the philosophy of education. His point was that happiness is not the consequence of doing-as-you-please, because the unwise may likely choose to do things that bring harm to themselves. Happiness comes from doing what is wise and just, and that requires education. In the dialogue Socrates set up a deep division between the philosophy of power and the philosophy of education, based on the mistaken assumption that power is *nothing more* than the use of force. Education has not recovered from this ancient expurgation because the other forms of power that are more compatible with the aim's of education have not been clearly set out in contrast with force.

Fiction

The central task in the exercise of power is eliciting from others consent to one's plan. One has to influence either the behavior or the beliefs, attitudes, and feelings in some other person(s) so as to put one's plan into effect. As I said above, one can force compliance with threatened or actual physical harm. But consent can be won with words and ideas and images, too. A person who is good at using words to turn ideas into images in the minds of listeners and readers is a person of great potential power. I will use the image of the storyteller for this form of power.

I should explain that I am using *story* in a broad sense to include all of the meanings that are reported in *Webster's New International Dictionary*, (a) a report, (d) an anecdote, (e) a fictitious narrative, (f) a falsehood, (g) a tradition or legend. In this view, story describes all kinds of verbal expression from history and philosophy to fantasy and lies. (Some would not take that to be a very broad range, I know.)

It is important to think of a storyteller as someone who uses words to create a sense of meaning, or a structure to use for interpreting a collection of events. All such senses or structures of meaning are *inventions*, they are created for the purpose of helping to sort out and give value to different bits of experience. These inventions are, in an important way, the necessary fictions of mental life. We cannot live without them – or at least we cannot live and communicate together without them.

Stories, then, and storytellers purvey their power by creating ways of thinking about certain plans. They are agents of change, calling for conditional assent to a certain way of thinking. If the key for an effective power relationship is eliciting consent to help achieve a plan for action, one good way to get that consent is to create a belief in the plan itself. This can be done by telling stories that appeal somehow to the core of meanings that support and transform beliefs. A good storyteller can induce belief and arouse commitment in the listener.

This fiction form of power should not be equated with deliberate deception and ignoble propaganda. It is much more versatile than that, capable of dealing with many subjects and many purposes. While it is clear that politicians use this form of power to win elections, raise taxes, and make war, it is less clear – but no less true – that scientists use it to introduce new theories and explanations of the microphysical nature of things (do you believe in "quarks"?) and the astrophysical ("quasars"? "black holes"?). Then we have the metaphysical philosophers whose stories about "quintessences" are still taken seriously by some, and sometimes even used to create "churches" that generate huge revenues.

Teachers use their own stories, too, as pedagogical techniques in motivating students to do better than the students believe they can do. Every history book is composed of stories (conceptual structures invented to help interpret events – "The Dark Ages," "The Causes of the Civil War," "Republicanism," "The Cold War"). The curriculum itself is a structure invented for the purpose of interpreting a collection of experiences as "education." To accept a curriculum, to believe that it represents the meaning of education, is to consent to the curriculum planners' plan for action and to help perform it.

The point to emphasize here is that this form of power shows up in many places, good and bad. It is used by good and bad people for good and bad reasons. Its purpose is to affect commitment by way of belief, not by way of force. Power as fiction is a product of civilization and a certain sort of victory over violence. In this sense, with apologies to Socrates, power as fiction is the beginning, rather than the antithesis, of a philosophy of culture or education. Because this form of power works through the mind to the heart, its potential is many times greater than that of physical force.

Finance

This is the third general class of power relations. It is most easily understood and commonly recognized as an offer of reward for services made within the rules of some theory of economic exchange. The reward need not he money, but it must always be something valued by the one who performs the service, just as the service must be valued by the one who offers the reward. In short, cooperation is achieved by the exchange of costs and benefits.

I have chosen finance (the science of revenue, or income from any source) as the name for this form to avoid too close an association with economic and exchange theories of power,[10] while borrowing some ideas from them. In the simplest words, this form of power has to do with adjusting social conditions to become more consistent with a given plan by offering rewards to or withholding them from other people. It is buying help. An employer buys time and labor from individuals with wages. A warden buys good behavior from prisoners with a reduction in sentence or parole. A military officer buys extra effort from his men with promotions and medals. An animal trainer buys obedience with bits of sugar and affection.

In education, the finance form of power can be seen in the assignment of grades, promotions, honors, recommendations and the like in exchange for hard work, high achievement, and good behavior, All that, I think, is obvious enough not to require argument. Perhaps less obvious, but more interesting for power theory, is the practice of behavioral modification programs.

The manipulation of costs and benefits is the talent of market modification. The manipulation of contingencies and reinforcement is the talent of behavior modification. This particular psychological theory, which has found recent wide favor in the schools, is a variation of exchange theory. The power of both consists in restricting the range of choices open to others by using a variety of means for contingency management and selective reinforcement. Theoretically, perfect control of a given set of contingencies will yield perfectly predictable behavior – the behavioral science equivalent of a market monopoly (raising similar questions about antitrust violation?). Empirically, however, and thank God, such perfect control of behavior is not possible in ordinary life because not all relevant contingencies can be managed perfectly at one time.

Teachers do control rewards in classrooms, however imperfectly, as a general feature of most that goes on there. And to the extent that the teacher is able to enlist the cooperation of students in adopting the teacher's plan for action, the teacher is exercising power. A student becomes school-wise by learning the skills of compliance and cooperation with the teacher's plan. These are skills of performance, which produce benefits in the currency of school success, namely, good evaluations.

One of the first and most obvious jobs a student has to do in adjusting to school is learning

> to behave in such a way as to enhance the likelihood of praise and reduce the likelihood of punishment. In other words, he must learn how the reward system of the classroom operates and then use that knowledge to increase the flow of rewards to himself.[11]

Adaptation to the teacher's power of delegation is a major task of all students. In this way of thinking, the teacher is like a banker who controls evaluation, which is the currency of the classroom (and greater educational) economy. To push the analogy one small step further, one could say the evaluations are loan notes that the student repays with interest, and that may be called in by the bank at any time. It is very likely in this system of exchange that if the student shows great interest, that is, pays a lot of attention, then the loan of a positive evaluation is secure.

The system of rewards in which students and teachers find themselves operates with regard to two curricula: the overt one of educational objectives, and the hidden one of classroom custom and institutional mores. It becomes apparent early in the school year who the "good" and "not-so-good" students are because the evaluations of educational performance are often public. In addition,

> every school child quickly learns what makes teachers angry. He learns that in most classrooms the behavior that triggers the teacher's ire has little to do with wrong answers or other indicators of scholastic failure. Rather, it is violations of institutional expectations that really get under the teacher's skin.[12]

Conforming to classroom custom must be seen as a cost the student bears for the prized benefit of praise in the reward system of the hidden curriculum.

It is not at all comforting to think that schools, through an unreflective use of this form of power, are creating a generation of graduates who may have learned that passive conformity – mindless consent and obedience, rather than informed agreement – pays off in school success more often than active curiosity and aggressive imagination. If this is the case, schools are creating the basis of an extremely serious power problem. Imagination is disruptive in its very nature and spoils the prospects of passive conformity. A nation schooled to avoid the disruptions of imagination in favor of the quiet, meager benefits of adaptation for the sake of teacher's praise is a nation about to lose its morality. (Perhaps I should stress the point that not *all* imagination is valuable and not *all* obedience is a threat to morality. It is the implicit pattern of sacrificing imaginative thought for adaptive thoughtlessness that is the threat.)

On the more positive side, teachers are well advised that passivity breeds boredom, and boredom breeds inattention. Inattention is a kind of withdrawal of consent to the existing plan of activities, and as such it constitutes a threat to the teacher's control of the plan – that is, the teacher's power. The management of attention, then, becomes a central power issue in teaching.

In broad terms, the bargain struck in the classroom is an exchange of attentiveness (at least the appearance of attentiveness), or involvement, for the teacher's positive evaluation. The costs are slight for some students because their plans do not seriously conflict with the teacher's plans, and what conflict there is may require little more than a postponement of desire. But others pay a much higher price by losing their sense of curiosity, individuality, and social responsibility in a glaze of thoughtless, obedient fulfillment of someone else's expectations.

In this form of power, as in the fiction form, the point is to get students as individuals, and as whole classes, to develop a commitment to a particular educational activity. The educational purpose of the exchange of reward for services is to attract attention, develop interest, cultivate involvement, and crown the effort with a witting, voluntary, wholehearted commitment to something worth the price of that effort.

Fealty

This is perhaps the most controversial part of my conception of power. Fealty (faithfulness or loyalty that is based on trust and mutuality) is close to love, and love is commonly thought to be not at all like power. And yet if the analysis of power done so far is correct, fealty emerges as one of its most stable forms. I have argued that power is present in all social situations in which at least two people are related through a plan for action. The task in such power relations is to secure consent to the plan and cooperation in putting it into effect. We have seen how this can be done by force, storytelling, and the exchange of rewards for services. How else can it be done?

To answer this question, we must imagine two or more people *who have the same plan, who share all information* relevant to that plan, and who have achieved a *balanced trust* with each other. Consent is assumed and needs no management, no enforcement. All resources that would otherwise be used in such management and enforcement are freed to be directed at the plan itself. Time, energy, and attention can be concentrated on the tasks required by the plan, and not dissipated in suspicion and fear. The kind of human organization that achieves these characteristics, whether between two people or among many, is very powerful indeed.

It is not unusual in power theory, or in educational philosophy, to feel a temptation at this point to commit a common fallacy. The fallacy is to say that when a relationship achieves a condition of balanced trust, shared understanding, and a mutual plan for action, then we are no longer talking about power. We are talking about something else. I would argue that we are not talking about something else, something to be *contrasted* with power, but we are talking about the highest form of power in a relationship that contains all of the necessary basic conditions in their most stable conformation. The governing point is this: Stability in power relations increases as the degree of informed cooperation increases. As power takes on forms that more and more closely approximate balanced trust, shared understanding, and a mutual plan for action, then more and more of one's available resources can be directed to the plan itself since they will not be needed to guarantee the enforcement of consent. As consent approaches complete willingness, based on informed judgment and invigorated by a personal motivation to accomplish the plan in question, then delegation and consent mingle into a sort of mutual cooperation that requires no vigilance, coercion, or force. No one in such a relationship needs to be watchful of revolt and withdrawal of the other(s). This form of power is efficient because all of the collective resources available through the relationship can be applied directly to accomplishing the plan. As a description of effective cooperation this form of power could apply equally well to a revolutionary army, a law firm, a hockey club, a trapeze act, a class project, or a marriage.

The application of this form of power to education would begin with a reconsideration of the ways in which educators learn to work with each other and with students. At present there is too little emphasis on learning how to develop trust, to share information, and to work cooperatively on educational plans that are genuinely and personally held to be mutual by teachers and students alike – not to mention the administrators.

The Ethics of Power

While I have implied an ethical progression from power as force to power as fealty, I have not spelled this out clearly. Nor have I tried to explain how schools and individual teachers can be moved along such a progression. These omissions are not the result of neglect or oversight. While it is easy to infer a real progression of ethical worth from the ordinal progression in my analysis of the forms, such an inference is suspect and probably unsound as well because it takes the shape of a naturalistic fallacy. One cannot confidently infer ethical conclusions from descriptive premises alone. I have tried to provide a descriptive analysis of the logical structure of power, emphasizing its four forms and the structural differences among them. In this regard, the analysis is normatively neutral. What determines the ethics of power is the use to which it is put, and the reasons that justify its uses – in any of its forms.

I have described fealty as the most stable and the most efficient form of power – these are descriptive terms, not ethical ones. I have described force as the most primitive and least stable, again trying to avoid a normative emphasis in favor of the more descriptive. The same is true of the presentation of fiction and finance as the two remaining forms. Setting force aside as the exception for a moment, I would not know how to order an ethical progression among the descriptive categories remaining. Each may be judged for its ethical character every time, and in each set of circumstances it is used.

Teachers can be taught knowledge about power more easily than they can be taught to hold the moral principles that will guide its application. The question of whether one has knowledge about power must be kept distinct from the question of whether one has the conscience and the will to use it morally. My intention is to reduce the use of force as much as possible by providing alternatives that are even more effective for accomplishing plans, and to increase the general distribution of knowledge about these alternatives. My hope is that such knowledge will be used wisely and justly.

The greater danger is not the growth of knowledge about power, but foolishness, as G. B. Shaw reminds us: "Power does not corrupt men; fools, however, if they get into a position of power, corrupt power."[13]

Notes

A much more extensive treatment of these issues can be found in the author's book Power Over Power *(Cornell University Press 1981).*

1. Books that thus imply a discussion of power include: *Power, Presidents, and Professors* by N. J. Demerath, R. W. Stephens, and R. R. Taylor (New York: Basic Books, 1967), has a brief summary (six pages) of a survey done on the question of the degree to which "esteem" is correlated with "decision-making influence" as an index of power in academic departments. But nowhere is there an analysis of what power means, or how it is related conceptually to esteem, decision-making influence, or anything else. The book is not about power at all; it is about university administrative organization.

   Power and Conflict in the University, by J. V. Baldridge (New York: John Wiley, 1971), alludes to the Hunter, Dahl, and Polsby studies in "community power" at one place, and describes some work done in social psychology on "power in groups" (Cartwright, French, and Raven) at another. Elsewhere, "power" turns up unsystematically in such phrases as "student power," "power plays," "powerful people," and so on, Baldridge's interest is not in the analysis of power, but in academic governance and decision making in universities.

   Power and Authority: Transformation of Campus Governance, ed. H. L. Hodgkinson and L. R. Meeth (San Francisco: Jossey-Bass, 1971), contains twelve essays, of which five have "power" in their titles, only one definition of power (p. 187, repeated on pp. 26–28), and no discussion of power at all.

   Power and Process: The Formulation and Limits of Federal Educational Policy, by H. L. Summerfield (Berkeley: McCutchan, 1974), is not about the concept of power, but rather about the role and process of government policymaking.

   Education as Power, by Theodore Brameld (New York: Holt, Rinehart & Winston, 1965), offers no definition and no analysis of power other than a seven-page agreement with Bacon's dictum that "knowledge is power." Brameld argues that both power – whatever that means – and knowledge should be used for the moral purposes of a "democratic world order."

   Education for Power, by A. Czartoryski (London: Davis-Poynter, 1975), posits power as "the name we give to the relationship between the dominating and the dominated," and goes on to argue for an active, participative democracy. The author rightly notes that power is inherent in social organization, but narrowly construes power to be always corrupting and self-serving: "Power extirpates from the mind every humane and gentle virtue." There is no deeper look at power than this.

   Power to Change: Issues for the Innovative Educator, ed. C. M. Culver and G. J. Hoban (New York: McGraw-Hill, 1973), offers no definition and no analysis of power.

Power to the Teacher: How America's Educators Became Militant, by M. O. Donley, Jr., (Bloomington: Indiana University Press/Phi Delta Kappa, 1976), does not even list power in the index. The book is a description of the growth of the NEA, AFT, and other teacher unions.

Power and Ideology in Education, ed. J. Karabel and A. H. Halsey (New York: Oxford University Press, 1977). Power is an explicit if unanalyzed theme in the contribution by Basil Bernstein and that of Pierre Bourdieu. Their research on the relations between the content of knowledge and the "structure of power" in society is perhaps the most promising in sociology of education with regard to our understanding of the concept of power in education. Bernstein in particular seems on track in his studies of the underlying principles of power that lie embedded in the language of education and the organization of controlled information in the school curriculum. But as Bernstein himself has pointed out, one of the main unresolved problems of his work is how "power relationships penetrate the organization, distribution and evaluation of knowledge through the social context" (quoted in Karabel and Halsey, p. 71).

2. R. S. Peters, *Ethics and Education* (London: Allen and Unwin, 1976), p. 239: "Authority is most in evidence in the sphere of social control where we have authority systems; we speak of those 'in authority' or 'the authorities.' In this sphere it must be distinguished from power with which it is too often confused by political theorists and sociologists alike. 'Power' basically denotes ways in which an individual subjects others to his will by means of physical coercion (e.g., infliction of pain, restriction of movement), or by psychological coercion (e.g., withholding food, water, shelter, or access to means of attaining such necessities), or by the use of less dire forms of sanction and rewards (e.g., by manipulating access to material resources and rewards, sexual satisfaction, etc.), or by personal influences such as hypnotism or sexual attraction. Authority, on the other hand, involves the appeal to an impersonal normative order or value system which regulates behavior basically because of acceptance of it on the part of those who comply."

3. Dorwin Cartwright, "Power: A Neglected Variable in Social Psychology," in *Studies in Social Power*, ed. Dorwin Cartwright (Ann Arbor: University of Michigan, Research Center for Group Dynamics, 1959), p. 2.

4. Bertrand Russell, *Power* (New York: W. W. Norton, 1938), p. 12.

5. Hannah Arendt, *On Violence* (New York: Harcourt, Brace & World, 1970), p. 38.

6. E. E. Schattschneider, *The Semisovereign People* (New York: Holt, Rinechart & Winston, 1960), 30.

7. Others disagree on this point, *See Felix Oppenheim, Dimensions of Freedom* (New York: St. Martin's Press, 1961), pp. 92–95; Stewart Clegg, *The Theory of Power and Organization* (London: Routledge & Kegan Paul, 1979), pp. 36–45; and Steven Lukes, *Power: A Radical View* (London: Macmillan, 1974).

8. Étienne de la Boétie, *The Politics of Obedience: The Discourse of Voluntary Servitude* (New York: Free Life Editions, 1975), pp. 46.

9. Adolph A. Berle, *Power* (New York: Harcourt, Brace & World, 1969), pp. 66–67.

10. See Peter M. Blau, *Exchange and Power in Social Life*, (New York: John Wiley, 1964); and Brian Barry, ed., *Power and Political Theory: Some European Perspectives* (New York: John Wiley, 1976).

11. Philip W. Jackson, *Life in Classrooms* (New York: Holt, Rinehart & Winston, 1968), p. 26.

12. Ibid., p. 22.

13. Quoted in W. H. Auden and Louis Kronenberger, eds., *The Viking Book of Aphorisms* (New York: Viking, 1966), p. 301.

75

Bodyreading

Madeleine R. Grumet

What does it mean to be a bodyreader? The term is drawn from Merleau-Ponty's term *the body subject*.[1] He used that phrase to rescue thought from its exile to the vast, inaccessible reaches of idealism. Despite the great complexity of his analyses, to read his work is to feel oneself come home, to gather up our politics, our psychology, our history, our literature, and our science, and to carry them like this week's groceries over the snowbank that blocks the driveway, up the stairs through the storm door and into the house. To the place where we live.

To bring what we know to where we live has always been the particular project of curriculum, and we can name the converse, to bring how we live to what we know as the project of curriculum inquiry. Our current concern about the distance between what we know and how we live is mirrored in our fear that our children do not read. It is a serious concern. It is the fear that what we know, the symbolic inscription of our collective experience in the world, moves away from them like an ice floe and leaves them stranded, separated from the past, and, we fear, from the future as well. We have seen the impulses to grasp that which seems to be escaping us expressed in the reactionary back-to-basics drills, and in the school reports that encourage us to extend, tighten, and enforce all sorts of requirements. I think that the new concerns about reading acknowledge, at least tacitly, the many ways in which reading is contingent, tangled up with the world from which texts and readers come. The act of reading requires what Ricoeur calls both sense and reference, both what we know and how we live.[2] The sense is the *what* of the text. The reference is *what it is about*. Ricoeur establishes these categories to undermine idealism, that confusion which Sartre describes as taking the word for the world. In *Interpretation Theory* Ricoeur maintains that "language is not a world of its own. It is not even a world. But because we are in the world, because we are affected by situations, and because we orient ourselves comprehensively in those situations, we have something to say, we have experience to bring to language."[3]

Source: *Teachers College Record*, 87(2) (1985): 175–193.

Ricoeur's work is drawn from an enterprise that we call hermeneutics. This word, which refers to the various methods that we employ to draw meaning from texts, comes from the name of the messenger of the Greek gods, Hermes. Both in literature and in cult, Hermes was identified as a protector of cattle and sheep, a point that may not seem immediately significant but that is, as I shall try to demonstrate, essential to this argument. Representations of Hermes show him either in flight, hence his winged feet, or in a more pastoral moment, carrying a shepherd's staff, a sheep slung over his shoulder. Whereas hermeneutics was originally grounded in philology, as interpreters of the Bible endeavored to justify their interpretations of text through recourse to historical and comparative linguistics, contemporary hermeneutics provides what Suleiman calls "the self-conscious moment of all criticism, when criticism turns to reflect on its own intentions, assumptions, and positions."[4] I have created the persona of the bodyreader to bring to reading what Merleau-Ponty's figure of the body subject brings to epistemology, the sense that reading is an act that is oriented toward what the subject can do in the world. Bodyreading is strung between the poles of our actual situation, crowded as it is with our own intentions, assumptions, and positions, and the possibilities that texts point to. Contemporary feminist theories of the text and programs of literary criticism such as post-structuralism or deconstruction have also pitted themselves against the idealism that imputes a meaning to the word, the sentence, the text, that is distinct from the actual and possible world of their readers. Their analyses reveal the ways that reading throbs with the conflicts that shape our mortal condition: the dialectics of birth and death, of private and public meaning, of gender, of class. Reading instruction in the public schools is not exempt from these concerns. These are human concerns, and reading is a most human activity. It would be a gesture of shallow arrogance to suggest that we can resolve these issues. What I hope to suggest are ways of working with teachers and students that honor them, ways that permit the sorrow and celebration that Yeats seeks in the poetry of the mortal condition: "Soul clap its hands and sing, and louder sing, for every tatter in its mortal dress."[5]

Decentered, lost in thought, locked into the courtesies and protocols of our very formal operations, we forget that the symbolic systems of language, number, art, and culture are part of our lived worlds. Even though Saussure has convinced us that language is not the echo of nature,[6] we need not think that the arbitrary character of the signifier is proof that we live locked into a linguistic fiction. Merleau-Ponty maintains that "words, vowels and phonemes are so many ways of 'singing' the world, and that their function is to represent things not, as the naive onomatopoeic theory had it, by reason of an objective resemblance, but because they extract, and literally express, their emotional essence."[7] I have argued that curriculum, like language, is a moving form; conceived as an aspiration, the object and hope of our intentionality, it comes to form and slips, at the moment of its actualization, into the ground of our action. It becomes part of our situation.[8] And of course it is this fluidity that Ricoeur and Merleau-Ponty are trying to recover for language. It is more difficult to grasp the protean nature of the word once it has become the text. "So long lives this and this gives life to thee."[9] I will not take time now to recount the history that has bonded text to class and caste, made it the emblem of authority, the sign of immortality and a rebuke to the lively imagination. Literacy has traveled a long and winding path from reading entrails to answering multiple choice reading comprehension questions on the Scholastic Aptitude Test, although on second thought both enterprises may be seen as attempts to control the future by making the correct interpretation. One wonders whether the priest ever looked up and muttered "none of the above."

I recognize that there is certain sadness that clings to the notion of bodyreading. The very need to present it seems to come from a sense that it expresses a continuity and an integration that we have lost – that it describes a place where we once were, a way of being that we can only remember. Psychoanalytic theories of language reinforce this sense as they establish desire as the precondition of symbol formation. They predicate the presence of the word on the absence of pleasure. To think, to speak, to read, to write, is to celebrate the presence of an absence. It follows then that all our assertions become suspect, like television commercials that push the very features that their products lack. Perhaps I do produce the bodyreader to recover what is lost. The bodyreader denies our terror of being lost in the world. It denies the sad intuition that the world as we have named it and now manipulate it is no longer a world that will sustain our bodies or those of our children. It repeats that tendency to impute to the past the ideal we wish for the future. Our lives are full of such histories – Marx's species community, Freud's infantile symbiosis. Perhaps a bodyreader is such a fantasy and Lacan is right when he suggests that the word is a sign of our alienation, that language is the expression of desire that is predicated on loss.[10]

But this melancholy sense of language sings our sadness, and it is our responsibility as educators not to be caught in an understanding of symbol systems that reduces them to elegies for lost worlds. Language can lead us somewhere else, to the place where we live, to the world, and to the world as it might be, and bodyreading need not be seen as a nostalgic fantasy, but as a practical necessity, the exploration of a world where we can live. When we consult the etymology of the word *read*, we find that *read* is lodged in the very guts of the word *ruminate*, which means to think things over. Nevertheless, *ruminate* is not associated with a group of animals noted for their erudition. Ruminants are cattle, also sheep (enter Hermes), goats, antelope, giraffe, and deer. "The skeletal and muscular systems of the ruminant together form a perfectly constructed running mechanism; their digestive system is also elaborately planned so that they may hastily snatch a meal in some favorable grazing ground and store the food temporarily in a special compartment of the stomach until they have found a refuge where they can masticate and digest it at leisure."[11]

The ruminant does not give up the world in order to think about it. On the hoof it stores the world that it consumes in multiple stomachs until it has found a place of safety to bring back what has been swallowed in haste for a good chew. Actually the ruminant's stomach has four compartments and it is the very last compartment, that has gastric glands in its walls for secretion of digestive juices. It is this fourth stomach that is called the read. The Oxford English Dictionary (OED) offers us a citation from 1450 where the *reid* is not only associated with the stomach of a cow but is used to signify the stomach of a human as well: 1450 Holland Howla, "He cry'd 'Allace . . . revyn is my reid. I am ungraciously gorrit, halthe guttis and gall.'" Some of us have had a similar response to what we take as being misread. The OED also tells us that "the original senses of the Teutonic verb [*reden*] are those of taking or giving counsel, taking care or charge of a thing, having or exercising control over something else." (Can we then assume that the Angles, the Saxons, and the Jutes were more interested in comprehension strategies than in decoding?) "The sense of considering or explaining something obscure or mysterious is also common to various languages," the OED tells us, and it is this sense of mystery that I hope to recover for our work with children and texts when I maintain that we have not lost our stomach for reading.[12]

The anatomy of mystery that lodges explanation in the stomach of the cow suggests that reading was and may still be a ritual of divination, for ritual, in the words of Meyer Fortes, prehends the occult and makes it patent.[13] It seeks what is hidden, internal, unseen in our experience. The reader pores over the text, like the priest reading the entrails, seeking signs of how to live. Nevertheless, unlike our ancient predecessors, we are plagued by our intolerance for ambiguity. Embarrassed that we cannot make the task clear and simple, we misrepresent it to children, suggesting that meaning is hidden in the folds of the topic sentence or the story structure. That is the positivism that characterizes most of the language arts curriculum as well as reading in the content areas. Its simplistic certainties are balanced by the solipsism of what we call recreational reading where we surrender to prose, cherishing reading experiences that envelop us in fantasies that confirm our individuality, drawn from unrealized selves that no one else could ever know. This tendency to locate meaning either in the words, sentences, structures of texts, or in the secret thoughts of the reader tells us that both community and curriculum are defunct, an impression that has been confirmed in the narratives of educational experiences written by students who have studied philosophy of education with me. Some of those students are practicing teachers, some teachers in training. Rarely are experiences related to reading as part of the school curriculum presented as educational.

When reading presents itself under the category of educational experience, it is usually presented as a process that creates privacy, substituting self-satisfaction for a relation that originally required another, usually a mother.

> Even before I can consciously remember, I know that I was read to every night of my early childhood. I loved to be read to. At ages three and four,

my brother and I would each pick out a book for my mother to read to us. John always picked 'Boy' books such as the Little Tug Boat and the Little Engine that Could. I picked fairy tales and Peter Pan, and Winnie the Pooh. We would both get ready for bed and go into John's room and listen to his story, which I always loved almost as much as my own. Then, although he is two years older than I, he would go to sleep and my mother would read my story in my room. . . . I loved the stories so much that I would memorize them and tell/read them to the amazed cleaning lady the next morning turning the pages at the appropriate times.

Finally I was old enough to go [to] the first grade. I knew the alphabet already and soon I learned all kinds of amazing things about vowels and consonant blends. Then it seemed one day that I just suddenly knew how to read.[14] It was the most incredible gift. I could do for myself the thing my mother had always had to do for me. I remember reading ahead in my first Dick and Jane reader, amazed at my own ability to find out what would happen next. I read an entire book before dinner that I received on Christmas morning. I read almost all the books in my age section of the children's room at the library. I had the most construction paper balloons on the wall for summer reading books.

The novelty of reading has worn off to a certain extent. However, I still Find myself engrossed in novel after novel, upset and dazed when I am forced back into the real world outside my book. I still read every night before I go to bed, it is force of habit I guess.[15]

The narratives evoke reading as a form of comfort and safety, reading in bed, surrounded by pillows and quilts, reading surreptitiously by the light of the flashlight, giving oneself to the text as one dare not surrender oneself to the world. Rarely do the readers in these tales offer an account of their reading experience to anyone else. It is a private pleasure. "We read," Stanley Elkin says "to die, . . . it has something to do with being alone, shutting the world out, doing books like beads, a mantra, the flu. Some perfect, hermetic concentration sealed as canned goods or pharmaceuticals. . . . Not so much a way of forgetting ourselves as of engaging the totality of our attentions, as racing car drivers or mountain climbers engage them, as surgeons and chess masters do."[16] It is rare to find a reading narrative that presents this kind of negotiation:

Later in France. A summer day. I remember a sleeveless dress. The poster was big with red, black and white colors. It showed two hands holding each other tightly, and the caption read as follows: "Workers, unite against poverty for freedom and justice!" Very impressed, I stood in front of it. With all the wisdom of my eight years I thought it was great. I did not really know why, I just liked it. My aunt, by that time, had caught up with me. "Isn't it beautiful?" I asked her, still contemplating the poster. "What?" "The poster," I answered, wondering how she could have missed it. She grabbed my hand, pulled me away and told me with a harsh voice, "Never, do you understand, never read posters like this one. They tell lies. They are bad. They are communist."[17]

Often, when schooling is the location of the reading narrative, meaning falls into one of the two forms presented in these stories. It is either an individual's fantasy, sensual, ideal, offering visions of power and control to the reader that are uncontested, or meaning is imposed, negating the reader's interpretation of the text and substituting a rebuke for negotiation. In *With Respect to Readers* Slatoff decries this dualism:

> Most aestheticians and critics . . . speak as though there were only two sorts of readers: the absolutely particular individual human being with all his prejudices, idiosyncrasies, personal history, knowledge, needs and anxieties, who experiences the work of art in solely "personal" terms, and the ideal or universal reader whose response is impersonal and aesthetic. Most actual readers except for the most naive, I think, transform themselves as they read into beings somewhere between these extremes. They learn, that is, to set aside many of the particular conditions, concerns and idiosyncrasies which help to define them in every day affairs.[18]

It is this process of gauging the context for meaning that helps us to constitute understandings that make us members of what Fish calls interpretive communities.[19] Discriminating the idiosyncratic from the general is delicate business. It is the basis of the prediction that Frank Smith defines as the prior elimination of unlikely alternatives.[20] But what reading is about, very much like writing, is bridging the gap between private and public worlds. Its purpose is not to reduce mystery to what is obvious, patent, nor to confirm solipsism, but to provide a passage between the images, impulses, and glimpses of meaning that constitute being in the world and our encoded representations of chat world. If we were to transpose the terms of hermeneutics into ego psychology, translating what we consider to be idiosyncratic on one hand, and general on the other, into the terms internal and external nonego, respectively, we would have to acknowledge that like ego identity, meaning is the provisional achievement of a dynamic and somewhat risky process. If reading is a passage between the public and the private worlds, the journey is fraught with danger. To give oneself up to the text is to relinquish the world in order to have the world, it is a birth and a death. And so it should not surprise us to find a child wary of reading, reluctant to follow that line across the page without knowing where it leads. Permit me to read to you. I promise that we will not go too far, just far enough to share Galway Kinnell's childhood discoveries of the mysteries of birth and death and culture. Once again, it is a ruminant that leads us into the light as well as the darkness:

Freedom, New Hampshire
  by Galway Kinnell

We came to visit the cow
Dying of fever,
Towle said it was already
Shoveled under, in a secret

Burial place in the woods
Weeks, we never

Found where. Other
Children other summers
Must have found the place
And asked, Why is it
Green here? The rich
Guess a grave, maybe,
The poor think a pit

For dung, like the one
We shoveled in in the fall
That came up green
The next year, and that,
For all that shows, may as well
Have been the grave
Of a cow or something.

We found a cowskull once; we thought it was
From one of the asses in the Bible, for the sun
Shone into the holes through which it had seen
Earth as an endless belt carrying gravel, had heard
Its truculence cursed, had learned how sweat
Stinks, and had brayed – shone into the holes
With solemn and majestic light, as if some
Skull somewhere could be Baalbek or the Parthenon.

That night passing Towle's Barn
We saw lights. Towle had lassoed a calf
By its hind legs, and he tugged against the grip
Of the darkness. The cow stood by chewing millet.
Derry and I took hold, too, and hauled
It was sopping with darkness when it came free.
It was a bullcalf. The cow mopped it awhile,
And we walked around it with a lantern

And it was sunburned, somehow, and beautiful.
It took a dug as the first business
And sneezed and drank at the milk of light.
When we got it balanced on its legs, it went wobbling
Toward the night. Walking home in darkness
We saw the July moon looking on Freedom, New Hampshire,
We smelled the fall in the air, it was the summer,
We thought, Oh this is but the summer![21]

Well, I think this is a poem about reading. And if the first few pages of this article succeeded, schema theory maintains that you now share the assumptions, associations, vocabulary, and expectations that confirm this interpretation.[22] Together we appropriate this text with impunity; we use it to make sense of the work we have to do. As the poem continues, it becomes clear that what concerns the poet is not the way that the corpse of the cow, nor its sun-drenched, time-filled skull, nor its damp, milky calf encode birth, death, and the passage of time called civilization. What concerns the poet is the death of his brother, Derry, who along with the speaker constitutes the *we* of the tale, the *we* who search for the buried cow, the *we* who find the cow skull, the *we* who see the Parthenon in it, the *we* who attend the birth of the calf. And Derry is not a mere witness of these moments, for the world and its symbols evolve within human relationships. It is Derry's presence that makes such a reading possible. Every text, every symbol, every word, is a passage between one consciousness and another. In almost every story of reading that my students tell, someone else is there in some way to witness the symbolic act, to receive or repudiate the reader's interpretation. Even when reading is a refuge from society, from friends, from parents, they are there, hovering on the other side of the door. Just as the capacity to have a world is mediated by other people for the body subject, the capacity to read a world is mediated by other people for the bodyreader.

Now it becomes clear to us why the "great debate" about reading instruction in the primary grades has been waged with such passion ever since Icklesamer published a primer in 1527 in Germany entitled *The Shortest Way to Reading* that proposed introducing children to speech sounds associated with well-known words before teaching them letters as the basic unit of instruction.[23] The issue about whether phonics or sight words provide the best foundation for beginning readers is now generally conceded to be a nonissue as it is now recognized that the complexity and richness of the reading process is hospitable to multiple instructional approaches. What is interesting to note at this point is that in this controversy we find not only a history of ideas about cognition, but a history of the human relationships that each form and unit of instruction implied. The feminist challenge to the status of the text and of language as a bulwark of patriarchal privilege has led us once again to look at the human relationships within which symbolic competence develops.

The debate over whether to privilege sight or sound in reading instruction becomes pertinent to our understandings of the epistemologies and cognitive styles associated with male and female gender identities. Despite the drill sequences and the repetitious and highly organized character of phonics, the mimesis and recitation of sounds that it requires is reminiscent of the echolalia that constitutes the babble of infants and early speech. This is the preoedipal discourse of mother and child, highly inflected, immediately echoed – the original language, the mother tongue, sounds that communicate intimacy without denotative meaning. A differential response to a mother's voice precedes the specific response to her face, a response that does not develop until later. Identification with mother is the original subject and object relation for both male and female babies, who are born into a nurturant field in which both are initially matrisexual.

Chodorow argues that the processes of gender identification that male and female children experience involve different responses to this early preoedipal relation, to what is simultaneously the other, mother, the world.[24] Girls, permitted to sustain the original identifications with their mothers, need not repress sound and touch as significant ways of being attached to the world. For males, on the other hand, gender identity requires a repudiation of preoedipal experience. To be male is to be, in effect, not mother, and that early identification as well as the sensual modalities that dominated it are repressed so that an identification with a father whose presence and relation depend more on sight than on sound or touch can be achieved. Linguistic competence and literacy are the achievement of the older child, whose object relations have enlarged to include its father in what Chodorow calls the relational triangle. In "Upright Man," Erwin Straus argues that it is the upright posture that gives sight its epistemological primacy in human thought.[25] Surrendering the detail, the intimacy and texture that touch and sound provide, sight provides us with a view and privileges the structural relations of abstract and rational thought. These speculations drawn from object relations theory and phenomenology suggest that coming to know the world may differ for boys and girls, orienting them to epistemologies at particular stages of their development that are gender specific. Such theories are less useful in predicting who will read well when than they are in reminding us that symbolic competence is generated within intense human relationships, and that our understanding of the relation of gender to language acquisition cannot be limited to sexual stereotypes and the sexual politics of the classroom but must also address the evolution of language in the mediation of desire and the constitution of the ego.

Touch and the voice are the sensual passages between parent and child. Because these modes of contact are associated with the intimacy of familial or erotic relations, they are barred from the classroom, where sensuality in any form is anathema.[26] Even if early reading instruction maintains the singsong chant of children's voices, that maternal modality soon gives way to silence. Recitation is replaced by workbooks, and the look dominates the classroom. Now it does sound as if I am taking the phonics side in this dispute as I invoke echolalia and the maternal voice as the foundation of linguistic competence. And I want to make it clear that I am quite convinced that Frank Smith is right when he maintains that phonics works only when you have a rough idea of what the word is that you are trying to read and some sense about how it sounds when you say it.[27] Smith has some difficulty accounting for the success of phonics given his conviction that it is merely epiphenomenal to the process that attaches meaning to print and that its complexity and artifice estrange those children whom we later call dyslexic from texts. What Smith needs to acknowledge is the ceremony that surrounds phonics. The physical activity is stimulating. The turn to phonics in many systems has been accompanied by the move to decrease the teacher/pupil ratio by hiring aides to work with children.

In *Divinity and Experience*, Godfrey Lienhardt observes that the rituals of the Dinka require that all ceremonial utterances of the priest be repeated by everyone in attendance at the ritual.[28] Prayers and incantations have no efficacy if muttered in private. Performative utterances rely on social confirmation to be compelling. (And that is probably why I run around telling everyone I know that I am starting a new diet when I decide to try to start a new diet.) And so, if as Merleau-Ponty maintains, speech sings the world, phonics provides a choral grasp of meaning that brings a social and emotional resonance to the meaning of texts.

Now I acknowledge that a goal in the development of reading skill is to release us from the physical marking and iteration of sound. And even Julia Kristeva, who invokes the sensuality and intimacy of echolalia to assert the epistemological claims of the first language, the mother tongue, warns feminists not to sink into its rhythms and secrets, not to forsake the public and political sign for the private, familial sound.[29] Like the ruminants, we must learn to swallow print without chewing it. The problem is that when we stop to think it over, we lose our sense of where the thought came from, and confusing the contents of long-term memory with memory itself, we fall into insidious idealism. If cattle treated grass the way we treat text, they would soon starve to death, thinking that they are the producers of their own cud. The problem is that in the silence of the secondary classroom, too often, nothing is happening, no grazing, no galloping, no chewing, no mooing, no nothing. Even babble is preferable to that kind of silence.

The bodyreader who is still alive and well in many elementary classrooms where language experience, directed reading-thinking activities, and phonics provide a rich and varied sensory and interpersonal ground for learning soon gives way to the reader who discriminates the private self from the public text. Meaning is either in here or out there. When it is in here it is identified with feeling, sensuality, and imagination that cannot be communicated and cannot be negotiated into any statement that deserves or attains the status of knowledge. When it is out there, it belongs to the text and to the teacher and understanding means that the reader stands under the text, under the gaze of the teacher, and learns to anticipate and repeat the interpretation that is an index of comprehension.

The world, Merleau-Ponty has told us, is the answer to the body's question. What we discover is what we can look for. "One's own body is the third term, always tacitly understood, in the figure-background structure, and every figure stands out against the double horizon of external and bodily space."[30] The body that makes it possible for us to have a world does not assemble a motley group of objects around it that it crowns with the title of objectivity. The world we have is the world that rises to meet our intentionality; it coheres around our needs, wishes, possibilities, real and imagined. The coherence of the text, like that of the world, is the possible and actual ground of our action. Meaning is something we make out of what we find when we look at texts. It is not in the text. Now this is hardly news, but I am sorry to tell you that the myth of the meaningful text still flourishes in the secondary classroom. Abandoned by cognitive theories, by epistemology, by aesthetic and literary theory, the secondary school curriculum stands alone, proclaiming the authority of the text. Using single textbooks, sometimes supplemented with library readings or handouts, the students are sent to read unburdened by motives, interests, questions, tasks, rationales, or expectations. If there is such a thing as a pure read, the textbooks of the secondary curriculum get it. All the baggage that I have just listed appears after the fact, when it appears at all, usually in some evaluation format.

We can see an example of this approach in Harold Herber's text *Teaching Reading in the Content Areas*, a book that is widely used by reading specialists. Herber identifies three levels of comprehension: the literal, the interpretive, and the applied. Herber presents these levels as a sequence:

> . . . first, the reader examines the words of the author and determines what is being said, what information is being presented. Second, the reader looks for relationships among statements within the materials, and from these intrinsic relationships derives various meanings. . . . Third the reader takes the product of the literal – what the author has said – and the interpretive – what the author meant by what he said – and applies it to other knowledge that she already possesses, thereby deepening the understanding.[31]

The absurdity of this sequence would only be matched if I took out flour, sugar and butter, milk, eggs, vanilla, cardamon, and baking powder, mixed them all in a bowl, observed the blend, noting its texture and flavor, applied this information to my previous experience, and hypothesized that I might be making either a cake, a pudding, an omelette or a quiche, a blintz, a crepe, or a pancake. As Frank Smith has noted, only in schools are we so stupid. Only in schools does the text become a spectacle, and do we, the dazed spectators, eyes glazed, sit in mute reception, waiting for something to appear. No, television has not ruined reading. Reading in school has trained us for television.

Let me stop this tirade, or at least turn its energy to something more useful. First, we must ask how the very women and men who bake cakes, drive cars, and maybe even write poetry come to banish intentionality from human action when they teach children to read. That question takes two forms in the work that I have done and would like to do. It leads us to the history of reading in the culture of schooling and to an understanding of the status of the text as a guarantor of patriarchy.[32]

Because schooling is a complex, ceremonial, and ritual form, it is important to study the status of texts in the exchange systems, totem systems of the classroom. For we have displaced school bodies with school texts. I do not ask my students, "Do you understand me?" Instead I ask them to understand my reading of the text. We pass texts between us. We touch the text instead of each other and make our marks on it, rather than each other. The text is material, it has texture, it is woven, we pull and tug at it, it winds around us, we are tangled up in it.

We need to work with teachers to investigate our understandings and experience of reading. Writing projects have shown us that the process of composition is very different from the ways that it has been conceived and taught in the school curriculum. Writing does not record preaccomplished thought; the act of writing constitutes thought. The Bay Area Writing Project and its spinoffs in the National Writing Project[33] are projects aimed at engaging teachers in writing so that together they may participate in the activities that bring thought to expression and name those processes. Reading seminars for teachers drawn from various disciplines may provide us with the opportunity to reclaim reading as intentional activity. It is no accident that the analysis of writing comes to mind when we think about reading. Attention to the moments of composition have revealed the contingencies, elisions, contradictions, and explosions that constitute the text.

Think of the repugnance one often feels for a text that is recently completed. There, clinging to all the lines, are shreds of the ideas that never quite made it to expression, fragments of the negative example, the other possibility, that the sentence, the chapter, the ideology, the deadline, the habit, the defense mechanism, just could not admit. Only time and forgetfulness smooth these rough edges so that we no longer remember what has been left behind, and then the text that has seemed so partial, merely provisional, prevarication, becomes *THE TEXT*, clear, complete, necessary, and sufficient. Some of the reader-response research done in Indiana by David Bleich and Eugene Kintgen confirms my own impressions from engaging students in that process we call "close reading" of texts.[34] We see that both writing and reading require what Kris[35] has named regression in the service of the ego. The interpretation of theoretical texts and dense prose often calls on students to draw from their own store of associations, and very free ones at that, in order to construct the world that the word can live in.

The clarity and apparent independence of the complete text are illusions that contemporary literary criticism has assailed. It does seem unfair and unkind to keep children playing in the shadow of the authority of the text, while the grown-ups dismantle it and revel in the newfound light. Whereas structuralists had seen the oppositions in a text as functioning to maintain its shape and integrity, deconstructionists celebrate the discovery of contradictions that undermine the authority of the text. They study the sense of the text to discover its multiple and conflicting references. Here is Eagleton's portrayal of the "writable" text, a text filled with what Barthes has called double signs, signs that reveal that they are merely provisional, material, historical signifiers that can barely contain the meanings that leak from their searns, boil over their rims, cascade over their banks into a new channel.

> The "writable" text, usually a modernist one, has no determinate meaning, no settled signifieds, but is plural and diffuse, an inexhaustible tissue or galaxy of signifiers, a seamless weave of codes and fragments of codes, through which the critic may cut his own errant path. There are no beginnings and no ends, no sequences h which cannot be reversed, no hierarchy of textual

"levels" to tell you what is more or less significant. All literary texts are woven out of other texts, not in the conventional sense that they bear the traces of "influence" but in the more radical sense that every word, phrase or segment is a reworking of other writings which precede or surround the individual work. There is no such thing as the "first" literary work: all literature is intertextual. A specific piece of writing thus has no clearly defined boundaries: it spills over constantly into the works clustered around it, generating a hundred different perspectives which dwindle to vanishing point. The work cannot be sprung shut, rendered determinate, by an appeal to the author, for the "death of the author" is a slogan that modern criticism is now confidently able to proclaim.[36]

Well, Hallelujah. Ding dong the witch is dead, dissolved in the spillage of those liquid texts. Barthes's playfulness, his nihilism, may be the most extreme, antic spirit to undo the text. Because most of us are more didactic than he, we cannot quite accept the telos of a vanishing point and rush to grab hold of meaning before it disappears around the bend of signification. (Our experience also suggests that vanishing points provide a teleology that has a poor track record with most school boards.) Nevertheless, his assassination of the text is a coup d'etat that can return the text to teachers and students, once again material, maleable, to be fashioned by them into what it is they need. Intertextuality invites us to use multiple texts, splicing them, interweaving them with each other, with our commentaries, with our questions. This is the promise of word processing, not some video version of the questions at the end of the chapter, but the presentation of text that can disappear at the touch of the delete button. There are no sacred texts. Let the cursor unravel the binding of the text as readers erase what they do not believe, or add whatever it is that the author left out. Why not invite them to weave their questions, responses, and arguments into the texts themselves, and so acknowledge the wisdom of graffiti?

The deconstructionist approach of Derrida is less jocular. He works, as Eagleton says, to embarrass the text, to show where the text, in spite of itself, slips up, says what it does not mean, means what it does not say. The work is more serious, and more abstruse. Supported by the theory of Lacan and the critiques of the French feminists, deconstructionism exposes meaning as an alias, a false identity constructed to disguise the plurality of meanings that is the text. But this openness to meaning does not collapse into an absence of meaning. It allows meaning to be provisional, lively, fluttering. It allows interpretation to be an act that transforms the text, and the world and the interpreters as well. Barthes has returned the pleasure of reading to us, its sensuality, its power. Over and over again he shows us how the passages that lead us into and out of texts are also forms of intentionality that we bring to the world around us:

To be with the one I love and to think of something else: this is how I have my best ideas, how I best invent what is necessary to my work. Likewise for the text, it produces in me, the best pleasure if it manages to make itself heard indirectly; if, reading it, I am led to look up often, to listen to something else. I am not necessarily *captivated* by the text of pleasure; it can be an act that is slight, complex, tenuous, almost scatterbrained: a sudden movement of the head like a bird who understands nothing of what we hear, who hears what we do not understand.[37]

Barthes's own texts show us that the glimpses of our world that our reading of another world provides need not slip from consciousness because they are not in themselves complete or elaborate literary forms. His texts about reading resymbolize his experience, gathering up not only the sense and reference of the text, but the sense and reference of his own intentionality as well, and winding it into a new spool.

Less outrageous than Barthes, less destructive than Derrida, are the reader-response theorists. Those who have been very much influenced by Piaget's epistemology contend that meaning does not reside in the text, nor in the schemes of the reader, but that it symbolizes the reader's experience of the text. While these theorists offer us some information about the processes of individual readers, reader-response founders in the classroom where even Stanley Fish, who has placed meaning in the response of the reader to the text, falters and accedes to interpretive communities who can, according to their own consensual light, privilege some interpretations as being better than others. Holland's identity themes provide a psychoanalytic frame for reader responses that portrays them as unconscious ego adaptations revealing readers' identity themes, thus conflating the reality principal with the text. Bleich solicits the writing of response statements, documents that record readers' associations and interpretations. He does not reduce these documents to case histories or diagnoses, but he does have difficulty when he talks about the contribution of response statements to the negotiation of meaning. It is not clear what is being negotiated and what the protocol for that negotiation is.[38]

It is an easy task to find the flaws in each of the reader-response schemes for the identification of meaning. Each of these critics has been kind enough to attack the rationales and claims of the others.[39] Their disputes reveal that despite these theorists' apparent readiness to return meaning to readers, those meanings and the ways they are articulated and negotiated are still claimed as the property of the critics. Sensing each others' attachment to this capital, they accuse each other of being Indian givers, and delight in finding the deeds that ensure that the property will revert to its original owner, the critic, of course, hidden under the mattress of every reader-response theory. But their property squabbles need not undermine our sense that the text is a new territory for our explorations with students. And their work is very important to us because it acknowledges the classroom as an interpretive community and makes its protocols and curriculum absolutely essential to this process we call reading.

If we can just wrest meaning from the grip of knowledge and return it to art, we will be able to given students something to do with texts. Activity-based curricula that are bonded to social, political, and physical action cannot contain the possibilities of meaning. The world is too unwieldy, the classroom too constricting. Exhausted, confusing the reference of the text with tomorrow, those teachers who have sensed the glory of engagement too often are disappointed and retreat to the cynical postures of critical thinking – adversarial, analytic attacks on meaning, where students are endlessly playing the seconds in their teacher/critics' duels.

Because art forms express knowledge about feeling they provide a bridge between public and private readings. Because aesthetic activity requires the making of things, comprehension is made palpable and accessible to the perception and response of other readers. Every time a text is drawn into performance, it is the reading of the text, and never the text itself, that is performed. We need to cultivate the irreverence of theater director Jerzy Grotowski if we are to recover the mystery that our ancestors associated with reading:

> For both actor and producer the author's text is a sort of scalpel, enabling us to open ourselves, to transcend ourselves, to find what is hidden in us all. In the theater, if you like, the text has the same function as the myth had for the poet of ancient times. The author of Prometheus found in the Prometheus myth both an act of defiance and a springboard, perhaps even the source of his own creation. . . . For me, a creator of theater, the important thing is not the words but what we do with these words, what gives life to the inanimate words of the text, what transforms them into The Word.[40]

Meaning is continually deferred. Like Io, ranging over the earth, pursued by the gadfly of Hera, meaning never rests in The Word, but in our ceaseless rumination and resymbolizations. Ricoeur is clear that the reference of the text, what the text is about, can never be identified as either the author's or the reader's situation. "The sense of the text is not behind the text, but in front of it. It is not something hidden, but something disclosed. What has to be understood is not the initial situation of discourse, but what points to a possible world."[41]

Theater is the enactment of possible worlds. It places action in time and space. Literally, the action takes place. Something happens, and what theater displays is the comprehension of the bodyreader. Performance simultaneously confirms and undermines the text. The body of the actor, like the body of the text, stumbles into ambiguity, insinuating more than words can say with gesture, movement, intonation. Mimesis tumbles into transformation and meaning, taken from the text, rescued from the underworld of negotiation, becomes the very ground of action.

Suzanne Langer sees this as the function of theater. Neither show biz nor ritual, theater's function is "to delimit the world where virtual action takes place."[42] And this, I suggest to you, is what curriculum can bring to reading.

It not only brings purpose to the reading process by providing a ground for intentionality, it also provides another stage where the possible worlds that the text points to can be identified and experienced as good places for grazing.

Notes

1. Maurice Merleau-Ponty, *The Phenomenology of Perception*, trans. Colin Smith (New York: Humanities Press, 1962).
2. Paul Ricoeur, *Interpretation Theory: Discourse and the Surplus of Meaning* (Fort Worth: Texas Christian University Press, 1976).
3. Ibid., p. 20.
4. Susan Suleiman, "Introduction: Varieties of Audience-Oriented Criticism," in *The Reader in the Text*, ed. Susan Suleiman and Inge Crossman (Princeton, N.J.: Princeton University Press, 1980), p. 38.
5. William Butler Yeats, "Sailing to Byzantium," in *Modern American and Modern British Poetry*, ed. Louis Untermeyer (New York: Harcourt, Brace, 1955), p. 475.
6. Ferdinand de Saussure, *Course in General Linguistics*, Charles Bally and Albert Sechahaye, eds., trans. Roy Harris (London: Duckworth, 1983).
7. Merleau-Ponty, *Phenomenology of Perception*, p. 187.
8. Madeleine R. Grumet, "Songs and Situations," in *Qualitative Evaluation*, ed. George Willis (Berkeley: McCutchan, 1978).
9. William Shakespeare, "Sonnet 18," in *The Riverside Shakespeare* (Boston: Houghton Mifflin, 1974), p. 1752.
10. Jacques Lacan, *The Language of the Self*, trans. Anthony Wilden (New York: Dell Publishing, 1968).
11. *Encyclopaedia Britannica* (Chicago: William Benton, 1962), vol. 19, p. 657.
12. *The Compact Edition of the Oxford English Dictionary* (London: Oxford University Press, 1971), vol. 2, p. 2427.
13. Meyer Fortes, "Religious Premises and Logical Technique in Divinatory Ritual," *Philosophical Transactions of the Royal Society* 251, no. 722 (1966): 409–26.
14. Frank Smith's theories of reading are supported by this portrayal of reading competence as a gestalt that arises from a complex communication situation. See his *Understanding Reading* (New York: Holt, Rinehart & Winston, 1973).
15. Elizabeth Keim, Hobart and William Smith Colleges, unpublished manuscript.
16. Stanley Elkin, "Where I Read What I Read," *Antaeus* 45/46 (Spring/Summer 1982): 57.
17. Marie-France Etienne, Hobart and William Smith Colleges, unpublished manuscript.
18. Walter Slatoff, *With Respect to Readers: Dimensions of Literary Response* (Ithaca, N.Y.: Cornell University Press, 1970), p. 54.
19. Stanley Fish, *Is There a Text in This Class?* (Cambridge: Harvard University Press, 1980).
20. Smith, *Understanding Reading*.
21. From Selected Poems by Galway Kinnell, published by Houghton Mifflin Company, Boston. Copyright © 1982 by Galway Kinnell. Reprinted by permission.
22. Schema theory addresses the relation between a particular interpretation or understanding of text and the expectations, assumptions, and particular experiences that readers bring to it. See the work of Richard C. Anderson, Jean Osborn, and Robert J. Tierney, *Learning to Read in American Schools* (Hillsdale, N.J.: Lawrence Erlbaum Associates, 1984).
23. Mitford Mathews, *Teaching to Read* (Chicago: The University of Chicago Press, 1966).
24. Nancy Chodorow, *The Reproduction of Mothering* (Berkeley: University of Chicago Press, 1978).
25. Erwin Straus, "Upright Man," in *Essays in Phenomenology*, ed. Maurie Natanson (The Hague: Martinus Nijhoff, 1966).

26. In "My Face Is Thine Eye, Thine in Mine Appeares: The Look in Parenting and Pedagogy," *Phenomenology and Pedagogy* 1, no. 1 (1982): 45–58, I have discussed the ways of being with children that sound, touch, and sight provide.

27. Smith, *Understanding Reading.*

28. Godfrey Lienhardt, *Divinity and Experience* (Oxford: Clarendon Press, 1961).

29. Julia Kristeva's writings explore the epistemology and politics of the "mother tongue." See her *About Chinese Women*, trans. A. Burrows (London: Marion Boyars, 1977); and idem, "Women's Time," trans. Alice Jardine and Harry Blake, in *Feminist Theory*, ed. N. O. Keohane, M. Z. Rosaldo, and B. C. Gelpi (Chicago: The University of Chicago Press, 1982).

30. Merleau-Ponty, *Phenomenology of Perception*, p. 10.

31. Harold Herber, *Teaching Reading in Content Areas* (Englewood Cliffs, N.J.: Prentice-Hall, 1978), p. 40.

32. In "Pedagogy for Patriarchy: The Feminization of Teaching," *Interchange* 12, no. 2/3 (1981): 165–205, I have examined the situations of the young women who taught in the common schools following industrialization to discover what induced them to deny their own experiences of childhood, or nurturance, and of desire as they complied with the ethics and epistemologies of schooling. Their experiences of reading, given the school's repudiation of sensuality, fantasy, and emotion, must have been literally unspeakable.

33. M. F. Goldberg, "An Update on the National Project Writing," *Kappan* 65, no. 5 (1984): 356–57.

34. David Bleich, *Subjective Criticism* (Baltimore: Johns Hopkins Press, 1978); and Eugene Kintgen, "Reading Response and Stylistics," *Style* 11, no. 1 (Winter 1977): 1–18.

35. Ernst Kris, *Psychoanalytic Explorations in Art* (New York: International Press, 1952).

36. Terry Eagleton, *Literary Theory* (Minneapolis: University of Minnesota Press, 1983), p. 138.

37. Roland Barthes, *The Pleasure of the Text*, trans. Richard Miller (New York: Hill and Wang, 1975), p. 24. Emphasis in original.

38. In addition to the works of Bleich and Fish already cited, see Norman Holland, *The Dynamics of Literary Response* (New York: Norton, 1975).

39. See *New Literary History* 7 (1976) for articles by David Bleich, "The Subjective Paradigm"; and Norman Holland, "The New Paradigm: Subjective or Transactive?"

40. Jerzy Grotowski, *Towards a Poor Theatre* (New York: Simon and Schuster, 1968), p. 57.

41. Ricoeur, *Interpretation Theory*, p. 87.

42. Suzanne Langer, *Feeling and Form* (New York: Charles Scribner's Sons, 1953), p. 322.

76

Valuing Teachers:
The Making of a Profession

Linda Darling-Hammond

This article argues that the most critical issue facing American education today is the professionalization of teaching. Professionalization involves not only the status and compensation accorded to the members of an occupation; it involves the extent to which members of that occupation maintain control over the content of their work and the degree to which society values the work of that occupation.

Communities and school organizations place an implicit value on teaching work in the ways in which they structure personnel practices and the conduct of schooling. These include the care and thoughtfulness, along with the resources, devoted to the training and preparation of teachers; the time and expertise allocated to the induction of teachers in the first years of their teaching experience; resources devoted to the selection, evaluation, and continuing professional development of teachers; and the degree to which value is placed on teachers' time for instruction as opposed to hall duty, bus duty, bathroom duty, and clerical chores. Value is measured also by the extent to which policymakers listen to teachers when they voice their concerns about instruction, about students, and about educational reforms. Ultimately, these factors reflect the degree to which we value students; for if we devalue the act of teaching, we devalue the act of learning as well. These issues are not new, but are, I believe, the necessary preconditions for real educational improvement in this country.

We have all heard a great deal about educational reform over the past two years. If we think about the types of changes that schools are being asked to make in the wake of the current educational reform movement, we can see that there are a number of mandates that assume an infrastructure of material resources and human capital for their implementation. The reforms include new course requirements for students – more and more advanced courses in science, social studies, English, mathematics, and foreign language; more

Source: *Teachers College Record*, 87(2) (1985): 205–218.

instructional hours in the school day and more days in the school year; more testing of students and more standardization of school curricula; more evaluation of teachers and more screening of prospective teachers, primarily through tests but also through more complicated certification requirements. Furthermore, this set of current reforms contains some paradoxes. As we find it harder and harder to attract and retain qualified teachers, we are increasing the demand for those teachers (through mandates for new courses and increased time) while we restrict the supply (through new screens to the profession).

We are facing a situation now where, in the face of these increased demands on schools and requirements of students, we simply do not have a sufficient number of adequately trained teachers to staff the courses we currently expect students to take. The widely acknowledged shortage of math and science teachers exemplifies the problem, but it is really just the tip of the proverbial iceberg. As state legislatures are busy mandating increased graduation requirements for students, we have for many years been asking teachers not trained in the fields where we are promoting these increased requirements to teach many of the courses we currently offer.

As an example of this dilemma, fewer than a third of American high schools now have a physics teacher on their faculties. In 1981 the nation's colleges granted fewer than 1,400 bachelor degrees in mathematics and science education combined. Fewer than half of those graduates went on into teaching.[1] This number represents less than one math or science teacher for every twenty school districts in the United States. In the following year, about 18,000 math and science teachers left their teaching posts; about half of them left the profession altogether.[2] This means that for every one newly trained mathematics or science teacher who entered the profession, about twelve left. The situation since then has grown only more grim. Officials in state departments of education and school district personnel offices report that they can identify only a handful of candidates qualified in these areas.

As a consequence of this situation, even in 1981 fewer than half of the teachers who were newly hired to teach mathematics and science were certified or even certifiable in those areas.[3] In practical terms, what this means is that – since their preparation includes at least a few of the relevant courses – physical education teachers are increasingly assigned to teach science courses and home economics teachers are increasingly assigned to teach math courses. Elementary teachers are assigned to teach junior high school courses in mathematics, science, and other areas of short supply. In some school districts this is the predominant mode of teacher assignment, rather than an exception to the rule. These teachers are generally not trained to teach upper-level courses, so this practice poses the dilemma of whether such courses should be taught poorly or not at all.

This is not a short-term problem. According to at least one set of estimates, of the current total teaching force of 200,000 mathematics and science teachers now teaching in our classrooms, about 30 percent are not fully qualified to teach the subjects they are teaching, and over 40 percent will retire within the next decade. The National Science Teachers Association estimates that in ten years we will need 300,000 *new* math and science teachers – which is 50 percent more than the total number we currently have.[4] Where will they come from?

The shortages, though, are not limited to this subset of teachers. They extend to nearly all secondary subject areas and will soon extend to elementary education as well. In 1981, more than a third of the newly hired social studies and English teachers were not certified or certifiable to teach those subjects.[5] By 1988, most projections indicate that only 70 to 80 percent of the total demand for new teachers will be satisfied by the supply of new teachers.[6]

This shortage is the result of sharp declines in the number of students preparing to become teachers,[7] combined with increases in the proportions of teachers who are or will be retiring and an increase in the number of young children about to enter the schools.

This is not a new occurrence. We have had shortages of teachers before, and we have somehow managed to keep the schools open and the classrooms staffed. What is new is this: We have lost the captive labor force for teaching on which we have relied for most of this century. This labor force has been freed by increased equality of opportunity in the broader society over the last ten years. Talented women and minorities, who once "chose" teaching because they had relatively few professional occupations available to them, are now comparing the relative salaries and the working conditions available in teaching and other careers; not surprisingly, many are opting out of education.

In one short decade, between 1970 and 1981, the proportion of women receiving bachelor degrees in education decreased by more than half – from 36 percent to 17 percent.[8] In a shorter period of time, between 1975 and 1981, the proportion of black students receiving degrees in education decreased by more than a third, and the same pattern was obvious for other minorities as well.[9] Defections from teaching have been primarily among the most academically able members of these groups,[10] who are now increasingly choosing degrees in business and commerce, the health professions, the sciences and engineering, over the "traditional" career paths open to them in the past.[11]

Where fifteen years ago, one out of every five college graduates received a degree in education, now the number of students planning to do so is only one in twenty.[12] And of all intended majors, the average Scholastic Aptitude Test (SAT) scores of college-bound seniors planning to major in education rank lower than all courses of study except vocational education and home economics.[13] Furthermore, most of the few top scorers who are recruited to teaching leave the profession within a few years.[14]

There are a number of reasons for these changes. Widely publicized surpluses of teachers in the 1970s have undoubtedly had some effect on supply, but even in areas of the country where enrollments were growing during that period of time, the supply of entering teachers has continued to shrink.

Most obvious is the fact that financial inducements to teaching are, to put it bluntly, terrible. Even when beginning teaching salaries are adjusted to reflect a twelve-month equivalent, they fall short of the next lowest category of wages offered to college graduates.[15] Between 1971 and 1981, average salaries for teachers declined by nearly 15 percent in real-dollar terms, while the average salaries of other college-educated workers increased.[16] This occurred even while the education and experience levels of the teaching force were increasing over that period of time. Furthermore, the proportion of educational expenditures allocated to teachers' salaries dropped during that decade from 49 percent of school expenditures to only 38 percent.[17]

Teachers also report being more dissatisfied with their work now than at any time in the recent past. Nearly 40 percent say that, if they had it to do over again, they would not choose teaching as a career. This compares with fewer than 10 percent only ten years earlier.[18] Fewer than half of current teachers plan to stay in teaching until retirement.[19] Recent research indicates that the most academically qualified teachers are the most dissatisfied with their working conditions and are most likely to say they will leave teaching.[20]

We have to ask ourselves what is going wrong. It is easy to summarize the factors that contribute to teacher dissatisfaction. Teachers feel that they lack support – physical support in terms of adequate facilities and materials; support services such as clerical help for typing, duplicating, and paperwork chores; and administrative support that would provide a school environment in which their work is valued and supported rather than obstructed by interruptions and proliferations of nonteaching tasks.[21] They see their ability to teach hampered by large classes, non-teaching duties, and bureaucratic requirements that demand standardized teaching practices that fail to meet the unstandardized needs of students. And they have little or no input into the decisions that critically affect their work environment.[22]

It is not just that the discrete components of a teacher's job deflect attention from teaching work to other, time-consuming and less rewarding tasks. It is that the generally adopted conception of teaching implicit in a factory model of schooling is both degrading to teachers and educationally counterproductive. Viewing teachers as semiskilled, low-paid workers in the mass production of education, policymakers have sought to change education, to improve it, by "teacher-proofing" it. Over the past decade we have seen a proliferation of elaborate accountability schemes that go by acronyms like MBO (management by objectives), PBBS (performance-based budgeting systems), CBE (competency-based education), CBTE (competency-based teacher education), and MCT (minimum competency testing).

This alphabet soup of educational reform is based on the notion that if teachers do exactly as they are told, students will learn just as they should.[23] Instead, we have found that highly prescriptive teaching policies often limit the curriculum to those subjects and modes of performance that are most easily tested; they create paperwork burdens that detract from teaching time;

and they sometimes prevent the use of alternative teaching strategies that are more appropriate to students' needs and to the development of higher-order cognitive abilities.[24]

In a Rand study of teachers views' of the effect of educational policies on their classroom practices, we learned from teachers that in response to policies that prescribe teaching practices and outcomes, they spend less time on untested subjects, such as science and social studies; they use less writing in their classrooms in order to gear assignments to the format of standardized tests; they resort to lectures rather than classroom discussions in order to cover the prescribed behavioral objectives without getting "off the track"; they are precluded from using teaching materials that are not on prescribed textbook lists, even when they think these materials are essential to meet the needs of some of their students; and they feel constrained from following up on expressed student interests that lie outside the bounds of mandated curricula. We also heard the frustration that results from the dual-accountability dilemma experienced by teachers when they must follow strictures from above that collide with their view of what they should responsibly do to meet the needs of their students. And 45 percent of the teachers in this study told us that the single thing that would make them leave teaching was the increased prescriptiveness of teaching content and methods – in short, the continuing deprofessionalization of teaching.[25]

Ironically, what makes many teachers leave the classroom is the sense that teaching work is not important in school. In a variety of ways teachers receive signals that filling out forms, meeting schedules, policing hallways, and enforcing rules are more essential to school life than is teaching. When preparation time is chewed up with nonteaching duties, when staff meetings are limited to conveying administrative directives, when classes are interrupted by announcements and record-keeping tasks, when innovative teaching ideas take a back seat to attendance and test reports, teachers find their work devalued and their effectiveness diminished.

These bureaucratic aspects of schooling are, of course, important to administrators responsible for monitoring what goes on in classrooms, but when they become the means for holding teachers accountable, they undermine the real work of teaching. As one teacher remarked to us: "If we could just get the administration to leave us alone and teach, we'd be able to. We spend probably 30 percent or more of our time doing paperwork. A good percentage of that is totally unnecessary and another percentage is something that could be done by a teacher's aide or secretary. We're doing paperwork during time that we could and should be using to teach. Most of it is a waste of time."

Another teacher described what happens: "So much of the teacher's time is spent in things other than teaching: recordkeeping, the rigid curriculum guide, the pre- and post-testing, and the massive record system to keep tiny little bits of it; when it is presented, when it is mastered, when it is re-taught and reinforced and post-tested. It is just mammoth. A great deal of time and energy is spent with these sorts of things, and it limits meeting the interests of children."

Another said: "The thing that would make me leave teaching is if they ever computerize all those objectives and I have to sit there and check off forms for 38 kids and 250 different objectives. I think if it got down to that I would just leave because I'd be spending more time on forms than kids."

And another: "I feel sorry for any teacher who is interested in teaching. For those who like the recordkeeping, and there are plenty of them, pathetic teachers but great recordkeepers, this will be a way of moving them up the ladder. It won't help the good teachers. It will help the people who teach by the book [because] it is safe and it doesn't require any imagination."

And another: "It's just another nail in the coffin driving a lot of would-be good teachers out of the profession."

Prescribed practices and paperwork are, of course, the means by which others in the school hierarchy hold teachers accountable for what is happening in the classroom. And our ever-burgeoning school bureaucracies (there is now one administrator for every ten teachers in American schools) find more and more ways to exert remote control over classroom teaching. Reports of attendance, teaching objectives, and test scores are meant to ensure that teachers are teaching and students are learning. But they have other effects. They deflect teachers' time and attention from students to narrowly configured procedural requirements. They limit teachers' flexibility in deciding how to teach. They discourage creativity on the part of both students and teachers. And they sacrifice the most precious teaching resource of all – the teachable moment – to externally determined goals and activities. They leave little room for exploration, inquiry, or critical thinking as they press inexorably for the one best multiple-choice answer to questions that ought to be the subject of reflection and debate.

As John Goodlad found in his examination of over one thousand American classrooms, students in most classrooms do certain things but not others. They listen, they read short passages, and they answer fill-in-the-blank or multiple-choice questions on tests and worksheets. They respond to short-answer, recall, and regurgitation-type questions. But rarely do they plan their own work, engage in projects requiring conception and application of concepts and ideas, read whole books, or write analytic themes. Goodlad comments:

> Teachers are sensitive to the pressures that state and district testing programs place on them. They get the message. The other messages – that there are goals beyond those that the tests measure, that pursing such goals calls for alternative teaching strategies, that the fundamentals of the curriculum transcend grade-level requirements – are faint to begin with, and they are drowned out by the more immediate and stronger message.[26]

It is worth noting that, while teachers report these changes in their teaching practices, the National Assessment of Educational Progress (NAEP) tests have recorded declines in students' understanding of science; in their abilities to read and write analytically; and in their abilities to use problem-solving skills in math and other areas.[27] Officials of NAEP, the National Science Foundation, and the National Councils of Teachers of Mathematics and English have attributed these declines to our last reform effort – to the "back to the basics" movement. Perhaps it is time that we use a different approach to educational policymaking – an approach that replaces bureaucratic accountability mechanisms with a professional accountability model that will be based on adequate preparation of teachers so that they can be entrusted to practice their profession.

Research on effective teaching lends support to that model. A number of studies over the last two decades have indicated that students have different learning styles, that effective teaching techniques vary for students of different characteristics and at different stages in their development, for different subject areas, and for different learning goals.[28] These studies have made it clear that professional judgment is a prerequisite for effective teaching, because unless students are treated according to their particular learning needs, they will be mistreated. Standardized practice is, in effect, malpractice. Unless we prepare teachers to responsibly exercise professional judgment, and then allow them to do so, we will have little hope of improving educational quality. This means restructuring schools and teaching so that professionalism can exist.

What does this mysterious quotient, professionalism, really consist of? And how can we achieve it? We can start by defining what it is not.

Professionalism is not blind conformity to state, local, or even school-level policies. At the core of the definition of a profession is the notion that its members must define and enforce their own standards of practice. As Barber puts it, "An essential attribute of professional role is autonomy and self-control regarding the development and application of the body of generalized knowledge in which they [professionals] alone are expert."[29]

It is not simply because professions lay claim to a body of knowledge that they must exercise self-control. Boreham explains that it is the *indetermination* of that knowledge – its inability to be reduced to rules or prescriptions for practice – that is the most powerful basis for professions' arguments that they must have autonomy from administrative control in determining occupational tasks and functions.[30] Friedson summarizes this argument in explaining the organization of professional tasks through the authority of institutionalized expertise rather than through rational-legal administrative authority: "Knowledge-based work, the work of . . . professionals . . . is by its very nature not amenable to mechanization and rationalization. . . . If it is true that management cannot rationalize such work . . . then it can only maintain an administrative framework around it."[31]

The place of judgment and non-standardizable skill in the work of professionals predicts resistance to codification or task determination by outsiders. Control and review of practice and practitioners, it is argued, must be conducted by peers.

Furthermore, professionals incur a special obligation toward their clients. The professional must do whatever will best serve the client's interest and welfare, using standards of practice that are based on the application of specialized knowledge to the unique circumstances of the client, even if that conflicts with rules and procedures that are imposed externally. Professionalism does not mean standardized practice, it means *appropriate* practice, which is far more complex – and in today's schools sometimes requires a fair amount of courage.

One rather extreme example of bureaucratically imposed teaching controls displays the ethical conflict that teachers experience. In a school district not far from where I live, a new teacher arrived on the first day of class to teach her kindergarten students and was handed the county's curriculum guide. She was told by her principal that she should give the students their first test as part of the competency-based education system. They were to write their numerals from one to two hundred. Although she protested that the task seemed unreasonable for beginning kindergarten students, she was compelled to comply. When she asked the students to perform this task, some of them scribbled on their papers, and some of them put their heads down and cried in confusion and fear. Of course, everyone failed the objective.

After continuing for two weeks with other activities more suited to the developmental needs of the children, the teacher was told to retest the students on their ability to write their numerals from one to two hundred. Her protests were again overruled, and the exercise was conducted with the same result. That teacher did not last long in teaching. The point, though, is that it is unethical for a teacher to conform to prescribed practices that are ultimately harmful to children. Yet that is what teachers are required to do by policies that are pedagogically inappropriate for some or all of their students.

When teachers are evaluated on the basis of conformity to these policies, their ethical dilemma is heightened, and their professionalism is undermined. But if we are to find another way to evaluate teachers and teaching, we must develop professional standards of practice that can guide the technical decision making that is rightfully and necessarily the role of teachers.

This means, among other things, teacher education that includes much more than courses in methods of teaching reading, methods of teaching social studies, and so on. The current curriculum in many schools of education could be compared to training doctors in methods of treating cancer and techniques for treating heart disease without any grounding in anatomy, physiology, or biology. Technique without theory and knowledge of content does not provide a basis for professional decision making. Thoughtful, reflective, and effective teaching requires that teachers have rigorous grounding in cognitive psychology so that they understand how people learn; in developmental psychology so that they know when children are ready to learn particular things in particular ways; in learning theory and pedagogy; and in professional ethics, which is one of the key elements missing from our system of teacher education.

Teachers must understand the structure and transmittal of knowledge. They ought to know about test theory and measurement, not just so they can explain what a stanine is, but so that they can critically examine and construct instruments for evaluating students, and they will know what a test score really tells them about student performance and what it does not. These things must be learned as students also acquire disciplinary expertise and have opportunities to apply this knowledge. This will require reshaping not only the types of courses in schools of education and the structure of teacher education programs, but also the resources devoted to teacher training. Teacher education institutions have long been revenue producers for their universities, and have often received fewer resources in return to devote to the serious preparation of teachers.

The development of professional standards of practice will require intensively supervised induction for teachers. This does not mean four evaluations instead of two every year, or two evaluators filling out the checklist instead of one. What is needed is a type of induction in which expert, experienced practitioners in the same teaching area as the intern consult frequently and continuously, and provide assistance and feedback over an extended period of time to new teachers so that they can learn to translate theory into practice – so they can have some possibility, indeed, probability of becoming effective teachers.

Teaching is the only profession in which there is so little concern for clients that we are willing to give new practitioners the most difficult and burdensome assignments, leave them without teaching materials, close the door, and tell them to sink or swim on their own. This is not only a disservice to new teachers (half of whom leave within a few years, in part because of this lack of support), but it is also, of course, a tremendous injustice to students.

Finally, for meaningful standards of practice to develop, there must be opportunities for discourse and inquiry among classroom teachers about real, immediate problems of practice. This is quite a different notion from that of in-service days where teachers are "in-serviced" on the latest textbook or a new teaching technique after which they return to the problems of their classrooms without satisfactory answers to the challenges they face. Teacher isolation, which is a fact in American schools, is not only a major cause of teacher attrition; it is deadening for professional growth and for the evolution and transmittal of professional knowledge.[32] Teachers need opportunities to observe and be observed by their colleagues, to jointly diagnose school problems and invent new approaches, to share teaching ideas, to develop programs and curricula, to assess the progress of their school and the students, and to learn from each other.

Ultimately, professionalism requires collective control by teachers over the technical decisions that define teaching work and collective responsibility for the appropriate treatment of students. This means not only peer review of practice, but also peer involvement in the prevention of malpractice. It also means a reconception of administration as a support function for teaching rather than a mechanism for the control of teaching.

And, of course, we need improved salaries and working conditions. We need wages that are professionally competitive and time for teachers to prepare and teach. Paraprofessionals ought to assume the nonteaching tasks that teachers have so that we can truly value the teaching acts that teachers must engage in if they are going to improve the quality of education for students.

Most of these reforms involve time and money as well as difficult reformulations of virtually all aspects of schooling. However, these conditions are much more nearly met in many other industrialized countries and their investments are paying off in ways that ours are not. In Japan, for example, teachers are paid as well as engineers and other professionals. A typical high school teacher teaches only seventeen hours out of a forty-hour school week. The remainder of that time is used for preparation and for consultations with parents, students, and colleagues.[33] The Japanese find a way to afford and structure schools that will allow teacher professionalism and teaching excellence.

While we consider the costs of fundamental reform, we should also consider the alternatives: Unless we change the incentives that operate in schools so that we can both attract and retain talented individuals in teaching, we will in only a few years face serious shortages of qualified teachers in virtually all subject areas and in virtually all regions of the country. We will be forced to hire the least academically able college students to fill those vacancies, and they will become the tenured teaching force for the next two generations of American school children.

Furthermore, to the extent that this crisis in teaching materializes, it will be – and it already is – primarily a crisis in equity. Schools in those districts that are least able to offer higher salaries and attractive working conditions will bear the brunt of the teacher supply problem. It is poor and minority children, primarily, whose educational opportunities are – and will increasingly be – diminished as they are taught by ill-prepared teachers, by inexperienced teachers without support, by a parade of short- and long-term substitutes, and by teachers who are forced to teach outside their fields of preparation. Teachers are already the most inequitably distributed of all school resources, and the instructional inequities will only be compounded if we fail to meet this challenge.

Finally, alongside the public quest for excellence being pursued in the public policymaking arena, parents who can afford to are conducting their own private quest for excellence, increasingly outside the public educational sector. With a growing number of two-income households accustomed to devoting a portion of their income to day care and private preschool education, the unquestioned use of public schools is waning. These parents are looking for stimulating, responsive educational settings where the individual needs of their children can be met. They do not choose private schools because such schools offer minimum competency testing or because they offer elaborate bureaucratic accountability mechanisms. They choose such schools because they sense a professional commitment and competence and a client-oriented value structure that allows for creative and responsive teaching.

If we are serious about improving the quality of public education, we will have to make more than marginal changes in the attractiveness of teaching. We will need to consciously and explicitly value teachers and the act of responsible, responsive teaching in all of our reform endeavors.

Notes

1. National Center for Education Statistics (henceforth NCES), *The Condition of Education, 1983 Edition* (Washington, D.C.: U.S. Department of Education, 1983), p. 188.
2. National Education Association, *Teacher Supply and Demand in Public Schools, 1981–82* (Washington, D.C.: NEA, 1983).
3. NCES, *The Condition of Education*, p. 206.
4. National Science Teachers Association Survey, December 1982, reported in Hope Aldrich, "Teacher Shortage: Likely to Get Worse Before It Gets Better," *Education Week*, July 27, 1983, pp. 9–12.
5. NCES, *The Condition of Education*, p. 206.
6. NCES, *Projections of Education Statistics to 1988–89* (Washington, D.C.: U.S. Department of Education, 1980); and National Education Association, *Teacher Supply and Demand in Public Schools*, p. 22.
7. NCES, *The Condition of Education*, p. 184.
8. Ibid.
9. William T. Trent, "Equity Considerations in Higher Education: Race and Sex Differences in Degree Attainment and Major Field from 1976 through 1981," *American Journal of Education*, May 1984, pp. 280–305.
10. See, for example, Victor S. Vance and Phillip C. Schlechty, "Recruitment, Selection, and Retention: The Shape of the Teaching Force," *Elementary School Journal* 83, no. 4 (1983): 469–87; and Sandra D. Roberson, Timothy Z. Keith, and Ellis B. Page, "Now Who Aspires to Teach?" *Educational Researcher*, June/July 1983, pp. 13–21.
11. Bureau of the Census, *Statistical Abstract of the United States: 1984*, 104th ed. (Washington, D.C.: U.S. Department of Commerce, 1983), p. 166; and idem, *Statistical Abstract of the United States: 1973*, 94th ed. (Washington, D.C.: U.S. Department of Commerce, 1973), p. 133.
12. College Entrance Examination Board, *Profiles of College-Bound Seniors, 1981* (New York: CEEB, 1982).
13. Ibid.
14. For example, 28 percent of the lowest quintile of SAT scorers from the high school class of 1973 went into teaching, and more than half of them planned to stay in the profession. By contrast, only 8 percent of the highest quintile went into teaching, and only 25 percent of them planned to stay (Victor S. Vance and Phillip C. Schlechty, "The Structure of the Teaching Occupation and the Characteristics of Teachers: A Sociological Interpretation," [Paper presented at the National Institute of Education Conference at Airleigh House, Virginia, February 25–27, 1982]). See also, Phillip C. Schlechty and Victor S. Vance, "Do Academically Able Teachers Leave Education? The North Carolina Case," *Phi Delta Kappan* 63 (1981): 106–12.

15. Data are for the 1981–1982 school year. National Education Association, *Prices, Budgets, Salaries, and Income: 1983* (Washington, D.C.: NEA. 1983), p. 22.

16. NCES, *The Condition of Education*, pp. 102–03.

17. C. Emily Feistritzer, *The Condition of Teaching: A State by State Analysis* (Washington, D.C.: The Carnegie Foundation for the Advancement of Teaching, 1983), p. 50.

18. National Education Association, *Status of the American Public School Teacher, 1980–81* (Washington, D.C.: NEA, 1982), pp. 73–76.

19. Ibid.

20. Linda Darling-Hammond, *Beyond the Commission Reports: The Coming Crisis in Teaching*, R-3177-RC (Santa Monica, Calif.: The Rand Corporation, July 1984).

21. Ibid., pp. 76–78; National Education Association, *Nationwide Teacher Opinion Poll, 1983* (Washington, D.C.: NEA, 1983), p. 9; and American Federation of Teachers, *School as a Workplace: The Realities of Stress*, vol. 1 (Washington, D.C.: AFT, 1983), pp. 15–17.

22. See, for example, Linda Darling-Hammond and Arthur E. Wise, "Teaching Standards or Standardized Teaching?," *Educational Leadership*, October 1983, pp. 66–69; Susan J. Rosenholtz and Mark A. Smylie, "Teacher Compensation and Career Ladders: Policy Implications from Research" (Paper commissioned by the Tennessee General Assembly's Select Committee on Education, December 1983); D. W. Chapman and S. M. Hutcheson, "Attrition from Teaching Careers: A Discriminant Analysis," *American Educational Research Journal* 19 (1982): 893–905; M. D. Litt and D. C. Turk, "Stress, Dissatisfaction, and Intention to Leave Teaching in Experienced Public High School Teachers" (Paper presented at the annual meeting of the American Educational Research Association, Montreal, April 1983).

23. Arthur E. Wise, *Legislated Learning: The Bureaucratization of the American Classroom* (Berkeley: University of California Press, 1979).

24. See Linda Darling-Hammond and Arthur E. Wise, "Beyond Standardization: State Standards and School Improvement," *Elementary School Journal* 85, no. 3 (January 1985): 315–36; Anne M. Bussis, "Burn It at the Casket: Research, Reading Instruction, and Children's Learning of the First R," *Phi Delta Kappan*, December 1982, pp. 237–41; Constance Kamii, "Encouraging Thinking in Mathematics," *Phi Delta Kappan*, December 1982, pp. 247–51: and Harriet Talmage and Sue Pinzur Rasher. "Unanticipated Outcomes: The Perils to Curriculum Goals." *Phi Delta Kappan*, September 1980, pp. 30–32, 71.

25. Darling-Hammond and Wise, "Beyond Standardization"; and Darling-Hammond, *Beyond the Commission Reports*.

26. John I. Goodlad, "A Study of Schooling: Some Findings and Hypotheses," *Phi Delta Kappan*, March 1983, p. 470.

27. National Assessment of Educational Progress, *Changes in Mathematical Achievement, 1973–78* (Denver: NAEP, 1979); idem, *Reading, Thinking and Writing: Results from the 1979–80 National Assessment of Reading and Literature* (Denver: NAEP, 1981); and National Research Council, *The State of School Science* (Washington, D.C.: Commission on Human Resources, 1979).

28. See, for example, W. Doyle, "Paradigms for Research on Teacher Effectiveness," in *Review of Research in Education*, ed. Lee S. Shulman, vol. 5 (Itasca, Ill.: F. E. Peacock. 1978); M. J. Durkin and B. J. Biddle, *The Study of Teaching* (New York: Holt, Rinehart & Winston, 1974); F. J. McDonald and P. Elias, *Executive Summary Report: Beginning Teacher Evaluation Study, Phase II* (Princeton, N.J.: Educational Testing Service, 1976); L. J. Cronbach and R. E. Snow, *Aptitudes and Instructional Methods: A Handbook for Research on Interactions* (New York: Irvington, 1977); N. L. Gage, *The Scientific Basis of the Art of Teaching* (New York: Teachers College Press, 1978); and J. E. Brophy and C. M. Evertson, *Learning from Teaching: A Developmental Perspective* (Boston: Allyn and Bacon, 1976).

29. L. W. Barber, "Teacher Evaluation and Merit Pay," Working Paper No. TF-83-5 (Background paper for the Task Force on Education for Economic Growth, 1984).

30. P. Boreham, "Indetermination: Professional Knowledge, Organization and Control," *Sociological Review* 32 (November 1983): 693–718.
31. E. Friedson, "Professionalization and the Organization of Middle Class Labour in Post-Industrial Society," in *Professionalization and Social Change*, ed. P. Halmas, Sociological Review Monograph 20 (Keele, England: University of Keele, 1973), p. 50.
32. Rosenholtz and Smylie, *Teacher Compensation and Career Ladders*.
33. Nobuo K. Shimahara, "Japanese Education and Its Implications for U.S. Education," *Phi Delta Kappan*, February 1985, pp. 418–21.

77

Imagination and Learning

Kieran Egan

I magination is difficult stuff to get any firm grasp on, and notoriously difficult to study. Most educational research has difficulty enough dealing with things like knowledge, learning, or development. These are things our methods of research seem able to get some kind of hold on. And so we have a great deal of research on the more easily grasped stuff and very little on imagination.

Unfortunately, what we focus on tends to take a disproportionate space in our field of vision. If you were to try to draw from memory a proportionate picture of the moon in the night sky, you would undoubtedly find on comparing it with reality that you had drawn your moon much too big. The moon is what we usually focus on in our casual looks up at the night sky. Similarly what we study within the broad realm of education tends to be disproportionately influential on our thinking about educational practice.

Everyone acknowledges the importance of imagination in education. But we do not have large and energetic programs of research focused on imagination that are constantly feeding their findings and implications into educational practice. We do see such influences on practice from educational psychology, philosophy, sociology, and so on, in all of which imagination is largely ignored.

The individual teacher or curriculum designer tends not to be excessively influenced by particular research studies or theories, of course. We compose our views gradually and eclectically from a wide range of theories and research findings in light of our own experience. From these we tend to form what I may perhaps call "*ad hoc* principles" that guide our teaching or curriculum choices. If research and theories contribute to these *ad hoc* principles, and this research and these theories tend to ignore imagination, we may expect to find these principles seriously deficient. My purpose in this article is to argue that some of the most influential principles presently in vogue about teaching and curricula tend to suppress children's imagination and undermine some of its potential educational uses.

Source: *Teachers College Record*, 87(2) (1985): 155–174.

Let me take a few such *ad hoc* principles. I choose these because they are enormously influential and I am sure every teacher has heard them in one form or another, and also because I suspect most teachers and other educators accept them as providing useful guidance. Educational development proceeds, these principles inform us, from the concrete to the abstract, from the simple to the complex, from the known to the unknown, from active manipulation to symbolic conceptualization. These principles are not, of course, usually taken as universally true. (Language learning is a complex, abstract task mastered very early; certain simple insights come only after long study.) But I think it is fair to say that these principles have a pervasive and profound influence on teaching practice and on curriculum design.

Most teachers of young children learn in their professional preparation that children's active manipulation of concrete objects should precede abstract or symbolic learning. It is a commonplace of such programs that in planning teaching we should begin with familiar knowledge and experiences and expand gradually toward new material. These principles are also powerfully influential in shaping the elementary school curriculum. They are most clearly evident in social studies; we begin with the child and present concrete experiences, then focus on the family, then on to communities, working gradually outward to the broader society and cultural realms of the world.

And what role does imagination play in shaping these *ad hoc* principles? Well, what *is* imagination? According to a standard dictionary definition it is "the act or power of forming mental images of what is not actually present," or "the act or power of creating mental images of what has never been actually experienced."

Imagination seems to have had no influence at all on the *ad hoc* principles. The sense of the child as an energetic creator of mental images of what may never have been experienced seems, on the face of it at least, to conflict with the sense of the child presented in the principles that have been so influential in education. Is the manipulator of concrete materials derived from everyday experience the same child whose mind is brimming with starwarriors, monsters, and wicked witches? And is it more or less important for future educational development that a child be able to create and mentally manipulate these imaginary creatures than that the child be able to conserve liquid volume?

If we focus on education by means of, say, psychological development and we are focused onto that topic by, say, Piaget's theory, then we think in terms of logico-mathematical structures.[1] (Many influential voices encourage just such a focus. David Elkind wrote recently: "My own belief is that educators need to be first and foremost child development specialists."[2]) The influence of Piaget's theory on education has been very great, not necessarily in its direct application, but in providing additional support and definition to some of the *ad hoc* principles mentioned above.

If we focus on education by means of, say, an epistemological concern with the nature or structures of knowledge, then our educational conclusions will be framed in terms of the appropriate range and kinds of knowledge that being educated requires, or the logical forms and sequences in which knowledge may be accumulated.

Now logico-mathematical structures are not in competition with imagination. Nor is the accumulation of knowledge to be contrasted with freedom and expansion of the imagination. But the influential *ad hoc* principles have been formulated by focusing on education from these perspectives, and imagination has played virtually no role. The cost, I will argue, is pervasive mechanistic procedures and an impoverished curriculum. I will explore what might happen to some of these principles if we consider them while holding firmly to a sense of the educational importance of imagination.

I will look at some of these *ad hoc* principles, then, in the light of some kind of intellectual activity in which we can see imagination energetically at work. I will begin by considering how just a few features of young children's fantasy might influence or challenge these principles.

From the Concrete to the Abstract

I have suggested that there is an apparent conflict between the images of the child that emerge from the *ad hoc* principles on the one hand and from our common observations of children's imaginativeness on the other. Let us consider whether this conflict is not more than merely apparent. If we accept the principle that children's learning progresses from the concrete to the abstract, for example, how do we deal with fantasy stories?

In education this principle is used quite widely, to support both the claim that we should begin teaching with concrete *material* things and move from these toward abstract concepts, and also that in learning any subject we should work from particulars within the experience of the child in the direction of greater abstraction. One problem with applying this principle with regard to children's thinking is that all mental entities are abstract in some sense or other. But there are degrees of "abstractness," and "concrete" is perhaps the obvious term to use for those more particular, less general concepts.

If we take a story such as *Cinderella*, which seems to cause few comprehension problems for the average five-year-old, or those jolly narratives in which Mr. Worm and Mrs. Butterfly chat casually about the weather as they go about their various middle-class tasks of shopping or gardening, it is clear that such stories are structured on the relationship of various underlying concepts. In the case of *Cinderella*, we can immediately see conflicts of fear/hope, kindness/cruelty, and, of course good/bad. These are enormously general, abstract concepts. There is an obvious sense in which children must "have" these abstract concepts for the "concrete" story of Cinderella to make sense. That is, the abstraction is prior and prerequisite to being able to understand the concrete story.

An immediate objection to this conclusion is that the abstract concepts – fear/hope, good/bad – have been generated from earlier concrete experiences. We will return to this idea.

Another apparent counter-example to the *ad hoc* principle will be evident to anyone who has read a book like *The Lord of the Rings* to a child. The parts of the narrative that are most comprehensible and engaging are those whose meaning turns on the child's understanding of abstract concepts like loyalty/betrayal, courage/cowardice, honor/selfishness. Without such concepts most of the concrete action in the book is meaningless. Such concepts are not generated by the actions; the abstract concepts have to be already understood for the action to make sense. Those parts of the narrative that are least engaging and comprehensible are indeed concrete descriptions of landscape, weather, flora, and so on. Now obviously we can provide explanations of such observations; their point here is only that they seem to conflict with the principle that children's understanding proceeds from the concrete to the abstract.

It has been argued that we do not – cannot – infer grammar from the scattered examples of speech that we hear. Similarly, and perhaps more obviously, we do not infer plot forms from hearing a few particular concrete stories. Stories make sense as stories only if we already have some abstract notion of plot to organize and make meaningful the affective force of the story. Very young children, for example, know that the satisfaction of certain expectations, set up in the beginning, signals the end of the story. The abstract underlying plot-rhythm of expectation and satisfaction, then, precedes and is prerequisite to stories' being meaningful.

Here, then, are three examples that – superficially at least – seem to conflict with the *ad hoc* principle that we proceed from the concrete to the abstract. Nor are they trivial or arcane matters. Indeed, the centrality of these abstract organizing tools that young children deploy so readily making sense of all kinds of things may make us wonder whether the *ad hoc* principle has not got matters entirely the wrong way round, and that children's educational development should proceed from the abstract to the concrete.

Well, we would obviously be unwise to try to swing to the opposite extreme. The plausibility of the *ad hoc* principle depends on its being able to reflect something about how we learn various kinds of skills. We come to understand chess by learning the particular, concrete moves of each piece and then putting these together until we achieve an abstract understanding of the rules that govern the game. Also, in mastering a language – and this is perhaps the most persuasive support for the principle – more concrete terms seem to precede abstract terms. Children seem to use concrete terms more readily and easily and often have difficulty with abstract terms.

From such support the *ad hoc* principle may move to a counterattack against my observations from children's fantasy stories. It might be argued that our ability to understand *Cinderella* or *The Lord of the Rings* comes from prior concrete experience having generated the abstract concepts required for comprehension of the story. And even grasp of plot forms comes from prior concrete experiences, such as the rhythm of expectation and satisfaction that the baby knows in getting hungry and being fed.

Now it will perhaps be obvious that this argument can merrily chug along for some time. The problems with where it is chugging us to are, at least, twofold. First, it is moving us increasingly far from the way the *ad hoc* principle is understood and put into practice in education. In education it is used to support, for example, beginning mathematics teaching with blocks or fruit-pips, and with organizing the social studies curriculum so that families and neighborhoods precede history. Second, it is taking us into one of the most complex and contentious of philosophical questions, one that has been intensely debated from the time of the ancient Greeks.

I will not resolve these philosophical questions here, or anywhere. But I can think of no way of avoiding them. To challenge the *ad hoc* principle, then, requires that I at least indicate that its counterattack against my earlier examples is itself not immune from attack. The counterattack is that all abstractions that we see young children using are themselves the product of prior concrete experiences.

Before my counter-counterattack I should perhaps stress that as far as educational uses of the principle are concerned the earlier observations carry some weight. The principle has been used gradually to leach out of the curriculum and teaching practice a reliance on or use of abstract concepts. The irrefutable point made by the examples of children's fantasy is that even though young children might not articulate abstract terms and have difficulty with *certain kinds* of abstract concepts, it is not true that abstract concepts in general are difficult for young children. Indeed, we see children constantly use flexibly and easily the most abstract concepts, such as good/bad. So while the *ad hoc* principle is supported by certain learning processes in young children, it is not valid for all kinds of things that young children can do. It is, in its usual educational interpretation, appropriate only in some respects some of the time, and when taken as generally valid that is the beginning of serious imbalance and educational problems.

A medieval equivalent of Cole's Notes summed up Aristotle's view of knowledge as *nihil in intellectu quod non prius in sensu* (There is nothing in the mind that did not get there by passing through the senses). In this view, knowledge, however abstract, is achieved only from concrete particulars. In a more modern formulation we find it encapsulated in William James's plausible, indeed imaginative, picture of the baby experiencing a "blooming, buzzing confusion," out of which and from the particulars of which we gradually induce abstract concepts.

The conflicting, anti-empiricist view is that we arrive in the world with minds structured in particular ways and predisposed to recognize certain patterns and make sense of the world and experience in certain ways. The baby, in this view, experiences a structured world in which certain particulars gradually become distinct as they can be fitted to the mental structures that we are born with. Knowledge is thus not merely composed by experience, but the mind constructively makes its own contribution. In this view, all our knowledge and all our actions are governed by abstract rules, which we "have" and use even though we are not necessarily conscious of them.

The philosophical and psychological support for this view is considerable, and becoming dominant it seems fair to say. But my point here is not to amass the arguments in favor of it so much as to indicate that the counterattack made by the *ad hoc* principle is hardly itself unassailable.

I am not trying to establish the primacy of the abstract in children's learning (for such an argument see Hayek[3]) but only trying to counter the claim for the primacy of the concrete. What can most sensibly be concluded about human learning at present is that the phenomena are vastly more complex than any of our psychological models or the *ad hoc* principles educators derive from them. We can also sensibly question the *adequacy* of the *ad hoc* principle for the educational uses it is made to serve, and consequently question the educational adequacy of those practices and curricula based on the principle. Influenced by this principle, the experience of young children in elementary school classrooms is predominantly involved with the simple and concrete. There is an avoidance of abstraction because the *ad hoc* principle has persuaded teachers and curriculum developers that abstract concepts are beyond the comprehension of young children. At the simplest level we may say that there is a confusion between children's ability to articulate abstractions and their ability to use them. It may be that typical five-year-olds could not adequately define loyalty or courage, but they use such concepts clearly in making sense of all kinds of stories.

I think it is fair to conclude that seeing the process of education as a development from the concrete to the abstract is a result of focusing on certain limited intellectual activities. Nor is it an accident that such – what I will inadequately call – logical processes have formed the focus of research attention. Most of that research has been conducted in the empiricist tradition and not surprisingly shaped its questions and accepted its answers according to the presuppositions of empiricism. But if we make vivid imaginative intellectual activity the focus of our attention, the general adequacy of the *ad hoc* principle is brought into question. It is at best a partial truth, but also a partial falsehood. As such we would undoubtedly be better off abandoning it and looking for a more adequate *ad hoc* principle. Of course children have difficulty learning some things, but we should give up accepting as an adequate explanation of those difficulties that there is inherent in children's intellectual development a progression from the concrete to the abstract.

From the Known to the Unknown

What about the related *ad hoc* principle about moving from the known to the unknown? If this is true, how can we explain children's easy engagement with star-warriors, wicked witches, and talking middle-class worms? We are not here looking for a psychological or psychoanalytic explanation. We could line up the competing arguments about why such creatures are so prominent in young children's mental lives, but these explanations do not help us with the educational claim that children's learning progresses gradually "outward" from present, local experience to the unknown.

This *ad hoc* principle, again, is not some trivial or arcane matter in education; it is enormously influential. Along with the previous principle, it offers about the only organizing element to the curriculum jumble called social studies, and it is prominently invoked in designing lessons and units of study at all levels of schooling.

By considering the content of young children's fantasy stories and their own imaginative games we are surely forced to wonder about the general adequacy of a principle that claims that our knowledge of the world and experience accumulates gradually from the known to the unknown. Are wicked witches and talking middle-class worms so prominent a part of the known world of children? Well, in one sense of course we must say yes. Such figures are all around them in books and on television. But this only moves the problem to a different context. Why are such fantastic creatures so engaging to young children? It is not enough to conclude simply that such creatures are foisted on children by grown-ups. They fill the world's myth-stories and haunt our dreams. They represent something about the vivid imaginative creativity of the human mind.

If we view children's education in terms of the progressive mastery of practical tasks and logical sequences of discipline areas then we can reasonably invoke the known-to-unknown principle. It will guide us to begin with children's present experiences and move gradually outward along lines of content associations. This principle indeed does shape our curricula, and we are no doubt all familiar with charts that gradually plod outward in such logical sequences from what is assumed to be the contents of children's experience.

Whatever the organizing value of this principle, we surely recognize – without having to analyze children's fantasy – that it inadequately describes our own educational development. Consider how you learned whatever you consider most valuable. We pick up bits and pieces, suddenly see connections; these break or defract, and are recomposed in new ways with disparate pieces.

If we consider briefly children's fantasy stories, and recall the objections to the previous principle, we can surely recognize that we directly make sense of all kinds of new knowledge by fitting it to our abstract schemes. Frodo's journey to Mordor *makes sense* (even before we consider the story's affective power) because we can fit all the new elements and events to our abstract categories of good/bad, courage/cowardice, honor/greed, and so on. That is, we see in such simple cases that we can readily understand all kinds of new material by a principle that does not at all require us to move outward along lines of content associations, connecting new knowledge to that which the child already has. We can introduce any knowledge as long as we ensure that it fits the abstract conceptual structures the child has in place.[4]

History, for example, need not remain untouched in the primary school – its absence at present being justified on the grounds that children lack the abstract concepts that are necessary to make history meaningful: chronological time, causality, and so on. From observing how children make sense of fantasy stories, we can see that they do have available the conceptual tools that can make history meaningful. They may lack an abstract logical conception of causality, but they clearly have available the sense of causality that holds stories together and moves them along: The conceptual tools that can make sense of *Cinderella* and *The Lord of the Rings* can be used to make sense of the Athenians' struggle for freedom against the tyrannous Persian Empire, or the monks' struggle to preserve civilized learning against the ravages of the Vikings. Nor need such understanding of history be trivial. Young children have the conceptual tools to learn the most profound things about our past as a struggle for freedom against arbitrary violence, for security against fear, for knowledge against ignorance, and so on. *They do not learn those concepts; they already have them. They use those concepts to learn about the world and experience.*

Now we might want to engage in all kinds of arguments about the educational value of such history at the beginning of children's schooling. The only point I am making here is that the known-to-unknown principle is an inadequate guide to what children can learn.

If we consider a little further how we progressively apply our abstract organizing categories to making fuller sense of experience, we might even further reject the known-to-unknown principle. One common procedure we see at work in children's learning is the dialectical process of forming binary opposites and mediating between them. For example, in learning the temperature continuum, children tend first to learn the binary opposite concepts of "hot" and "cold." Next they mediate between these and learn the concept "warm." This is elaborated by then mediating between, say, "warm" and "cold," and the concept of "cool" or "fairly cold" is established. Some people claim this is a fundamental structure of all human learning (Lévi-Strauss[5] and neo-Hegelians of all kinds). We need accept this no more than we need accept the known-to-unknown principle. What we can commonly observe, however, are examples of this binary opposite formation and mediation at work. It is a model that conflicts with the *ad hoc* principle that determines so much educational practice.

Just in passing we might consider the pervasiveness of this binary opposites and mediation process. It seems to be one of the mind's commoner procedures for trying to make sense of the world and experience. It suggests interesting explanations for much of the fantastic content of children's thinking. If you look at the world through the eyes of a child, and you use the reliable dialectical process that is helping to make sense of much of what you see, then you will note what seems like an empirically sound binary distinction between nature and culture. If you are a child you will probably not put it in these terms, of course, but you will notice that however much you talk to the cat, it does not talk back, and however much you encourage them, the guinea pig and the gerbil will not make clothes for themselves nor tables and chairs for their cage. If you try to use the mediating process that has done you so well in being able to make sense of the talk about continua of temperature, and speed, size, and much else, you will search for categories that mediate between nature and culture. If you cannot find them, that mental process will create them. So you will generate things like talking middle-class worms. Such a creature is a mediation between nature and culture, as warm is a mediation between hot and cold. Similarly, you will observe a binary distinction between life and death. You will mediate and create ghosts, spirits, and all kinds of beings that are both alive and dead, as warm is hot and cold and middle-class worms are natural and cultural. My point here is only that this particular process of learning seems to be derived from the way the mind is programmed to learn, and proceeds even in the face of empirical reality, generating mediations that require imaginative creation. The logical plodding known-to-unknown principle does not account for this most powerful tool.[6]

Now it might be argued that the known-to-unknown principle *does* account for this and any other counter-examples. It might be claimed that in the case of the abstract categories that allow us to make sense of any new content organized on them the abstract categories are "the known" and we use them to make sense of the "unknown" content. And in the previous example, it may be claimed that the binary opposites are the known and we mediate from them to an unknown. Certainly this interpretation saves the principle. And the value of the principle may be reinterpreted as pointing up that we need to be sure that new content can be structured on "known" abstract categories, or that it be a mediation between known binary opposites. Its purpose remains to remind us that there needs to be some coherence in the sequencing of children's learning.

We *can* save the principle this way, but two points need to be made. First, it is saved by widening its interpretation to the point of making it a rather vacuous truism. Second, its interpretation so far has been used to support a curriculum and teaching practices based on expanding content associations. By focusing briefly on children's imaginative activities, we see that learning can expand a number of different ways, and that some of them seem much more pervasive and powerful than that captured in the known-to-unknown principle. The principle has been an instrument of highlighting one process of learning at the expense of others, especially at the expense of those associated with the use of imagination. Of course there are senses in which the *ad hoc* principle represents some truth, but it has falsified more than it has clarified. Its acceptance as generally true is to see the whole night sky filled with moon.

The remaining principles I mentioned at the beginning of this article – from the simple to the complex and from active manipulation to symbolic conceptualization – are clearly related to the two I have discussed. Given more space, those too could be discussed in detail, and we could also consider the history of these principles. They are all principles that have emerged from viewing the child as a prosaic thinker with not well developed capacities for dealing with certain logical and technical tasks. They have emerged from conceptions of education that stress the need to produce competent citizens who have the technical capabilities required by the dominant economic system.

They are principles that can survive only by ignoring the highly developed imaginative capacities of children and the immensely energetic forms of learning that they clearly use constantly and that can be seen more readily if we focus on imaginative activities. Teaching practices and curricula that are derived from research that views the child's imagination as largely irrelevant to learning are not calculated either to use or to develop the imaginative capacities of children.

My point is not that we should increase the fantasy content of school curricula. Others adequately make the case for the use of the arts in general as stimulants of these capacities. My point is that we need, for the educational benefit of children, to reconstruct our curricula and teaching methods in light of a richer image of the child as an imaginative as well as a logico-mathematical thinker. What we call imagination is also a tool of learning – in the early years perhaps the most energetic and powerful one. The influence of the *ad hoc* principles I have been discussing has been to produce a curriculum and teaching methods that, have excluded much of the richness of human experience that young children can have direct access to because it cannot be fitted to such an arid and impoverished image of the child. What cannot be made concretely manipulable and directly tied to some simple content within the child's immediate experience has been increasingly forced out of the early school curriculum. We are treating young children as fools. Our early childhood curricula and practices are largely filled with trivia – except where the imaginative work of individual teachers counters the influence of these principles. The most powerful and energetic intellectual tools children bring to school are largely ignored and excluded when research is conducted on children's learning, intelligence, development, and so on. The products of that research then seep into education and support the kinds of *ad hoc* principles considered above, and these have been powerfully if subtly influential in shaping curricula and in forming teachers' preconceptions about what and how children can best learn.

Perhaps ironically my conclusion from a focus on children's fantasy is that a more academically rich curriculum is appropriate in the early years. Children's imaginative capacities, let me stress, do not only find an outlet in fantasy stories; they find their real work and growth in being applied to history, mathematics, and the sciences as well.

An impoverished empiricist view of science has misused the authority of science to promote in education a narrow kind of logical thinking at the expense of those forms of thinking that we see most clearly in children's imaginative activities. The prevalence of this view has served to push imagination to the educational "sidelines" – to the "frills" of art, music, and so on, from which it can less easily be displaced. As this essentially nineteenth-century view of science finally recedes, and a more balanced view of science as a human activity becomes dominant, we in education might sensibly try to establish a more balanced view of children's thinking and learning. The *ad hoc* principles I have discussed are the remnants of the old unbalanced view. My purpose here has been to argue that imagination is a powerful and neglected tool of learning, and that we need to rethink our teaching practices and curricula with a more balanced appreciation of children's intellectual capacities. Prominent among those intellectual capacities is imagination. By ridding ourselves of the influential and restrictive *ad hoc* principles, we can see our way to enormously enriching the primary school curriculum. We can provide children with things to think about that challenge and stimulate the imaginative powers they have to think with.

Notes

1. Some might want to point out that Piaget has derived his theory from a study of play, dreams, and many other aspects of children's thinking that are centrally concerned with imagination. The subject matter of his research indeed included such material, but the aim is not to study fantasy or imagination so much as to uncover from children's responses the logico-mathematical forms that underlie them. The *sauvage*, free, imaginative content is typically given short shrift: "One would like to be able to rule out romancing with the same severity as [those answers designed to please the questioner]" (Jean Piaget, *Plays, Dreams, and Imitation in Childhood* [New York: Norton, 1951]). For a fuller criticism of Piaget's influence on education see Kieran Egan, *Education and Psychology: Plato, Piaget, and Scientific Psychology* (New York: Teachers College Press, 1983).
2. David Elkind, "Education for Educators," *Contemporary Psychology* 29, no. 8 (1984): 644.
3. F. A. Hayek, "The Primacy of the Abstract", in *Beyond Reductionism*, ed. Arthur Koestler and J. R. Smythies (New York: Macmillan, 1969).
4. This process seems common in adults as well, of course. If we hear that there has been a revolution in Africa or South America, in order to make sense of it we want to know whether the rebels were, say, backed by the CIA or had Cuban advisors. Such facts help us to make sense of the event by enabling us to fit it to abstract ideological categories we already have in place. The facts by themselves are largely meaningless; it is only by fitting them to such abstract categories that we make them meaningful.
5. C. Lévi-Strauss, *The Savage Mind* (Chicago: University of Chicago Press, 1966).
6. If this is indeed an adequate explanation of much of the fantasy content of children's stories, then we clearly can make hay with many psychoanalytic explanations, and we also have an additional argument against crude empiricism. This explanation fulfills the first requirement for an adequate theory: making plausible sense of the phenomena in question. How one might advance it against competing psychological or psychoanalytic explanations is less easy to see, and is, fortunately, not necessary here.

Imagination and Learning: A Reply to Kieran Egan

Maxine Greene

I welcome Professor Egan's drawing attention to the importance of the imagination, as I welcome his discussion of the narrow focus of education governed by what he calls the *"ad hoc* principles." Both are of particular importance at this time of educational prescription and reform. The word *imagination* does not appear in the major government and foundation reports or recommendations; the focus throughout tends to be on what Egan calls "the progressive mastery of practical tasks and logical sequences of discipline areas." We are in agreement that this is not an adequate account of educational development.

We are not, however, in total agreement on the nature of imagination, on the meaning of the concrete, or on the abstract categories or conceptual tools that (for Egan) account for children's comprehension of fantasy stories. I want to introduce some alternative views, in the hope that the argument can be enriched but not undermined. It is altogether necessary to sustain Egan's focal point: that existing "curriculum and teaching methods . . . have excluded much of the richness of human experience that young children can have direct access to." I wish to draw on different resources and take a rather different perspective.

It may well be that there has been little research concerned with imagination and that it has been "largely ignored" in educational psychology and philosophy. I do not believe we should overlook, however, the significant tradition of philosophical and literary writing on imagination, a tradition that remains to be tapped by educational thinkers and curriculum makers. I have Immanual Kant's *Critique of Judgement*[1] in mind, of course, as well as Samuel Taylor Coleridge's work and that of William Wordsworth.[2] For all the differences in emphasis, there is throughout a concern for imagination as the capacity to create new orders in experience, to open up new possibilities, and to disclose alternative realities.

All this is closely related to the image-making function, the ability to envisage the "nonactual," the "unreal." There is also, in John Dewey's work, for instance, a concern for imagination in its meaning-giving role. In *Art as Experience*, he wrote:

> For while the roots of every experience are found in the interaction of a live creature with its environment, that experience becomes conscious, a matter of perception, only when meanings enter it that are derived from prior experiences. Imagination is the only gateway through which these meanings can find their way into a present interaction; or rather . . . the conscious adjustment of the new and old *is* imagination. Interaction of a living being with an environment is found in vegetative and animal life. But the experience

enacted is human and conscious only as that which is given here and now is extended by meanings and values drawn from what is absent in fact and presented only imaginatively.[3]

Jean-Paul Sartre, similarly, saw imagination as giving intelligibility to the present moment. Somewhat like Dewey, he suggested that in any interpretation of what is perceived, there is a dimension of awareness of the past and of the future, of what is not or what is not yet.[4]

I would prefer to think of the "concrete" in terms of what is perceived, rather than what is sensed. Maurice Merleau-Ponty, for example, emphasizes "the primacy of perception," the experience of perception as "a nascent *logos*."[5] As he saw it, perceiving is a process of configuring, of patterning the lived world; it is a process mediated by the body that registers the presence of the objects and events around. It is an active process, and the field opened by perception is continually enlarged by imagination, which opens up the possible. Again, as in Dewey's viewing, the imagination effects connections between what is already known and understood and what is newly given. This is quite different from the mediation process Egan describes, even as it involves a movement from the known to the unknown, an opening outward to what is not yet.

Merleau-Ponty, considering the child's perceptive capacities as a mode of organizing experience, went on to say that we cannot "assimilate what is called the *image* in the child to a kind of degraded, weakened copy of preceding perceptions." Imagination provided still another way of ordering experience: "What is called imagination is an emotional conduct." It had to do with something occuring "*beneath* the relation of the knowing subject to the known object . . . a primordial operation by which the child organizes the imaginary, just as he organizes the perceived."[6] Clearly, this is an alternative to a conception of programming, of the "abstract categories" Egan turns to, to account for the child's making sense of Frodo's journey or *Cinderella*, or his or her ability to summon up unicorns.

He might, of course, say that this does not adequately explain the child's ability to grasp plot lines and so on. Louise Rosenblatt, talking about transactions with different texts, emphasized the "action of the reader in relating one episode or one element or one aspect of the events to the others decoded from the text." She went on: "A child may look at the separate squares of a comic strip, and see them as separate and distinct. Plot begins to emerge when he sees that the characters and situation of a second square can be related to the first, usually as later in time and as developing from the situation of the situation indicated in the first and so on, so that the comic strip becomes a narrative. This is a simpler version of a process carried on in the reading of a play or a novel."[7] As Rosenblatt sees it, it is a matter of the reader's *living* through a series of events, relating them, and organizing his or her emotional responses to them. For her, the reader "provides the experimental ligatures" between the events as they proceed; this, again, seems to be quite different from a "way the mind is programmed to learn."[8]

Of equal interest in this regard is Jerome Bruner's notion of what he calls the "narrative and paradigmatic modes of thought."[9] He believes that there are two modes of cognitive functioning, each of which provides a way of "ordering experience, of constructing reality." The paradigmatic mode is the logico-scientific one; the narrative mode is a temporal, story-telling mode, which constructs two landscapes simultaneously. "One is the landscape of action, where the constituents are the arguments of action: agent, intention or goal, situation, instrument. Its other landscape is the landscape of consciousness: what those involved in the action know, think, or feel."[10] Now it is clear enough that the paradigmatic mode makes truth claims possible; the narrative mode allows for verisimilitude or believability. Both modes, Bruner says, can be imaginatively applied: That is how we get good theory, logical proof, and so on, on one side, and how we get "good stories, gripping drama, believable historical accounts" on the other.[11] It seems to me to be at least possible that Egan's questions about children's capacities to deal with stories can be partially resolved by a recognition that storytelling and the understanding of stories involve an alternative mode of world-making or interpretation. They may not need to be reduced to conceptual schemes.

Of course it is the case that children's sense-making abilities are belittled in too many schools. To read some of the accounts presented by some of the phenomenologists of childhood[12] is to be reminded of this. To read of such teaching adventures as those reported by Gareth B. Matthews in *Philosophy and the Young Child*[13] of what good (philosophical) teaching can elicit does the same. (Matthews also believes that "Piaget's low regard for the thinking of young children is unwarranted."[14]) And who can disagree that a neglect of imagination is a neglect of a significant dimension of mind and mindfulness? My problem is that I scent a kind of reductionism in Egan's work, a neo-Kantian subsuming of imagination under schematization and conceptualization.

I find suggestive Mary Warnock's words at the end of her book, called *Imagination*, when she writes about educational policy. She believes, as Egan and I do, that the education of children should indeed be directed to their imagination. She believes this should not necessarily be done through an emphasis on self-expression, but by enabling them "to read and to look at the works of other people . . . grown-ups, or the works of nature." And then: "In so far as they begin to feel the significance of the forms they perceive, they will make their own attempts to interpret this significance. It is the emotional sense of the infinity or inexhaustibleness of things which will give point to their experience."[15]

She seems to believe, as I do, that imagination is what sees the meanings in the objects of which we become conscious in the course of our perceiving. Imagination may order, effect connections, and sometimes disorder or transform. And it may suggest "that there are vast unexplored areas, huge spaces of which we may get only an occasional aweinspiring glimpse, questions raised by experience about whose answers we can only with hesitation speculate."[16] That, to me, explains the power of imagination in learning: It draws toward the unexplored, toward the possible. It opens windows in the actual and the taken-for-granted toward what might be and is not yet.

Notes

1. Immanuel Kant, *Critique of Judgement* (Oxford: Oxford University Press, 1952).
2. See Harold Bloom, *A Reading of English Romantic Poetry* (Garden City: Doubleday Anchor Books, 1960), pp. 132–249.
3. John Dewey, *Art as Experience* (New York: Minton, Balch & Company, 1934), p. 272.
4. Jean-Paul Sartre, *The Psychology of Imagination* (New York: The Citadel Press, 1963), pp. 3–77.
5. Maurice Merleau-Ponty, *The Primacy of Perception* (Evanston, Ill.: Northwestern University Press, 1964), p. 25.
6. Ibid., p. 98.
7. Louise M. Rosenblatt, *The Reader, the Text, the Poem* (Carbondale: Southern Illinois University Press, 1978), p. 92.
8. Ibid.
9. Jerome Bruner, "Narrative and Paradigmatic Modes of Thought," in *Learning and Teaching: The Ways of Knowing*, Eighty-fourth Yearbook of the National Society for the Study of Education, ed. Elliot W. Eisner (Chicago: The University of Chicago Press, 1985), pp. 97–115.
10. Ibid., p. 99.
11. Ibid., p. 98.
12. See, e.g., Martinus J. Langeveld, "How Does the Child Experience the World of Things?" *Phenomenology and Pedagogy* 2, no. 3 (1984): 215–23; and Valerie Suransky, *The Erosion of Childhood* (Chicago: The University of Chicago Press, 1982).
13. Gareth B. Matthews, *Philosophy & the Young Child* (Cambridge: Harvard University Press, 1980).
14. Ibid., p. 48.
15. Mary Warnock, *Imagination* (Berkeley: University of California Press, 1978), p. 207.
16. Ibid., p. 208.

Imagination and Learning: A Response to Maxine Greene

Kieran Egan

Maxine Greene's comments seem to me to provide an important enriching dimension to my paper and to sound an important caveat. The enrichment is of course to the concept of imagination and the caveat, as I see it, concerns the suggestion of reductionism in my use of schemes such as a polarization/mediation, and simplistic distinctions between the concrete and the abstract, and inappropriate notions of conceptualization in imaginative activity. I suspect that the areas of our actual disagreement are rather less than she has inferred from what I see now as some unfortunate phrases and my choice of strategy for making the argument. Perhaps I may provide a whiff of exculpation to overwhelm the scent of reductionism.

She has provided a brief sketch of a series of important aspects of imagination, pointing out that we do have available, and should pay more heed to, rich resources on which to draw in thinking about the nature and roles of imagination in life and education. (In anyone else's account these resources would have included reference to her own work.) In composing the article I decided to take a minimal notion of imagination, in order to argue that commonplace observations about the most simple imaginative activities raise very serious problems for some of the principles that are at present enormously influential in teacher-education programs and in curriculum development. The article says hardly anything about imagination, but attempts rather naively to point to its commonest meaning and ask why we persist in accepting, and allowing our thinking and practice to be dominated by, principles that patently ignore "half" of the child's mind – and arguably the more energetic half.

The scent of reductionism is due, I think, less to my holding some constrained or mechanistic view of imagination and how it works, and more to my failure to qualify and elaborate some rather naively used terms and phrases. The insensitive use of "the way the mind is programmed to learn" is not intended to mean anything that is inconsistent with the kinds of mental activity characterized by Rosenblatt. Given our present degree of conceptual sophistication, imagination is largely ineffable. Most of our accounts are little more than elaborations of metaphors that seem more or less able to grasp at some aspect of it. My use of the notions of "abstract categories" or "polarization/mediation" are not products of reifying neo-Kantian categories so much as attempts to make my argument as clear as possible, without – I hoped – violating any reasonable conception of imagination. The schematizing evident in, say, polarizing/mediating has a somewhat different motive, which I will return to.

My discussion of polarizing/mediating in terms of underlying abstract categories was not intended as a general argument about how children generate imaginative forms, or organize imagery, or comprehend stories. Rather it was intended as an attempt to characterize a common process that exemplifies thinking that is not perception-dominated, in the sense taken from the classic Piagetian experiments. None of this seems to me necessarily inconsistent with Merleau-Ponty's or Mary Warnock's points, and I acknowledge that using a more sophisticated notion of perception might have allowed me to make the point more adequately. We are, it seems to me, talking about a somewhat different level of imaginative phenomena in somewhat different ways – but ways that seem to me not necessarily incompatible. Mine is certainly a more superficial way of dealing with children's imaginative activity, but I think it is adequate to the point I wanted to make. No doubt a fuller account would use more sophisticated concepts, but I think the point about the inadequacy of the common notion of children's thinking being perception dominated remains valid and has far-reaching implications. Similarly, Dewey's notion of imagination as forging connections between what is known and what is new seems to me to be addressing something rather different from my point about the inadequacy of the principle that children's learning moves from the known to the unknown. The limited point I make is not to be read as an attempt at a comprehensive explanation. "Mediation" indeed does not suggest the "opening outwards to what is not yet," and the two are clearly different, but I do not intend polarizing/mediating to be an exhaustive account of imaginative engagements with, or generation of, the new. Dewey's account is different in at least the respect of being much more comprehensive, and one might interpret polarization/mediation as just one of a number of processes that could be comprehended within his account.

The schematizing, evident in the polarizing/mediating discussion, is not so much a product of a mechanistic notion of imagination as an attempt to work toward techniques for planning teaching and designing curricula so that they may better evoke imaginative activity. There are many techniques, models, schemes for planning teaching and curricula derived from mechanistic learning theories. We lack such techniques derived from analysis of the imaginative "half" of the child. This is a little like letting the devil have all the best tunes. We can, for example, examine children's stories and games, and try to derive from them some principles that will help us to plan more meaningful and engaging lessons and units of study. If we do this sensitively we can provide the teacher and curriculum designer with models, schemes, techniques that will focus attention onto what is humanly important and what encourages imaginative activity, as well as ensure the progressive mastery of practical tasks and logical sequences of discipline areas.[1]

Imagination is obviously of crucial importance to education and, as Greene observes, we have wonderful but neglected sources that can educate us about its forms and importance. But what a strange pass we have come to in the training of professional educators when we are expected to be familiar with much material of most dubious value, and it is thought odd to recommend close familiarity with Wordsworth's *Prelude*.

Note

1. For some stumbles in this direction see Kieran Egan, *Educational Development* (New York: Oxford University Press, 1979); and idem, *Teaching as Story Telling* (London, Ontario: The Althouse Press, 1986).

78

In Search of a Critical Pedagogy

Maxine Greene

In what Jean Baudrillard describes as "the shadow of silent majorities"[1] in an administered and media-mystified world, we try to reconceive what a critical pedagogy relevant to this time and place ought to mean. This is a moment when great numbers of Americans find their expectations and hopes for their children being fed by talk of "educational reform." Yet the reform reports speak of those very children as "human resources" for the expansion of productivity, as means to the end of maintaining our nation's economic competitiveness and military primacy in the world. Of course we want to empower the young for meaningful work, we want to nurture the achievement of diverse literacies. But the world we inhabit is palpably deficient: there are unwarranted inequities, shattered communities, unfulfilled lives. We cannot help but hunger for traces of utopian visions, of critical or dialectical engagements with social and economic realities. And yet, when we reach out, we experience a kind of blankness. We sense people living under a weight, a nameless inertial mass. How are we to justify our concern for their awakening? Where are the sources of questioning, of restlessness? How are we to move the young to break with the given, the taken-for-granted – to move towards what might be, what is not yet?

Confronting all of this, I am moved to make some poets' voices audible at the start. Poets are exceptional, of course; they are not considered educators in the ordinary sense. But they remind us of absence, ambiguity, embodiments of existential possibility. More often than not they do so with passion; and passion has been called the power of possibility. This is because it is the source of our interests and our purposes. Passion signifies mood, emotion, desire: modes of grasping the appearances of things. It is one of the important ways of recognizing possibility, "the presence of the future as *that which is lacking* and that which, by its very absence, reveals reality."[2] Poets move us to give play to our imaginations, to enlarge the scope of lived experience and reach

Source: *Harvard Educational Review*, 56(4) (1986): 427–441.

beyond from our own grounds. Poets do not give us answers; they do not solve the problems of critical pedagogy. They can, however, if we will them to do so, awaken us to reflectiveness, to a recovery of lost landscapes and lost spontaneities. Against such a background, educators might now and then be moved to go in search of a critical pedagogy of significance for themselves.

Let us hear Walt Whitman, for one:

I am the poet of the Body and I am the poet of the Soul,
The pleasures of heaven are with me and the pains of hell are with me.
The first I graft and increase upon myself, the latter I translate into a
new tongue.
I am the poet of the woman the same as the man,
And I say it is as great to be a woman as to be a man,
. . . .
I chant the chant of dilation or pride.
We have had ducking and deprecating about enough,
I show that size is only development.
Have you outstript the rest? are you the President?,
It is a trifle, they will more than arrive there every one,
and still pass on.[3]

Whitman calls himself the poet of the "barbaric yawp"; he is also the poet of the child going forth, of the grass, of comradeship and communion and the "en masse." And of noticing, naming, caring, feeling. In a systematized, technicized moment, a moment of violations and of shrinking "minimal" selves, we ought to be able to drink from the fountain of his work.

There is Wallace Stevens, explorer of multiple perspectives and imagination, challenger of objectified, quantified realities – what he calls the "ABC of being . . . the vital, arrogant, fatal, dominant X," questioner as well of the conventional "lights and definitions" presented as "the plain sense of things." We ought to think of states of things, he says, phases of movements, polarities.

But in the centre of our lives, this time, this day, It is a state, this spring among the politicians Playing cards. In a village of the indigenes, One would still have to discover. Among the dogs and dung, One would continue to contend with one's ideas.[4]

One's ideas, yes, and blue guitars as well, and – always and always – "the never-resting mind," the "flawed words and stubborn sounds."

And there is Marianne Moore, reminding us that every poem represents what Robert Frost described as "the triumph of the spirit over the materialism by which we are being smothered," enunciating four precepts:

Feed imagination food that invigorates.
Whatever it is, do with all your might.
Never do to another what you would not wish done to yourself.
Say to yourself, "I will be responsible."

Put these principles to the test, and you will be inconvenienced by being overtrusted, overbefriended, overconsulted, half adopted, and have no leisure. Face that when you come to it.[5]

Another woman's voice arises: Muriel Rukeyser's, in the poem "Käthe Kollwitz."

What would happen if one woman told the truth about her life? The world would split open[6]

The idea of an officially defined "world" splitting open when a repressed truth is revealed holds all sorts of implications for those who see reality as opaque, bland and burnished, resistant both to protest and to change.

Last, and in a different mood, let us listen to these lines by Adrienne Rich:

A clear night in which two planets
seem to clasp each other in which the earthly grasses
shift like silk in starlight
If the mind were clear
and if the mind were simple you could take this mind this particular state
and say
This is how I would live if I could choose: this is what is possible[7]

The poem is called "What Is Possible," but the speaker knows well that no mind can be "simple," or "abstract and pure." She realizes that the mind has "a different mission in the universe," that there are sounds and configurations still needing to be deciphered; she knows that the mind must be "wrapped in battle" in what can only be a resistant world. She voices her sense of the contrast between the mind as contemplative and the mind in a dialectical relation with what surrounds.

They create spaces, these poets, between themselves and what envelops and surrounds. Where there are spaces like that, desire arises, along with hope and expectation. We may sense that something is lacking that must be surpassed or repaired. Often, therefore, poems address our freedom; they call on us to move beyond where we are, to break with submergence, to transform. To transform what – and how? To move beyond ourselves – and where? Reading such works within the contexts of schools and education, those of us still preoccupied with human freedom and human growth may well find our questions more perplexing. We may become more passionate about the possibility of a critical pedagogy in these uncritical times. How can we (decently, morally, intelligently) address ourselves both to desire and to purpose and obligation? How can we awaken others to possibility and the need for action in the name of possibility? How can we communicate the importance of opening spaces in the imagination where persons can reach beyond where they are?

Poets, of course, are not alone in the effort to make us see and to de-familiarize our commonsense worlds. The critical impulse is an ancient one in the Western tradition: we have only to recall the prisoners released from the cave in *The Republic*, Socrates trying to arouse the "sleeping ox" that was the Athenian public, Francis Bacon goading his readers to break with the "idols" that obscured their vision and distorted their rational capacities, David Hume calling for the exposure of the "sophistries and illusions" by which so many have habitually lived. In philosophy, in the arts, in the sciences, men and women repeatedly have come forward to urge their audiences to break with what William Blake called "mind-forg'd manacles." Not only did such manacles shackle consciousness; their effectiveness assured the continuing existence of systems of domination – monarchies, churches, land-holding arrangements, and armed forces of whatever kind.

The American tradition originated in such an insight and in the critical atmosphere specific to the European Enlightenment. It was an atmosphere created in large measure by rational, autonomous voices engaging in dialogue for the sake of bringing into being a public sphere. These were, most often, the voices of an emerging middle class concerned for their own independence from anachronistic and unjust restraints. Their "rights" were being trampled, they asserted, rights sanctioned by natural and moral laws. Among these rights were "life, liberty, and the pursuit of happiness," which (especially when joined to justice or equity) remain normative for this nation: they are goods *to be* secured. Liberty, at the time of the founding of our nation, meant liberation from interference by the state, church, or army in the lives of individuals. For some, sharing such beliefs as those articulated by the British philosopher John Stuart Mill, liberty also meant each person's right to think for himself or herself, "to follow his intellect to whatever conclusions it may lead" in an atmosphere that forbade "mental slavery."[8]

The founders were calling, through a distinctive critical challenge, for opportunities to give their energies free play. That meant the unhindered exercise of their particular talents: inventing, exploring, building, pursuing material and social success. To be able to do so, they had to secure power, which they confirmed through the establishment of a constitutional republic. For Hannah Arendt, this sort of power is kept in existence through an ongoing process of "binding and promising, combining and covenanting." As she saw it, power springs up between human beings when they act to con-stitute "a worldly structure to house, as it were, their combined power of action."[9] When we consider the numbers of people excluded from this process over the generations, we have to regard this view of power as normative as well. It is usual to affirm that power belongs to "the people" at large; but, knowing that this has not been the case, we are obligated to expand the "wordly structure" until it contains the "combined power" of increasing numbers of articulate persons. A critical pedagogy for Americans, it would seem, must take this into account.

For the school reformers of the early nineteenth century, the apparent mass power accompanying the expansion of manhood suffrage created a need for "self-control" and a "voluntary compliance" with the laws of righteousness.[10] Without a common school to promote such control and compliance, the social order might be threatened. Moreover, the other obligation of the school – to prepare the young to "create wealth" – could not be adequately met. Even while recognizing the importance of providing public education for the masses of children, we have to acknowledge that great numbers of them were being socialized into factory life and wage labor in an expanding capitalist society. Like working classes everywhere, they could not but find themselves alienated from their own productive energies. The persisting dream of opportunity, however, kept most of them from confronting their literal powerlessness. The consciousness of objectively real "open" spaces (whether on the frontier, "downtown," or out at sea) prevented them from thinking seriously about changing the order of things; theoretically, there was always an alternative, a "territory ahead."[11] It followed that few were likely to conceive of themselves in a dialectical relation with what surrounded them, no matter how exploitative or cruel. As the laggard and uneven development of trade unions indicates, few were given to viewing themselves as members of a "class" with a project to pull them forward, a role to play in history.

The appearance of utopian communities and socialist societies throughout the early nineteenth century did call repeatedly into question some of the assumptions of the American ideology, especially those having to do with individualism. The founders of the experimental colonies (Robert Owen, Frances Wright, Albert Brisbane, and others) spoke of communalism, mental freedom, the integration of physical and intellectual work, and the discovery of a common good. Socialists called for a more humane and rational social arrangement and for critical insight into what Orestes Brownson described as the "crisis as to the relation of wealth and labor." He said, "It is useless to shut our eyes to the fact and, like the ostrich, fancy ourselves secure because we have so concealed our heads that we see not the danger."[12] Important as their insights were, such people were addressing themselves to educated humanitarians whose good offices might be enlisted in improving and perfecting mankind. Critical though they were of exploitation, greed, and the division of labor, they did not speak of engaging the exploited ones in their own quests for emancipation. No particular pedagogy seemed required, and none was proposed, except within the specific contexts of utopian communities. Once a decent community or society was created, it was believed, the members would be educated in accord with its ideals.

There were, it is true, efforts to invent liberating ways of teaching for children in the larger society, although most were undertaken outside the confines of the common schools. Elizabeth Peabody and Bronson Alcott, among others, through "conversations" with actual persons in classrooms, toiled to inspire self-knowledge, creativity, and communion. Like Ralph Waldo Emerson, they were all hostile to the "joint-stock company" that society seemed to have become, a company "in which the members agree, for the better securing of his bread to each shareholder, to surrender the liberty and culture of the eater."[13] Like Emerson as well, they were all hostile to blind conformity, to the ethos of "Trade" that created false relations among human beings, to the chilling routines of institutional life. It is the case that they were largely apolitical; but their restiveness in the face of an imperfect society led them to find various modes of defiance. Those at Brook Farm tried to find a communal way of challenging the social order: Fuller found feminism; Emerson, ways of speaking intended to rouse his listeners to create their own meanings, to think for themselves.

The most potent exemplar of all this was Henry David Thoreau, deliberately addressing readers "in the first person," provoking them to use their intellects to "burrow" through the taken-for-granted, the conventional, the genteel. He wanted them to reject their own self-exploitation, to refuse what we would now call false consciousness and artificial needs. He connected the "wide-awakeness" to actual work in the world, to projects. He knew that people needed to be released from internal and external constraints if they were to shape and make and articulate, to leave their own thumbprints on the world. He understood about economic tyranny on the railroads and in the factories, and he knew that it could make political freedom meaningless. His writing and his abolitionism constituted his protests; both *Walden* and *On Civil Disobedience* function as pedagogies in the sense that they seemed aimed at raising the consciousness of those willing to pay heed. His concern, unquestionably, was with his "private state" rather than with a public space; but he helped create the alternative tradition in the United States at a moment of expansion and materialism. And there are strands of his thinking, even today, that can be woven into a critical pedagogy. Whether building his house, hoeing his beans, hunting woodchucks, or finding patterns in the ice melting on the wall, he was intent on *naming* his lived world.

There were more overtly rebellious figures among escaped slaves, abolitionists, and campaigners for women's rights; but the language of people like Frederick Douglass, Harriet Tubman, Sarah Grimke, Susan B. Anthony, and Elizabeth Cady Stanton was very much the language of those who carried on the original demand for independence. The power they sought, however, was not the power to expand and control. For them – slaves, oppressed women, freedmen and freedwomen – the idea of freedom as endowment solved little; they had to take action to *achieve* their freedom, which they saw as the power to act and to choose. Thomas Jefferson, years before, had provided the metaphor of *polis* for Americans, signifying a space where persons could come together to bring into being the "worldly structure" spoken of above. Great romantics like Emerson and Thoreau gave voice to the passion for autonomy and authenticity. Black leaders, including Douglass, W. E. B. Du Bois, the Reverend Martin Luther King, and Malcolm X, not only engaged dialectically with the resistant environment in their pursuit of freedom; they invented languages and pedagogies to enable people to overcome internalized oppression.

Struggling for their rights in widening public spheres, they struggled also against what the Reverend King called "nobodiness" as they marched and engaged in a civil disobedience grounded in experiences of the past. Du Bois was in many ways exemplary when he spoke of the "vocation" of twentieth-century youth. Attacking the industrial system "which creates poverty and the children of poverty . . . ignorance and disease and crime," he called for "young women and young men of devotion to lift again the banner of humanity and to walk toward a civilization which will be free and intelligent, which will be healthy and unafraid."[14] The words hold intimations of what Paulo Freire was to say years later when he, too, spoke of the "vocation" of oppressed people, one he identified with "humanization."[15] And the very notion of walking "toward a civilization" suggests the sense of future possibility without which a pedagogy must fail.

Public school teachers, subordinated as they were in the solidifying educational bureaucracies, seldom spoke the language of resistance or transcendence. It is well to remember, however, the courageous ones who dared to go south after the Civil War in the freedmen's schools. Not only did they suffer persecution in their efforts to invent their own "pedagogy of the oppressed" – or of the newly liberated; they often fought for their own human rights against male missionary administrators and even against the missionary concept itself.[16] It is well to remember, too, the transformation of the missionary impulse into settlement house and social work by women like Jane Addams and Lillian Wald. Committing themselves to support systems and adult education for newcomers to the country and for the neighborhood poor, they supported union organization with an explicitly political awareness of what they were about in a class-ridden society. They were able, more often than not, to avoid what Freire calls "malefic generosity" and develop the critical empathy needed for enabling the "other" to find his or her own way.

For all the preoccupations with control, for all the schooling "to order," as David Nasaw puts it,[17] there were always people hostile to regimentation and manipulation, critical of constraints of consciousness. Viewed from a contemporary perspective, for example, Colonel Francis Parker's work with teachers at the Cook County Normal School at the end of the nineteenth century placed a dramatic emphasis on freeing children from competitive environments and compulsions. He encouraged the arts and spontaneous activities; he encouraged shared work. He believed that, if democratized, the school could become "the one central means by which the great problem of human liberty is to be worked out."[18] Trying to help teachers understand the natural learning processes of the young, he was specifically concerned with resisting the corruptions and distortions of an increasingly corporate America. In the Emersonian tradition, he envisioned a sound community life emerging from the liberation and regeneration of individuals. And indeed, there were many libertarians and romantic progressives following him in the presumption that a society of truly free individuals would be a humane and sustaining one.

This confidence may account for the contradictions in the American critical heritage, especially as it informed education within and outside the schools. Structural changes, if mentioned at all, were expected to follow the emancipation of persons (or the appropriate molding of persons); and the schools, apparently depoliticized, were relied upon to effect the required reform and bring about a better world. If individual children were properly equipped for the work they had to do, it was believed, and trained to resist the excesses of competition, there would be no necessity for political action to transform economic relations. The street children, the tenement children, those afflicted and crippled by poverty and social neglect, were often thrust into invisibility because their very existence denied that claim.

John Dewey was aware of such young people, certainly in Chicago, where he saw them against his own memories of face-to-face community life in Burlington, Vermont. Convinced of the necessity for cooperation and community support if individual powers were to be released, he tried in some sense to recreate the Burlington of his youth in the "miniature community" he hoped to see in each classroom.[19] In those classrooms as well, there would be continuing and open communication, the kind of learning that would feed into practice, and inquiries arising out of questioning in the midst of life. Critical thinking modeled on the scientific method, active and probing intelligence: these, for Dewey, were the stuff of a pedagogy that would equip the young to resist fixities and stock responses, repressive and deceiving authorities. Unlike the libertarians and romantics, he directed attention to the "social medium" in which the individual growth occurred and to the mutuality of significant concerns.

Even as we question the small-town paradigm in Dewey's treatment of community, even as we wonder about his use of the scientific model for social inquiry, we still ought to be aware of Dewey's sensitivity to what would later be called the "hegemony," or the ideological control, implicit in the dominant point of view of a given society. He understood, for instance, the "religious aureole" protecting institutions like the Supreme Court, the Constitution, and private property. He was aware that the principles and assumptions that gave rise even to public school curricula were so taken for granted that they were considered wholly natural, fundamentally unquestionable. In *The Public and Its Problems*, he called what we think of as ideological control a "social pathology," which "works powerfully against effective inquiry into social institutions and conditions." He went on, "It manifests itself in a thousand ways: in querulousness, in impotent drifting, in uneasy snatching at distractions, in idealization of the long established, in a facile optimism assumed as a cloak, in riotous glorification of things 'as they are,' in intimidation of all dissenters – ways which depress and dissipate thought all the more effectually because they operate with subtle and unconscious pervasiveness."[20] A method of social inquiry had to be developed, he said, to reduce the "pathology" that led to denial and to acquiescence in the status quo. For all his commitment to scientific method, however, he stressed the "human function" of the physical sciences and the importance of seeing them in human terms. Inquiry, communication, "contemporary and quotidian" knowledge of consequence for shared social life: these fed into his conceptions of pedagogy.

His core concern for individual fulfillment was rooted in a recognition that fulfillment could only be attained in the midst of "associated" or inter-subjective life. Troubled as we must be fifty years later by the "eclipse of the public," he saw as one of the prime pedagogical tasks the education of an "articulate public." For him, the public sphere came into being when the consequences of certain private transactions created a common interest among people, one that demanded deliberate and cooperative action. Using somewhat different language, we might say that a public emerges when people come freely together in speech and action to take *care* of something that needs caring for, to repair some evident deficiency in their common world. We might think of homelessness as a consequence of the private dealings of landlords, an arms build-up as a consequence of corporate decisions, racial exclusion as a consequence of a private property-holder's choice. And then we might think of what it would mean to educate to the end of caring for something and taking action to repair. That would be *public* education informed by a critical pedagogy; and it would weave together a number of American themes.

Certain of these themes found a new articulation in the 1930s, during the publication of *The Social Frontier* at Teachers College. An educational journal, it was addressed "to the task of considering the broad role of education in advancing the welfare and interests of the great masses of the people who do the work of society – those who labor on farms and ships and in the mines, shops, and factories of the world."[21] Dewey was among the contributors; and, although it had little impact on New Deal policy or even on specific educational practices, the magazine did open out to a future when more and more "liberals" would take a critical view of monopoly capitalism and industrial culture with all their implications for a supposedly "common" school.

In some respect, this represented a resurgence of the Enlightenment faith. Rational insight and dialogue, linked to scientific intelligence, were expected to reduce inequities and exploitation. A reconceived educational effort would advance the welfare and interests of the masses. Ironically, it was mainly in the private schools that educational progressivism had an influence. Critical discussions took place there; attention was paid to the posing of worthwhile problems arising out of the tensions and uncertainties of everyday life; social intelligence was nurtured; social commitments affirmed. In the larger domains of public education, where school people were struggling to meet the challenges of mass education, the emphasis tended to be on "life-adjustment," preparation for future life and work, and "physical, mental, and emotional health."

There is irony in the fact that the progressive social vision, with its integrating of moral with epistemic concerns, its hopes for a social order transformed by the schools, was shattered by the Second World War. The terrible revelations at Auschwitz and Hiroshima demonstrated what could happen when the old dream of knowledge as power was finally fulfilled. Science was viewed as losing its innocence in its wedding to advanced technology. Bureaucracy, with all its impersonality and literal irresponsibility, brought with it almost unrecognizable political and social realities. It took time, as is well known, for anything resembling a progressive vision to reconstitute itself; there was almost no recognition of the role now being played by "instrumental rationality,"[22] or what it would come to signify. On the educational side, after the war, there were efforts to remake curriculum in the light of new inquiries into knowledge structures in the disciplinary fields. On the side of the general public, there were tax revolts and rejections of the critical and the controversial, even as the McCarthyite subversion was occurring in the larger world. Only a few years after the Sputnik panic, with the talent searches it occasioned, and the frantic encouragement of scientific training, the long-invisible poor of America suddenly took center stage. The Civil Rights Movement, taking form since the Supreme Court decision on integration in 1954, relit flames of critical pedagogy, as it set people marching to achieve their freedom and their human rights.

Viewed from the perspective of a critical tradition in this country, the 1960s appear to have brought all the latent tendencies to the surface. The Civil Rights Movement, alive with its particular traditions of liberation, provided the spark; the war in Vietnam gave a lurid illumination to the system's deficiencies: its incipient violence; its injustices; its racism; its indifference to public opinion and demand. The short-lived effort to reform education and provide compensation for damages done by poverty and discrimination could not halt the radical critique of America's schools. And that many-faceted critique – libertarian, Marxist, romantic, democratic – variously realized the critical potentialities of American pedagogies. Without an Emerson or a Thoreau or a Parker, there would not have been a Free School movement or a "deschooling" movement. Without a Du Bois, there would not have been liberation or storefront schools. Without a social reformist tradition, there would have been no Marxist voices asking (as, for instance, Samuel Bowles and Herbert Gintis did) for a "mass-based organization of working people powerfully articulating a clear alternative to corporate capitalism as the basis for a progressive educational system."[23] Without a Dewey, there would have been little concern for "participatory democracy," for "consensus," for the reconstitution of a public sphere.

Yes, the silence fell at the end of the following decade; privatization increased, along with consumerism and cynicism and the attrition of the public space. We became aware of living in what Europeans called an "administered society";[24] we became conscious of technicism and positivism and of the one-dimensionality Herbert Marcuse described.[25] Popular culture, most particularly as embodied in the media, was recognized (with the help of the critical theorist Theodor Adorno) as a major source of mystification.[26]

The schools were recognized as agents of "cultural reproduction," oriented to a differential distribution of knowledge.[27] Numerous restive educational thinkers, seeking new modes of articulating the impacts of ideological control and manipulation, turned towards European neo-Marxist scholarship for clues to a critical pedagogy. In an American tradition, they were concerned for the individual, for the subject, which late Marxism appeared to have ignored; and the humanist dimension of Frankfurt School philosophies held an unexpected appeal. Moreover, what with its concern for critical consciousness and communicative competence, Frankfurt School thinking held echoes of the Enlightenment faith; and, in some profound way, it was recognized.

There is, of course, an important sense in which the Frankfurt School has reappropriated philosophical traditions (Kantian, Hegelian, phenomenological, psychological, psychoanalytical) which are ours as well or which, at least, have fed our intellectual past. But it also seems necessary to hold in mind the fact that European memories are not our memories. The sources of European critical theory are to be found in responses to the destruction of the Workers' Councils after the First World War, the decline of the Weimar Republic, the rise of Stalinism, the spread of fascism, the Holocaust, the corruptions of social democracy. As climactic as any contemporary insight was the realization that reason (viewed as universal in an Enlightenment sense) could be used to justify the application of technical expertise in torture and extermination. Europeans saw a connection between this and the rationalization of society by means of bureaucracy, and in the separating off of moral considerations long viewed as intrinsic to civilized life. The intimations of all this could be seen in European literature for many years: in Dostoevsky's and Kafka's renderings of human beings as insects; in Musil's anticipations of the collapse of European orders; in Camus's pestilence, in Sartre's nausea, in the Dionysian and bestial shapes haunting the structures of the arts. We have had a tragic literature, a critical literature, in the United States. We need only recall Twain, Melville, Crane, Wharton, Hemingway, Fitzgerald. But it has been a literature rendered tragic by a consciousness of a dream betrayed, of a New World corrupted by exploitation and materialism and greed. In background memory, there are images of Jeffersonian agrarianism, of public spheres, of democratic and free-swinging communities. We do not find these in European literature, *nor* in the writings of the critical theorists.

One of the few explicit attempts to articulate aspects of the Western tradition for educators has been the courageous work of Freire, who stands astride both hemispheres. He has been the pioneer of a pedagogy informed by both Marxist and existential-phenomenological thought; his conception of critical reflectiveness has reawakened the themes of a tradition dating back to Plato and forward to the theologies of liberation that have taken hold in oppressed areas of the Western world. His background awareness, however, and that of the largely Catholic peasants with whom he has worked, are not that of most North Americans. It must be granted that his own culture and education transcend his Brazilian origins and make him something of a world citizen when it comes to the life of ideas. Like his European colleagues, however, he reaches back to predecessors other than Jefferson and Emerson and Thoreau and William James and Dewey; his social vision is not that of our particular democracy. This is not intended as criticism, but as a reminder that a critical pedagogy relevant to the United States today must go beyond – calling on different memories, repossessing another history.

We live, after all, in dark times, times with little historical memory of any kind. There are vast dislocations in industrial towns, erosions of trade unions; there is little sign of class consciousness today. Our great cities are burnished on the surfaces, building high technologies, displaying astonishing consumer goods. And on the side streets, in the crevices, in the burnt-out neighborhoods, there are the rootless, the dependent, the sick, the permanently unemployed. There is little sense of agency, even among the brightly successful; there is little capacity to look at things as if they could be otherwise.

Where education is concerned, the discourse widens, and the promises multiply. The official reform reports, ranging from *A Nation at Risk* to the Carnegie Forum's *A Nation Prepared*, call for a restructuring of schools and of teacher education to the end of raising the levels of literacy in accord with the requirements of an economy based on high technology.[28] The mass of students in the schools, including the one third who will be "minorities," are to be enabled to develop "higher order skills" in preparation for "the unexpected, the nonroutine world they will face in the future."[29] The implicit promise is that, if the quality of teachers is improved (and "excellent" teachers rewarded and recognized), the majority of young people will be equipped for meaningful participation in an advanced knowledge-based economy wholly different from the mass-production economy familiar in the past.

On the other hand, there are predictions that we will never enjoy full employment in this country, that few people stand any real chance of securing meaningful work. If the military juggernaut keeps rolling on, draining funds and support from social utilities, daycare centers, arts institutions, schools and universities, we will find ourselves devoid of all those things that might make life healthier, gentler, more inviting and more challenging. At once we are reminded (although not by the authors of the educational reports) of the dread of nuclear destruction (or of Chernobyls, or of Bhopal) that lies below the surface of apparent hope for the future. This dread, whether repressed or confronted, leads numbers of people to a sense of fatalism and futility with respect to interventions in the social world. For others, it leads to a sad and often narcissistic focus on the "now." For still others, it evokes denial and accompanying extravagances: consumerism increases; a desire for heightened sensation, for vicarious violence, grows. And for many millions, it makes peculiarly appealing the talk of salvation broadcast by evangelists and television preachers; it makes seductive the promise of Armageddon.

As young people find it increasingly difficult to project a long-range future, intergenerational continuity becomes problematic. So does the confidence in education as a way of keeping the culture alive, or of initiating newcomers into learning communities, or of providing the means for pursuing a satisfying life. Uncertain whether we can share or constitute a common world, except in its most fabricated and trivialized form, we wonder what the great conversation can now include and whether it is worth keeping alive. Michael Oakeshott spoke eloquently of that conversation, "begun in the primeval forests and extended and made more articulate in the course of centuries." He said it involves passages of argument and inquiry, going on in public and in private, that it is an "unrehearsed intellectual adventure. . . ." Education, for him, "is an initiation into the skill and partnership of this conversation," which gives character in the end "to every human activity and utterance."[30] We know now how many thousands of voices have been excluded from that conversation over the years. We know how, with its oppositions and hierarchies, it demeaned. As we listen to the prescriptions raining down for "common learnings" (which may or may not include the traditions of people of color, feminist criticism and literature, Eastern philosophies) and "cultural literacy," we cannot but wonder how those of us in education can renew and expand the conversation, reconstitute what we can call a common world.

Yes, there are insights into humane teaching in the latest reports; but, taking the wide view, we find mystification increasing, along with the speechlessness. We have learned about the diverse ways we Americans interpret our traditions: about those who identify with the old individualism, those who yearn for old communities, those who seek new modes of justice, those who want to lose themselves in a cause.[31] We know something about the persistence of a commitment to freedom, variously defined, and to the idea of equity. At once, we are bound to confront such extremes as a moral majority usurping talk of intimacy and family values, while neoliberals seek out technocratic, depersonalized solutions to quantified problems and speak a cost-benefit language beyond the reach of those still striving for public dialogue.

People have never, despite all that, had such vast amounts of information transmitted to them – not merely about murders and accidents and scandals, but about crucial matters on which public decisions may some day have to be made: nuclear energy, space vehicles, racism, homelessness, life-support systems, chemotherapies, joblessness, terrorism, abused children, fanatics, saints. There are whole domains of information that arouse frustration or pointless outrage. All we need to do is think of the persecution of the sanctuary-movement leaders, of children living in shelters, of the *contras* in Honduras, of adolescent suicides, of overcrowded jails. At the same time, no population has ever been so deliberately entertained, amused, and soothed into avoidance, denial, and neglect. We hear the cacophonous voices of special interest groups, we hear of discrete acts of sacrifice and martyrdom; we seldom hear of intentionally organized collaborative action to repair what is felt to be missing, or known to be wrong.

Complacency and malaise; upward mobility and despair. Sometimes we detect feelings of shame and helplessness perceived as personal failure. To be dependent, to be on welfare, is to be certified as in some manner deviant or irresponsible since good Americans are expected to fend for themselves. Even as oppressed peasants internalize their oppressors' images of them as helpless creatures, so unsuccessful Americans (young or old) internalize the system's description of them as ineffectual. They are unable to live up to the culture's mandate to control their own lives and contribute to the productivity of the whole. Our institutional responses are ordinarily technical (and we are drawn to technical solutions out of benevolence, as well as out of helplessnesss). Yet we know that to think mainly in terms of techniques or cures or remedies is often to render others and the earth itself as objects to be acted upon, treated, controlled, or used. It is to distance what we believe has to be done (efficiently, effectively) from our own existential projects, from our own becoming among other incomplete and questing human beings. It is to repress or deny the prereflective, tacit understandings that bind us together in a culture and connect us to our history.

Having said all this, I must ask again what a critical pedagogy might mean for those of us who teach the young at this peculiar and menacing time. Perhaps we might begin by releasing our imaginations and summoning up the traditions of freedom in which most of us were reared. We might try to make audible again the recurrent calls for justice and equality. We might reactivate the resistance to materialism and conformity. We might even try to inform with meaning the desire to educate "all the children" in a legitimately "common" school. Considering the technicism and the illusions of the time, we need to recognize that what we single out as most deficient and oppressive is in part a function of perspectives created by our past. It is a past in which our subjectivities are embedded, whether we are conscious of it or not. We have reached a point when that past must be reinterpreted and reincarnated in the light of what we have learned.

We understand that a mere removal of constraints or a mere relaxation of controls will not ensure the emergence of free and creative human beings. We understand that the freedom we cherish is not an endowment, that it must be achieved through dialectical engagements with the social and economic obstacles we find standing in our way, those we have to learn to name. We understand that a plurality of American voices must be attended to, that a plurality of life-stories must be heeded if a meaningful power is to spring up through a new "binding and promising, combining and covenanting." We understand that the Enlightenment heritage must be repossessed and reinterpreted, so that we can overcome the positivism that awaits on one side, the empty universalism on the other. But we cannot and ought not escape our own history and memories, not if we are to keep alive the awarenesses that ground our identities and connect us to the persons turning for fulfillment to our schools.

We cannot negate the fact of power. But we can undertake a resistance, a reaching out towards becoming *persons* among other persons, for all the talk of human resources, for all the orienting of education to the economy. To engage with our students as persons is to affirm our own incompleteness, our consciousness of spaces still to be explored, desires still to be tapped, possibilities still to be opened and pursued. At once, it is to rediscover the value of care, to reach back to experiences of caring and being cared for (as Nel Noddings writes) as sources of an ethical ideal. It is, Noddings says, an ideal to be nurtured through "dialogue, practice, and confirmation,"[32] processes much akin to those involved in opening a public sphere. We have to find out how to open such spheres, such spaces, where a better state of things can be imagined; because it is only through the projection of a better social order that we can perceive the gaps in what exists and try to transform and repair. I would like to think that this can happen in classrooms, in corridors, in schoolyards, in the streets around.

I would like to think of teachers moving the young into their own interpretations of their lives and their lived worlds, opening wider and wider perspectives as they do so. I would like to see teachers ardent in their efforts to make the range of symbol systems available to the young for the ordering of experience, even as they maintain regard for their vernaculars. I would like to see teachers tapping the spectrum of intelligences, encouraging multiple readings of written texts and readings of the world.

In "the shadow of silent majorities," then, as teachers learning along with those we try to provoke to learn, we may be able to inspire hitherto unheard voices. We may be able to empower people to rediscover their own memories and articulate them in the presence of others, whose space they can share. Such a project demands the capacity to unveil and disclose. It demands the exercise of imagination, enlivened by works of art, by situations of speaking and making. Perhaps we can at last devise reflective communities in the interstices of colleges and schools. Perhaps we can invent ways of freeing people to feel and express indignation, to break through the opaqueness, to refuse the silences. We need to teach in such a way as to arouse passion now and then; we need a new camaraderie, a new en masse. These are dark and shadowed times, and we need to live them, standing before one another, open to the world.

Notes

1. Baudrillard, *In the Shadow of Silent Majorities* (New York: Semiotexte, 1983).
2. Jean-Paul Sartre, *Search for a Method* (New York: Knopf, 1968), p. 94.
3. Whitman, *Leaves of Grass* (New York: Aventine Press, 1931), pp. 49–50.
4. Stevens, *Collected Poems* (New York: Knopf, 1963), p. 198.
5. Moore, *Tell Me, Tell Me* (New York: Viking Press, 1966), p. 24.
6. Rukeyser, "Käthe Kollwitz," in *By a Woman Writt*, ed. Joan Goulianos (New York: Bobbs Merrill, 1973), p. 374.
7. Rich, *A Wild Patience Has Taken Me This Far* (New York: Norton, 1981), p. 23.
8. Mill, "On Liberty," in *The Six Great Humanistic Essays* (New York: Washington Square Press, 1963), p. 158.
9. Arendt, *On Revolution* (New York: Viking Press, 1963), pp. 174–175.

10. Horace Mann, "Ninth Annual Report," in *The Republic and the School: Horace Mann on the Education of Free Men*, ed. Lawrence A. Cremin (New York: Teachers College Press, 1957), p. 57.
11. Mark Twain, *The Adventures of Huckleberry Finn* (New York: New American Library, 1959), p. 283.
12. Brownson, "The Laboring Classes," in *Ideology and Power in the Age of Jackson*, ed. Edwin C. Rozwenc (Garden City, NY: Anchor Books, 1964), p. 321.
13. Emerson, "Self-Reliance," in *Emerson on Education*, ed. Howard Mumford Jones (New York: Teachers College Press, 1966), p. 105.
14. Du Bois, *W. E. B. Du Bois: A Reader*, ed. Meyer Weinberg (New York: Harper Torchbooks, 1970), pp. 153–154.
15. Freire, *Pedagogy of the Oppressed* (New York: Continuum, 1970), pp. 27 ff.
16. Jacqueline Jones, "Women Who Were More Than Men: Sex and Status in Freedmen's Teaching," *History of Education Quarterly*, 19 (1979), 47–59.
17. Nasaw, *Schooled to Order* (New York: Oxford University Press, 1981).
18. Parker, *Talks on Pedagogics* (New York: Harper, 1894).
19. Dewey, "The School and Society," in *Dewey on Education*, ed. Martin Dworkin (New York: Teachers College Press, 1959), p. 41.
20. Dewey, *The Public and Its Problems* (Athens, OH: Swallow Press, 1954).
21. Lawrence A. Cremin, *The Transformation of the School* (New York: Knopf, 1961), pp. 231–232.
22. Jürgen Habermas, *Knowledge and Human Interests* (Boston: Beacon Press, 1972).
23. Bowles and Gintis, *Schooling in Capitalist America* (New York: Basic Books, 1976), p. 266.
24. Marcuse, "Some Social Implications of Modern Technology," in *The Essential Frankfurt School Reader*, ed. Andrew Arato and Eike Gebhardt (New York: Urizen Books, 1978), pp. 138–162.
25. Marcuse, *One-Dimensional Man* (Boston: Beacon Press, 1966).
26. Adorno, "Cultural Criticism and Society," in *Prisms* (London: Neville Spearman, 1961), pp. 31–32 ff.
27. See Pierre Boudieu and Jean-Claude Passeron, *Reproduction* (Beverly Hills: Sage, 1977).
28. The National Commission on Excellence in Education, *A Nation at Risk: The Imperative for Educational Reform* (Washington: U.S. Department of Education, 1983); and Carnegie Forum on Education and the Economy, *A Nation Prepared: Teachers for the 21st Century* (New York: Carnegie Forum, 1986).
29. Carnegie Forum, *A Nation Prepared*, p. 25.
30. Oakeshott, *Rationalism in Politics and Other Essays* (London: Methuen, 1962), pp. 198–199.
31. Robert N. Bellah, Richard Madsen, William M. Sullivan, Ann Swidler, and Steve M. Tipton, *Habits of the Heart: Individualism and Commitment in American Life* (Berkeley: University of California Press, 1985).
32. Noddings, *Caring: A Feminine Approach to Ethics and Moral Education* (Berkeley: University of California Press, 1984).

79

The Functions and Uses of Literacy

Shirley Brice Heath

Since the initiation of the public school system in the United States, national leaders have periodically issued statements of a ("literacy crisis") and have launched reform programs designed to eliminate illiteracy and to ensure that the schools produce functional literates. But the concept of literacy covers a multiplicity of meanings, and definitions of literacy carry implicit but generally unrecognized views of its functions (what literacy can do for individuals) and its uses (what individuals can do with literacy skills).

Current definitions of literacy held by policy-making groups are widely varied, and they differ markedly in the relationship they bear to the purposes and goals of reading and writing in the lives of individuals. Public schools (and the widespread minimum competency movement) see literacy as an individual accomplishment measured by psychometric scales of reading ability. A survey conducted for the National Reading Council defined literacy as "the ability to respond to practical tasks of daily life" (Harris & Associates, 1970). A compilation of surveys of employer attitudes toward the preparation of youth for work defined literacy as the integration of mathematical and linguistic skills necessary for filling out a job application, filing, conducting routine correspondence, monitoring inventories, and expressing oneself clearly in writing (Research for Better Schools, 1978). The Adult Performance Level Project defined the standard for literacy as the performance of people at given conjoint levels of low income, low job status, and few years of schooling (Northcutt, 1975). The National Census defines a literate individual as one who has completed six or more grades of school and has the "ability to read and write a simple message in any language." In the past decade, however, those studying literacy in societies throughout the world have challenged these definitions, primarily on the basis that the generally assumed functions and uses of literacy which underlie them do not

Source: Suzanne de Castell, Allan Luke and Kieran Egan (eds), *Literacy, Society and Schooling* (New York: Cambridge University Press, 1986), pp. 15–26.

correspond to the social meanings of reading and writing across either time periods, cultures, or contexts of use.

A number of historians (Davis, 1975; Eisenstein, 1979; and see Graff, this volume) have asked of social groups in certain places and times: What does it matter whether or not a person can read? What social consequences does literacy have for the group? What responses have societies made to the introduction of writing systems or print? Some unexpected patterns have emerged from the attempts to answer these questions. For example, knowledge of the possibility of written language (or the possibilities of print) does not in itself ensure that writing systems will be adopted. Furthermore, even in societies in which writing systems and/or print have been accepted, the uses of literacy have often been very much circumscribed, because only a small elite or particular craftsmen have had access to literacy. Finally, a restricted literate class can increase the range of functions of written language without increasing the size of the literate population.

In a study of the impact of printing on the unlettered masses of 17th-century France, Davis (1975) found a major paradox in the functions of literacy. Printing destroyed traditional monopolies on knowledge, and widely disseminated both information and works of imagination. But printing also made possible new kinds of control over the people. Until the appearance of the printing press, oral culture and popular, community-based social organizations seemed strong enough to resist standardization and thrusts for uniformity; but when the printing press appeared, people began to measure themselves against a widespread norm and to doubt their own worth. In today's American society, similar reasons are behind the desire of some American Indians who do not want their languages written (Walker, 1981), and of some religious groups, such as the Amish, who do not wish their children to move beyond certain levels of schooling.

The frequent assertion that literacy leads to improved economic status and participation in benevolent causes has been challenged by a number of studies. In 17th- and 18th-century New England, according to Lockridge (1974), distinction in occupational status was neither created nor reinforced by substantial differences in literacy. In addition, rising literacy in the general population erased former associations between wealth and literacy for individuals. Among the working classes of 19th-century England and Scotland, reading was learned in many situations outside formal education, and its purposes and consequences were varied (Webb, 1950, 1954). Economic laws of supply and demand with respect to job opportunities in 18th-century England dictated levels of literacy and secondary education that were set as ideals, but there was no direct relationship between skills achieved in secondary education and job success.

The equating of reading evaluation in the United States with an emphasis on oral reading style and correct responses to standardized performance seems to stem from late-19th-century teaching rationales (de Castell & Luke, this volume). Reading for comprehension and transferring the ability to the outside world were less readily assessed and were discounted in the general society. Soltow and Stevens (1977, 1981) point out the extent to which these standardized measures were lauded by parents of the late 19th century and suggest that such performance convinced parents that their children would be able to achieve occupational mobility. Whether or not the schools taught children to read at skill levels that made a difference in their chances for upward occupational mobility is not at all clear. Nevertheless, if students acquired the moral values, social norms, and general rational and cultural behaviors of literate citizens (even though their skills of comprehension were questionable), occupational mobility often resulted. These and other studies of the effects of printing and learning to read and write throw considerable doubt on time-honored beliefs regarding the consequences of literacy and formal schooling for individual social mobility.

Traditionally, the functions and uses of literacy have been examined at the level of the society. Kroeber (1948) traced the invention and diffusion of writing systems. Goody and Watt (1968) and Havelock (1963, 1976) suggested that the advent of alphabetic writing systems and the spread of literacy changed forms of social and individual memory of past events and useful information. Others (Goody, 1977; Olson, 1975, 1977) have proposed that societies also developed certain logical operations that led them to be able to classify and categorize the world about them in new ways.

However, studies of single societies (Goody, Cole, & Scribner, 1977; Scribner & Cole, 1981) or communities (Scollon & Scollon, 1979; Heath, 1983) have found that the functions of literacy suggested by Goody, Havelock, and others cannot be universally attributed, and that the methods of learning literacy skills, as well as their consequences, vary considerably across societies. For example, literacy may decline if it becomes nonfunctional in a society, or if the goals it has been thought to accomplish are not achieved. For example, in cargo cults, the millenarian movements that grew up in New Guinea and Melanesia at various times during the 20th century, members were initially anxious to have their young and old learn to read for the economic and religious benefits promised by missionaries. However, when the population recognized that they remained poor despite their sons' learning to read and write, they withdrew from literacy and maintained it only for select purposes in religious ceremonies (Meggitt, 1968).

Societies also differ with respect to the perceived benefits and functions of literacy. The Tuareg society in the Sahara has a centuries-old writing system, the *tifinagh*, which is adequate for representing their Berber language, and many members of the group are literate in the script. However, they use it only rarely – for graffiti on rocks in the desert, for certain kinds of talismans, and for brief love notes (Cohen, 1958). Among some American Indian groups who have developed and maintained a native literacy, it serves a variety of purposes: the practice of religion, the conduct of business, the recording of native medical practices, correspondence with relatives in distant places. In some cases, the proportion of literates within the group has actually decreased in the 20th century, although literacy is still highly valued even among those who do not read. Take the Cherokee as a good example. The Cherokee do not expect all members of their community to become literate; instead, certain individuals who play specific roles become literate, so that virtually every household has access to someone who can read and write (Walker, 1981). They do not insist that literacy be learned formally among the young; nor do they withhold literacy instruction from those who did not acquire literacy while they were young, or regard these people as failures. Those who become literate as adults do so by watching literates read and write and practicing by themselves for some time before trying it out before others. There is a long period of pre-learning, integrated into natural routines of home, church, and extended family, before one is expected to exercise the skill. Attempts to use formal educational methods at home may be viewed as coercive, and children do not learn from them. Later, however, as adults, they may remember and reactivate these early experiences.

Literacy without schooling was also studied by Scribner and Cole (1981) among the Vai of northwestern Liberia. Their work suggested that literacy is a culturally organized system of skills and values learned in specific settings. Moreover, generalizations about oral and literate modes of thought and their causative links to abilities in hypothetical reasoning, abstract thinking, or logical organization of ideas have not been borne out in cross-cultural studies of literacy. Literacy acquisition is often a function of society-specific tasks, which are sometimes far removed from those of formal schooling, and are not conceived of as resulting from effort expended by "teacher" and "learners." Indeed, the historically conditioned instructional strategies and social values and norms for literacy may not be related to those promoted today by some sectors of the population (see Coe; de Castell & Luke, this volume). Thus, much more must be known about the psychological and social consequences of both illiteracy and nonschooled literacy before pushing ahead with goals such as UNESCO's mission to eradicate illiteracy in the world before the year 2000 (San Francisco Chronicle, October 24, 1979).

Since reading varies in its functions and uses across history and cultures, it must also vary across contexts of use as defined by particular communities. For example, the highly publicized "Black English" court decision in the case of *Martin Luther King, Jr., Elementary School Children v. Ann Arbor School District Board* held that the school should provide appropriate models for students to follow in developing images of themselves as readers. The school's responsibility was seen as particularly important for those students whose parents and/or siblings did not read at home and did not view reading as having a positive effect on their lives. The expert witnesses and the court decision assumed here that children who were not successful readers by school standards were not exposed to types of reading and writing at home that could be transferred to their school experience (Labov, 1982). However, we know very little about the actual types, functions, or uses of literacy in the homes of these children, or in "constant television" homes, or, in general, in the homes of unskilled or semiskilled workers.

Numerous surveys have characterized the kinds of reading promoted in the homes of successful, academically oriented families and industrialized, urbanized populations (e.g., Hall & Carlton, 1977; Staiger, 1979; U.S. National Commission for UNESCO, 1978), but even these surveys provide only a limited picture of reading habits. In particular we expect surveys by questionnaire to tell us little about the actual reading and writing of lower-class or working-class families. Recently, ethnographers of education (Szwed, 1981; Spindler, 1982; Heath, 1983, 1984; Taylor, 1983) have suggested that participation in and observation of the lives of social groups can provide a more comprehensive picture of the uses of literacy and its component skills.

To find out who reads and writes, for what purposes, and in what circumstances, we observed reading and writing behavior in one community between 1969 and 1978 (Heath, 1983). We participated in the ongoing daily life of an all-black working-class community in the Southeastern United States and recorded the literacy behaviors of approximately 90 individuals in community, work, school, and home settings. Most households in the community had one or more members between the ages of 21 and 45 who worked at jobs providing salaries equal to or above those of beginning public school teachers in the area. Jobs were semiskilled, many residents being employed in the local textile mill, and many of the residents gardened, repaired homes, or worked on cars in their spare time.

Of particular importance in the study of reading and writing behaviors in the context of community life were questions related to how the adults participated in preschoolers' experience with print. Preschoolers were able to read many types of information available in their environment. Yet the adults did not read to the children, or consciously model or demonstrate reading and writing behaviors for them. Instead, the adults let the children find their own reading and writing tasks (defined, e.g., in terms of the trade names of bicycles or cars, house numbers and license plates, and the content of television messages), and they made their instructions fit the requirements of the tasks. Sometimes they helped with hard items, corrected errors of fact, and pointed out features of certain sounds (especially rhyming sounds). But in general, they kept their distance and let the children do what they could within their capabilities. Thus the children read to learn information they judged necessary in their lives. They watched others reading and writing for a variety of purposes, cooperated and participated in the process with older children and adults, and finally read, and often wrote, independently at very young ages.

Adults did not provide reading tasks unless children either wanted or needed to know something; nor did adults encourage older children to provide younger ones with graded tasks. While fulfilling responsibilities shared with older siblings, the children found reading tasks in their environment (reading the names of railroad lines on passing trains, reciting ads for taxi companies, noting changing prices of items in the store, etc.). On occasion, older siblings tried to provide school-like tasks for younger brothers and sisters, but these were rejected except when put in special frameworks, such as games. Thus the children did not necessarily require verbal reinforcement from parents or older siblings, and they needed neither teaching by overt demonstration nor talk about the reading process.

In effect, these children achieved some mastery of environmental print without being taught. They learned names of cereals or the meanings of railroad names, not because these were pointed out each time or because their letters were sounded out, but because of their juxtaposition with a spoken word or an action that carried meaning. The relevant context or set of circumstances of the material was often recalled by the children when the word later appeared in a different context. For these children, comprehension was the context rather than the outcome of learning to read. They acquired the skill without formal instruction or reading-readiness activities generally used by school-oriented parents with their preschoolers (cf. Harste, Woodward, & Burke, 1984).

These children's methods of dealing with print were different from those encouraged by parents whose reading goals for their children were oriented to school success (cf. Heath, 1982). Similarly, adults in this community used literacy in ways that differed from those of academically motivated parents. Among these adults, reading was social activity, involving more than the individual reader. Solitary reading, in fact, was often interpreted as an indication that one had not succeeded socially; thus, women who read "romance" magazines or men who read "girlie" magazines were charged with having to read to meet social needs they could not handle in real life. Written materials were often used in connection with oral explanation, narratives, and jokes about what the written materials meant or did not mean. The authority of the materials was established through social negotiation by the readers (see Heath, this volume).

From the uses of reading in the community, we could describe seven uses of literacy:

1. Instrumental. Literacy provided information about practical problems of daily life (price tags, checks, bills, advertisements, street signs, traffic signs, house numbers).
2. Social interactional. Literacy provided information pertinent to social relationships (greeting cards, cartoons, bumper stickers, posters, letters, recipes).
3. News related. Literacy provided information about third parties or distant events (newspaper items, political flyers, messages from local city offices about incidents of vandalism, etc.).
4. Memory-supportive. Literacy served as a memory aid (messages written on calendars and in address and telephone books; inoculation records).
5. Substitutes for oral messages. Literacy was used when direct oral communication was not possible or would prove embarrassing

(messages left by parent for child coming home after parent left for work, notes explaining tardiness to school).

6. Provision of permanent record. Literacy was used when legal records were necessary or required by other institutions (birth certificates, loan notes, tax forms).

7. Confirmation. Literacy provided support for attitudes or ideas already held, as in settling disagreements or for one's own reassurance (advertising brochures on cars, directions for putting items together, the Bible).

It is significant that these types do not include those uses – critical, aesthetic, organizational, and recreational (e.g., Staiger, 1979) – usually highlighted in school-oriented discussions of literacy uses.

Within each of these community uses, reading was highly contextualized. For example, a price tag on a roll of plastic tape might contain ten separate pieces of information, but community residents would scan the tag for the critical cue – the decimal point – and then read the price of the item. Similarly, only specific parts of soup cans, detergent boxes, brochures on automobiles, etc., were read, not because the individuals were incapable of reading the other information, but because it served no evident purpose for them to do so. They searched each item for only those messages they judged meaningful. For example, boys who modified their bicycles for sometimes unique effects selectively read portions of brochures on bicycles and instructions for using tool sets.

Reading of the local paper was selective and generally followed the sequence of obituaries first, followed by employment listings, ads for grocery and department store sales, captions beneath pictures, and headlines. Because the television was on most of the time in these households, family members tended to hear national news stories repeated frequently and to learn of news about the metropolitan center from which the local television shows originated. News from their small town, however, rarely was reported on these programs. Individuals therefore found it useful to read local news stories, but not national or metropolitan stories.

On the job, community members were not often called on to read. The employment officer wrote in the necessary information. Employees were "walked through" their new tasks with oral explanations. Bulletin boards contained general information about insurance, new regulations related to production, and occasionally news clippings from local newspapers – especially features about textile mill employees. However, most of the information on these boards was given to employees in oral as well as in written form, and employees thus did not find it necessary to read the bulletin board notices. Briefings were held with foremen and other senior employees when new production strategies were initiated; these employees, in turn, explained changes to employees on the line. Time charts and safety records were routinely filled out by employees without apparent difficulties.

The point of gathering this information on actual reading and writing practices is not to make judgments about how these uses of literacy compare with those of the school-oriented segments of society. It is to recognize that the extent to which physiologically normal individuals learn to read and write depends greatly on the role literacy plays in their families, communities, and jobs. Research from this study, as well as from historical and other social science studies, suggests that all normal individuals can learn to read and write, provided they have a setting or context in which there is a need to be literate, they are exposed to literacy, and they get some help from those who are already literate. This help, however, need not be formal instruction, nor must it necessarily follow what are frequently believed to be the basic tenets of reading instruction in school: graded tasks, isolated skill hierarchies, and a tight, linear order of instruction in sets and subsets of skills. Within this system of instruction, a student's success is measured by a sequenced move through a hierarchy of skills, and it is believed that acquiring these skills – that is, *learning to read*, is necessary before a student is *reading to learn*.

Typically, in order to help students improve their reading performance in school (that is, read school materials successfully and perform reading-related school tasks acceptably), standard reading programs are slowed down and broken into smaller and smaller fragments of skills, and high-interest, low-level reading materials are used along with numerous reading resources. When parents and community groups are asked to aid in this process, they are expected to continue and to reinforce the classroom practices, often being instructed in an explicit pedagogy. In many cases, the result of imposing this formal structure on parents is that the experience is fraught with feelings of inadequacy and frustration, and little measurable academic gain is realized by their children.

This process need not be the only way to teach reading. In a class of first-graders from the community reported here, a teacher built her reading program on the following philosophy, presented in various ways to her students throughout the year:

> Reading and writing are things you do all the time – at home, on the bus, riding your bike, at the barber shop. You can read, and you do every day before you ever come to school. You can also play baseball. Reading and writing are like baseball or football. You play baseball and football at home, at the park, wherever you want to, but when you come to school or go to a summer program at the Neighborhood Center, you get help on techniques, the gloves to buy, the way to throw, and the way to slide. School does that for reading and writing. We all read and write a lot of the time, lots of places. School isn't much different except that here we work on techniques, and we practice a lot – under a coach. I'm the coach.

This teacher's views of literacy, its uses and functions, were obviously very different from those implicit in the standardized tests which had judged these students to be lacking in reading-readiness skills and having little potential for success in the first grade. Throughout the year, traditional teaching methods (basal readers, phonics lessons, work sheets) emphasized *learning to read*, but equal stress was given to *reading to learn*. Store advertisements, price tags, movie titles, instructions for new toys and games, and classroom notices were used. The teacher's approach to reading enabled these students to define themselves as readers and writers by their community norms, and to grow with confidence into being readers by school criteria.

The challenge posed to a uniform definition of functional literacy, and to universal patterns of functions and uses, may alter not only methods and goals of reading instruction, but also assessments of the accountability of schools in meeting society's needs. For example, the dramatic societal and cultural shifts caused by the mechanization and automation of production have turned reading and writing into social events and instrumental actions for many segments of the population. The current state of literacy research suggests, therefore, expanding the definitions, measures, methods, and materials behind literacy teaching to incorporate not only school-based skills, uses, and functions of literacy, but also the counterparts and modifications of these in out-of-school contexts.

Furthermore, those literacy skills taught and reinforced in the college-bound or general track of public schools are often not valued by potential employers, an increasing number of whom do not see school-rewarded reading and writing skills as marketable. Instead, as indicated in a recent survey of employer attitudes toward potential employees, employers want an integration of mathematical and linguistic skills, displays of the capability of learning "on one's own," and listening and speaking skills required to understand and give instructions and describe problems (Research for Better Schools, 1978).

Both research findings and community/business needs, therefore, suggest several conclusions about literacy skills and needs. First, reading and writing need not be taught exclusively in the schools. In fact, a strict adherence to formal methods of teaching and evaluating literacy may limit potential opportunities for literacy learning and maintenance in homes and communities, by alienating parents and creating feelings of inadequacy about their own competencies. Second, literacy acquisition does not require a tight, linear order of instruction that breaks down small sets and subsets of skills into isolated, sequential hierarchies. Third, learners frequently possess and display in out-of-school contexts skills relevant to using literacy that are not effectively exploited in school learning environments. Finally, for a large percentage of the population, learning and sustaining reading and writing skills are not primarily motivated by a faith in their academic utility. For many families and communities, the major benefits of reading and writing may not include such traditionally assigned rewards as social mobility, job preparation, intellectual creativity, critical reasoning, and public information access. In short, literacy has different meanings for members of different groups, with a corresponding variety of acquisition modes, functions, and uses; these differences have yet to be taken into account by policy-makers.

Note

An earlier version of this paper appeared in the *Journal of Communication*, 30:1, 1980 (reprinted with permission).

References

Cohen, M. (1958). *La Grande Invention de l'escriture et Son Evolution*. Paris: Imprimerie Nationale.

Davis, N. (1975). *Society and Culture in Early Modern France*. Stanford, CA.: Stanford University Press.

Eisenstein, E. L. (1979). *The Printing Press as an Agent of Change* (2 vols.). Cambridge: Cambridge University Press:

Goody, J. (1977). *Domestication of the Savage Mind*. Cambridge: Cambridge University Press.

Goody, J., & Watt, I. (1968). The Consequences of Literacy. In J. Goody (Ed.). *Literacy in Traditional Societies*. Cambridge: Cambridge University Press.

Goody, J., Cole, M., & Scribner, S. (1977). Writing and Formal Operations: A Case Study among the Vai. *Africa*, 47, 289–304.

Hall, D., & Carlton, R. (1977). *Basic Skills at School and Work*. Toronto: Ontario Economic Council.

Harste, J. C., Woodward, V. A., & Burke, C. L. (1984). *Language Stories and Literacy Lessons*. Portsmouth, N.H.: Heinemann Educational Books.

Harris, Louis & Associates (1970). *Survival Literacy Study*. New York: Louis Harris & Associates.

Havelock, E. (1963). *Preface to Plato*. Cambridge, Ma.: Harvard University Press.

Havelock, E. (1976). *Origins of Western literacy*. Toronto: Ontario Institute for Studies in Education.

Heath, S. B. (1982). What no Bedtime Story Means: Narrative Skills at Home and School. *Language in Society*, 11, 49–76.

Heath, S. B. (1983). *Ways with Words: Language, Life, and Work in Communities and Classrooms*. Cambridge: Cambridge University Press.

Heath, S. B. (1984). Oral and Literate Traditions. *International Social Science Journal*, 99, 41–58.

Kroeber, A. (1948). *Anthropology*. New York: Harcourt, Brace.

Labov, W. (1982). Objectivity and Commitment in Linguistic Science: The Case of the Black English Trial in Ann Arbor. *Language in Society*, 11, 165–202.

Lockridge, K. (1974). *Literacy in Colonial New England*. New York: Norton.

Meggitt, M. (1968). Uses of Literacy in New Guinea and Melanesia. In J. Goody (Ed.). *Literacy in Traditional Societies*. Cambridge: Cambridge University Press.

Northcutt, N. (1975). *Adult Performance Level Project: Adult Functional Competency: A Report to the Office of Education Dissemination Review Panel*. Austin, Tex.: University of Texas, Division of Extension.

Olson, D. (1975). *Review of Toward a Literate Society*, ed. J. B. Carroll & J. S. Chall. In *Proceedings of the National Academy of Education*, 2, 109–178.

Olson, D. (1977). From Utterance to Text: The Bias of Language in Speech and Writing. *Harvard Educational Review*. 47, 257–281.

Research for Better Schools (1978). *Employer Attitudes toward the Preparation of Youth for Work*. Philadelphia, Pa.: Research for Better Schools.

Scollon, R., & Scollon, B. K. (1979). *Linguistic Convergence: An Ethnography of Speaking at Fort Chipewyan, Alberta*. New York: Academic Press.

Scribner, S., & Cole, M. (1981). *The Psychology of Literacy*. Cambridge, Ma.: Harvard University Press.

Soltow, L., & Stevens, E. (1977). Economic Aspects of School Participation in Mid-nineteenth Century United States. *Journal of Interdisciplinary History*, 8, 221–243.

Soltow, L., & Stevens, E. (1981). The Rise of Literacy and the Common School in the United States: A Socioeconomic Analysis to 1870. Chicago: University of Chicago Press.

Spindler, G. (1982) (Ed.) *Doing the Ethnography of Schooling: Educational Anthropology in Action*. New York: Holt, Rinehart & Winston.

Staiger, R. (1979). Motivation for Reading: An International Bibliography. In R. C. Staiger (Ed.), *Roads to Reading*. Paris: UNESCO.

Szwed, J. (1981). The Ethnography of Literacy. In M. F. Whiteman (Ed.), *Variations in Writing: Functional and Linguistic-Cultural Differences*. Baltimore, Ma.: Lawrence Erlbaum Associates.

Taylor, D. (1983). *Family Literacy: Young Children Learning to Read and Write*. Exeter, N.H.: Heinemann Educational Books.

United States National Commission for UNESCO (1978). *A Reason to Read: A Report on an International Symposium on the Promotion of the Reading Habit*. New York: UNESCO.

Walker, W. (1981). Native American Writing Systems. In C. A. Ferguson & S. B. Heath (Eds.), *Language in the USA*. Cambridge: Cambridge University Press.

Webb, R. K. (1950). Working Class Readers in Early Victorian England. *English Historical Review*, 65, 333–351.

Webb, R. K. (1954). Literacy among the Working Classes in Ninteenth-Century Scotland. *Scottish Historical Review*, 33, 110–114.

80

The Silenced Dialogue: Power and Pedagogy in Educating Other People's Children

Lisa Delpit

A black male graduate student who is also a special education teacher in a predominantly black community is talking about his experiences in predominantly white university classes:

> There comes a moment in every class where we have to discuss "The Black Issue" and what's appropriate education for black children. I tell you, I'm tired of arguing with those white people, because they won't listen. Well, I don't know if they really don't listen or if they just don't believe you. It seems like if you can't quote Vygotsky or something, then you don't have any validity to speak about your *own* kids. Anyway, I'm not bothering with it anymore, now I'm just in it for a grade.

A black woman teacher in a multicultural urban elementary school is talking about her experiences in discussions with her predominantly white fellow teachers about how they should organize reading instruction to best serve students of color:

> When you're talking to white people they still want it to be their way. You can try to talk to them and give them examples, but they're so headstrong, they think they know what's best for *everybody*, for *everybody's* children. They won't listen; white folks are going to do what they want to do *anyway*.
>
> It's really hard. They just don't listen well. No, they listen, but they don't *hear* – you know how your mama used to say you listen to the radio, but you *hear* your mother? Well they don't *hear* me.
>
> So I just try to shut them out so I can hold my temper. You can only beat your head against a brick wall for so long before you draw blood. If I try to stop arguing with them I can't help myself from getting angry. Then I end up

---

Source: *Harvard Educational Review*, 58(3) (1988): 280–298.

walking around praying all day "Please Lord, remove the bile I feel for these people so I can sleep tonight." It's funny, but it can become a cancer, a sore.

So, I shut them out. I go back to my own little cubby, my classroom, and I try to teach the way I know will work, no matter what those folk say. And when I get black kids, I just try to undo the damage they did.

I'm not going to let any man, woman, or child drive me crazy – white folks will try to do that to you if you let them. You just have to stop talking to them, that's what I do. I just keep smiling, but I won't talk to them.

A soft-spoken Native Alaskan woman in her forties is a student in the Education Department of the University of Alaska. One day she storms into a black professor's office and very uncharacteristically slams the door. She plops down in a chair and, still fuming, says, "Please tell those people, just don't help us anymore! I give up. I won't talk to them again!"

And finally, a black woman principal who is also a doctoral student at a well-known university on the West Coast is talking about her university experiences, particularly about when a professor lectures on issues concerning educating black children:

If you try to suggest that's not quite the way it is, they get defensive, then you get defensive, then they'll start reciting research.

I try to give them my experiences, to explain. They just look and nod. The more I try to explain, they just look and nod, just keep looking and nodding. They don't really hear me.

Then, when it's time for class to be over, the professor tells me to come to his office to talk more. So I go. He asks for more examples of what I'm talking about, and he looks and nods while I give them. Then he says that that's just *my* experience. It doesn't really apply to most black people.

It becomes futile because they think they know everything about every-body. What you have to say about your life, your children, doesn't mean anything. They don't really want to hear what you have to say. They wear blinders and earplugs. They only want to go on research they've read that other white people have written.

It just doesn't make any sense to keep talking to them.

Thus was the first half of the title of this text born: "The Silenced Dia-logue." One of the tragedies in this field of education is that scenarios such as these are enacted daily around the country. The saddest element is that the individuals that the black and Native Alaskan educators speak of in these statements are seldom aware that the dialogue *has* been silenced. Most likely the white educators believe that their colleagues of color did, in the end, agree with their logic. After all, they stopped disagreeing, didn't they?

I have collected these statements since completing a recently published article, a somewhat autobiographical account entitled "Skills and Other Dilemmas of a Progressive Black Educator," in which I discuss my perspective as a product of a skills-oriented approach to writing and as a teacher of process-oriented approaches.[1] I described the estrangement that I and many teachers of color feel from the progressive movement when writing process advocates dismiss us as too "skills oriented." I ended the article suggesting that it was incumbent upon writing process advocates, or indeed, advocates of any progressive movement, to enter into dialogue with teachers of color, who may not share their enthusiasm about so-called new, liberal, or progressive ideas.

In response to this article, which presented no research data and did not even cite a reference, I received numerous calls and letters from teachers, professors, and even state school personnel from around the country, both black and white. All of the white respondents, except one, have wished to talk more about the question of skills versus process approaches – to support or reject what they perceive to be my position. On the other hand, *all* of the nonwhite respondents have spoken passionately on being left out of the dialogue about how best to educate children of color.

How can such complete communication blocks exist when both parties truly believe they have the same aims? How can the bitterness and resentment expressed by the educators of color be drained so that the sores can heal? What can be done?

I believe the answer to these questions lies in ethnographic analysis, that is, in identifying and giving voice to alternative worldviews. Thus, I will attempt to address the concerns raised by white and black respondents to my article "Skills and Other Dilemmas." My charge here is not to determine the best instructional methodology; I believe that the actual practice of good teachers of all colors typically incorporates a range of pedagogical orientations. Rather, I suggest that the differing perspectives on the debate over "skills" versus "process" approaches can lead to an understanding of the alienation and miscommunication, and thereby to an understanding of the "silenced dialogue."

In thinking through these issues, I have found what I believe to be a connecting and complex theme: what I have come to call "the culture of power." There are five aspects of power I would like to propose as given for this presentation:

1. Issues of power are enacted in classrooms.
2. There are codes or rules for participating in power; rhat is, there is a "culture of power."
3. The rules of the culture of power are a reflection of the rules of the culture of chose who have power.
4. If you are not already a participant in the culture of power, being told explicitly the rules of that culture makes acquiring power easier.
5. Those with power are frequently least aware of – or least willing to acknowledge – its existence. Those with less power are often most aware of its existence.

The first three are by now basic tenets in the literature of the sociology of education, but the last two have seldom been addressed. The following discussion will explicate these aspects of power and their relevance to the schism between liberal educational movements and that of non-white, non-middle-class teachers and communities.[2]

1. **Issues of power are enacted in classrooms.** These issues include: the power of the teacher over the students; the power of the publishers of textbooks and of the developers of the curriculum to determine the view of the world presented; the power of the state in enforcing compulsory schooling; and the power of an individual or group to determine another's intelligence or "normalcy." Finally, if schooling prepares people for jobs, and the kind of job a person has determines her or his economic status and, therefore, power, then schooling is intimately related to that power.

2. **There are codes or rules for participating in power; that is, there is a "culture of power."** The codes or rules I'm speaking of relate to linguistic forms, communicative strategies, and presentation of self; that is, ways of talking, ways of writing, ways of dressing, and ways of interacting.

3. **The rules of the culture of power are a reflection of the rules of the culture of those who have power.** This means that success in institutions – schools, workplaces, and so on – is predicated upon acquisition of the culture of those who are in power. Children from middle-class homes tend to do better in school than those from non-middle-class homes because the culture of the school is based on the culture of the upper and middle classes – of those in power. The upper and middle classes send their children to school with all the accoutrements of the culture of power; children from other kinds of families operate within perfectly wonderful and viable cultures but not cultures that carry the codes or rules of power.

4. **If you are not already a participant in the culture of power, being told explicitly the rules of that culture makes acquiring power easier.** In my work within and between diverse cultures, I have come to conclude that members of any culture transmit information implicitly to co-members. However, when implicit codes are attempted across cultures, communication frequently breaks down. Each cultural group is left saying, "Why don't those people say what they mean?" as well as, "What's wrong wich them, why don't they understand?"

   Anyone who has had to enter new cultures, especially to accomplish a specific task, will know of what I speak. When I lived in several Papua New Guinea villages for extended periods to collect data, and when I go to Alaskan villages for work with Native Alaskan communities, I have found it unquestionably easier, psychologically and pragmatically, when some kind soul has directly informed me about such matters as appropriate dress, interactional styles, embedded meanings, and taboo words or actions. I contend that it is much the same for anyone seeking to learn the rules of the culture of power. Unless one has the leisure of a lifetime of "immersion" to learn them, explicit presentation makes learning immeasurably easier.

And now, to the fifth and last premise:

5. **Those with power are frequently least aware of – or least willing to acknowledge – its existence. Those with less power are often most aware of its existence.** For many who consider themselves members of liberal or radical camps, acknowledging personal power and admitting participation in the culture of power is distinctly uncomfortable. On the other hand, those who are less powerful in any situation are most likely to recognize the power variable most acutely. My guess is that the white colleagues and instructors of those previously quoted did not perceive themselves to have power over the nonwhite speakers. However, either by virtue of their position, their numbers, or their access to that particular code of power of calling upon research to validate one's position, the white educators had the authority to establish what was to be considered "truth" regardless of the opinions of the people of color, and the latter were well aware of that fact.

A related phenomenon is that liberals (and here I am using the term "liberal" to refer to those whose beliefs include striving for a society based upon maximum individual freedom and autonomy) seem to act under the assumption that to make any rules or expectations explicit is to act against liberal principles, to limit the freedom and autonomy of those subjected to the explicitness.

I thank Fred Erickson for a comment that led me to look again at a tape by John Gumperz on cultural dissonance in cross-cultural interactions.[3] One of the episodes showed an East Indian interviewing for a job with an all-white committee. The interview was a complete failure, even though several of the interviewers appeared to really want to help the applicant. As the interview rolled steadily downhill, these "helpers" became more and more indirect in their questioning, which exacerbated the problems the applicant had in performing appropriately. Operating from a different cultural perspective, he got fewer and fewer clear clues as to what was expected of him, which ultimately resulted in his failure to secure the position.

I contend that as the applicant showed less and less aptitude for handling the interview, the power differential became ever more evident to the interviewers. The "helpful" interviewers, unwilling to acknowledge themselves as having power over the applicant, became more and more uncomfortable. Their indirectness was an attempt to lessen the power differential and their discomfort by lessening the power-revealing explicitness of their questions and comments.

When acknowledging and expressing power, one tends towards explicitness (as in yelling at your ten-year-old, "Turn that radio down!"). When deemphasizing power, there is a move toward indirect communication. Therefore, in the interview setting, those who sought to help, to express their egalitarianism wirh the East Indian applicant, became more and more indirect – and less and less helpful – in their questions and comments.

In literacy instruction, explicitness might be equated with direct instruction. Perhaps the ultimate expression of explicitness and direct instruction in the primary classroom is Distar. This reading program is based on a behaviorist model in which reading is taught through the direct instruction of phonics generalizations and blending. The teacher's role is to maintain the full attention of the group by continuous questioning, eye contact, finger snaps, hand claps, and other gestures, and by eliciting choral responses and initiating some sort of award system.

When the program was introduced, it arrived with a flurry of research data that "proved" that all children – even those who were "culturally deprived" – could learn to read using this method. Soon there was a strong response, first from academics and later from many classroom teachers, stating that the program was terrible. What I find particularly interesting, however, is that the primary issue of the conflict over Distar has not been over its instructional efficacy – usually the students did learn to read – but the expression of explicit power in the classroom. The liberal educators opposed the methods – the direct instruction, the explicit control exhibited by the teacher. As a matter of fact, it was not unusual (even now) to hear of the program spoken of as "fascist."

I am not an advocate of Distar, but I will return to some of the issues that the program, and direct instruction in general, raises in understanding the differences between progressive white educators and educators of color.

To explore those differences, I would like to present several statements typical of those made with the best of intentions by middle-class liberal educators. To the surprise of the speakers, it is not unusual for such content to be met by vocal opposition or stony silence from people of color. My attempt here is to examine the underlying assumptions of both camps.

"I want the same thing for everyone else's children as I want for mine."

To provide schooling for everyone's children that reflects liberal, middle-class values and aspirations is to ensure the maintenance of the status quo, to ensure that power, the culture of power, remains in the hands of those who already have it. Some children corne to school with more accoutrements of the culture of power already in place – "cultural capital," as some critical theorists refer to it[4] – some with less. Many liberal educators hold that the primary goal for education is for children to become autonomous, to develop fully who they are in the classroom setting without having arbitrary, outside standards forced upon them. This is a very reasonable goal for people whose children are already participants in the culture of power and who have already internalized its codes.

But parents who don't function within that culture often want something else. It's not that They disagree with the former aim, it's just that they want something more. They want to ensure that the school provides their children with discourse patterns, interactional styles, and spoken and written language codes that will allow them success in the larger society.

It was the lack of attention to this concern that created such a negative outcry in the black community when well-intentioned white liberal educators introduced "dialect readers." These were seen as a plot to prevent the schools from teaching the linguistic aspects of the culture of power, thus dooming black children to a permanent outsider caste. As one parent demanded, "My kids know how to be black – you all teach them how to be successful in the white man's world."

Several black teachers have said to me recently that as much as they'd like to believe otherwise, they cannot help but conclude that many of the "progressive" educational strategies imposed by liberals upon black and poor children could only be based on a desire to ensure that the liberals' children get sole access to the dwindling pool of American jobs. Some have added that the liberal educators believe themselves to be operating with good intentions, but that these good intentions are only conscious delusions about their unconscious true motives. One of the black anthropologist John Gwaltney's informants in *Drylongso* reflects this perspective with her tongue-in-cheek observation that the biggest difference between black folks and white folks is that black folks *know* when they're lying!

Let me try to clarify how this might work in literacy instruction. A few years ago I worked on an analysis of two popular reading programs, Distar and a progressive program that focused on higher-level critical thinking skills. In one of the first lessons of the progressive program, the children are introduced to the names of the letters *m* and *e*. In the same lesson they are then taught the sound made by each of the letters, how to write each of the letters, and that when the two are blended together they produce the word *me*.

As an experienced first-grade teacher, I am convinced that a child needs to be familiar with a significant number of these concepts to be able to assimilate so much new knowledge in one sitting. By contrast, Distar presents the same information in about forty lessons.

I would not argue for the pace of Distar lessons – such a slow pace would only bore most kids – but what happened in the other lesson is that it merely provided an opportunity for those who already knew the content to exhibit that they knew it, or at most perhaps to build one new concept onto what was already known. This meant that the child who did not come to school already primed with what was to be presented would be labeled as needing "remedial" instruction from day one; indeed, this determination would be made before he or she was ever taught. In fact, Distar was "successful" because it actually *taught* new information to children who had not already acquired it at home. Although the more progressive system was ideal for some children, for others it was a disaster.

I do not advocate a simplistic "basic skills" approach for children outside of the culture of power. It would be (and has been) tragic to operate as if these children were incapable of critical and higher-order thinking and reasoning. Rather, I suggest that schools must provide these children the content that other families from a different cultural orientation provide at home. This does not mean separating children according to family background, but instead, ensuring that each classroom incorporate strategies appropriate for all the children in its confines.

And I do not advocate that it is the school's job to attempt to change the homes of poor and nonwhite children to match the homes of those in the culture of power. That may indeed be a form of cultural genocide. I have frequently heard schools call poor parents "uncaring" when parents respond to the school's urging, saying, "But that's the school's job." What the school personnel fail to understand is that if the parents were members of the culture of power and lived by its rules and codes, then they would transmit those codes to their children. In fact, they transmit another culture that children must learn at home in order to survive in their communities.

> *"Child-centered, whole language, and process approaches are needed in order to allow a democratic state of free, autonomous, empowered adults, and because research has shown that children learn best through these methods."*

People of color are, in general, skeptical of research as a determiner of our fates. Academic research has, after all, found us genetically inferior, culturally deprived, and verbally deficient. But beyond that general caveat, and despite my or others' personal preferences, there is little research data supporting the major tenets of process approaches over other forms of literacy instruction, and virtually no evidence that such approaches are more efficacious for children of color.[5]

Although the problem is not necessarily inherent in the method, in some instances adherents of process approaches to writing create situations in which students ultimately find themselves held accountable for knowing a set of rules about which no one has ever directly informed them. Teachers do students no service to suggest, even implicitly, that "product" is not important. In this country, students will be judged on their product regardless of the process they utilized to achieve it. And that product, based as it is on the specific codes of a particular culture, is more readily produced when the directives of how to produce it are made explicit.

If such explicitness is not provided to students, what it feels like to people who are old enough to judge is that there are secrets being kept, that time is being wasted, that the teacher is abdicating his or her duty to teach. A doctoral student of my acquaintance was assigned to a writing class to hone his writing skills. The student was placed in the section led by a white professor who utilized a process approach, consisting primarily of having the students write essays and then assemble into groups to edit each other's papers. Thar procedure infuriated this particular student. He had many angry encounters with the teacher about what she was doing. In his words:

I didn't feel she was teaching us anything. She wanted us to correct each other's papers and we were there to learn from her. She didn't teach anything, absolutely nothing.

Maybe they're trying to learn what black folks knew all the time. We understand how to improvise, how to express ourselves creatively. When I'm in a classroom, I'm not looking for that, I'm looking for structure, the more formal language.

Now my buddy was in [a] black teacher's class. And that lady was very good. She went through and explained and defined each part of the structure. This [white] teacher didn't get along with that black teacher. She said that she didn't agree with her methods. But *I* don't think that white teacher *had* any methods.

When I told this gentleman that what the teacher was doing was called a process method of teaching writing, his response was, "Well, at least now I know that she *thought* she was doing *something*. I thought she was just a fool who couldn't teach and didn't want to try."

This sense of being-cheated can be so strong that the student may be completely turned off to the educational system. Amanda Branscombe, an accomplished white teacher, recently wrote a letter discussing her work with working-class black and white students at a community college in Alabama. She had given these students my "Skills and Other Dilemmas" article to read and discuss, and wrote that her students really understood and identified with what I was saying. To quote her letter:

One young man said that he had dropped out of high school because he failed the exit exam. He noted that he had then passed the GED without a problem after three weeks of prep. He said that his high school English teacher claimed to use a process approach, but what she really did was hide behind fancy words to give herself permission to do nothing in the classroom.

The students I have spoken of seem to be saying that the teacher has denied them access to herself as the source of knowledge necessary to learn the forms they need to succeed. Again, I tentatively attribute the problem to teachers' resistance to exhibiting power in the classroom. Somehow, to exhibit one's personal power as expert source is viewed as disempowering one's students.

Two qualifiers are necessary, however. The teacher cannot be the only expert in the classroom. To deny students their own expert knowledge *is* to disempower them. Amanda Branscombe, when she was working with black high school students classified as "slow learners," had the students analyze rap songs to discover their underlying patterns. The students became the experts in explaining to the teacher the rules for creating a new rap song. The teacher then used the patterns the students identified as a base to begin an explanation of the structure of grammar, and then of Shakepeare's plays. Both student and teacher are expert at what they know best.

The second qualifier is that merely adopting direct instruction is not the answer. Actual writing for real audiences and real purposes is a vital element in helping students to understand that they have an important voice in their own learning processes. E. V. Siddle examines the results of various kinds of interventions in a primarily process-oriented writing class for black students.[6] Based on readers' blind assessments, she found that the intervention that produced the most positive changes in the students' writing was a "mini-lesson" consisting of direct instruction about some standard writing convention. But what produced the *second* highest number of positive changes was a subsequent student-centered conference with the teacher. (Peer conferencing in this group of black students who were not members of the culture of power produced the least number of changes in students' writing. However, the classroom teacher maintained – and I concur – that such activities are necessary to introduce the elements of "real audience" into the task, along with more teacher-directed strategies.)

> *"It's really a shame but she (that black teacher upstairs) seems to be so authoritarian, so focused on skills and so teacher directed. Those poor kids never seem to be allowed to really express their creativity. (And she even yells at them.)"*

This statement directly concerns the display of power and authority in the classroom. One way to understand the difference in perspective between black teachers and their progressive colleagues on this issue is to explore culturally influenced oral interactions.

In *Ways with Words*, Shirley Brice Heath quotes the verbal directives given by the middle-class "townspeople" teachers:[7]
  – "Is this where the scissors belong?"
  – "You want to do your best work today."
By contrast, many black teachers are more likely to say:
  – "Put those scissors on that shelf."
  – "Put your name on the papers and make sure to get the right answer for each question."
Is one oral style more authoritarian than another?

Other researchers have identified differences in middle-class and working-class speech to children. Snow and others, for example, report that working-class mothers use more directives to their children than do middle- and upper-class parents.[8] Middle-class parents are likely to give the directive to a child to take his bath as, "Isn't it time for your bath?" Even though the utterance is couched as a question, both child and adult understand it as a directive. The child may respond with "Aw, Mom, can't I wait until...," but whether or not negotiation is attempted, both conversants understand the intent of the utterance.

By contrast, a black mother, in whose house I was recently a guest, said to her eight-year-old son, "Boy, get your rusty behind in that bathtub." Now, I happen to know that this woman loves her son as much as any mother, but she would never have posed the directive to her son to take a bath in the form of a question. Were she to ask, "Would you like to take your bath now?"

she would not have been issuing a directive but offering a true alternative. Consequently, as Heath suggests, upon entering school the child from such a family may not understand the indirect statement of the teacher as a direct command. Both white and black working-class children in the communities Heath studied "had difficulty interpreting these indirect requests for adherence to an unstated set of rules."[9]

But those veiled commands are commands nonetheless, representing true power, and with true consequences for disobedience. If veiled commands are ignored, the child will be labeled a behavior problem and possibly officially classified as behavior disordered. In other words, the attempt by the teacher to reduce an exhibition of power by expressing herself in indirect terms may remove the very explicitness that the child needs to understand the rules of the new classroom culture.

A black elementary school principal in Fairbanks, Alaska, reported to me that she has a lot of difficulty with black children who are placed in some white teachers' classrooms. The teachers often send the children to the office for disobeying teacher directives. Their parents are frequently called in for conferences. The parents' response to the teacher is usually the same. "They do what I say; if you just *tell* them what to do, they'll do it. I tell them at home that they have to listen to what you say." And so, does not the power still exist? Its veiled nature only makes it more difficult for some children to respond appropriately, but that in no way mitigates its existence.

I don't mean to imply, however, that the only time the black child disobeys the teacher is when he or she misunderstands the request for certain behavior. There are other factors that may produce such behavior. Black children expect an authority figure to act with authority. When the teacher instead acts as a "chum," the message sent is that this adult has no authority, and the children react accordingly. One reason that is so, is that black people often view issues of power and authority differently than people from mainstream middle-class backgrounds.[10] Many people of color expect authority to be earned by personal efforts and exhibited by personal characteristics. In other words, "the authoritative person gets to be a teacher because she is authoritative." Some members of middle-class cultures, by contrast, expect one to achieve authority by the acquisition of an authoritative role. That is, "the teacher is the authority because she is the teacher."

In the first instance, because authority is earned, the teacher must consistently prove the characteristics that give her authority. These characteristics may vary across cultures, but in the black community they tend to cluster around several abilities. The authoritative teacher can control the class through exhibition of personal power; establishes meaningful interpersonal relationships that garner student respect; exhibits a strong belief that all students can learn; establishes a standard of achievement and "pushes" the students to achieve that standard; and holds the attention of the students by incorporating interactional features of black communicative style in his or her teaching.

By contrast, the teacher whose authority is vested in the role has many more options of behavior at her disposal. For instance, she does not need to express any sense of personal power because her authority does not come from anything she herself does or says. Hence, the power she actually holds may be veiled in such questions/commands as "Would you like to sit down now?" If the children in her class understand authority as she does, it is mutually agreed upon that they are to obey her no matter how indirect, soft-spoken, or unassuming she may be. Her indirectness and soft-spokenness may indeed be, as I suggested earlier, an attempt to reduce the implication of overt power in order to establish a more egalitarian and nonauthoritarian classroom atmosphere.

If the children operate under another notion of authority, however, then there is trouble. The black child may perceive the middle-class teacher as weak, ineffectual, and incapable of taking on the role of being the teacher; therefore, there is no need to follow her directives. In her dissertation, Michelle Foster quotes one young black man describing such a teacher:

> She is boring, boring. She could do something creative. Instead she just stands there. She can't control the class, doesn't know how to control the class. She asked me what she was doing wrong. I told her she just stands there like she's meditating. I told her she could be meditating for all I know. She says that we're supposed to know what to do. I told her I don't know nothin' unless she tells me. She just can't control the class. I hope we don't have her next semester.[11]

But of course the teacher may not view the problem as residing in herself but in the student, and the child may once again become the behavior-disordered black boy in special education.

What characteristics do black students attribute to the good teacher? Again, Foster's dissertation provides a quotation that supports my experience with black students. A young black man is discussing a former teacher with a group of friends:

> We had fun in her class, but she was mean. I can remember she used to say, "Tell me what's in the story, Wayne." She pushed, she used to get on me and push me to know. She made us learn. We had to get in the books. There was this tall guy and he tried to take her on, but she was in charge of that class and she didn't let anyone run her. I still have this book we used in her class. It has a bunch of stories in it. I just read one on Coca-Cola again the other day.[12]

To clarify, this student was *proud* of the teacher's "meanness," an attribute he seemed to describe as the ability to run the class and pushing and expecting students to learn. Now, does the liberal perspective of the negatively authoritarian black teacher really hold up? I suggest that although all "explicit" black teachers are not also good teachers, there are different attitudes in different cultural groups about which characteristics make for a good teacher. Thus, it is impossible to create a model for the good teacher without taking issues of culture and community context into account.

And now to the final comment I present for examination:

"Children have the right to their own language, their own culture. We must fight cultural hegemony and fight the system by insisting that children be allowed to express themselves in their own language style. It is not they, the children, who must change, but the schools. To push children to do anything else is repressive and reactionary."

A statement such as this originally inspired me to write the "Skills and Other Dilemmas" article. It was first written as a letter to a colleague in response to a situation that had developed in our department. I was teaching a senior-level teacher education course. Students were asked to prepare a written autobiographical document for the class that would also be shared with their placement school prior to their student teaching.

One student, a talented young Native American woman, submitted a paper in which the ideas were lost because of technical problems – from spelling to sentence structure to paragraph structure. Removing her name, I duplicated the paper for a discussion with some faculty members. I had hoped to initiate a discussion about what we could do to ensure that our students did not reach the senior level without getting assistance in technical writing skills when they needed them.

I was amazed at the response. Some faculty implied that the student should never have been allowed into the teacher education program. Others, some of the more progressive minded, suggested that I was attempting to function as gatekeeper by raising the issue, and had internalized repressive and disempowering forces of the power elite to suggest that something was wrong with a Native American student just because she had another style of writing. With few exceptions, I found myself alone in arguing against both camps.

No, this student should not have been denied entry to the program. To deny her entry under the notion of upholding standards is to blame the victim for the crime. We cannot justifiably enlist exclusionary standards when the reason this student lacked the skills demanded was poor teaching at best and institutionalized racism at worst.

However, to bring this student into the program and pass her through without attending to obvious deficits in the codes needed for her to function effectively as a teacher is equally criminal – for though we may assuage our own consciences for not participating in victim blaming, she will surely be accused and convicted as soon as she leaves the university. As Native Alaskans were quick to tell me, and as I understood through my own experience in the black community, not only would she not be hired as a teacher, but those who did not hire her would make the (false) assumption that the university was putting out only incompetent Natives and that they should stop looking seriously at any Native applicants. A white applicant who exhibits problems is an individual with problems. A person of color who exhibits problems immediately becomes a representative of her cultural group.

No, either stance is criminal. The answer is to *accept* students but also to take responsibility to *teach* them. I decided to talk to the student and found out she had recognized that she needed some assistance in the technical aspects of writing soon after she entered the university as a freshman. She had gone to various members of the education faculty and received the same two kinds of responses I met with four years later: faculty members told her either that she should not even attempt to be a teacher, or that it didn't matter and that she shouldn't worry about such trivial issues. In her desperation, she had found a helpful professor in the English Department, but he left the university when she was in her sophomore year.

We sat down together, worked out a plan for attending to specific areas of writing competence, and set up regular meetings. I stressed to her the need to use her own learning process as insight into how best to teach her future students those "skills" that her own schooling had failed to teach her. I gave her some explicit rules to follow in some areas; for others, we devised various kinds of journals that, along with readings about the structure of the language, allowed her to find her own insights into how the language worked. All that happened two years ago, and the young woman is now successfully teaching. What the experience led me to understand is that pretending that gatekeeping points don't exist is to ensure that many students will not pass through them.

Now you may have inferred that I believe that because there is a culture of power, everyone should learn the codes to participate in it, and that is how the world should be. Actually, nothing could be further from the truth. I believe in a diversity of style, and I believe the world will be diminished if cultural diversity is ever obliterated. Further, I believe strongly, as do my liberal colleagues, that each cultural group should have the right to maintain its own language style. When I speak, therefore, of the culture of power, I don't speak of how I wish things to be but of how they are.

I further believe that to act as if power does not exist is to ensure that the power status quo remains the same. To imply to children or adults (but of course the adults won't believe you anyway) that it doesn't matter how you talk or how you write is to ensure their ultimate failure. I prefer to be honest with my students. I tell them that their language and cultural style is unique and wonderful but that there is a political power game that is also being played, and if they want to be in on that game there are certain games that they too must play.

But don't think that I let the onus of change rest entirely with the students. I am also involved in political work both inside and outside of the educational system, and that political work demands that I place myself to influence as many gatekeeping points as possible. And it is there that I agitate for change, pushing gatekeepers to open their doors to a variety of styles and codes. What I'm saying, however, is that I do not believe that political change toward diversity can be effected from the bottom up, as do some of my colleagues. They seem to believe that if we accept and encourage diversity within classrooms of children, then diversity will automatically be accepted at gatekeeping points.

I believe that will never happen. What will happen is that the students who reach the gatekeeping points – like Amanda Branscombe's student who dropped out of high school because he failed his exit exam – will understand that they have been lied to and will react accordingly. No, I am certain that if we are truly to effect societal change, we cannot do so from the bottom up, but we must push and agitate from the top down. And in the meantime, we must take the responsibility to *teach*, to provide for students who do not already possess them, the additional codes of power.[13]

But I also do not believe that we should teach students to passively adopt an alternate code. They must be encouraged to understand the value of the code they already possess as well as to understand the power realities in this country. Otherwise they will be unable to work to change these realities. And how does one do that?

Martha Demientieff, a masterful Native Alaskan teacher of Athabaskan Indian students, tells me that her students, who live in a small, isolated, rural village of less than two hundred people, are not aware that there are different codes in English. She takes their writing and analyzes it for features of what has been referred to by Alaskan linguists as "Village English," and then covers half a bulletin board with words or phrases from the students' writing, which she labels "Our Heritage Language." On the other half of the bulletin board she puts the equivalent statements in "Standard English," which she labels "Formal English."

She and the students spend a long time on the "Heritage English" section, savoring the words, discussing the nuances. She tells the students, "That's the way we say things. Doesn't it feel good? Isn't it the absolute best way of getting that idea across?" Then she turns to the other side of the board. She tells the students that there are people, not like those in the village, who judge others by the way they talk or write.

> We listen to the way people talk, not to judge them, but to tell what part of the river they come from. These other people are not like that. They think everybody needs to talk like them. Unlike us, they have a hard time hearing what people say if they don't talk exactly like them. Their way of talking and writing is called "Formal English."
>
> We have to feel a little sorry for them because they have only one way to talk. We're going to learn two ways to say things. Isn't that better? One way will be our Heritage way. The other will be Formal English. Then, when we go to get jobs, we'll be able to talk like those people who only know and can only really listen to one way. Maybe after we get the jobs we can help them to learn how it feels to have another language, like ours, that feels so good. We'll talk like them when we have to, but we'll always know our way is best.

Martha then does all sorts of activities with the notions of Formal and Heritage or informal English. She tells the students,

In the village, everyone speaks informally most of the time unless there's a potlatch or something. You don't think about it, you don't worry about following any rules – it's sort of like how you eat food at a picnic – nobody pays attention to whether you use your fingers or a fork, and it feels *so* good. Now, Formal English is more like a formal dinner. There are rules to follow about where the knife and fork belong, about where people sit, about how you eat. That can be really nice, too, because it's nice to dress up sometimes.

The students then prepare a formal dinner in the class, for which they dress up and set a big table with fancy tablecloths, china, silverware. They speak only Formal English at this meal. Then they prepare a picnic where only informal English is allowed.

She also contrasts the "wordy" academic way of saying things with the metaphoric style of Athabaskan. The students discuss how book language always uses more words, but in Heritage language, the shorter way of saying something is always better. Students then write papers in the academic way, discussing with Martha and with each other whether they believe they've said enough to sound like a book. Finally, students further reduce the message to a "saying" brief enough to go on the front of a T-shirt, and the sayings are put on little paper T-shirts that the students cut out and hang throughout the room. Sometimes the students reduce other authors' wordy texts to their essential meanings as well.

The following transcript provides another example. It is from a conversation between a black teacher and a Southern black high school student named Joey, who is a speaker of Black English. The teacher believes it very important to discuss openly and honestly the issues of language diversity and power. She has begun the discussion by giving the student a children's book written in Black English to read.

> TEACHER: What do you think about that book?
> JOEY: I think it's nice.
> TEACHER: Why?
> JOEY: I don't know. It just told about a black family, that's all.
> TEACHER: Was it difficult to read?
> JOEY: No.
> TEACHER: Was the text different from what you have seen in other books?
> JOEY: Yeah. The writing was.
> TEACHER: How?
> JOEY: It use more of a southern-like accent in this book.
> TEACHER: Uhm-hmm. Do you think that's good or bad?
> JOEY: Well, uh, I don't think it's good for people down this-a-way, cause that's the way they grow up talking anyway.
> They ought to get the right way to talk.
> TEACHER: Oh. So you think it's wrong to talk like that?
> JOEY: Well...*(Laughs)*
> TEACHER: Hard question, huh?
> JOEY: Uhm-hmm, that's a hard question. But I think they shouldn't make books like that.

TEACHER: Why?

JOEY: Because they are not using the right way to talk and in school they take off for that, and li'l chirren grow up talking like that and reading like that so they might think that's right, and all the time they getting bad grades in school, talking like that and writing like that.

TEACHER: Do you think they should be getting bad grades for talking like that?

JOEY: *(Pauses, answers very slowly)* No...no.

TEACHER: So you don't think that it matters whether you talk one way or another?

JOEY: No, not long as you understood.

TEACHER: Uhm-hmm. Well, that's a hard question for me to answer, too. It's, ah, that's a question that's come up in a lot of schools now as to whether they should correct children who speak the way we speak all the time. Cause when we're talking to each other we talk like that even though we might not talk like than when we get into other situations, and who's to say whether it's –

JOEY: *(Interrupting)* Right or wrong.

TEACHER: Yeah.

JOEY: Maybe they ought to come up with another kind of...maybe Black English or something. A course in Black English. Maybe Black folks would be good in that cause people talk, I mean black people talk like that, so... but I guess there's a right way and wrong way to talk, you know, not regarding what race. I don't know.

TEACHER: But who decided what's right or wrong?

JOEY: Well that's true...I guess white people did.

(Laughter. End of tape.)

Notice how throughout the conversation Joey's consciousness has been raised by thinking about codes of language. This teacher further advocates having students interview various personnel officers in actual workplaces about their attitudes toward divergent styles in oral and written language. Students begin to understand how arbitrary language standards are, but also how politically charged they are. They compare various pieces written in different styles, discuss the impact of different styles on the message by making translations and back translations across styles, and discuss the history, apparent purpose, and contextual appropriateness of each of the technical writing rules presented by their teacher. *And* they practice writing different forms to different audiences based on rules appropriate for each audience. Such a program not only "teaches" standard linguistic forms, but also explores aspects of power as exhibited through linguistic forms.

Tony Burgess, in a study of secondary writing in England by Britton, Burgess, Martin, McLeod, and Rosen, suggests that we should not teach "iron conventions...imposed without rationale or grounding in communicative intent," but "critical and ultimately cultural awareness."[14] Courtney Cazden calls for a two-pronged approach:

1. Continuous opportunities for writers to participate in some authentic bit of the unending conversation...thereby becoming part of a vital community of talkers and writers in a particular domain, and
2. Periodic, temporary focus on conventions of form, taught as cultural conventions expected in a particular community.[15]

Just so that there is no confusion about what Cazden means by a focus on conventions of form, or about what I mean by "skills," let me stress that neither of us is speaking of page after page of "skill sheets" creating compound words or identifying nouns and adverbs, but rather about helping students gain a useful knowledge of the conventions of print while engaging in real and useful communicative activities. Kay Rowe Grubis, a junior high school teacher in a multicultural school, makes lists of certain technical rules for her eighth graders' review and then gives them papers from a third grade to "correct." The students not only have to correct other students' work, but also tell them why they have changed or questioned aspects of the writing.

A village teacher, Howard Cloud, teaches his high school students the conventions of formal letter writing and the formulation of careful questions in the context of issues surrounding the amendment of the Alaska Land Claims Settlement Act. Native Alaskan leaders hold differing views on this issue, critical to the future of local sovereignty and land rights. The students compose letters to leaders who reside in different areas of the state seeking their perspectives, set up audioconference calls for interview/debate sessions, and, finally, develop a videotape to present the differing views.

To summarize, I suggest that students must be *taught* the codes needed to participate fully in the mainstream of American life, not by being forced to attend to hollow, inane, de-contextualized subskills, but rather within the context of meaningful communicative endeavors; that they must be allowed the resource of the teacher's expert knowledge, while being helped to acknowledge their own "expertness" as well; and that even while students are assisted in learning the culture of power, they must also be helped to learn about the arbitrariness of those codes and about the power relationships they represent.

I am also suggesting that appropriate education for poor children and children of color can only be devised in consultation with adults who share their culture. Black parents, teachers of color, and members of poor communities must be allowed to participate fully in the discussion of what kind of instruction is in their children's best interest. Good liberal intentions are not enough. In an insighful 1975 study entitled "Racism without Racists: Institutional Racism in Urban Schools," Massey, Scott, and Dornbusch found that under the pressures of teaching, and with all intentions of "being nice," teachers had essentially stopped attempting to teach black children.[16] In their words: "We have shown that oppression can arise out of warmth, friendliness, and concern. Paternalism and a lack of challenging standards are creating a distorted system of evaluation in the schools." Educators must open themselves to, and allow themselves to be affected by, these alternative voices.

In conclusion, I am proposing a resolution for the skills/process debate. In short, the debate is fallacious; the dichotomy is false. The issue is really an illusion created initially not by teachers but by academics whose worldview demands the creation of categorical divisions – not for the purpose of better teaching, but for the goal of easier analysis. As I have been reminded by many teachers since the publication of my article, those who are most skillful at educating black and poor children do not allow themselves to be placed in "skills" or "process" boxes. They understand the need for both approaches, the need to help students establish their own voices, and to coach those voices to produce notes that will be heard clearly in the larger society.

The dilemma is not really in the debate over instructional methodology, but rather in communicating across cultures and in addressing the more fundamental issue of power, of whose voice gets to be heard in determining what is best for poor children and children of color. Will black teachers and parents continue to be silenced by the very forces that claim to "give voice" to our children? Such an outcome would be tragic, for both groups truly have something to say to one another. As a result of careful listening to alternative points of view, I have myself come to a viable synthesis of perspectives. But both sides do need to be able to listen, and I contend that it is those with the most power, those in the majority, who must take the greater responsibility for initiating the process.

To do so takes a very special kind of listening, listening that requires not only open eyes and ears, but open hearts and minds. We do not really see through our eyes or hear through our ears, but through our beliefs. To put our beliefs on hold is to cease to exist as ourselves for a moment – and that is not easy. It is painful as well, because it means turning yourself inside out, giving up your own sense of who you are, and being willing to see yourself in the unflattering light of another's angry gaze. It is not easy, but it is the only way to learn what it might feel like to be someone else and the only way to start the dialogue.

There are several guidelines. We must keep the perspective that people are experts on their own lives. There are certainly aspects of the outside world of which they may not be aware, but they can be the only authentic chroniclers of their own experience. We must not be too quick to deny their interpretations, or accuse them of "false consciousness." We must believe that people are rational beings, and therefore always act rationally. We may not understand their rationales, but that in no way militates against the existence of these rationales or reduces our responsibility to attempt to apprehend them. And finally, we must learn to be vulnerable enough to allow our world to turn upside down in order to allow the realities of others to edge themselves into our consciousness. In other words, we must become ethnographers in the true sense.

Teachers are in an ideal position to play this role, to attempt to get all of the issues on the table in order to initiate true dialogue. This can only be done, however, by seeking out those whose perspectives may differ most, by learning to give their words complete attention, by understanding one's own power, even if that power stems merely from being in the majority, by being unafraid to raise questions about discrimination and voicelessness with people of color, and to listen, no, to *hear* what they say. I suggest that the results of such interactions may be the most powerful and empowering coalescence yet seen in the educational realm – for *all* teachers and for *all* the students they teach.

81

Postmodernism and the Discourse of Educational Criticism

Henry A. Giroux

> Genealogical practice transforms history from a judgment on the past in the name of a present truth to a "counter-memory" that combats our current modes of truth and justice, helping us to understand and change the present by placing it in a new relation to the past. (Foucault, 1977, p. 160)

Educational theory and practice has always been strongly wedded to the language and assumptions of modernism. Educators as diverse as John Dewey (1916), Ralph Tyler (1950), Herb Gintis (Bowles & Gintis, 1976), John Goodlad (1984), and Martin Carnoy (Carnoy & Levin, 1985) have shared a faith in those modernist ideals which stress the capacity of individuals to think critically, to exercise social responsibility, and to remake the world in the interest of the Enlightenment dream of reason and freedom. Central to this view of education and modernity has been an abiding faith in the ability of individuals to situate themselves as self-motivating subjects within the wider discourse of public life. For many educators, modernism is synonymous with "the continual progress of the sciences and of techniques, the rational division of industrial work, and the intensification of human labor and of human domination over nature" (Baudrillard, 1987, pp. 65–66). A faith in rationality, science, and technology buttresses the modernist belief in permanent change, and in the continual and progressive unfolding of history. Similarly, education provides the socializing processes and legitimating codes by which the grand narrative of progress and human development can be passed onto future generations.

The moral, political, and social technologies that structure and drive the imperatives of public schooling are drawn from the modernist view of the *individual* student and educator as the guarantor of the delicate balance between private and public life, as the safeguard who can guarantee that the economy and the democratic state will function in a mutually determining manner. Within the discourse of modernism, knowledge draws its boundaries

---

Source: *Journal of Education*, 170(3) (1988): 5–30.

almost exclusively from a European model of culture and civilization. Civilization in this script is an extension of what Jean-Francois Lyotard (1984) calls the "great story" of the Enlightenment. In addition, modernism has been largely drawn from cultural scripts written by white males whose work is often privileged as a model of high culture informed by an elite sensibility that sets it off from what is often dismissed as popular or mass culture. While it is not the purpose of this essay to write either the story of modernism[1] or its specific expressions in the history of educational theory and practice, it is important to note that modernism in both its progressive and reactionary forms has provided the central categories that have given rise to various versions of educational theory and practice. To question the most basic principles of modernity is tantamount, not only to redefining the meaning of schooling, but also to calling into question the very basis of our history, our cultural criticism, and our manifestations and expressions of public life. In effect, to challenge modernism is to redraw and remap the very nature of our social, political, and cultural geography. It is for this reason alone that the challenge currently being posed by various postmodernist discourses needs to be taken up and examined critically by educators.

In this paper, I want to argue that the challenge of postmodernism is important for educators because it raises crucial questions regarding certain hegemonic aspects of modernism and by implication how these have affected the meaning and dynamics of present-day schooling. Postmodern criticism is also important because it offers the promise of deterritorializing and redrawing the political, social, and cultural boundaries of modernism while simultaneously affirming a politics of racial, gender, and ethnic difference. Moreover, postmodern criticism does not merely challenge dominant Western cultural models with their attendant notion of universally valid knowledge; it also resituates us within a world that bears little resemblance to the one that inspired the grand narratives of Marx and Freud. In effect, postmodern criticism calls attention to the shifting boundaries related to the increasing influence of the electronic mass media and information technology, the changing nature of class and social formations in post-industrialized capitalist societies, and the growing transgression of boundaries between life and art, high and popular culture, and image and reality.

I will argue in this essay that postmodern criticism offers a combination of reactionary and progressive possibilities and that its various discourses have to be examined with great care if we are to benefit politically and pedagogically from its assumptions and analyses. I will also argue that the basis for a critical pedagogy is not to be developed around a choice between modernism and postmodernism. As Ernesto Laclau (1988) aptly states, "postmodernism cannot be a simple rejection of modernity; rather, it involves a different modulation of its themes and categories" (p. 65).[2] Moreover, both dicourses as forms of cultural criticism are flawed; they need to be examined for the ways in which each cancels out the worst dimensions of the other. They each contain elements of strength, and educators have an opportunity to fashion a critical pedagogy that draws on the best insights of each. Most importantly, I will argue that those ideals of the project of modernity which link memory, agency, and reason to the construction of a democratic public sphere need to be defended as part of a discourse of critical pedagogy within (rather than in opposition to) the existing conditions of a postmodern world. At issue here is the task of delineating the broader cultural complexities that inform what I shall call a postmodern sensibility and criticism. Such a delineation needs to take place within the boundaries of a pedagogy and politics that reclaims and reinvigorates, rather than denies or is indifferent to, the possibilities of a radical democracy.

The argument that is developed in this paper unfolds as follows: First, I will provide some theoretical groundwork for developing a broad map of what constitutes both the meaning of postmodernism and what can be called the postmodern condition. Briefly put, the postmodern condition refers to the various discursive and structural transformations that characterize what can be called a postmodern culture in the era of late capitalism. Second, I will articulate some of the central and most critical themes that have emerged from the various discourses on postmodern theory. In this section I will examine the conservative and radical implications of these positions. Third, I will argue that in order to develop a more adequate theory of schooling as a form of cultural politics it is important that contemporary educators integrate the central theoretical features of a postmodernism of resistance with the more radical elements of modernist discourse.

The Meaning of Postmodernism

Though postmodernism has influenced a wide variety of fields – including music, fiction, film, drama, architecture, criticism, anthropology, sociology, and the visual arts – there is no agreed-upon meaning for the term.[3] In keeping with the multiplicity of difference that it celebrates, postmodernism is not only subject to different ideological appropriations, it is also marked by a wide variety of interpretations. This can be illustrated by briefly looking at the different views of postmodernism articulated by two of its leading theorists, Jean-Francois Lyotard (1984) and Fredric Jameson (1984, 1988).

Lyotard has described postmodernism as a rejection of grand narratives, metaphysical philosophies, and any other form of totalizing thought. In Lyotard's view, the meaning of postmodernism is inextricably related to the changing conditions of knowledge and technology which are producing forms of social organization that are undermining the old habits, bonds, and social practices of modernity. For Lyotard, the postmodern is defined through the diffusion throughout Western societies of computers, scientific knowledge, advanced technology, and electronic texts, each of which accents and privileges diversity, locality, specificity, and the contingent against the totalitizing narratives of the previous age. According to Lyotard, technical, scientific, and artistic innovations are creating a world where individuals must make their own way without the benefit of fixed referents or traditional philosophical moorings. Total mastery and liberation are dismissed as the discourses of terror and forced consensus. In its place postmodernism appears as an ideological and political marker for referencing a world without stability, a world where knowledge is constantly changing and where meaning can no longer be anchored in a ideological view of history.

Fredric Jameson's (1984, 1988) writings on postmodernism challenge the nihilism implicit in many theories of postmodernism. Jameson defines postmodernism as the "cultural logic" which represents not only the third great stage of late capitalism, but also the new cultural dominant of the times in Western societies. For Jameson (1984), postmodernism is an epochal shift that alerts us to the present remapping of social space and the creation of new social formations. If postmodernism represents new forms of fragmentation, the creation of new constellations of forms, and the emergence of new technological and artistic developments in capitalist society, Jameson does not respond either by calling for the death of grand narratives or by celebrating the electronic spectacles that substitute images for reality. Instead, he argues for new cognitive maps, different forms of representation that provide a systematic reading of the new age.

Douglas Kellner (1988) is right in arguing that Jameson's view of postmodernism is quite different from that of Lyotard and a number of other prominent theorists of the postmodern. Kellner writes:

> In any case, one sees how, against Lyotard, Jameson employs the form of a grand narrative, of a totalizing theory of society and history that makes specific claims about features of postmodernism – which interprets as "the cultural logic of capital" rather than as a code word for a new (post)historical condition – as do Lyotard and Baudrillard (however much they reject totalizing thought). Obviously, Jameson wishes to preserve Marxism as the Master Narrative and to relativize all competing theories as sectorial or regional theories to be subsumed in their proper place within the Marxian Master Narrative, (p. 262)

Postmodernism's refusal of grand narratives, its rejection of universal reason as a foundation for human affairs, its decentering of the humanist subject, its radical problematization of representation, and its celebration of plurality and the politics of racial, gender, and ethnic difference have sparked a major debate among conservatives, liberals, and radicals in an increasingly diverse number of fields. For example, conservative cultural critics such as Alan Bloom (1987) argue that postmodernism represents "the last, predictable stage in the suppression of reason and the denial of the possibility of truth" (p. 379). In a similar fashion, conservatives such as Daniel Bell (1976) claim that postmodernism extends the adversarial and hedonistic tendencies of modernism to destructive extremes. For a host of other conservatives, postmodernism as it is expressed in the arts, music, film, and fiction is pejoratively dismissed as "a reflection of . . . the present wave of (destructive) political reaction sweeping the Western world" (Gott, 1986, p. 10).

Liberals such as Jurgen Habermas and Richard Rorty take opposing positions on the relevance of postmodernism. Habermas (1983) sees it as a threat to the foundations of democratic public life, while Rorty (1985) appropriates its central assumptions as part of the defense of liberal capitalist society. Among left-wing radicals, postmodernism runs a theoretical gamut that ranges from adulation, to condemnation, to a cautious skepticism. Radical critics such as Terry Eagleton (1985), Perry Anderson (1984), and Barbara Christian (1987) see postmodernism as either a threat to or a flight from the real world of politics and struggle. Hal Foster (1983), Andreas Huyssen (1986), Stuart Hall (1986), and a number of feminist critics such as Teresa De Lauretis (1987) and Meghan Morris (1988) approach the discourse of postmodernism cautiously by interrogating critically its claims and absences. Radical avant-garde theorists such as Jean Baudrillard (1988) and Jean-Francois Lyotard (1984) utilize postmodern discourses as a theoretical weapon to articulate either the nihilism of capitalist society and its alleged collapse of meaning or the tyranny implicit in the totalizing narratives characteristic of modernity.

While it would be easy to dismiss postmodernism as simply a code word for a new theoretical fashion, the term is important because it directs our attention to a number of changes and challenges that are a part of the contemporary age. For some social theorists, postmodernism may be on the verge of becoming an empty signifier, while others credit it with a theoretical and heuristic relevance deriving from its capacity to provide a focus for a number of historically significant debates. As Dick Hebdige (1986) points out, there can be little doubt that the term postmodern appears to "have occupied a semantic ground in which something precious and important was felt to be embedded" (p. 79). The discourse of postmodernism is worth struggling over, and not merely as a semantic category that needs to be subjected to ever more precise definitional rigor. Rather, it is important to mine its contradictory and oppositional insights for possible use in the service of a radical cultural politics and a critical theory of pedagogy.

As a referent for understanding its political and cultural insights, I want to argue that postmodernism in the broadest sense refers both to an intellectual position (a form of cultural criticism) and to an emerging set of social, cultural, and economic conditions that have come to characterize the age of global capitalism and industrialism. In the first instance, postmodernism represents a form of cultural criticism that presents a radical questioning of the logic of foundations that has become the epistemological cornerstone of modernism. In the second instance, postmodernism refers to an increasingly radical change in the relations of production, the nature of the nation state, the development of new technologies that have redefined the fields of telecommunications and information processing, and the forces at work in the growing globalization and interdependence of the economic, political, and cultural spheres. All of these issues will be taken up below in more specific detail.

Mapping the Postmodern Condition

Before enumerating what I think are the basic assumptions that the various discourses of postmodernism have in common, I want to briefly elaborate on some of the conditions that have come to characterize what can be called a postmodern age. I don't believe that postmodernism represents a drastic break or rupture from modernity as much as it signals a shift toward a set of social conditions that are reconstituting the social, cultural, and geopolitical map of the world, while simultaneously producing new forms of cultural criticism. Such a shift represents a break away from certain definitive features of modernism, "with the emphasis firmly on the sense of the relational move away" (Featherstone, 1988, p. 197). At the same time, I believe that the various discourses of postmodernism have underplayed the continuities that mark the transition from one age to another within the current capitalist countries. Modernism is far from dead – its central categories are simply being written within a plurality of narratives that are attempting to address the new set of social, political, technical, and scientific configurations that constitute the current age. Stuart Hall (1986) captures the complexity of the relationship between modernity and postmodernism in the following comment:

> But I don't know that with "postmodernism" we are dealing with something totally and fundamentally different from that break at the turn of the century. I don't mean to deny that we've gone through profound qualitative changes between then and now. There are, therefore, now some very perplexing features to contemporary culture that certainly tend to outrun the critical and theoretical concepts generated in the early modernist period. We have, in that sense to constantly update our theories and to be dealing with new experiences. I also accept that these changes may constitute new subjects – positions and social identities for people. But I don't think there is any such absolutely novel and unified thing as the postmodern condition. It's another version of that historical amnesia characteristic of American culture – the tyranny of the New. (p. 47)

In what follows I will discuss some of the major features of the postmodern condition. In doing so, I will draw on a variety of different theoretical perspectives regarding the nature and meaning of these conditions.

The postmodern condition has to be seen as part of an ongoing shift related to global structural changes as well as a radical change in the way in which culture is produced, circulated, read, and consumed. Such shifts cannot be seen as part of the old Marxist base/superstructure model. Instead, they have to be viewed as part of a series of uneven developments that have emerged out of the conflict between traditional economic models and new cultural formations and modes of criticism, on the one hand, and related discourses that mark out the terrains of certain aspects of modernism and postmodernism on the other. On an ideological level, the deterritorialization and remapping characteristic of the postmodern condition can be seen in the effort by many theorists and critics to challenge and rewrite in oppositional terms the modernist ideals of rationality, totality, certainty, and progress along with its "globalizing, integrative vision of the individual's place in history and society" (Richards, 1987/1988, p. 6).

But the struggle against the ideals of modernity is not limited to the rewriting of its major texts and assumptions. For example, such a struggle cannot be seen exclusively as a matter of challenging a privileged modernist aesthetic, which calls into question the oppressive organization of space and experience that characterizes institutions such as schools, museums, and the workplace, nor can the struggle against modernity be read simply as a call to open up texts to the heterogeneity of meanings they embody and mediate. These sites of struggle and contestation are important, but the postmodern condition is also rooted in those fundamental political and technological shifts that undermine the central modernist notion that there exists "a legitimate center – a unique and superior position from which to establish control and to determine hierarchies" (Richard, 1987/1988, p. 6). This center refers to the privileging of Western patriarchal culture with its representations of domination rooted in a Eurocentric conception of the world and to the technological, political, economic, and military resources that once were almost exclusively dominated by the Western industrial countries. In effect, the basic elements of the postmodern condition have been created by major changes in the global redistribution of political power and cultural legitimation, the deterritorialization and decentering of power in the West, the transformations in the nature of the forces of production, and the emergence of new forms of cultural criticism. In what follows, I will spell these out in greater detail.

The economic and political conditions that have come about in the Western nations since World War II have been extensively analyzed by theorists such as Stanley Aronowitz (1987/1988), Scott Lash and John Urry (1987), and Jean Baudrillard (1988). Although these theorists hold differing positions on the importance of postmodernism, each of them believes that postmodernism can only be understood in terms of its problematic relationship with central features of the modernist tradition. Each of their analyses is important. For Aronowitz (1987/1988), modernity's faith in the nation-state is receding on a world-wide level as the forces of production that drive the global economy are increasingly dispersed through the multinationalism of the corporations and the emergence of economic powers outside of the Western industrialized nations. Moreover, Aronowitz believes that the legitimating narratives of modernity regarding public life no longer have either the power of conviction nor the ideological cohesiveness they once had. Ideological support has given way to bad faith. This can be seen in the various ways in which sexual and power hierarchies, electoral politics, and faith in industrialism are now under attack from a wider variety of groups at the same time that they are more deeply entrenched in elite public discourse and politics.

For Lash and Urry (1987), capitalism has become increasingly disorganized. They argue that this process, while not contributing directly to the development of postmodernist culture, represents a powerful force in the emergence of many of the elements that make up the postmodern condition. The central changes that Lash and Urry point to include: the deconcentration of capital as national markets become less regulated by national corporations; the decline in the number of blue-collar workers as de-industrialization reconstructs the centers of production and changes the makeup of the labor force; a dramatic expansion of the white-collar workforce as well as a distinctive service class; an increase in cultural pluralism and the development of new cultural/ethnic/political formations; and demographic changes involving the financial collapse of inner cities and the growth of rural and suburban populations. And, finally, though they touch on a number of other considerations, Lash and Urry emphasize the appearance of an ideological/ cultural apparatus in which the production of information and symbols not only becomes a central aspect of the making and remaking of everyday life, but contributes to the breakdown of the division between reality and image.

In Jean Baudrillard's (1988) discourse, the postmodern condition represents more than a massive transgression of the boundaries that are essential to the logic of modernism; it represents a form of hyperreality, an infinite proliferation of meanings in which all boundaries collapse into models of simulation. In this perspective, there is no relevance to an epistemology that searches out the higher elevations of truth, exercises a depth reading, or tries to penetrate reality in order to uncover the essence of meaning. Reality is on the surface. Ideology, alienation, and values are all jettisoned in this version of postmodern discourse, subsumed within the orbit of a society saturated with media messages that have no meaning or content in the rationalist sense. In this view, information as noise is passively consumed by the masses whose brutish indifference obliterates the ground of mediation, politics, and resistance. In emphasizing the glitter of the everyday and the spectacle, Baudrillard points to the new forms of technology and information that have become central to a reproductive order which blurs the lines between past and present, art and life, and commitment and experience.

But Baudrillard's society of simulations, a society in which "signs replace the logic of production and class conflict as key constituents of contemporary capitalist societies" (Kellner, in press, p. 11), translates less into a provocative analysis of the changing contours and features of the age than it does into a nihilism that undermines its own radical intent. Fatalism replaces struggle and irony resigns itself to a "mediascape" that offers the opportunity for a form of refusal defined simply as play. Foundationalism is out, and language has become a signifier, floating anchorless in a terrain of images that refuse definition and spell the end of representation. In Baudrillard's postmodern world, history is finished, subsumed in a vertigo of electronic fantasy-images that privilege inertia as reality. For theorists like Baudrillard, the masses have become the black hole into which all meaning simply disappears. Domination now takes place through the proliferation of signs, images, and signifiers that envelop us without a hint of either where they come from or what they mean. The task is not to interpret but to consume – to revel in the plurality of uncertainties that claim no boundaries and seek no resolutions. This is the world of the spectacle and the simulacra, a world in which the modernist notion of the "aura" of a work, personality, or text no longer exists (Benjamin, 1969). Everything is a copy, everything and everyone is networked into a communication system in which we are all electronically wired, pulsating in response to the simulations that keep us watching and consuming. In Baudrillard's world, the postmodern condition is science fiction, meaning is an affront to reality, and pedagogy vanishes except as form because there are no more experts.

In spite of the different politics and analyses presented by each of these positions, they all respectively concede that we are living in a transitional era in which emerging social conditions call into question the ability of old orthodoxies to name and understand the changes that are ushering us into the 21st century. Whether these changes suggest a break between modernity and postmodernity may not be as important an issue as understanding the nature of the changes and what their implications might be for reconstituting a radical cultural politics appropriate to our own rime and place. We need to understand more clearly what changes are taking place in various artistic, intellectual, and academic spheres regarding the production, distribution, and reception of various theories and discourses. We also need to better understand how a broader shift in the balance of power in the wider cultural sphere either opens up or restricts the possibilities for developing a discourse of public life, one which can draw from both a critical modernism and a postmodernism of resistance. Finally, we need to understand how the field of the everyday is being reconstituted not simply as a commodity sphere but as a site of contestation that offers new possibilities for engaging the memories, histories, and stories of those who offer not simply otherness but an oppositional resistance to various forms of domination. All of these concerns and changes involve pedagogical and political issues, not only because they focus on the ways in which power is being redistributed and taken up by different social formations making new and radical demands both within and outside societies, but also because they illuminate the need to understand how these changes are actually taken up by different groups in particular historical and cultural contexts.

Postmodern Problematics: Reactionary vs. Progressive Appropriations

In what follows, I shall address some of the productive contradictions inherent in some of the more important thematic considerations that cut across a number of postmodernist discourses. Following Linda Hutcheon (1988), I maintain that the various theories and practices that constitute the postmodern field represent what can in effect be called postmodern problematics: "a set of problems and basic issues that have been created by the various discourses of postmodernism, issues that were not particularly problematic before but certainly are now" (Hutcheon, 1988, p. 5). The problematics that will be analyzed below make clear some of the major paradoxes of postmodernist discourse; they also illuminate the difficulties and possibilities for both rereading and rewriting the major categories of educational theory and cultural criticism.

(a) Postmodernism and the Crisis of Totality and Foundationalism

We have paid a high enough price for the nostalgia of the whole and the one, for the reconciliation of the concept and the sensible, of the transparent and the communicable experience. . . . Let us wage war on totality; let us be witnesses to the unpresentable; let us activate the differences and save the honor of the name. (Lyotard, 1984, pp. 81–82)

In the above quote, Lyotard articulates an antagonism that has become a central feature of postmodernist discourse. That is, postmodernism rejects those aspects of the Enlightenment and Western philosophical tradition that rely on master narratives "which set out to address a transcendental Subject, to define an essential human nature, to prescribe a global human destiny or to proscribe collective human goals" (Hebdige, 1986, p. 81). Within this perspective all claims to universal reason and impartial competence are rejected in favor of the partiality and specificity of discourse. General abstractions that deny the specificity and particularity of everyday life, that generalize out of existence the particular and the local, that smother difference under the banner of universalizing categories are rejected as totalitarian and terroristic.

The postmodern critique of totality also represents a rejection of foundational claims that wrap themselves in an appeal to science, objectivity, neutrality, and scholarly disinterestedness. Validity claims that rest on essentializing and transcendent meta-discourses are viewed with suspicion and skepticism and regarded as ideological expressions of particular discourses embodying normative interests and legitimating historically specific relations of power. This is especially true of those grand narratives that encompass sweeping global claims regarding human destiny and happiness. In this case, postmodern discourse rejects, for example, the totalizing theories of Marxism, Hegelianism, Christianity, and any other philosophy of history based on notions of causality and all-encompassing global resolutions regarding human destiny. For Lyotard (1984), totalizing narratives need to be opposed as part of the wider struggle against modernity.

I will use the term modern to designate any science that legitimates itself with reference to a metadiscourse of this land making an explicit appeal to some grand narrative, such as the dialectics of Spirit, the hermeneutics of meaning, the emancipation of the rational or working subject, or the creation of wealth. (p. xxii)

But there is more at stake here than simply an argument against the grand narrative or the claims of universal reason; there is also an attack on those intellectuals who would designate themselves as the emancipatory vanguard, an intellectual elite who have deemed themselves above history only to attempt to shape it through their pretensions to what Dick Hebdige (1986) calls an "illusory Faustian omnipotence" (p. 91). In some versions of the postmodern, totality and foundationalism do not lead to the truth or emancipation, but to periods of great suffering and violence. The postmodernist attack on the grand narrative is simultaneously a criticism of an inflated teleological self-confidence, a dangerous transcendentalism, and a rejection of the omniscient narrator (Feher, 1988, pp. 197–198). Read in more positive terms, postmodernists are arguing for a plurality of voices and narratives, that is, for different narratives that present the unrepresentable, for stories that emerge from historically specific struggles. Similarly, postmodern discourse is attempting with its emphasis on the specific and the normative to situate reason and knowledge within rather than outside particular configurations of space, place, time, and power. Partiality in this case becomes a political necessity as part of the discourse of locating oneself within rather than outside of history and ideology. Stanley Aronowitz (1987/1988) captures this issue in the following comment:

> Postmodern thought . . . is bound to discourse, literally narratives about the world that are admittedly partial. Indeed, one of the crucial features of discourse is the intimate tie between knowledge and interest, the latter being understood as "standpoint" from which to grasp "reality? Putting these terms in inverted commas signifies the will to abandon scientificity, science as a set of propositions claiming validity by any given competent investigatory. What postmodernists deny is precisely this category of impartial competence. For competence is constituted as a series of exclusions – of women, of people of color, of nature as a historical agent, of the truth value of art. (p. 103)

The postmodern attack on totality and grand narratives needs to be dialectically construed if it is to contribute to a radical theory of education and cultural politics. At one level the critique of master narratives is important because it makes us attentive to those mythic elements of foundationalism which give history, society, nature, and human relations an ultimate and unproblematic meaning. In this case, the critique of master narratives is synonymous with an attack on those forms of theoretical terrorism that deny contingency, values, struggle, and human agency. Moreover, by denying an ultimate ground upon which human action is construed, the critique of totality/master narratives opens up the possibility for a wider proliferation of discourses and forms of political action (Laclau, 1988, pp. 78–79). In effect, this form of critique rejects totality and the notion of master narratives as an ontological notion. On the other hand, to reject all notions of totality is to run the risk of being trapped in particularistic theories that cannot explain how the various diverse relations that constitute larger social, political, and global systems interrelate or mutually determine and constrain each other. In order to retain a relationship between postmodern discourse and the primacy of the political, it is imperative that the notion of totality be embraced as a heuristic device rather than an ontological category. In other words, we need to preserve a notion of totality that privileges forms of analyses in which it is possible to make visible those mediations, interrelations, and interdependencies that give shape and power to larger political and social systems. We need theories which express and articulate difference but we also need to understand how the relations in which differences are constituted operate as part of a wider set of social, political, and cultural practices. Doug Kellner (1988) is incisive on this issue as he modifies the postmodernist position on totality with a more critical and dialectical view by arguing for a distinction between vhat he calls grand and master narratives:

> Against Lyotard, we might want to distinguish between "master narratives" that attempt to subsume every particular, every specific viewpoint, and every key point into one totalizing theory (as in some versions of Marxism, feminism, Weber, etc.) from "grand narratives" which attempt to tell a Big Story, such as the rise of capital, patriarchy or the colonial subject. (p. 253)

(b) Postmodernism, Culture, and the Problematic of Otherness

Related to the critique of master narratives and theories of totality is another major concern of postmodernism: the development of a politics that addresses popular culture as a serious object of aesthetic and cultural criticism, on the one hand, and signals and affirms the importance of minority cultures as historically specific forms of cultural production on the other. Postmodernism's attack on universalism, in part, has translated into a refusal of modernism's relentless hostility to mass culture, and its reproduction of the elitist division between high and low culture (Foster, 1983; Huyssen, 1986). Not only has postmodernism's reaffirmation of popular culture challenged the aesthetic and epistemological divisions supportive of academic disciplines and the contours of what has been considered "serious" taste, it has also resulted in new forms of art, writing, film-making, and types of aesthetic and social criticism.[4] Similarly, postmodernism has provided the conditions necessary for exploring and recuperating traditions of various forms of otherness as a fundamental dimension of both the cultural and the sociopolitical sphere.

What postmodernism has done in problematizing the cultural sphere is threefold. First, it has pointed to those changing conditions of knowledge embedded in the age of electronically mediated culture, cybernetic steering systems, and computer engineering (Lyotard, 1984). Second, it has helped to raise new questions about the terrain of culture as a field of both domination and contestation. More specifically, various discourses of postmodernism have challenged the ethnocentricity that rests on the assumption that America and Europe represent universalized models of civilization and culture (Ross, 1988). In doing so postmodernism has helped to redefine the relationship between power and culture, representation and domination, and language and subjectivity. Third, postmodernism has provided a theoretical foundation for engaging the Other not only as a deterritorialized object of domination, but also as a source of struggle, collective resistance, and historical affirmation. In other words, postmodernism's stress on the problematic of otherness has included: a focus on the importance of history as a form of counter-memory (Kaplan, 1987); an emphasis on the value of the everyday as a source of agency and empowerment (Grossberg, 1988); a renewed understanding of gender as an irreducible historical and social practice constituted in a plurality of self and social representations (De Lauretis, 1987, Morris, 1988); and an insertion of the contingent, the discontinuous, and the unrepresentable as coordinates for remapping and rethinking the borders that define one's existence and place in the world.

By pointing to the increasingly powerful and complex role of the new electronic mass media in constituting individual identities, cultural languages, and social formations, the various discourses of postmodernism have provided a powerful new language that enables us to understand the changing nature of domination and resistance in late capitalist societies. This is particularly true in its understanding of how the conditions for the production of knowledge have changed within the last two decades with respect to the electronic and information processing technologies of production, the types of knowledge produced, and the impact they have had both at the level of everyday life and in larger global terms (Kellner, in press). By incorporating these changes in the cultural sphere into its discourse, postmodernism not only questions the relevance of traditional discourses such as Marxism, it also raises serious ideological questions about the academic boundaries that structure the organization of canons and knowledge formations. Within many postmodernist discourses, the established academic canons are criticized for ignoring the socially constructed nature of their form and content and for narrowly defining their relationship and impact on the larger world. The importance of this form of postmodern criticism can be seen in the ways it has been taken up in the various debates on the status and ideological nature of the canon in higher education.[5]

Of course, there is no systematic theory of culture at work in postmodernism; instead, there are a variety of theoretical positions and cultural practices ranging from Baudrillard's (1988) darker vision of the collapse of meaning into simulations or simulacra to less pessimistic theoretical attempts to challenge new forms of cultural production and domination while simultaneously creating alternative artistic and cultural spheres (Foster, 1983; Kellner, 1988). At stake here is a politics and cultural analysis that provides the conditions for challenging the formalist and institutionalized boundaries of art and culture which characterize those public spheres that trade in and profit from the reproduction and production of signs, images, and representations, whether they be the museum, school, city planning commission, or the state. Similarly, there is also the increasing proliferation of alternative forms of cultural criticism in which the use of pastiche, irony, and parody allow us to deepen our understanding of "the kinds of men, women, and biographical experiences that the late postmodern period makes available to its members" (Denzin, 1988, p. 461).

The postmodern problematic of culture and otherness is not without its ambiguities and problems. In spite of its dazzling display of cultural criticism, postmodern critics say very little regarding how the characteristic experiences of the postmodern are actually experienced and taken up by different groups. There is little if any sense of pedagogy in this discourse, which is overly focused on the performance of reading cultural texts without a concomitant understanding of how people make choices or invest in signs, signifiers, images, and discourses that actively construct their identities and social relations. Similarly, postmodernism has a tendency to democratize the notion of difference in a way that echoes a type of vapid liberal pluralism. There is in this discourse the danger of affirming difference simply as an end in itself without acknowledging how difference is formed, erased, and re-suscitated within and despite asymmetrical relations of power. Lost here is any understanding of how difference is forged in both domination and opposition. While the rediscovery of difference as an aesthetic and cultural issue is to be applauded, there is a theoretical tendency in many postmodernist discourses to abstract the primacy of the relations of power and politics from the discussion of marginalized others. Difference in this sense often slips into a theoretically harmless and politically deracinated notion of pastiche. As Cornel West points out, the revolt "against the center by those constituted as marginals [should be viewed in terms of] an oppositional difference. . . . These American attacks on universality in the name of difference, these 'postmodern' issues of Otherness (Afro-Americans, Native Americans, women, gays) are in fact an implicit critique of certain French postmodern discourses about Otherness that really serve to hide and conceal the power of the voices and movements of Others" (Stephanson, 1988, p. 273).

The position that West is criticizing is best exemplified in the work of the liberal postmodernist Richard Rorty (1979, 1985). Rorty's postmodernism attempts to allow space for the diverse voices of marginalized groups by including them in conversations that expand the notions of solidarity and human community. But in Rorty's version, solidarity is given a liberal twist which removes it from relations of power, resistance, and struggle. The community in which Rorty's conversation takes place engages a notion of pluralism in which various groups appear to have an equal voice. As George Yudice (1988) convincingly reveals, there is a failure within this type of analysis to develop forms of social analysis, critique, or understanding of how particular voices and social formations are formed in oppositional struggle, rather than in dialogue. That is, there is little or no theoretical attempt to illustrate how dominant and subordinate voices are formed in the ideological and material contexts of real conflict and oppression. There is no clear understanding in Rorty's position why marginalized Others may not be able or willing to participate in such a conversation. Similarly, there is little sense of how subordinate groups, as part of an oppositional cultural politics, first need to participate in the struggle to constitute themselves as both the subject and object of history. Put another way, some versions of postmodern discourse want to recognize and privilege the marginal without engaging the important issue of what social conditions need to exist before such groups can actually exercise forms of self and social empowerment. In similar fashion, what needs to be dealt with in postmodernist discourse regarding the problematic of otherness is how subordinate groups can struggle collectively to create conditions that enable them to both better understand how their identities have been constructed within dominant and subordinate relations of power and what it takes to struggle for their own voices and visions while simultaneously working to transform the social and material conditions that have oppressed them (Hartsock, 1987; Yudice, 1988). There is no pure space from which to develop either a politics of resistance or a politics of identity. Indeed, the struggle for voice and collective empowerment has to be forged within, not outside of, the mediating traditions and histories that link the center and the margins of late capitalism.

Within the postmodern discourses of culture and otherness, there is a privileging of space, textuality, signs, and surfaces which runs the risk of abandoning all forms of historicity. While some critics rightly argue that postmodernism offers the opportunity to repossess those human histories barred from the script of dominant historical narratives as well as the possibility of reworking history from another vantage point (Chambers, 1986; Feher, 1988), more often than not, such opportunities remain concretely unrealized. For in the vast territory of postmodern commentary and cultural production, history either gets lost in the effacement of boundaries orchestrated in the reworkings of pastiche or is displaced into forms of parody and nostalgia. For example, films like *Blue Velvet* and *Wetherby* depict a postmodernist experience which, while sometimes fascinating, effaces most connecting boundaries between the past and the present (Denzin, 1988). In these films, either history collapses into an attack on nostalgia which becomes synonymous with terror as in *Blue Velvet* or, as in *Wetherby*, history dissolves in a dissolution of narrative structure itself. In both films, historical understanding gives way to a pastiche in which the film characters become so free floating as to become lost in a web of self-parody. In these films, style is subsumed into celebration of the grotesque, collapsing into a display of the strange and unrepresentable and impeding the audience's ability to critically engage the politics of the film. In these films, style disguises rather than illuminates their underlying political machinery. For instance, *Blue Velvet* may successfully employ parody in its depiction of small-town America, but it also denigrates working-class life and women in nothing less than reactionary terms. Otherness in these films is depicted within hegemonic categories that undermine and restrict a progressive reading or identification with subordinate groups. These are films without a critical sense of history and politics. To a large extent, these films reflect some of the deeper problems characteristic of postmodern cultural forms and criticism in general.

(c) Postmodernism and the Crisis of Language, Representation, and Agency

Perhaps the most important feature of postmodernism is its stress on the centrality of language and subjectivity as new fronts from which to rethink the issues of meaning, identity, and politics. Postmodern discourse has retheorized the nature of language as a system of signs structured in the infinite play of difference, and in doing so has undermined the dominant, positivist notion of language as either a genetic code structured in permanence or simply a linguistic, transparent medium for transmitting ideas and meaning. Jacques Derrida (1976), in particular, has played a major role in retheorizing language through the principle of what he calls difference. This view suggests that meaning is the product of a language constructed out of and subject to the endless play of differences between signifiers. What constitutes the meaning of a signifier is defined by the shifting, changing relations of difference that characterize the referential play of language. What Derrida, Laclau and Mouffe (1985), and a host of other critics have demonstrated is "the increasing difficulty of defining the limits of language, or, more accurately, of defining the specific identity of the linguistic object" (Laclau, 1988, p. 67). But more is at stake here than theoretically demonstrating that meaning can never be fixed once and for all. Postmodernism has also offered powerful new modes of criticism in which various cultural objects can be read textually in the manner of a socially constructed language. In effect, by constituting cultural objects as languages, it has become possible to radically question the hegemonic view of representation which argues that knowledge, truth, and reason are governed by linguistic codes and regulations which are essentially neutral and apolitical (Cherryholmes, 1988; McLaren, 1986). The most politically charged aspect of the postmodern view of discourse is that "it challenges reason on its own ground and demonstrates that what gets called reason and knowledge is simply a particular way of organizing perception and communication, a way of organizing and categorizing experience that is social and contingent but whose socially constructed nature and contingency have been suppressed" (Peller, 1987, p. 30). For traditionalists, the postmodern emphasis on the contingency of language represents a retreat into nihilism, but, in effect, it does just the opposite by making problematic the very nature of language, representation, and meaning. In this view, truth, science, and ethics do not cease to exist; instead, they become representations that need to be problematized rather than accepted as received canons and truths.

The postmodern emphasis on the centrality of discourse has also resulted in a major rethinking of the notion of subjectivity. In particular, various postmodern discourses have offered a massive critique of the liberal humanist notion of subjectivity which is predicated on the notion of a unified, rational, self-determining consciousness. In this view, the individual subject is the source of self-knowledge and his or her view of the world is constituted through the exercise of a rational and autonomous mode of understanding and knowing. What postmodern discourse challenges is liberal humanism's notion of the subject "as a kind of free, autonomous, universal sensibility, indifferent to any particular or moral contents" (Eagleton, 1985/1986, p. 101). Chris Weeden (1987) offers a succinct commentary on postmodernism's challenge to this position:

> Language is the place where actual and possible forms of social organization and their likely social and political consequences are defined and contested. Yet it is also the place where our sense of ourselves, our subjectivity, is constructed. The assumption that subjectivity is constructed implies that it is not innate, not genetically determined, but socially produced. Subjectivity is produced in a whole range of discursive practices – economic, social and political – the meanings of which are a constant site of struggle over power. Language is not the expression of unique individuality; it constructs die individual's subjectivity in ways which are socially specific. . . . subjectivity is neither unified nor fixed. Unlike humanism, which implies a conscious, knowing, unified, rational subject [postmodernism] theorizes subjectivity as a site of disunity and conflict, central to the process of political change and to pre-serving the status quo. (p. 21)

The importance of postmodernism's retheorizing of subjectivity cannot be overemphasized. In this view, subjectivity is no longer assigned to the apolitical wasteland of essences and essentialism. Subjectivity is now read as multiple, layered, and non-unitary; rather than being constituted in a unified and integrated ego, the "self" is seen as being "constituted out of and by difference and remains contradictory" (Hall, 1986, p. 56). No longer viewed as merely the repository of consciousness and creativity, the self is constructed as a terrain of conflict and struggle, and subjectivity is seen as site of both liberation and subjugation. How subjectivity relates to issues of identity, intentionality, and desire is a deeply political issue that is inextricably related to social and cultural forces that extend far beyond the self-consciousness of the so-called humanist subject. Both the very nature of subjectivity and its capacities for self- and social determination can no longer be situated within the guarantees of transcendent phenomena or metaphysical essences. Within this perspective, the basis for a cultural politics and the struggle for power has been opened up to include the issues of language and identity.

The theoretical status and political viability of various postmodern discourses regarding the issues of language, textuality, and the subject are a matter of intense debate among diverse progressive groups. What appears to be at stake in these debates is less a matter of accepting the theoretical and political credibility of these categories than a matter of deepening and extending their radical potential for a viable and critical theory of cultural practice. While the questions raised around these categories are important and politically necessary, what remains subject to serious criticism are the theoretical and political absences that have characterized the way in which the issues of language and subjectivity have been developed in some American versions of postmodernism. In what follows, I will develop some of the more important criticisms aimed at radicalizing rather than rejecting the notions of language and subjectivity as part of a wider discourse of educational and cultural struggle.

The postmodern emphasis on language and textuality is marked by a number of problems that need to be addressed. In the United States, the postmodern/deconstructive emphasis on treating social and cultural forms as texts has become increasingly reductionistic in its overly exclusive reliance on literature as its object of analysis. Confined largely to literary and film studies, textual criticism has failed to move beyond the boundaries of the book or screen. Consequently, such analyses have not only become highly academicized, they have also retreated into a formalism that fails to link their own semiological productions to wider institutional and social practices. By failing to incorporate the complexity of determinations that constitute the cultural, political, and economic aspects of the society, postmodern criticism often fails to confront those aspects of hegemonic power that cannot be captured in merely linguistic models. This limited focus on textual analysis runs the risk of dissolving into a kind of self-congratulatory form of academic hyperbole, one that, as many feminist theorists have noted, produces a form of sterile academic politics. Commenting on Jean-Francois Lyotard's (1984) revision of the theory of language games, Meaghan Morris (1988) offers an illuminating criticism of the postmodern emphasis on the endless deconstructive rereading and rewriting of texts:

> One of the problems now emerging as a result is that as the terms of such analyses become commodified to the point of become dated . . . they offer little resistance to the wearing effects of overuse. When any and every text can be read indifferently as another instance of "strategic rewriting," another illustration of an established general principle, something more (and something more specific) is needed to argue how and why a particular event of rewriting might matter. (p. 5)

Cornel West extends this criticism by arguing that "the multilevel operations of power within social practices" cannot be understood exclusively with reference to language and discourse" (Stephanson, 1988, p. 271). There is more at stake here than simply the play of difference, the reading of a text, or an interrogation of the social construction of meaning. The limits of the linguistic model, and of discourse in general, become apparent in understanding how the operations of power work as part of a deeper, nondiscursive sense of reality. Language is not the sole source of meaning; it cannot capture through a totalizing belief in textuality, the constellation of habits, practices, and social relations that constitute what can be called the "thick" side of human life. Those aspects of social practice in which power operates to maim and torture as well as to forge collective struggles whose strengths are rooted in lived experiences, felt empathy, and concrete solidarity exceeds the insights offered by way of linguistic models (Giroux & McLaren, 1989). Postmodernism performs a theoretical service by arguing that a new political front can be opened up in the sphere of language, but it must extend the implications of this analysis from the domain of the text to the real world and in doing so recognize the limits of its own forms of analyses.

Postmodernism is deeply indebted to various poststructuralist theories of the subject. In many of these discourses, the subject is constituted through language within a number of different subject positions prescribed by various cultural texts. Unfortunately, in too many of these accounts, the subject is not only decentered, but ceases to exist. In other accounts, the construction of the subject appears to be entirely attributable to textual and linguistic operations. The subject is constructed, but bears no responsibility for agency since he or she is merely a heap of fragments bereft of any self-consciousness regarding the contradictory nature of his or her own experience. There is little sense in many of these accounts of the ways in which different historical, social, and gendered representations of meaning and desire are actually mediated and taken up subjectively by real, concrete individuals. Paul Smith has addressed this question with more theoretical rigor than most. He argues convincingly that it is imperative that any theory of the subject address why certain subject positions offered in various ideologies that circulate in everyday life are rejected by some individuals and how it is possible to theorize beyond the "subjugation" of the subject in order to leave room in which "to envisage the agent of a real and effective resistance" (Smith, 1988, p. 39). In this view, the issue of how people become agents is seen as part of a broader attempt to reconstruct a theory of cultural politics, rather than subordinate politics to an overly structuralist theory of the subject.

It is also important to note that the postmodern emphasis on both the decentering and death of the subject has been criticized in political terms on the grounds that it undermines the possibility of those who have been excluded from the centers of power to name and experience themselves as individual and collective agents. Nancy Hartsock (1987) is worth repeating at length on this issue:

> Somehow it seems highly suspicious that it is at this moment in history, when so many groups are engaged in "nationalisms" which involve redefinitions

of the marginalized Others, that doubt arises in the academy about the nature of the "subject," about the possibilities for a general theory which can describe the world, about historical "progress." Why is it, exactly at the moment when so many of us who have been silenced begin to demand the right to name ourselves, to act as subjects rather than objects of history, that just then the concept of subjecthood becomes "problematic"? Just when we are forming our own theories about the world, uncertainty emerges about whether the world can be adequately theorized? Just when we are talking about the changes we want, ideas of progress and the possibility of "meaningfully" organizing human society become suspect? And why is it only now that critiques are made of the will to power inherent in the effort to create theory? (p. 196)

According to theorists such as Elizabeth Fox-Genovese (1986), the death of the subject seems not only theoretically premature, but also is ideologically suspect, especially since such a position is being touted principally by white male academics in mostly elite universities. In this case, some versions of postmodernism are being questioned not only because they offer a radically depoliticized notion of subjectivity, but also because they refuse to treat the issue of subjectivity in historical and political terms. Terry Eagleton (1985/1986) is right in arguing that as the production of certain forms of subjectivity in any society involves analyzing in historical terms the various technologies of power at work for "instilling . . . specific kinds of value, discipline, behaviour, and response in human subjects." He adds that "What these techniques at once map and produce, for the ends of social knowledge and order, are certain forms of value and response" (p. 97). While it is important to understand subjectivity as constructed and decentered, to extol the death of the subject and with it any notion of agency is to "jettison the chance of challenging the ideology of the subject (as male, white, and middle-class) by developing alternative and different notions of subjectivity" (Huyssen, 1986, p. 212).

For feminist theorists such as Teresa De Lauretis (1987), Linda Alcoff (1988), and Meaghan Morris, postmodern discourse is theoretically flawed on two related counts. First, it pays too little attention to the issue of how subjectivity can be linked to a notion of human agency in which self-reflective, capable political selves become possible. Second, by ignoring both the issue of gender and the contribution feminists have made in contributing to what Morris calls the formative and enabling aspects of the postmodern debate, postmodernism becomes complicitous with other discourses which leave "a woman no place from which to speak, or nothing to say" (Morris, 1988, p. 15). Unwilling either to explore the contributions of feminists or to articulate a concept of gendered subjectivity, postmodern discourse fails to link the emphasis on difference with an oppositional politics in which the particularities of gender, race, class, and ethnicity are seen as fundamental dimensions in the construction of subjectivity and the politics of voice and agency.

Conclusion

In spite of some of its theoretical failings, postmodernism offers educators a number of important insights that can be taken up as part of a broader theory of schooling and critical pedagogy. Moreover, rather than negating the modernist concern with public life and critical rationality, postmodernism provides the grounds on which to deepen and extend such concerns. Postmodern engagements with foundationalism, culture, difference, and subjectivity provide the basis for questioning the modernist ideal of what constitutes a decent, humane, and good life. Rather than celebrate the narratives of the "masters," postmodernism raises important questions about how narratives get constructed, what they mean, how they regulate particular forms of moral and social experience, and how they presuppose and embody particular epistemological and political views of the world. Similarly, postmodernism attempts to delineate how borders are named, it attempts to redraw the very maps of meaning, desire, and difference, it inscribes the social and individual body with new intellectual and emotional investments, and it calls into question traditional forms of power and its accompanying modes of legitimation.

For educators postmodernism offers new theoretical tools to rethink the broader and specific contexts in which authority is defined; it offers what Richard Bernstein calls a healthy "suspiciousness of all boundary-fixing and the hidden ways in which we subordinate, exclude, and marginalize" (Bernstein, 1988, p. 267). Postmodernism also offers educators a variety of discourses for interrogating modernism's reliance on totalizing theories based on a desire for certainty and absolutes. In addition, postmodernism provides educators with a discourse capable of engaging the importance of the contingent, specific, and historical as central aspects of a liberating and empowering pedagogy. But in the end, postmodernism is too suspicious of the modernist notion of public life and of the struggle for equality and liberty that has been an essential aspect of liberal democratic discourse. If postmodernism is going to make a valuable contribution to the notion of schooling as a form of cultural politics, educators must combine its most important theoretical insights with those strategic modernist elements that contribute to a politics of radical democracy. In this way, the project of radical democracy can be deepened by expanding its sphere of applicability to increasingly wider social relations and practices; in this case, encompassing individuals and groups who have been excluded by virtue of their class, gender, race, age, or ethnic origin. What is at stake here is the recognition that postmodernism provides educators with a more complex and insightful view of the relationship between culture, power, and knowledge. But for all of its theoretical and political virtues, postmodernism is inadequate to the task of rewriting the emancipatory possibilities of the language and practice of a revitalized democratic public life. This is not to suggest that postmodernism is useless to the task of creating a public philosophy that extends the possibilities of social justice and human freedom. But it does argue that postmodernism must extend and broaden the most democratic claims of modernism. When linked with the modernist language of public life, the notions of difference, power, and specificity can be understood as part of a public philosophy that broadens and deepens individual liberties and rights *through rather than against* a radical notion of democracy.

Talk about the public must be simultaneously about the discourse of an engaged plurality and critical citizenship. This must be a discourse that breathes life into the notion of democracy by stressing a notion of lived community that is *not* at odds with the issues of justice, liberty, and the good life. Such a discourse must be informed by a postmodern concern with establishing the material and ideological conditions that allow multiple, specific, and heterogeneous ways of life. For educators the modernist concern with enlightened subjects, when coupled with the postmodernist emphasis on diversity, contingency, and cultural pluralism, points to educating students for a type of citizenship that does not separate abstract rights from the realm of the everyday, and does not define community as the legitimating and unifying practice of a one-dimensional historical and cultural narrative. The postmodern emphasis on refusing forms of knowledge and pedagogy wrapped in the legitimizing discourse of the sacred and the priestly, its rejection of universal reason as a foundation for human affairs, its claim that all narratives are partial, and its call to perform a critical reading on all scientific, cultural, and social texts as historical and political constructions provide the pedagogical grounds for radicalizing the emancipatory possibilities of teaching and learning as part of a wider struggle for democratic public life and critical citizenship. In this view, pedagogy is not reduced to the lifeless methodological imperative of teaching conflicting interpretations of what counts as knowledge (Graff, 1987). Instead, pedagogy is informed by a political project that links the creation of citizens to the development of a critical democracy; that is, a political project that links education to the struggle for a public life in which dialogue, vision, and compassion are attentive to the rights and conditions that organize public life as a democratic social form rather than as a regime of terror and oppression. Difference and pluralism in this view do not mean reducing democracy to the equivalency of diverse interests; on the contrary, what is being argued for is a language in which different voices and traditions exist and flourish to the degree that they listen to the voices of others, engage in an ongoing attempt to eliminate forms of subjective and objective suffering, and maintain those conditions in which the act of communicating and living extends rather than restricts the creation of democratic public forms. This is as much a political as it is a pedagogical project, one that demands that educators combine a democratic public philosophy with a postmodern theory of resistance.

In the next article, I want to outline some elements of what I call border pedagogy of postmodern resistance. In effect, I will attempt to demonstrate how certain postmodern notions of culture, difference, and subjectivity when combined with modernist concerns such as the language of public life, the notion of counter-memory, and the feminist notion of political identity provide a number of elements for developing a more encompassing theory of schooling and critical pedagogy.

Acknowledgements

I would like to thank Michele Fine, Peter McLaren, Richard Quantz, and Candy Mitchell for their advice regarding this piece. I am solely responsible for its contents.

Notes

1. The now classic defense of modernity in the postmodern debate can be found in Jurgen Habermas (1983, 1987). For more extensive analyses of modernity, see: Marshall Berman (1982), Eugene Lunn (1982), David Frisby (1986), David Kolb (1986), and William Connolly (1988). An interesting comparison of two very different views on modernity can be found in Berman (1988) and Nelly Richard (1987/1988).
2. Ernesto Laclau (1988) is worth elaborating on this issue. For him, it is the ontological status of the central concepts of the various discourses of modernity that the postmodern sensibility calls into question. He writes:

   If something has characterized the discourses of modernity, it is their pretension to intellectually dominate the foundation of the social, to give a rational context to the notion of the totality of history, and to base in the latter the project of a global human emancipation. As such, they have been discourses about essences and fully present identities based in one way or another upon the myth of a transparent society. Postmodernity, on the contrary, begins when this fully present identity is threatened by an ungraspable exterior that introduces a dimension of pacity and pragmatism into the pretended immediacy and transparency of its categories. This gives rise to an unbreachable abyss between the real and concepts, thus weakening the absolutist pretensions of the latter. It should be stressed that this "weakening" does not in any way negate the contents of the project of modernity; it shows only the radical vulnerability of those contents to a plurality of contexts that redefine them in an unpredictable way. Once this vulnerability is accepted in all its radicality, what does not necesisarily follow is either the abandonment of the emancipatory values or a generalized skepticism concerning them, but rather, on the contrary, the awareness of the complex strategic-discursive operations implied by their affirmation and defense. (pp. 71–72)

3. Dick Hebdige (1986) provides a sense of the range of meanings, contexts and objects that can be associated with the postmodern:

   the decor of a room, the design of a building, the diegesis of a film, the construction of a record, or a "scratch" video, a TV commercial, or an arts documentary, or the "intertextual" relations between them, the layout of a page in a fashion magazine or critical journal, an anti-teleological tendency within epistemology, the attack on the "metaphysics of presence," a general attenuation of feeling, the collective chagrin and morbid projections of a post-War generation of Baby Boomers confronting disillusioned middle age, the "predicament" of reflexivity, a group of rhetorical tropes, a proliferation of surfaces, a new phase in commodity fetishism, a fascination for "images," codes and styles, a process of cultural, political or existential fragmentation and/or crisis, the "de-centering" of the subject, an "incredulity towards metanarratives," the replacement of unitary power axes by a pluralism of power/discourse formations, the "implosion," the collapse of cultural hierarchies, the dread engendered by the threat of nuclear self-destruction, the decline of the University, the functioning and effects of the new miniaturised technologies, broad societal and economic shifts into a "media," "consumer" or "multinational" phase, a sense (depending on whom you read) of "placelessness" or the abandonment of placelessness ("critical regionalism") or (even) a generalised substitution of spatial for temporal coordinates. (p. 78)

4. A characteristic example of this work can be seen in Foster (1983), Ross (1988), in the wide-ranging essays on culture, art, and social criticism in the journal *Zone* (1/2, 1988), Wallis (1988), and in *Utopia Post Utopia* (1988) published by the Institute of Contemporary Art, Boston.

5. See, for example, Aronowitz and Giroux (1988), Spanos (1987).

References

Alcoff, L. (1988). Cultural Feminism vs. Poststructuralism: The Identity Crisis in Feminist Theory. *Signs, 13*, 405–436.

Anderson, P. (1984). Modernity and Revolution, *New Left Review*, No. 144, pp. 96–113.

Aronowitz, S. (1987/1988). Postmodernism and Politics. *Social Text*, No. 18, pp. 94–114.

Aronowitz, S., & Giroux, H. A. (1988). Schooling, Culture, and Literacy in the Age of Broken Dreams, *Harvard Educational Review, 58*, 172–194.

Baudrillard, J. (1987). Modernity. *Canadian Journal of Political and Social Theory 11*(3), 63–72.

Baudrillard, J. (1988). *Selected Writings* (M. Poster, Ed.). Stanford: Stanford University Press.

Bell, D. (1976). *The Cultural Contradictions of Capitalism*. New York: Basic Books.

Benjamin, W. (1969). The Work of art in the Age of Mechanical Reproduction. In H. Arendt (Ed.), *Illuminations* (pp. 217–251). New York: Schocken.

Berman, M. (1982). *All that is Solid Melts into Air: The Experience of Modernity*. New York: Simon & Schuster.

Berman, M. (1988). Why Modernism still Matters, *Tikkun, 4*(1), 81–86.

Bernstein, R. (1988). Metaphysics, Critique, and Utopia. *Review of Metaphysics, 42*, 255–273.

Bloom, A. (1987). *The Closing of the American Mind*. New York: Simon & Schuster.

Bowles, S., & Gintis, H. (1976). *Schooling in Capitalist America*. New York: Basic Books.

Carnoy, M., & Levin, H. (1985). *Schooling and Work in the Democratic State*. Stanford: Stanford University Press.

Chambers, I. (1986). Waiting for the End of the World. *Journal of Communication Inquiry, 10*(2), 98–103.

Cherryholmes, C. (1988). *Power and Criticism: Poststructural Investigations in Education*. New York: Teachers College Press.

Christian, B. (1987). The Race for Theory. *Cultural Critique*, No. 6, pp. 51–64.

Connolly, W. (1988). *Political Theory and Modernity*. New York: Basil Blackwell.

De Lauretis, T. (1987). *Technologies of Gender*. Bloomington: Indiana University Press.

Denzin, N. (1988). Blue Velvet: Postmodern Contradictions. *Theory, Culture, and Society*, No. 5, pp. 461–473.

Derrida, J. (1976). *Of Grammatology* (G. Spivak, Trans.). Baltimore: Johns Hopkins University Press.

Dewey, J. (1916). *Democracy and Education*. New York: Macmillan.

Eagleton, T. (1985/1986). The Subject of Literature. *Cultural Critique*, No. 2, pp. 95–104.

Featherstone, M. (1988). In Pursuit of the Postmodern: An Introduction. *Theory, Culture and Society, 5*(2–3), 195–215.

Feher, F. (1988). The Status of Postmodernity. *Philosophy and Social Criticism, 13*(2), 195–206.

Foster, H. (Ed.). (1983). *The Anti-aesthetic: Essays on Postmodern Culture*. Port Townsend, Washington: Bay Press.

Foucault, M. (1977). *Language, Counter-memory, Practice: Selected Essays and Interviews* (D. Bouchard, Ed.). Ithaca: Cornell University Press.

Fox-Genovese, E. (1986). The Claims of a Common Culture: Gender, Race, Class and the Canon. *Salmagundi, 72*(Fall), 131–143.

Frisby, D. (1986). *Fragments of Modernity*. Cambridge: MIT Press.

Giroux, H., & McLaren, P. (Eds.). (1989). *Critical Pedagogy, the State, and Cultural Struggle*. Albany: State University of New York Press.

Goodlad, J. (1984). *A Place called School*. New York: McGraw-Hill.

Gott, R. (1986), December 1). The Crisis of Contemporary Culture. *The Guardian*, p. 10.

Graff, G. (1987). *Professing Literature: An Institutional History*. Chicago: University of Chicago Press.

Grossberg, L. (1988). Putting the Pop back into Postmodernism. In A. Ross (Ed.), *Universal abandon? The Politics of Postmodernism* (pp. 167–190). Minneapolis, MN: University of Minnesota Press.

Habermas, J. (1983). Modernity – An Incomplete Project. In H. Foster (Ed.), *The Anti-aesthetic: Essays on Postmodern Culture* (pp. 3–16). Port Townsend, WA: Bay Press.

Habermas, J. (1987). *The Philosophical Discourse of Modernity*. Cambridge: MIT Press.

Hall, S. (1986). On Postmodernism and Articulation: An Interview. *Journal of Communication Inquiry, 10*(2), 40–56.

Hartsock, N. (1987). Rethinking Modernism: Minority vs. Majority Theories. *Cultural Critique*, No. 7, pp. 187–206.

Hebdige, D. (1986). Postmodernism and "the Other Side." *Journal of Communication Inquiry, 10*(2), 78–99.

Hutcheon, L. (1988). Postmodern Problematic. In R. Merrill (Ed.), *Ethics/Aesthetics: Post-modern Positions* (pp. 1–10). Washington, DC: Maisonneuve Press.

Huyssen, A. (1986). *After the Great Divide*. Bloomington: Indiana University Press.

Institute of Contemporary Art, Boston. (1988). *Utopia Post Utopia: Configurations of Nature in Recent Sculpture and Photography*. Boston: Institute of Contemporary Art.

Jameson, F. (1984). Postmodernism or the Cultural Logic of Late Capitalism. *New Left Review*, No. 146, pp. 53–93.

Jameson, F. (1988). Regarding Postmodernism – A Conversation with Fredric Jameson. In A. Ross (Ed.), *Universal Abandon! The Politics of Postmodernism* (pp. 3–30). Minneapolis: University of Minnesota Press.

JanMohamed, A., & Lloyd, D. (1987). Introduction: Minority Discourse – What is to be Done? *Cultural Critique*, No. 7, pp. 5–17.

Kellner, D. (1988). Postmodernism as Social Theory: Some Challenges and Problems. *Theory, Culture and Society, 5*(2 & 3), 239–269.

Kellner, D. (in press). Boundaries and Borderlines: Reflections on Jean Baudrillard and Critical Theory. In *From Marxism to Postmodernism and Beyond: Critical Studies of Jean Baudrilland*. Oxford: Polity Press.

Kolb, D. (1986). *The Critique of Pure Modernity: Hegel, Heidegger, and After*. Chicago: University of Chicago Press.

Laclau, E. (1988). Politics and the Limits of Modernity. In A. Ross (Ed.). *Universal abandon? The Politics of Postmodernism* (pp. 63–82). Minneapolis: University of Minnesota Press.

Laclau, E., & Mouffe, C. (1985). *Hegemony and Socialist Strategy*. London: Verso Books.

Lash, S., & Urry, J. (1987). *The End of Organized Capitalism*. Madison: University of Wisconsin Press.

Lunn, E. (1982). *Marxism and Modernism*. Berkeley: University of California Press.

Lyotard, J. (1984). *The Postmodern Condition*. Minneapolis: University of Minnesota Press.

McLaren, P. (1986). Postmodernism and the Death of Politics: A Brazilian Reprieve. *Educational Theory, 36*(4), 389–401.

Morris, M. (1988). *The Pirate's Fiancee: Feminism, Reading, Postmodernism*. London: Verso Press.

Peller, G. (1987). Reason and the Mob: The Politics of Representation. *Tikkun, 2*(3), 28–31, 92–95.

Richard, N. (1987/1988). Postmodernism and Periphery. *Third Text, 2*, 5–12.

Rorty, R. (1979). *Philosophy and the Mirror of Nature*. Princeton: Princeton University Press.

Rorty, R. (1985). Habermas and Lyotard on Postmodernity. In Richard Bernstein (Ed.), *Habermas and Modernity* (pp. 161–176). Cambridge: MIT Press.

Ross, A. (Ed.), (1988). *Universal Abandon? The Politics of Postmodernism*. Minneapolis: University of Minnesota Press.

Shor, I. (1979). *Critical Teaching and Everyday Life*. Boston: South End Press.

Smith, P. (1988). *Discerning the Subject*. Minneapolis: University of Minnesota Press.

Spanos, W. (1987). *Repetitions: The Postmodern Occasion in Literature and Culture*. Baton Rouge: Louisiana State University Press.

Stephanson, A. (1988). Interview with Cornel West. In A. Ross (Ed.). *Universal Abandon? The Politics of Postmodernism* (pp. 269–287). Minneapolis: University of Minnesota Press.

Tyler, R. W. (1950). *Basic Principles of Curriculum and Instruction*. Chicago: University of Chicago Press.

Yudice, G. (1988). Marginality and the Ethics of Survival. In A. Ross (Ed.). *Universal abandon? The Politics of Postmodernism* (pp. 214–236). Minneapolis: University of Minnesota Press.

Wallis, B. (Ed.). (1988). *Blasted Allegories*. Cambridge: MIT Press.

Weeden, C. (1987). *Feminist Practice and Poststructuralist Theory*. London: Blackwell. *Zone*, 1/2(1988).

82

Metaphor and Meaning in the Language of Teachers

Eugene F. Provenzo, Jr., Gary N. McCloskey,
Robert B. Kottkamp and Marilyn M. Cohn

Commenting on the shortage of qualified teachers in the United States, Albert Shanker, the president of the American Federation of Teachers, has said: "Educated people today simply do not want to work in the kind of factory the traditional school has become, especially when they're treated like hired hands."[1] In making this observation, Shanker uses a metaphor to communicate his powerful image of the condition of the teaching profession.

An individual's creation of metaphor is part of a fundamental human impluse to find meaning in life. C. A. Bowers sees this impluse to use metaphors as a drive to name, to give meaning, and to categorize.[2] Much of the power of metaphor is contextual. Through its capacity to clarify meaning in complex settings, metaphor is able to go beyond the limitations of scientific language and description.

Working in the fundamentally ambiguous context of schools, teachers are in need of a language that enables them to clarify meaning in the midst of complexity. Metaphor meets this need, especially in the schools of a pluralistic culture such as the United States, whose very nature is fraught with multiple meanings and values. Metaphor becomes an extraordinarily powerful tool through which the teacher can express more fully the meaning of what he or she does in an ambiguous work setting. For the researcher, in turn, the metaphors used by teachers provide a tool for interpreting the meaning of what it is to be a teacher in American society.

This article is based on interview data from a larger research project investigating perceptions and attitudes of teachers toward their work.[3] We were struck by the images teachers consistently used in the interviews – struck by the use of metaphors to create meaning in ambiguous, complex situations.

Source: *Teachers College Record*, 90(4) (1989): 551–573.

Here we not only explore the importance of metaphor for teachers, but also examine the metaphorical language teachers use to describe their work experience. In examining teacher metaphors, we sketch an outline of the meaning of work as teachers experience it. In addition, we contrast teacher images and meanings with images imposed on them by the school systems in which they work and the society that employs them. Finally, we attempt to describe a perspective through which to view teaching as a profession, not from the standpoint of the school system or larger society, but instead from the experience of teachers.

Teachers' Use of Metaphors

In our review of the metaphors used by teachers in the interviews for this study, three major categories emerged. The first was the group of metaphors that addressed the question "What is a teacher?" The second explored "What does a teacher experience?" while the third addressed "How does a teacher function as part of a system?"

However, to understand fully the meanings of the metaphors teachers use, it is necessary to understand the use of metaphor as a means of communication. The philosopher Paul Ricoeur, in his studies of the use of language, has focused on the role of metaphor in the creation of meaning. In *The Rule of Metaphor*, Ricoeur outlines the historical and phenomenological interpretations of the use of metaphorical language. For Ricoeur, metaphor enables one to (1) describe the discrepancies between the expected and the experienced, (2) use expressions reflecting the experience of multiple meanings or values in a situation (pluralism), and (3) create new understandings in a given situation.[4]

Throughout this article we draw heavily on Ricoeur's ideas as a means of interpreting the metaphors we found teachers using to describe their work, because his theories provide explanations of how teachers use metaphors rather than a schema for categorizing teachers' metaphors.[5] For an initial inquiry, the usage of metaphor seems to us the more illuminating approach. Categorization by function and types of meaning (although important to a full understanding of teachers' use of metaphors) would be a future endeavor built on the insights gleaned from this study.

What is a Teacher?

Throughout the interviews, teachers used various metaphors to define what it means to be a teacher. Although they were never asked specifically to define the term *teacher*, the metaphors they used in answering other questions revealed a struggle to name what it is to be a teacher. No single metaphor predominated, but all those offered seem to reflect a view that teaching is a complex endeavor demanding that each individual, by virtue of personality, focus predominantly on one part of a range of meanings because the whole is too complex for one vision to control.

Among the classical metaphors used were the images of the teacher as a trainer or a nurturer of things that grow. One of the teachers mixed these two metaphors to present his understanding.

> I think I'm basically a trainer. I say that because I have trained horses and I loved it. I like to see accomplishment. I think this is my greatest satisfaction – seeing something grow. I am also into plants. I love to see plants grow. I like to see people grow. That's just any nature, to see things grow, to start with nothing, develop it and end up with a finished product. (23, M, W, Jr/H, Lang. Arts/Eng.)

Other respondents also used traditional metaphors. For example, one teacher explained her role as a life anchor for children when she said:

> Even as an adult you need something to hold onto. You need an anchor Children feel the same way. (63, F, B, Elem/H, Spec.Ed./V.E.)

Some teachers expressed their metaphors in terms of other professions. As one observed:

> Half the time I think I am a preacher. I seem to find myself constantly relating literature, even if it had been written 160 years ago, to the present day – to what these kids find as their major problems. (50, F, W, Sr/L, Lang. Arts/Eng.)

Even the difficulties teachers found with each other came to show the metaphorical conceptions teachers have of their work.

> You have the hanger-oners. You find those all over. Even when you're laying bricks you'll have the brick shirker. (66, F, W, Elem/H, 4th).

Sometimes, a focused concept like anchor, preacher, or even brick layer was too Confining and teachers attempted to describe their work by an all-inclusive catalogue of traditional metaphors. As the teacher who saw herself as an "anchor" explained:

> You've got to be the mother, the counselor, the doctor, the lawyer, the preacher, the teacher and everything. (63, F, B, Elem/H, Spec.Ed./ V.E.)

Despite the specificity of traditional metaphors, teachers did not necessarily feel restricted by them. In fact, teachers seemed to feel free to create non-traditional metaphors to express their highly articulate personal philosophies about teaching. One teacher expressed his thoughts, about teaching as molding lives, in this way:

> I think attitude is more important than knowledge and skill. You have to be a mold breaker more than an educator. If you can motivate kids to want to do it, they will do it. I think that's what makes successful teachers. (22, M, H, Sr/M, Phys.Ed./Dri.Ed.)

The fact that teachers are somewhow very special people, who not only do special things but have a special brand of determination, came through in a high school teacher's observation:

> In order to be a teacher you have to be cut from a special kind of cloth. You have to be able to take the work. You have to be able to take the hate, to use the word – insults. You have to be able to take the parent criticism. You have to know your place. You have to be determined that in spite of all this you will do a good job and enjoy it. Those teachers who don't feel that way are not really very good teachers. They burn out so very quickly. They leave for other fields. (25, F, W, Sr/L, Lang. Arts/Eng.)

Often the images conveyed in descriptive metaphors emphasized the uniqueness of a good teacher as a quality that cannot be given but only developed. The range of these images can be seen in the excerpts from one teacher interview:

> She could spot gum on a midnight without a moon with the lights off, just amazing perception. (51, M, W, Sr/L, Lang. Arts/Eng.)
>
> Everyone was a character. Maybe that's what I look for in a teacher. They are good actors. They can sell their subject. (51, M, W, Sr/L, Lang. Arts/Eng.)
>
> She's like a bottle of champagne, you shake it up and it's all over the place. . . . When she teaches she puts out more energy in that hour than I could in a week or a day. It's just pure love – energy absolute. What-ever she does puts me to shame. This gal is so eclectic, she goes from K to Z and back again. I feel like I am somewhere in the middle between k and N. (51, M, W, Sr/L, Lang.Arts/Eng.)

Whether it is being a mold breaker, someone cut from the special cloth of determination, someone able to spot gum in the dark, an actor/huckster, or the energy of a shaken-up bottle of champagne, these untraditional metaphors express the concept that the teacher brings unique qualities to his or her work. These are qualities that are not obtained through education but rather are parts of the personality that resonate with and enhance the teaching act.

What is a Teacher?: The Discrepancy between the Expected and Experience in Teaching

In the use of conventional metaphors to express a range of meaning, or even in the creation of unique metaphors, teachers expressed a tension between what they expected teaching to be and what they eventually experienced as professionals. This fits with Ricoeur's notion that by using metaphor, a statement is made that something resembles (is like) something else. This in turn implies that there is also an element of nonresemblance (that it is unlike). Therefore, within the metaphor there exists a tension between what is "like" and what is "unlike." In addition, because of the unlike element, the metaphor provides a shift in meaning for the expression. This shift allows the individual to assimilate and integrate the different, the unknown, and the unlike into what is already known and understood. Metaphor allows the understanding an individual already possesses to contribute to the interpretation of experience for which present understanding and descriptions are inadequate.[6]

An example of this can be seen in the quotation above in which a teacher tries to describe what he does with a combination of trainer and nurturer metaphors. Initially, an implicit analogy is made between educating children and training horses. Significantly, the metaphor is inadequate to describe the range of the teacher's feelings, so he turns to the metaphor of students being like plants, things that grow – things that begin as nothing, that develop and become fully grown. Each of the metaphors used by the teacher describes his experience in some way. Only through the use of both metaphors in conjunction with one another is it possible for him to express the range of his experience.[7] The conception is one of internal growth with a sense of external ordering. Using the trainer metaphor alone could give one the idea that education involves an external ordering only.

The metaphors that the teachers used not only expressed discrepancy between the expected and the experience but also outlined the meaning of the experience. According to Ricoeur, in a metaphor "the meaning is not something hidden but something disclosed."[8] In disclosing meaning, metaphor has two functions: rhetorical and poetic.[9] The rhetorical function can be seen when a word or phrase expresses contradiction through the way it is used, or in a proposition contradicting its usual reference. No one, for example, believes that a teacher is a shaken-up bottle of champagne, yet when the statement is made the meaning of the phrase – despite its rhetorical overtones – is immediately understood. Likewise, no one believes that a teacher's classroom is a railroad station, yet when the statement is made that "during lunch time my room was like Grand Central Station" (55, F, W, Sr/L, Spec.Ed./V.E.) the meaning is conveyed.

The poetic function, on the other hand, can be seen in a perception of reality that contradicts previous conceptions.[10] This poetic function involves the presentation of that tension between like and unlike, resemblance and nonresemblance.[11] A good example of this contradiction is the metaphor of mold-breaker. One has often heard teachers referred to as molders of youth, yet the teacher here sees the need to break the molds the students have been placed in, in order for these students to achieve their potential. To reach the growth that education is aimed at, the teacher has to break rather than make molds. Another example can be seen in the combination of nurturer and trainer. These separate conceptions, when put together in the tension spoken of above, present an element of contradiction. Training with its external locus of control and nurturance with its internal locus of control can be seen to contradict each other if we do not see the dynamic tension a teacher must make sense out of each day.

What the use of metaphor tells us about teachers' understanding of these conceptions is that to be a teacher one has to make sense for oneself out of the experiences and roles presented, and at times find new images. Teaching also demands a type of personality that has the determination to focus on the needs of the children in a particular classroom despite the contradictions presented by societal or organizational expectations. In addition, the various metaphors communicate the feeling that the formal training teachers received as students was inadequate, by itself, to meet the actual challenges faced by them in the profession. The traditional images were conveyed in teacher training, but the determination and the need to Find meaning for oneself were overlooked there, and thus entry into and continuance in the profession were jeopardized. In short, teaching for the interviewees involved strength of character, the ability to grow and to cope with complex and challenging environments as they sought to aid children in the development of their learning.

What does a Teacher Experience?

Listening to the metaphors used to describe a teacher one might naturally ask what is it that a teacher experiences in teaching. The teachers interviewed have already observed that the answer is not to be found in textbooks, but rather in the multiple experiences that combine with one another to define what it is that is going on in teaching. Through metaphor teachers have identified for themselves those things that they actually experience.

In many of the metaphors, interviewees describe highly idiosyncratic experiences of assuming authority within their circumstances and inductively defining the world of teaching. One teacher explained how he confronted the discrepancy between the expected and the realities of the classroom.

> I believe you should try every trick you know to motivate a person, to stimulate a person, to help. But if the person has other pressures upon him, whether it's innate lack of ability, or family problems, societal problems, where he's living, or the fact that mom is divorced, or mom has never been married and so forth. I don't think you're going to overcome this by some

teaching strategy. I think it's Pollyannish to think so. . . . It's like the Holy Grail. It's like my argument about democracy as I teach my students. We have a vested interest in the concept of democracy. I make my speech that we believe that the entire world should be democratic. Of course historically, it's completely foolish. (42, M, W, Sr/H, Soc.Stud.)

This teacher tries every trick in the book to cope with the pressures exerted on students by forces outside the school. Even his presentation on the concept of democracy does not always ring true, given the need to reconcile expectations and reality.

For some teachers, overcoming the discrepancy occurs as the result of a special experience that puts their work as teachers into a new light. A high school English teacher explained this process as follows:

We used to bowl over at the Congress Bowling Alleys on Monday nights. They were telling me, "You have to hold the ball just so. You take two steps and swing your arm." Whatever it was, it wasn't working too well. I heard a voice behind me say: "Mrs. – – – , you bowl like I do English." It suddenly dawned on me that as teachers we don't realize – we think it is easy to know a noun from a verb. Easy! Any damn fool can see a noun and a verb are not the same. But kids don't see it. This youngster was bowling 170–180, and all of a sudden he said, "You bowl like I do English." I think that made me a better English teacher. (25, F, W, Sr/L, Lang.Arts/Eng.)

In the experience of bowling, this teacher learned about the experience of learning and, in turn, teaching.

Coming to terms with one's own experience was clearly one of the important functions of metaphors for the teachers who were interviewed. Metaphors provided a means by which to cope with fears and apprehension about oneself and expectations about the job of being a teacher. One delightful example of this use of metaphor can be seen in the following description by a high school teacher.

I remember Ethel Barrymore. The day she didn't have stage fright before she went on stage was the day that she would have walked out. Ethel Merman said she never had it. She didn't know what it was. I'm the Ethel Barrymore type. I always have stage fright. When it's not going well, I feel it's not going well. (51, M, W, Sr/L, Lang.Arts/Eng.)

Beyond the images of Barrymore and Merman, enthusiasm and passion for what one experiences as a teacher were frequently communicated in the metaphors used by the interviewees. Often teachers described what they experienced as though they have to sell a product. Teaching for them not only involved assuming authority through enthusiasm with a touch of inspiration, but also a touch of salesmanship, perhaps even hucksterism.

I think you've got something to sell. I've got literature for sale. I present it and I am selling it to the kids. (50, F, W, Sr/L, Lang.Arts/Eng.)

Enthusiasm came through the interviews as a crucial element to support effective teaching over time.[12] However, enthusiasm in teaching is an embattled commodity. The enthusiasm that many of the teachers showed for their work was tempered by sobering perceptions of problems within the larger field of education. Concern regarding the rapid growth of knowledge and the complexity of what students had to learn was communicated by a high school teacher using a metaphor drawn from mathematics.

> You've got to realize that knowledge is increasing exponentially. Our ability to teach seems to be decreasing fractionally or increasing fractionally. . . . The more there is to know in this world, the less we're able to teach them each year. They've got a lot of other things to distract them. We've got to find a way to bring that measure of distraction into the school curriculum or we're going to lose them. (37, M, W, Sr/M, Lang.Arts)

A further sobering perception that the teachers interviewed dealt with was the experience of the loss of the prestige, authority, and power once attached to being a teacher. One teacher trying to maintain enthusiasm and overcome difficulties with her work explained how she coped with the pressures of her job by focusing on what was doable in her classroom.

> Sometimes you are up against a brick wall. You have a love of subject matter. Sometimes it's difficult to communicate that to a student. A student has other things going on in his mind, especially towards the end of the year. The kids are concerned with Grad Night and things like that. You're trying to get objectives across, and they're just not responding. You have to realize this is their problem and just try and forge ahead. If they're not receptive to the idea you try to reach the students that are. (38, F, W, Sr/L, Fine Arts/Art)

For some teachers, there is no reconciling perceived indignities experienced in teaching with their image of themselves as professionals. As one high school teacher complained:

> I don't like being assigned extra little duties that we don't really need, like lunch duty and hall duty and things like that. This is different from just covering for somebody for an hour or so, whenever they need it. I get coverage from coaching. But, when you only have about a forty-minute lunch break, you should not have to spend ten to fifteen minutes of that break on hall duty. My wife is a nurse. Why does she have to go around changing sheets? That is why they have aides, but she is still doing it. You are not doing what you are supposed to be doing. You should be teaching. You are more babysitting. (39, M, W, Sr/L, Industrial Arts)

Another teacher reacted against her practice that had become mechanical.

> I explained it to the children one day. I wasn't going to do it anymore after that. Have you ever seen at the zoo when an animal does a trick they get a

cookie or whatever? I said, "This is what it seems is going on there." They thought about it, and they said that's true. (43, F, B, Elem/M, 4th)

Clearly, this teacher needed to take action to eliminate the problem involved in using a prescribed method of special education instruction after she discovered that this method forced her into dealing with students in a way she felt was inappropriate. The image used is particularly striking because it emerged from a special education setting, where its full impact and significance might have been lost on the students.

Despite the travails of teaching, teachers do experience, at times, support and fellowship from their colleagues. As an elementary teacher explained:

My first teaching experience was teaching kindergarten in a private school. It was a parochial school. The faculty was very social and I enjoyed that aspect of it. They also weren't fuddy duddies. They smoked and they drank. They told dirty jokes, and they did everything that everybody else did. They were just plain human beings and I thoroughly enjoyed my year with them. (32, F, W, Elem/M, 4th)

The assistance provided by such mutual support and networking was indicated in the following:

There are programs where you get to meet and talk with other teachers. Oftentimes, we end up discussing concerns, problems, and we find out that we are the same – we're not the only pebble on the beach. There are other people out there with the same concerns, the same problems. You can network and provide a support team. (69, F, W, Jr/M, Spec.Ed./V.E.)

The realities experienced in teaching are rarely what most individuals anticipated. Yet despite this fact, the teachers interviewed consistently showed their flexibility and capacity to adapt themselves to different demands and needs. Through this flexiblity and adaptability teachers assumed authority in the world in which they worked. This need to assume authority did not seem, for the most part, to be some sort of need to show who is in charge. Rather it seemed to be the recognition on the part of teachers of their responsibility for children's learning. This is a responsibility in which they have not been supported by society or the bureaucratic structure. The authority that comes with responsibility is something that must be taken hold of since the present system is not going to give it, and at times does not support those who exercise it. The enthusiasm teachers see as necessary to their work relates to the absence of support for them as they assume the responsibility of teaching.

Another area in which teachers have difficulty finding the expected is in the search for rewards and satisfactions. The metaphors teachers used to describe the rewards and satisfactions they received from their work frequently repeated images they used to describe what it meant to be a teacher.

The metaphor, for example, of the teacher as nurturer and gaining satisfaction thereby is clearly evident in the following passage:

> I raise cactus and succulents. I had been doing it for a second income before I started teaching night school. . . . I like to see things grow. I like to go to the flea market and sell someone a cactus and have them say "Oh, how beautiful," or "I like your arrangement, I'll buy it." I get a high, and it's the same with seeing a student learn new vocabulary. "I didn't know that word." Then they start using it. . . . That's what makes me stay in the profession. I love to see the growth. (23, M, W, Jr/H, Lang.Arts/Eng.)

This image presumes that growth will be visible and that success and satisfaction in the teaching endeavor will be immediately apparent. Yet a number of teachers clearly expressed in their use of metaphors that the pleasures derived from teaching were neither consistent nor always readily apparent. As one teacher indicated:

> It's kind of like a roller coaster. Sometimes I feel that this is the best job in the world and I wouldn't do anything else. Other times I say, "God I wonder if I could find something else." But no, it depends on that particular year and how things are going. There've been some years where I just decided I didn't want to teach anymore. Other years, I've said, there isn't a better job in the world. I can't believe sometimes that they pay me for what I do. (22, M, H, Sr/M, Phys.Ed./Dri.Ed.)

Reflecting on the invisibility of many of the rewards found in teaching, one teacher offered the following advice to new teachers:

> I let them know that there are some good and bad parts to it. If they can handle it, it is a very rewarding job. But, if they don't have their eyes open to see the rewards, they are going to walk right by them. It's like knowing there's a pot of gold just under the sand. If all they're doing is looking out here, they're going to walk right over it. They've got to be able to dig a bit, and look for it. If they say teaching isn't rewarding, then I'll call them a liar, because it's very rewarding. But, you have to be able to know what to look for. (33, F, W, Sr/M, Sci.Bio.)

The pot of gold being sought is not at the end of the visible rainbow, but is instead hidden under the sand. Thus, the rewards of the profession must be searched for and can easily be missed. What teachers are looking for may not be as grand as a pot of gold. Their search may be simply for the little satisfactions in life:

> When I was a beginning teacher I was much more interested in just the academics. If the child learned, then that was sufficient for me. In little things I didn't take time to smell the flowers. I didn't look for the little things and I do that now. Little things can be very satisfying for me. (56, F, W, Elem/H, Kindergarten)

The need for rewards that were lacking in the professional structure of teaching was indicated in a number of other metaphors used by the teachers. Often the image of being "stroked" appeared. Particularly interesting was the fact that many teachers felt that the only time that they were recognized by the principal was when they were causing some sort of trouble. One teacher described the situation in the following terms:

> I look at it this way. . . . As long as you're driving and you don't run a red light, or you don't have an accident, nothing is said about it. You know you're doing all right. But as soon as you do something wrong then you're going to get a ticket. Well, I feel that if I do something right, someone should mention that. (28, F, B, Sr/M, Math./Geom.)

Another teacher saw positive stroking by administrators as being as helpful to the administrators themselves as to teachers. If administrators stroked teachers more it might be easier to get them to work more effectively and efficiently in meeting the goals of the administrator.

> In my situation other teachers are friendly and we compliment each other. But we don't get enough from the administration. We get some but we need more. We can go miles with it. We can get ten miles out of one mile worth of gas with stroking. . . . Every week the football team is complimented whether they win or lose. (51, M, W, Sr/L, Lang. Arts/Eng.)

Some teachers offered images that went contrary to the desire for stroking. For them rewards would always be intrinsic. As one teacher put it:

> My drive, my energy, just the devotion I have for the profession, . . . I don't look for my name in lights. I think that I would perform at a certain level regardless of pay or whatever. (29, M, B, Sr/M, Soc.Stud./Civ./Gov.)

Another teacher saw something unhealthy in the search for positive strokes.

> It's vying for the attention of the principal so that he, as a father figure, will say, "You were a good girl today." Psychologically that's about it. What it boils down to, backbiting or whatever it takes to get close to the principal. (34, F, W, Sr/H, Media Spec.)

Rewards and satisfactions for teachers, as expressed in their use of metaphors, emphasized the variety of needs that different teachers have. Any attempt to satisfy or reward teachers cannot rely on a single solution. Even pluralistic models of rewards and satisfactions must be used carefully since some teachers find certain types of rewards and satisfactions expected by other teachers inconsistent with their own professional goals and personas. Although they may not receive such a reward or satisfaction, the fact that it is given out at all is a problem for them.

What does a Teacher Experience? Polysemy as the Experience of Multiple Meanings

The review of ideas surrounding rewards and satisfactions presents a world of teachers with different and at times conflicting understandings of these ideas. However in this situation of multiple meaning (authority over the teaching act), teachers seem pretty consistent in maintaining that rewards and satisfactions are present in their experience but are hard to come by and must be gotten for oneself most of the time. This then presents teaching as a tension between the expected/desired and the experienced.

According to Ricoeur, by allowing such tension, the poetic aspect of metaphor "sketches a 'tensional' conception of truth."[13] The tension of truth within the metaphor does not determine the meaning the hearer draws from it. Although the speaker uses the tension to overcome contradiction, the nature of the contradiction and tension allows for multiple meaning. Even the individual words used in a metaphor can convey multiple meanings. Polysemy is this "property of words in natural language of having more than one meaning."[14]

An example of the use of polysemy can be seen in the following exchange between a veteran high school teacher with nearly forty years of experience and one of the interviewers:

INTERVIEWER: What are the things that bother you?

TEACHER: The fact that we get the blame for everything. We don't get much credit. I think like everyone else teachers are human. We would like to have our back rubbed once in a while. We have done a good job, and we appreciate recognition. "They" mark us down for doing something.

INTERVIEWER: "They" being?

TEACHER: They being the nebulous "they" that sits in the ivory tower.

INTERVIEWER: The social order or whatever?

TEACHER: Yeah, that sits in the ivory tower. (25, F, W, Sr/L, Lang. Arts/Eng.)

The use of "they" by the teacher allows her to express her feelings concerning the forces that are influencing and shaping her day-to-day work, without having to specify their actual source and origin. The use of language in this manner is highly problematic. As Ricoeur explains, there are decided advantages and disadvantages to the use of polysemy:

On the one hand, it satisfies the principle of economy, which is the basic principle for all kinds of languages, at the same time that it allows the contextual game to draw an infinite variety of meaningful effects from this economic structure. But on the other hand, it delivers language to the precarious and haphazard work of interpretation and, therefore, to the risks of ambiguity, equivocity and misunderstanding.[15]

Given the ambiguous, pluralistic contexts in which teachers typically find themselves working, polysemy can be useful, but also potentially highly misleading. People with different meanings for the same metaphor can believe themselves to be allied with other individuals when in fact the concerns they have are very different. "They" for one person may be society in general, while for another "they" may be the administrators in the school system. Risking the disadvantages of polysemy is the necessary condition for the advantages to come to the fore. As J. B. Thompson points out, "Polysemy, by endowing the word with a surplus of meaning that must be sifted through interpretation, provides the basis for the creative extension of meaning through metaphor."[16]

Reflecting on "what it is that they experience," teachers present a vision of reality that, although it is filled with many creative possibilities to be sifted through, is also fraught with problems and difficulties. Given the multiple understandings of the reality of teaching, terms like responsibility, authority, and rewards and satisfaction will always mean different things to different teachers. Despite this apparently idiosyncratic reality, whatever definitions teachers give to responsibility, authority, and rewards and satisfaction, each of these is always difficult to find. Even though education is a societal function, the metaphors underline the fact that the teacher, in reality, has little or no social status nor authority to act as a professional. Thus, they must work to gain respect. In order to gain this previously expected status and authority, the teacher must be flexible and focus on the manageable and doable. Rewards and satisfaction, although sometimes illusory, are obtainable if a teacher looks hard enough for them. Additionally, such rewards and satisfaction will not be given to the teachers by anyone, but must be sought after by themselves and in some way created by them through their own ingenuity. In the end, even though personal definitions of the reality of teaching are a reflection of the variety of experiences individual teachers possess, the metaphors teachers use outline the confrontation of a reality no teacher escapes, and a tension in the truth of their experiences that demands that they make sense out of teaching – a sense no one else can give them.

How does a Teacher Function as Part of a System?

As we studied the responses of teachers in the interviews, it became clear that they do not see their work as involving just classroom situations. Instead they also clearly saw themselves functioning in new ways within a larger social and bureaucratic system. Their responses reflect their struggle with new experiences of the question "How does a teacher function as part of a system?" For the teachers interviewed, the single most evident image that seemed symbolic of their work as part of a system was increasing amounts of "paper."

Victimization was a theme clearly expressed through the metaphor and image of paperwork. Teachers saw paperwork as evidence of teach-ers' taking the blame for society's problems. As one high school physical education teacher conceived it:

> Going back to English, because it's the one I know the best because my wife teaches it. She keeps a folder on each kid and a sheet on each kid and all these things. She spends more time on paperwork than actually what she's supposed to be doing. Mountains and mountains. Every time there's something in the paper that says our kids are not graduating with a good enough education we just get a few more forms to fill out. (22, M, H, Sr/M, Phys.Ed./Dri.Ed.)

For a veteran teacher the victimization had become debilitating.

> There's always something hanging over your head that has to be done. You still have to do more. It's like the pressure of it all. The mounds and mounds of paperwork, not children's work I'm talking about. But other kinds of forms and charts and other things that you have to turn in to the administration. It's not them that's putting it on – it's coming down through them. It's funneled down. They say "You must have your teachers do this." The administration says, "Teachers you must do this land that." The state is telling the system what they must do and that sort of thing. So all of this combined, it gets to be too much. I've had it. I've had enough of it. It's too much to expect of one person. (12, F, B, Elem/ H, 2nd)

Underlying this sense of victimization is a perception that the paperwork is meaningless, that is, it does not even accomplish its purpose. In the words of a teacher:

> When it comes to all the garbage that we have to do in addition to teaching, it is not going to make us a better teacher. (25, F, W, Sr/L, Lang. Arts/Eng.)

In all the references to teaching as a world of paper, the sense of a bureau-cracy that has no focus or control of its destiny comes through. The lack of focus, responsibility, or authority within the system often appears to the teachers as activities in playing a game. A teacher expressed it this way.

> The game sometimes bothers me. I feel if you're reaching the goals that you need to reach with those children you don't have to play a game. It's because of the system that you have to play games, and people play games with you. That's the only way things get done. That's not teaching. That's paperwork. I know what my principal wants when it comes to the grade book. I don't want a hard time, so I'll play her game. I'll do everything in blue ink, pretty things, and I'll make sure it is just so. (21, F, H, Jr/M, 6th)

When teachers accept the "game" aspect of participating in the system, that acceptance brings with it a determination to control one's own form of participation in the game. This can be seen in the remarks of two teachers. As one commented:

> I began to see this is a game. We'll play it their way, because the rules are stated here. Now I want to win. If those are the rules, we'll play by them. But I am awfully glad that I had my forty hours of chemistry that I can say, "That's something I can rely on." That's where I go for help. I don't go to the education books. (47, F, W, Sr/H, Gen.Sci.)

Although not as militant in her response, another teacher sees the game as imposing limits on the "other side."

> Teachers have to assert themselves. The school board has to play the game honestly. If they are going to talk about upgrading education, they have to allow us to do it as teachers. Parents can't call and say "I want my child in this class," and have us put the child in this class, whether or not he is capable of doing the work. (25, F, W, Sr/L, Lang.Arts/Eng.)

Conceiving the paperwork as the relation of teacher to system, teachers saw this as a classic bureaucratic experience. Even the paperwork game is a signal of a government bureaucracy at work.

> If you have a dedicated person you're not going to have to demand paperwork to prove it. If you have a person who is not dedicated, even then the mountain of paperwork that he passes through isn't going to say that he is performing. How do you bridge that? Governments like paperwork. (47, F, W, Sr/H, Gen.Sci.)

Going further, an elementary school teacher saw the school system as a bureaucracy within a bureaucracy. As she put it:

> Teachers feel that their hands are tied. What good does it do to say anything to the principal? The principal doesn't have control over it. What good does it even do to complain, if you could get there, to the superintendent of schools? He doesn't have any say in the matter. (36, F, W, Elem/L, Spec.Ed./L.D.)

Everyone's hands are tied. As a result, the origin of mandates and directives remains unclear.

From the images of paperwork and metaphors of bureaucracy, it is evident that teachers often do not understand the purpose of the educational system and the reasons for many of its programs. From the strength of the comments there appears to be a chasm between teachers and administrators. Yet, at other times, a sense of both sides being victims of some larger entity becomes a bridge over the chasm.

This victimization by the larger system of which education is but a part has led some teachers to conceive of addressing their plight by taking responsibility and acting. As one teacher sees it:

I'm afraid that we're going to have to launch a campaign. We are going to have to sell ourselves. We're going to have to sell what we're doing. We're going to have to use the media. We're going to have to go out and raise funds for ourselves to do this. Somebody is going to have to educate the public. Since nobody seems to read these days, we are going to have to do it with television. We better sit down and face the fact that we are going to have to raise funds to do some real fine publicity. We have to advertise ourselves. (50, F, W, Sr/L, Lang.Arts/Eng.)

Yet another teacher sees the problem as the poor self-image of individual teachers and of the profession as a whole – a self-image that continues to reinforce itself negatively.

If teachers don't teach well, they don't have any self-respect either. . . . It's a vicious cycle as far as I am concerned. It's like the non-achiever. He doesn't achieve so he doesn't try. He doesn't have success, so why should he try. It keeps going around in a circle. The teaching profession is very much the same. People used to think that education was a snap and say, "Boy I'll do that." (32, F, W, Elem/M, 4th)

It is interesting to note that this teacher views part of the problem as coming from an unrealistic original conception of what teaching is.

In trying to conceive of an image for the world of teaching, some teachers used the business world as an image to clarify problems they have with the system. As one teacher viewed it:

They said that even the people who have been there should float. So they have two rooms. I had three or four last year. . . . A business executive doesn't float around. He has an office and he can be more organized. To work under those conditions seems primitive and silly. (10, F, W, Sr/M, Soc.Stud./His.)

Other teachers' comments indicate that the business-world image is useful but flawed. In the words of one teacher:

It's not like being an accountant. Going in there they give you books. It's either a one or a seven or whatever. In teaching it's not like that. It's not either a one or a seven. You're dealing with human beings, kids that are abused, physically and mentally. You're dealing with all these personalities in one room. It's just you. You have to be able to cope. That is a very important skill. (21, F, H, Jr/M, 6th)

Another teacher saw unionization as borrowing an element from business that brought with it undesired and unexpected consequences:

People are becoming more complaisant. Unionization has maybe done some of it by bringing in the time clock. If they are going to sit there and punch you in and punch you out, and you have to be at the school at 8:20, then the whole school will be vacant at 3:40 – not a soul will be there working. If you start to leave at 3:40, then you start to think "Well I'm not going to take my work home." When it becomes a matter of "the union says you're getting paid for this and da, da, da, and you're not being paid another cent more," then people stop thinking as professionals. Then they start thinking like the blue collar worker who punches a clock and is here for x number of hours. You think they own you or they don't own you. I don't know one accountant who's successful, one doctor, dentist, attorney, or businessman or woman who thinks their day is over when they leave the office. (69, F, W, Jr/M, Spec.Ed./V.E.)

How does a Teacher Function as Part of a System? The Creation of New Meaning through Metaphor

The teachers' metaphors describing the relation of the individual teacher to the system of education reveal professionals who predominantly see themselves in the nontraditional role of victim. Such an image is a new understanding/ meaning for the term *teacher* – in fact, a somewhat frightening one.

To comprehend this new meaning there is a need to go one step further in understanding the use of metaphor. To this point the concepts outlined have assumed a case in which there is like and unlike and multiple meanings/values (pluralism). As stated earlier, Ricoeur sees metaphor as a circumstance in which the meaning is not something hidden but something disclosed. The disclosure property of metaphor implies that where metaphors are apparent in discourse, there is disclosure of circumstances in which like confronts unlike and multiple meanings/values are the order of the day. Implicit in the existence of metaphors is the description of a reality in which pluralism necessarily resides.

Revealing discrepancies and pluralism alone does not enable one to give order to the differences. Metaphors also provide the means to incorporate differences. They enable the speaker to fuse various horizons into one ordered conception.[17] One previously quoted teacher described teaching to people interested in entering the profession as the search for a pot of gold hidden beneath the sand. Usually a pot of gold is at the end of the rainbow. Because the rewards from teaching are not immediately evident for this teacher, her reshaping of the metaphor provides the means to demonstrate the order she finds in her personal experience. An ordered conception such as this is an interplay. "The identity and difference do not melt together but confront each other."[18]

The creation of metaphor reflects a power that is not simply responsive, but that goes beyond previous categorizations into new territory. "Metaphor not only shatters the previous structures of our language, but also the previous structures of what we call reality."[19] Metaphors are therefore iconoclastic.

This iconoclastic function of metaphors repeated itself time and again throughout the interviews. In a previously quoted metaphor, an elementary teacher involved in special education expressed her frustration over the use of behavior modification techniques. She did so by evoking an image of her students as animals at the zoo being given cookies to perform tricks. Through the use of this metaphor the teacher creates an iconoclastic image. Significantly, this iconoclastic function provides the means by which to create a new icon. Through the use of a powerful metaphor, an otherwise relatively inarticulate teacher is able not only to see the failure of an old conception, but also to formulate a new conception to take its place. In this case, the conception is the image of a real dialogue with special education students about their education. The teacher is not simply an icon breaker, but also an icon maker.

For Ricoeur, "the strategy of metaphor is heuristic fiction for the sake of redescribing reality."[20] Redescribing reality is a confirmation of "interest in emancipation."[21] It is clear from the context that the use of a zoo as the metaphor for schooling was an ironic expression of a desire to redescribe reality for the purpose of emancipating the students involved.

Thus, despite the fact that they see themselves as being victimized, teachers remain remarkably self-confident and firm in their conviction about what they are doing. This is so because they have struggled with ambiguity and have somewhat successfully reshaped their authority in the classroom. These are individuals who have taken responsibility for their lives and have, iconoclastically, given themselves new meaning within the context of their work. As a result, they are surviving as part of the bureaucracy. However, because the system does not provide the freedom necessary to do the work, these people become adept at playing bureaucratic games. In a society that often seems unclear about the purpose of education, the educational system seems reactive to every movement in society. In the teachers' perceived need to compare teaching to other professions, it would appear that the conception of teaching as a profession in its own right is unclear. This lack of clarity (meaning) in both the profession and the system may be a significant factor in the difficulty many teachers have in finding for themselves a clear role or a place (new meaning) in the system. The profession is unclear as to the authority, responsibility, and freedom teachers have when they teach, while the system is unclear as to what authority, responsibility, and freedom society has given to it.

Conclusion

Faced with unexpected situations in which the stock answers were inadequate to describe their experience, the teachers interviewed responded to the uncertainty by developing or reformulating answers through the use of metaphor. However, Dan Lortie, in *Schoolteacher*, maintains that in the face of such uncertainty

> eased entry and unstepped careers exacerbate rather than alleviate the feelings of uncertainty provoked by teaching tasks. Uncertainty, under these

conditions, can be transformed into diffuse anxiety and painful self-doubt, which reduce the psychic rewards of classroom teaching.[22]

Thus, because of the reduction of psychic rewards in the actual work of teaching, the teacher is confronted with critical questions. The answers that teachers develop enable them to assume authority and responsiblity in the situations confronting them. Ricoeur calls this use of metaphor as the means of taking control of the unknown and unexplained "appropriation."[23] For these teachers, metaphor provides a means by which they can construct and express their understanding of social reality when the definitions and understandings presented to them fail to provide adequate meaning.

Given the endemic uncertainties in teaching, how can a teacher learn the appropriate ways to assume authority and responsibility? Paulo Freire has proposed a theory of education and culture in which those being educated (and in turn teachers themselves) do not simply adapt to a given scenario. Rather, those being educated integrate themselves into their reality through their exercise of "the critical capacity to make choices and transform that reality."[24] Through the metaphors that teachers use, the process Freire calls "conscienticization" or "critical self-insertion into reality" takes place with respect to their identity as teachers.[25]

Despite the assertion of self-identity, and its attendant liberation, the metaphors teachers use continue to reveal a negative attitude toward both education as a social system and the preparation they received in teacher education. Freire observes that every announcement of critical consciousness brings with it a concomitant denunciation.[26] However, it seems that the denunciation has a deeper tone of estrangement – an estrangement from freedom – that exists in the face of apparent liberation through the assumption of authority and responsibility.

Maxine Greene sees this estrangement as endemic in teaching. The teacher as stranger is very much a "Hemingway hero."[27] This estrangement, reflected in a negative attitude toward education as a social system, may come from the failure to achieve effective praxis (the integration of theory and practice). True praxis, as Greene observes, is a collective not an individual project.[28] Facing education as an ineffective social system, the individual can continue to feel dominated and lacking in self-assurance. Yet teachers do experience a certain level of control. They find rewards in their teaching and see success. There is a sense of hope in the endeavor of education, even though their estrangement, at times, makes it an ambivalent hope. This estrangement marks the limits of appropriation, limits that the neophyte must learn to confront in the quest for critical self-insertion into reality. One may try to self-insert, but what if reality rejects the form of self-insertion?

Henry Giroux sees such a dilemma and its ambivalent hope as part of the experience of the hegemony of education as a social system. Hegemony used in this context is the predominant influence of one state of affairs over all others. Hope lies in the reality that the terrain of hegemony is a constantly shifting and active relation between ideology and power.[29] It is not a cohesive force. "It is riddled with contradictions and tensions that open up the possibility for counter-hegemonic struggle."[30] In the teacher metaphors described in this study, hope is found for a counter-hegemonic struggle to improve the praxis of education. Ambivalence results from the absence of ways to collectively harness teacher authority, responsibility, and freedom into a counter-hegemonic struggle. The absence of such a struggle may only reinforce the teacher's feeling of estrangement from the dominant hegemony.

Since effective praxis is a collective endeavor, how effective can education be as a social system if the work force is so disaffected? The metaphors of teachers demonstrate they have something clear and important to contribute to the talk about teaching. Teacher metaphors, as counter-hegemonic language, expose contradictions inherent in the existing fabric of the educational hegemony. A confrontation of both false assumptions and false practices is necessary to bring about improved practice, or even the effective praxis that the current hegemony itself claims to seek. Teacher metaphors related to education as a social system expose areas in which dialogue should begin.

Metaphors that demonstrate a negative attitude toward preparation received in teacher education appear to suggest another problem. Giroux observes that teacher education programs are, by and large, part of the dominant ideology and hegemony of social control.[31] Teacher metaphors have a contribution to make here by demonstrating critical areas unaddressed, or underaddressed, by teacher education programs. In metaphors, teachers name for themselves the critical experiences of their lives. Such naming, when it can be generalized to the experience of others, is what Freire calls "generative words."[32] Although Freire presents generative words as leading to literacy, for the teacher, the generative situations, or problem posing, that lead to metaphor are events or experiences that make them critically conscious about teaching rather than reading. Exploration of teacher metaphors on a larger scale can lead to the identification of critical events in teaching and how the teacher experiences them. Such events and experiences, if introduced into teacher education programs, can provide a dialectic for current programs in order to expand the repertoire of the teacher-to-be and illuminate his or her entry into the reality of the profession, as it is experienced. For teachers in the field, who experience these critical moments as interfering with their teaching performance, the use of metaphors and the events confronted through metaphor can enable them to appropriate as their successful colleagues do, that is, to envision ways to change their circumstances and deal with the basic contradictions and tensions found in the process of schooling.[33]

In the ambivalent hope evident in teacher metaphors one can observe in action Maxine Greene's perception that the teacher is "stranger, homecomer, questioner and goad to others."[34] Facing critical questions, the teacher, as individual, is "condemned to meaning and compelled to choose."[35] Such a choice becomes possible through the use of metaphor. Yet metaphor also reveals the distance of the individual from the agenda of both education as a social system and teacher education – a distance that needs to be bridged. Teacher metaphors, systematically understood, can become a basis for dialogue between teachers, corporately, and the educational system, as well as between the reality of teacher experience and teacher education programs. Such a corporate dialogue may result in teachers' being better able to go beyond the experience of endemic uncertainty as stranger and questioner to the achievement of the profession's traditional goal of the more psychically rewarding experience of a homecomer and goad to others.

Notes

1. Quoted in "On the Record," *Time*, February 24, 1986, p. 69.
2. C. A. Bowers, "Curriculum as Cultural Reproduction: An Examination of Metaphor as a Carrier of Ideology," *Teachers College Record* 82, no. 2 (Winter 1980): 270–71.
3. Sponsored by the National Institute of Education, U.S. Department of Education (Contract # NIE-G-83-0067), this project used as its baseline data collected by Dan C. Lortie in the mid-1960s for his classic work *Schoolteacher: A Sociological Study* (Chicago: University of Chicago Press, 1975). The research extended Lortie's work through the use of a teacher survey, an interview study, and the collection of historical data. A total of 73 teachers eventually participated in the interviews, of which 53 were women and 20 were men. The grade-level figures were 30 elementary, 17 junior high, and 26 senior high teachers. The ethnic mix was 47 whites, 16 blacks, and 10 Hispanics. In this article each of the quotes from the interviews is identified with a number assigned to each interviewee, a designation for sex, ethnicity (black, Hispanic, white), school grade level (elementary, junior, senior)/school socio-economic level (low, medium, high), and interviewee's teaching area. For example, (23, M, W, Jr/H, Lang.Arts) indicates interviewee 23, male, white, Jr. high, Language Arts.
   We have used the language of our interviewees, as it was transcribed from the interviews, without change except for light editing to make spoken language intelligible in writing.
4. Paraphrased from Paul Ricoeur, *The Rule of Metaphor: Multi-disciplinary Studies of the Creation of Meaning in Language*, trans. Robert Czerny et al. (Toronto: University of Toronto Press, 1977).
5. George Lakoff and Mark Johnson, in their *Metaphors We Live By* (Chicago: University of Chicago Press, 1980), speak of metaphors as a conceptual system. We believe that further inquiry beyond ours should explore the deeper systems of meaning revealed by the metaphors we outline here. We see this study as establishing a basis for that next endeavor.
6. Paul Ricoeur, "Biblical Hermeneutics," *Semeia* 4 (1975): 75–80.
7. The range of meaning of metaphor can be conveyed by what Ricoeur calls "The Family of Metaphor" (*The Rule of Metaphor*, p. 59). In this family are personification, allegory, and poetic fancy.
8. Paul Ricoeur, *Hermencutics and the Human Sciences: Essays on Language, Action and Interpretation*, ed. and trans. John B. Thompson (Cambridge: Cambridge University Press, 1981), p. 177.
9. Ricoeur, *The Rule of Metaphor*, p. 12.
10. Morny Joy, "Explorations in the Philosophy of Imagination: The Work of Gilbert Durand and Paul Ricoeur," in *Foundations of Religious Literacy*, ed. John V. Apczynski (Chico, Calif.: Scholars Press, 1983), pp. 49–50.
11. Ricoeur, *The Rule of Metaphor*, p. 247.
12. This has been identified in an earlier analysis of these interview data and reported in Marilyn M. Cohn et al., "Teachers' Perspectives on the Problems of the Profession: Implications for Policymakers and Practitioners" (Washington, D.C.: Office of Educational Research and Improvement, U.S. Department of Education, March 1987; Contract # ERI-P-86-3090).

13. Ricoeur, *The Rule of Metaphor*, p. 313.
14. Charles E. Reagan and David Stewart, eds., *The Philosophy of Paul Ricocur: Anthology of His Work* (Boston: Beacon Press, 1978), p. 124.
15. Ibid., p. 126.
16. Thompson quoted in Ricoeur, *Hermeneutics and the Human Sciences*, p. 12.
17. Reagan and Stewart, *The Philosophy of Paul Ricocur*, p. 91.
18. Ibid., p. 199.
19. Ibid., p. 132.
20. Ibid., p. 133.
21. Paul Ricoeur, *Political and Social Essays*, ed. David Stewart and Joseph Bien (Athens, Ohio: Ohio University Press, 1974), p. 266. Redescribing reality and the interest in emancipation are not for Ricoeur a factor of man as philosopher. These abilities are tied to the concrete reality of man as worker. The promotion of human living arises out of "the dialectic of speech and work" (ibid., p. 81). This dialectic allows people through the creation of multiple meaning to overcome the anxiety resulting from previous inadequate explanations. These multiple meanings strive to restore a previously felt wholeness. In describing the search for such a restoration from an ethical perspective, Ricoeur posits a demand, expectation, and hope (see Paul Ricoeur, *The Symbolism of Evil*, trans. Emerson Buchanan [New York: Harper & Row, 1967], p. 44).
22. Lortie, *Schoolteacher*, p. 161.
23. In Reagan and Stewart, *The Philosophy of Paul Ricoeur*, p. 91.
24. Paulo Freire, *Education for Critical Consciousness* (New York: The Seabury Press, 1974), p. 154.
25. Paulo Freire, *Cultural Action for Freedom* (Cambridge: Harvard Educational Review, 1970), pp. 21–22.
26. Ibid., p. 21.
27. Maxine Greene, *Teacher as Stranger: Educational Philosophy for the Modern Age* (Belmont, Calif.: Wadsworth Publishing Company, Inc., 1973), p. 4.
28. Maxine Greene, *Landscapes of Learning* (New York: Teachers College Press, 1978), p. 100.
29. Henry A. Giroux, *Ideology, Culture and the Process of Schooling* (Philadelphia: Temple University Press, 1981), p. 25.
30. Ibid., p. 24
31. Ibid., pp. 143–62.
32. Freire, *Cultural Action for Freedom*, p. 18.
33. Giroux, *Ideology, Culture and the Process of Schooling*, p. 98.
34. Greene, *Teacher as Stranger*, p. 298.
35. Ibid., p. 208.

83

The Violation of People at Work in Schools

Arthur G. Wirth

I have been a teacher-educator who has taken an eight-year detour into the world of American work. I think that there are parallel issues in work and in schools that we ought to be aware of.

A couple of quotations set the themes I will be referring to. The first is by Hazel Henderson, maverick economist: "For the first time in history morality has become pragmatic."[1] That is the good news. It has become *practical* to act morally. The bad news is that we may not be insightful or courageous enough to act on it. The second is by Mike Cooley, president of the British Union of Engineers, who one sunny morning on the banks of the Thames gave me this quotation from a book he was writing:

> Either we will have a future in which human beings are reduced to a sort of bee-like behavior, reacting to the systems and equipment specified for them; or we will have a future in which masses of people, conscious of their skills in both a political and technical sense, decide that they are going to be the architects of a new form of technological development which will enhance human creativity and mean more freedom of choice and expression rather than less. The truth is we shall have to make the profound decision whether we intend to act as architects or bees.[2]

The choice between architect and bee confronts Americans in both schools and work. It is true that the bee-like way of treating teachers and students in schools came from American industry. Unfortunately the chances of shifting toward the architect side may be better in American industry than in the schools.

The "violation of people" got in any title because institutions that treat us like bees violate who we are as human beings. Ernest Becker, in *The Structure of Evil*, helped me see that. Becker pointed out that since the rise of

Source: *Teachers College Record*, 90(4) (1989): 535–549.

science and the Enlightenment in the seventeenth and eighteenth centuries we have been confronted by two major images of humans: *l'homme machine* (the human as mechanism) and *homo poeta* (humans as meaning makers). The Newtonian image of the world as a physical mechanism moving according to mathematically regulated laws of force and motion gave powerful support to tendencies to see humans as manipulable objects within the grand mechanical design. That view was captured nicely by the eighteenth-century philosopher Julien Offray de la Mettrie in his phrase *l'homme machine*. The problem with that concept, according to Becker, is that it is in violation of our deeper needs as *homo poeta*. We create structures of evil, Becker said, whenever we create institutions that deny persons the opportunity to stage the world so they can act in it creatively as meaning makers.[3] In our time such institutions are not only immoral; they are also impractical, because our chance of meeting successfully the problems of turbulent change in the present period of momentous transition depends on utilizing the full range of our creative strengths as *homo poeta*.

It has taken me a while to see things this way. In the late seventies I was aware of the growing concern about lowered productivity in American industry and schools. I was aware, also, of the new press by educational policy-makers to start treating children's learning as a measurable production function – with the assumption that the only learning that counts is learning that can be counted, and the parallel assumption that teachers will be made accountable in terms of test-score results. What disturbed me was my growing awareness that the teachers I thought of as the most committed and creative were becoming demoralized and thinking of quitting. Some of the rest were cheating to beat the test-score pressures.

As parents we had learned that the best bet for getting our own kids "hooked on learning" was to have them with teachers whose creative energies were engaged – teachers who worked from what the Greeks called their *entheos*, the personal God within that is the source of *enthusiasmos* or enthusiasm. If the new reductionist emphasis – "teaching is teaching for tests" – did damage to that, and in addition taught children that adults will cheat when fearful and resentful, then I assumed that something crazy and crazy-making was going on. It was obvious that the new systems/efficiency rationale was coming from the scientific management tradition in industry at a time of new fears about growing foreign competition. The question occurred to me, "If the scientific-efficiency rationale is having crazy-making effects in schools, is anyone in management questioning its effects?"

About that time I was asked to join the interdisciplinary Human Resource Management program at my university, which helped me to get in touch with the new thinking emerging in American industry. I found that while American management was split, and still is, advanced thinkers in industry and labor were beginning to hold that the scientific-efficiency rationale was itself the source of productivity problems. These industry leaders in effect were saying to school people, "No, not that way! We're going the other way – that-a-way." So I began my detour into American industry. It took me into fascinating places, from a pioneering auto-mirror plant in Bolivar, Tennessee, to Work Research Institutes in Oslo, Stavenger, and Trondheim, Norway, to Sweden, to auto plants in Tarrytown, New York, Flint and Detroit, and to Anheuser Busch think tanks in St. Louis.

In *Productive Work in Industry and Schools* I described what I found. The alternative to scientific management was an emerging democratic socio-technical theory of work that claimed that the dominant management tradition is guilty of the technical-fix error, that is, the assumption that all system problems will yield to technical-type solutions. The new theorists were arguing that the reality of a human work system is that it is "socio" as well as "technical." "Socio" refers to the purposive, idea-generating, communicative-collaborative aspect of human beings.[4] The main-line efficiency model is out of touch with this dimension of reality, or worse yet, violates it. All of this gave me insight into what was crazy-making. To be out of touch with reality is crazy. Rational-efficiency models are out of touch with the uniquely human socio dimension of human work – the *homo poeta* dimension.

A vice president of General Motors in charge of new plant design helped me get the point. "GM used to boast," he said, "that the production line had been broken down into segments so small that any task could be taught in fifteen minutes or less; any idiot could do it. If workmanship and morale were poor, the answer was to step up supervision and control. GM is now convinced," he added, "that a model based on increased control by supervisors, of a bored, reluctant work force which produces shabby products is not viable for survival."[5]

The Oxford dictionary gave me further insight. "Crazy" comes from the old Norwegian word *krasa*, which means crushed or fragmented – not together. It showed up in fragmenting human work so that idiots could do it. It showed up in transforming school learning into information bits that would yield good test scores and ruin the enthusiasm and morale of teachers and students.

Where are we in industry and education by the end of the eighties? Management and labor are still split, but as we all know industry has made moves toward participative work design that assume that both the socio and the technical have to be taken with equal seriousness. What about American schools? It is hazardous, of course, to make generalizations about the sprawling American school phenomenon, where happily many things different from what I am describing are also going on. It is a safe guess, however, that for a large number of educational planners the search for technical-fix solutions is strongly under way.

To amplify the argument I want to turn to two very different types of materials: (1) some empirical data collected by a group of Massachusetts teachers and (2) some insights from the late French social theorist Michel Foucault.

The Boston Women's Teachers Group study, *The Effect of Teaching on Teachers*, was based on in-depth, fifteen-hour interviews of twenty-five women elementary school teachers over a two-year period.[6] About half of them had taught for fifteen years, the other half less. They were selected to match substantially the national teacher population in terms of socioeconomic and racial background, marital status, educational attainments, and father's occupation, within the limitations of the small sample. They had taught in impoverished urban schools as well as in affluent systems.

Lengthy analyses of the data over many months led the teacher-researchers to conclude that teachers' feelings with regard to burnout, isolation, job satisfaction, and sense of efficacy were rooted in the *working relations* and *institutional structures* of the schools. As one of the authors said, "Teacher stress is an institutionally derived problem not a result of individual personality failures, as teachers have been led to believe."[7]

I can only sketch a profile of what they found. Since the study illustrates what I have called "crazy-making" and "violation of people" I shall make a rough sort according to these categories. They are not unrelated.

The following statements – researcher commentaries and teacher statements – refer to that which is crushed or fragmented or out of touch with reality, the "crazy-making" factor.[8]

RESEARCHER: Teachers work in an institution which holds, in its rhetoric, that questioning and debating, risk and error develop one's thinking ability. But learning situations are structured to lead to one right answer, and both teachers and students are evaluated in ways that emphasize only quantifiable results.

TEACHER: The worst thing is that you get this printout and you're expected to find the profile of each individual child and then find material on those specific skills that they have to master . . . and then they take a multiple choice test where they have to choose a, b, or c. Well, the kids glance at the choices and figure out that one of those endings make a pretty good answer. They never read the whole sentence. They're used to a world of filling blanks without it meaning anything. I mean it's meaningless work.

TEACHER: This year my principal's evaluation said this: "Five kids looked up from their work and looked out of the window within a five-minute period. Now if you multiply five kids and five minutes in a period and you place it in an hour you get the percentage who are not doing their work and not involved."

Massachusetts is not alone in imposing this style. Deborah Meier, director of the Central Park East High School in New York City, reports on how evaluators prescribed hundreds of specific written goals. Example: "Given teacher supervision, praise and positive reinforcement, the student will attend difficult assignments for five minutes, three times out of four as recorded by teacher."[9] Now, I ask, who is crazy?

Commentary that points to violation of persons as *homo poeta* includes the following:

RESEARCHER: Teachers were continually perplexed by the admonition to be *professional* while the area in which their expertise could be applied became narrower and narrower.

TEACHER: The thing that aggravates me is that we as educators are not treated as adults. . . . They check up on you like you're children. . . . They walk into your room and you have to be within minutes of where your program card says.

TEACHER: Every Tuesday is a half day for faculty meetings. . . . People sit there deadpan because they don't want to commit themselves, you know, get themselves into any kind of hot water. Most of the stuff comes down from the central office that is really separate from the actual core of teaching.

TEACHER: One of the things that has bothered me about the hurried pace of teaching today is that a lot of the creativeness is taken away from you – the feeling that I'm going to think of a new, fresh way to do it. The curriculum gets reduced to: "Here is a book and teach it. You should be on page 200 by such and such a date." It has nothing to do with your kids and nothing to do with whatever ideas you might want to bring in.

TEACHER: I think the merit evaluation is even worse than seniority. Oh, my God. In this particular school it has destroyed any type of relations. I mean you look at the person next door to you and you say, "Gee, I wonder how many points she has." So instead of encouraging teachers to be more open about what they're doing, there isn't one bit of sharing. When you're in competition for your job, you're pitting one person against another. I think in this business you can't do that. Because we tell the kids that everybody is unique.

TEACHER: I started seeing myself not taking the risks I used to. I used to do all kinds of interesting things with my students – build things all over the classroom But every once in a while someone would notice that the classroom wasn't as neat as it should be . . . and since anything can be pointed to, you start to retrench. You feel a lack of growth and you look around. And I decided to leave.

This teacher left. For those who stay there are heavy pressures to yield to the technocratic rationale.

RESEARCHER: The teacher, under attack for failing to help children reach arbitrary grade level goals, accedes to the greater wisdom of the commercial test makers and the research academics. Once started on the road to quantification, the method becomes addictive. . . .

The new *objective* type *teacher* evaluations that have been introduced are examples of such quantitative methods. They take great pains to code and enumerate the type, number and direction of the interactions of the teacher with her pupils within the classroom.

The more quantitative measures and national exams are used to evaluate the teacher, the more she will feel the need to use such quantitative methods to judge her students and other teachers. She is now the in-class representative of the national norms and country-wide bell curves. Once she has entered the child's progress in her book, both she and her pupils are assumed to be easily understood and evaluated.

The same factors work on students. There is John Goodlad's famous observation that not even 1 percent of the instructional time in classes is devoted to discussion that "required some kind of open response involving reasoning or perhaps an opinion from students . . . the extraordinary degree of student passivity stands out."[10]

An example was furnished to me by Rita Roth from her observation journal:

TEACHER: Why aren't you doing your work, Alphonse?
ALPHONSE: I thought we were going to read today.
TEACHER: That's what we did – you just had reading group.
ALPHONSE: But I thought we would read today.
TEACHER: We just did, Alphonse, We lookwed for "s" sounds in your book, did two "s" sheets in your workbook and here is the worksheet you should be doing right now to find some more "s" words.
ALPHONSE: But I thought we would read today, you know *READ read*.[11]

Deborah Meier's comment on the parallel experience of New York City teachers once more is relevant: ". . . predictable multiple-choice questions replaced *conversation* about books. Reading scores went up, literacy collapsed. . . . Improved test scores, alas, are best achieved by ignoring real reading activity."[12]

We need to note that something profoundly important is contained in these statements of Alphonse and Deborah Meier. Hans-Georg Gadamer in *Reason in an Age of Science* reminded us that the *right of converse* – to dialogue with texts and each other in reaching for understanding about the world and ourselves – is *the* unique, distinctive characteristic of being human.[13] It is what Alphonse was asking for in his request to "*READ read.*" To diminish the right to that kind of learning by trivializing instruction is, I believe, violating the human rights of both students and teachers.

I have talked with many teachers who have expressed a feeling of helplessness about being able to articulate what is wrong with the model being forced on them. It seems so reasonable. An applicant to a medieval shoemaker's guild would be told: "You say you are a shoemaker – make a shoe." In a twentieth-century culture obsessed with bottom-line results it is assumed that reading teachers can be made accountable by simply telling them to "show us your reading scores results." What possibly can be wrong with that?

The issue, Denis Goulet suggests in *The Uncertain Promise: Value Conflicts in Technology Transfer*, is not whether to be for or against efficiency, but what *kind* of efficiency is right for human institutions. Western engineering-type efficiency, which worked wonders in closed mechanical systems by simple measures of inputs to outputs, can be dangerous to well-being in non-mechanical human systems. What we now need, says Goulet, is to explore ways of becoming *integrally efficient*: how to produce efficiently while optimizing social and human values.[14] Integral efficiency would tell us that if we are teaching so that scores are going up and real reading is going down we ought to stop it because it is inefficient.

Now I want to refer briefly to what I learned from the French social theorist Michel Foucault, who in *Discipline and Punish* helped me see why the rational efficiency assumptions seem so unassailable. The great truth we must constantly hold before ourselves, said Foucault, is the realization that the reason or rationality of the Enlightenment, which gave us the liberties, also invented the disciplines.[15] Foucault showed that, from the seventeenth and eighteenth centuries onward, there was a virtual take-off in the increase of calculated power to control people through state apparatuses such as the army, prisons, tax administration, and so on.

A vivid example is the transformation of the rowdy soldiers of the late middle ages into the eighteenth-century "redcoat" type soldiers who could be made into automatons by minute attention to detail in their training. As modern soldiers they would be taught to remain motionless, never to look at the ground, and to move on command with bold, uniform steps, later to become the goose step. "Very good," Grand Duke Mikhail remarked to a regiment, after having kept it for an hour presenting arms, "only they breathe."[16]

We find the new controls also, says Foucault, in the fashioning of the late seventeenth-century Christian Brothers Schools for the poor. Jean Baptiste de la Salle, the founder, said, "How grave and dangerous is the task of teachers in the Christian Schools. . . . We must be concerned above all with the little things, the minute things in the lives of our students and their teachers. The little things lead to great results." Foucault adds, "The meticulousness of the regulations, the fussiness of inspections, the supervision of the smallest fragments of life and of the body will soon provide, in the context of the school, the barracks, the hospital or the workplace a technical rationality for the mystical calculus of the infinitesimal."[17]

Foucault noted that Jeremy Bentham's panopticon proposals for prisons, factories, or schools in the early 1800s embodied the technically thought out disciplines required in the modern era. Panopticon comes from the Greek words *pan* (everything) and *opticon* (a place of sight) – thus, a place of sight to see everything. The general idea included a basic circular building, with cells for individual subjects around the inside of the circumference. In the center, facing the cells, is an Inspector's Tower with windows looking down on the cells. The observatory room at the top was constructed with a line of sight so that the inspector could see all, while being invisible to the inmates below. Thus, the basic principle was that "the persons to be inspected should always feel themselves as if under inspection."[18] The person to be supervised must never know if at any moment he is actually being observed; at the same time he must constantly feel that he might be. "He is seen, but he does not see, he is the object of information, never a subject of communication,"[19] The guiding concept, says Foucault, is the ideal of the Perfect Gaze, the gaze that can see everything constantly. It employs three instrumentalities: hierarchical surveillance – all of those intrusive gazes from the central office; normalizing judgment aimed at securing conformity; and the examination. The gist of his argument is in his comments on the *examination* by which individuals may be measured, classified, and judged. In the examination, says Foucault, we can find a whole domain of knowledge and type of power: (1) through techniques of the examination individuals are made *visible* – subject to "the gaze," and made into objects for measurement; (2) by *documentation* individuals and groups are encoded in written reports and files; they are organized into registers, classifications, and cumulative systems; (3) by collecting documentary records on each individual, each is *individualized as a case* and becomes an object of knowledge and power.[20]

The examination is now pervasive in modern institutions and is notably present, said Foucault, in the growth of larger, more systematized modern schools. The school has become, in fact, a sort of apparatus of uninterrupted examination, increasingly an arena for "a perpetual comparison of each and all that made it possible both to measure and judge."[21] My New York State informants tell me that a regent's student will take twenty-nine state-required examinations in twelve years. Only two years in the elementary school will be free of state-imposed examinations.

The extension of the panopticon rationale throughout the society coincided, Foucault says, with the rise of human sciences. In line with the ideal of the gaze, quantitative test scores and record keeping created the conditions for a technical matrix that changed discourse about policy issues into the neutral language of science. In schools, for example, talk about problems is limited to the lexicon of technocratic ideology. Thus teachers are taught to think of classrooms as management systems, and to talk about their teaching in terms of performance objectives, system components, sequencing of instruction, and so on. When the terminology of technical experts takes over, teachers may feel mute in the face of it: "Who are we to question scientific expertise?" If the system breaks down and does not work, the only answer of panopticon technicians is to do more of the same.

Retreat into acquiescence is not the only response, however. Resistance does break out: at work – in strikes, sabotage, and drug abuse; among teachers – as witnessed by the Massachusetts Women's Research Study; by a marvelous gadfly newspaper, *Rethinking Schools*, produced by Milwaukee teachers who are in rebellion against damaging, bureaucratic intrusions that harm their work; in Harold Berlak's *Democratic Schools*, providing a communication network for English, Canadian, and American teachers who resist the megamachine; and George Woods's lively Institute for Democratic Education at Ohio University. Foucault would not be surprised. He predicts resistance because, he says, panopticon manipulation and domination violate our human need for autonomy and freedom.

In industry there is a growing awareness that panopticon violation of people is impractical as well as immoral. There is, for example, *Technology and the American Economic Transition*, a massive report published in 1988 by the Office of Technology Assessment (OTA). The OTA says that we face a conjunction of two epochal events: the acceleration of the electronic information revolution and the fact that we now have to compete for economic survival in a one-world market. The challenge is how to confront *turbulent change* – change that is rapid and unpredictable. Our greatest need is for a well-educated, committed work force fully engaged in flexible interactions with high-tech equipment.[22]

Since I began thinking about work and schools ten years ago there has been a rapid expansion of awareness by some major corporations of the need to tap the brains of people at work, to move toward democratic sociotechnical work design. There is, for example, the plan for production of Saturn, GM's "car of the future." The goal is to lay the groundwork for combining robotics with a new style of work relationship. The agreements worked out with the United Automobile Workers change the status of assembly-line workers from hourly laborers to salaried employees. Union workers in small production work units will be involved in decision-making processes that formerly were the prerogative of management. They will perform their own quality control with electronic equipment.[23] If you compare workplaces like this with accountability routinization in the schools, which drives creative teachers to despair, it does not take a genius to see who is out of step.

A growing number of major leaders in industry and labor are becoming aware of the discrepancy. The 1985 statement *Investing in our Children* by the Committee for Economic Development (CED) is a case in point.[24] CED members include executive officers from major American corporations that are being transformed by the rush of computer technology. They are forthright in declaring that a work force educated by "old school basics" will not be equipped to meet the challenges of turbulent change.

The report presents the case of Proctor and Gamble as prototype. The strong trend now is for employees to perform a broad range of tasks including operating and maintaining equipment, performing their own quality control, and participating in goal setting, problem solving, and budgeting. With this view of work in America the report calls for "nothing less than a revolution in the role of the teacher and the management of schools."[25] High-tech firms, they say, are not served well by centralized, rigid bureaucracies that are hostile to creativity. They stifle it because their goal is to keep control in the hands of centralized authority. The essential obligation of organizations in the new era is "to nurture creativity." School policymakers must learn the lesson of industry: Give employees a stake in the system by decentralizing decision making to the lowest possible level.

The interaction of teachers, students, and administrators in individual schools becomes the key arena for action. The report assumes that able people will not choose teaching, nor choose to remain in it, if they are stifled by bureaucratic regimentation or shackled with "teacher-proof" materials. Teachers as creative actors will respond only if they are given a chance to exercise judgment and to reshape the working environment.[26] The authors ask for a view of teachers as carriers of liberal culture with a responsibility to teach higher-order learning – to think analytically, to cooperate as well as to compete, to assume responsibility, and to learn to learn.

They shy away from "merit plans," which often undermine collegial relations. Teachers working in a largely competitive environment, they say, will be less inclined to support the feeling of community that is essential for effective schools.[27]

Change in the corporate work world is widespread enough to lead to such recommendations. It would be a gross oversimplification, however, to assume that the issue about work in corporate life itself has been settled in this happy fashion. Since many corporations continue the narrow scientific management tradition, the issue of whether we will choose to become architects rather than bees is very much in doubt.

The Office of Technology Assessment says that a major challenge for both corporations and schools will be how they choose to make use of swiftly evolving computer technology. *Technology and the American Economic Transition* says that micro-electronic robotics and telecommunication technology combined with democratic work styles can provide an opportunity to revitalize the competiveness of American industry. A work force with high morale linked to imaginatively designed technology can move us toward an economy of high-tech, high-skilled, high-wage industries.[28] However, our habits and the control needs of those in charge push us toward rational, bureaucratic management. With this bias, computer electronics can become a force to intensify hierarchical controls and surveillance.

A Ted Koppel program, "Surveillance on the Job," illustrated the new electronic monitoring of performance of airline representatives.[29] One of the agents reported how she worked under a demerit system monitored by a computer. If she spends an average of more than 109 seconds talking to a customer about reservations or fares she gets one demerit. If she spends more than 11 seconds in between customers she gets two demerits. After 12 seconds a light flashes on the board of her supervisor, who comes in then with, "Anything wrong? May I help you?" Six demerits earn a warning; thirty-six, dismissal. Another agent reported the monitoring of her time between calls. When she was heard saying a swear word to herself it was evaluated as "evidence of a bad attitude," Six million clerical workers are now being watched by the unblinking gaze. Another four million technical and managerial people are about to be electronically evaluated in the next few years. We come closer to what Gadamer saw as the ultimate nightmare – when science expands into a total technocracy.[30]

We may take the road of deskilling and degrading work. The Office of Technology Assessment report says that if we do, we ought to know the consequences. Such a path not only downgrades American work and lowers our standard of living, but often includes sending hardware and software overseas to exploit the cheap labor and vulnerability of Third World women. It increases the gap between technical-managerial elites and a growing body of deskilled workers, often nonwhite.[31] As it exacerbates dualist divisions in the society and treats millions with disrespect, it violates the values of the democratic tradition.

The OTA report also says that a comparable issue will appear in the near future in education. The evidence of serious inadequacies in the *technical* skills of basic mathematical and verbal literacy of American students is clear. The OTA recommends that we undertake a major research effort immediately to explore how the new potential of computer-enhanced instruction might help us with the stubborn problems of skill training and conceptual learning.[32] It envisions two major policy choices.[33] The first, which it warns against, is to aim for a uniform national curriculum and examination system to which teachers everywhere will be made accountable. One of the major computer companies is now moving to what could become statewide or even nationwide mainframes through which uniform instructional materials could be piped. Electronic monitoring of scores could "keep book" on teachers and schools everywhere.

The other approach recommended by OTA is illustrated in an experiment by Apple, Inc. In anticipation of the near universal availabilty of computers ten years from now, Apple has created "computer-saturated" classrooms in seven different school communities throughout the United States, including a black urban school in Memphis, a rural school in Minnesota, and a Cupertino, California, school in Silicon Valley itself.[34] Students and teachers are provided with individual Macintosh computers at home as well as at school. Apple operates on the assumption that the culture of each school is different, and that teachers in each setting should be free to experiment with usages to help meet their own broader educational goals. In those seven different schools seven different strategies and designs are emerging. I could feel excitement and commitment by staff and students in the setting at West High School in Columbus, Ohio, which I visited. Here we see our capacity to create decentralized learning communities in which teachers can take initiatives in designing the use of computer technology to meet their goals. Students, administrators, and parents join with teachers in the explorations. Each new use opens other possibilities. It feels freeing instead of controlling. In terms of our educational history we could say that we need *both* Thorndike skill training and the Deweyan meaning-seeking parts of our tradition.

We need the will to make the powerful tool of computer-assisted instruction subordinate to the Deweyan meaning-seeking needs of both teachers and students.

It is time to close. A title like "The Violation of People at Work in Schools" conveys an impression of anger. I am angry about teachers feeling hurt, worn down, and resentful, yet unable to articulate what is wrong. One of our tasks as professors of education is to help with the articulation.

For me those women in the Boston teachers group put their finger on a key insight. Their message was: It is not teachers' psyches that need massaging. The source of trouble is in the structure of the schools and its effects on teachers' working relations with each other, with administrators, with students, and with learning.[35] Let us accept the working propositon that Deborah Meier articulated: "Serious rooted change cannot happen unless the knowledge of those who do the job is tapped."[36] That means putting teachers in charge by structural change that supports school-based initiative, inquiry, and decision making – changes that open time and space so that teachers have time to converse and plan together.

I am suggesting also that we can get to the deeper issues about that structural problem and begin to use blunt language about what is going on. Michael Harrington, in *The Politics at God's Funeral*, helps. The crisis of our time, he says, is a crisis of the human spirit, and we have to give up the illusion that we can talk adequately about the real problems of our lives and our work by using only the bland, value-free language of technocratic reform.[37]

Foucault and Becker helped me see that the structure those caring teachers were pointing to as the source of their burnout was a manifestation of a much broader structural problem – the lifeless bureaucratic "perfect-gaze" control systems that are killing our spirits in both late corporate capitalism and East Bloc communism. Rationalized functionalism, with hierarchical surveillance, impoverishes the human spirit by denying people access to their dignity and personal enthusiasms. It is crazy-making. Ernest Becker says that when these structures threaten the core of who we are as *homo poeta*, we should call them what they are – structures of evil.

The situation calls for resistance and school people need allies to resist. I was happy to find a budding challenge to sterile scientific management in the work world. The movement toward democratic sociotechnical work explores how democratic values can be combined with technological innovation – the same task that needs exploration in the schools. Our reach must be for the ideal stated by Kant: We must try to achieve maximum individuality within maximum community. Sterile control models allow access to *neither* individuality nor community. We are cheated of the strengths we need to meet the awesome challenges of the coming twenty-first century.

Having taken such a lofty conceptual flight I want to end by returning to the reality of contemporary school life. The choice between architect and bee is not fictional fantasy. It is being played out in two major American school systems.

In my home town of St. Louis a complex system of teacher evaluation has been introduced based, in part, on student scores on standardized tests. The predictable charges of cheating occur with lurid press headlines. A school board member responds by setting up his own system of surveillance: a telephone hotline that encourages students, teachers, or staff members to report to him anonymously suspicions of teacher cheating. The plummeting of trust, morale, and care are "externalities," not counted in the evaluation equations. By equating examination scores with significant learning this newest panopticon creates a facade of "educational excellence" that cheats the children who can least afford it.

Meanwhile, in Detroit, a very different and risky gamble is being tried with major support from Detroit unions, corporations, and foundations. An effort is being launched to introduce into the schools the philosophy and techniques of democratic sociotechnical work theory from the level of classroom practice, through teacher and administrator relationships, all the way up to the school board/teacher's union core committee. The project is directed by Neal Herrick, who has had a long history of pioneering such efforts through the United Automobile Workers and the Union of Public Employees. I deliberately use the term "risky gamble" because we need to recognize how difficult it may be to learn new habits after years of being bent by panopticon controls. Only the reality of desperation has led to this effort to break out.

In these examples we can see the schizophrenia within reform: simultaneous moves toward uniform centralized control and moves toward school-based autonomy with teacher participation and initiative. In both work and schools we confront the choice – architect or bee – the choice of who we want to be as a people for entering that third millennium.

Notes

This article was originally presented as the Charles DeGarmo Lecture for the Society of Professors of Education at New Orleans, April 6, 1988.

1. Hazel Henderson, "A New Economics," in *Work and Education*, ed. Dyckman Vermilye (San Francisco: Jossey-Bass, 1977), p. 235.
2. Mike Cooley, *Architect or Bee?* (Boston: South End Press, 1981), p. 100.
3. Ernest Becker, *The Structure of Evil: An Essay on the Unification of Science of Man* (New York: The Free Press, 1968), pp. 214–15.
4. Arthur G. Wirth, *Productive Work in Industry and Schools: Becoming Persons Again* (Lanham, Md.: University Press of America, 1983). See ch. 3.
5. Lecture by Dr. William Duffy, Director of Research in Work Innovation at General Motors, March 1980 (unpublished).
6. Sara Freedman, Jane Jackson, and Katherine Boles, *The Effect of Teaching on Teachers* (Bismarck: Center for Teaching and Learning, University of North Dakota, 1986).
7. Sara Freedman, "Classes Help Teachers Understand Burnout," *Boston Herald*, April 29, 1984, p. 25.

8. Freedman, Jackson, and Boles, *Effect of Teaching*, quotations selected pp. 11–20 *et passim*.

9. Deborah Meier, "Good Schools Are Still Possible," *Dissent*, Fall 1987, p. 546.

10. John I. Goodlad, *A Place Called School* (New York: McGraw-Hill, 1984), pp. 229–30.

11. Wirth, *Productive Work*, p. 133.

12. Meier, "Good Schools," p. 544.

13. Hans-George Gadamer, *Reason in an Age of Science* (Cambridge: The M.I.T. Press, 1981), pp. 11, 91–93, 113–37 *et passim*.

14. Denis Goulet, *The Uncertain Promise* (New York: IDOC/North America, 1977), p. 30.

15. Michel Foucault, *Discipline and Punish* (New York: Vintage Books, 1979), p. 222.

16. Quoted in ibid., p. 188.

17. Ibid., p. 140.

18. *The Works of Jeremy Bentham* (New York: Russell and Russell, Inc., 1962), vol. 4, p. 44.

19. Foucault, *Discipline and Punish*, p. 200.

20. Ibid., pp. 184–94 *et passim*.

21. Ibid., p. 186.

22. U.S. Congress, Office of Technology Assessment, *Technology and the American Economic Transition: Choices for the Future* (Washington, D.C.: U.S. Government Printing Office, 1988), pp. 3–4.

23. *The New York Times*, Aug. 4, 1985, p. E5.

24. *Investing in Our Children: Business and the Public Schools* (A Statement by the Research and Policy Committee of the Committee for Economic Development, 447 Madison Ave., New York, N.Y. 10022, pp. 15–17 *et passim*). I have been critical of this report in "Contemporary Work and the Quality of Life," *Society as Educator in an Age of Transition*, Eighty-sixth Yearbook of the National Society for the Study of Education, Part II, ed. Kenneth D. Benne and Steven Tozer (Chicago: University of Chicago Press, 1987. Here I report only on aspects relevant for the topic at hand. See also Denis P. Doyle and Marsha Levine, "Business and the Public Schools," *Phi Delta Kappan* 67, No. 2 (Oct. 1986): 113–15.

25. *Investing in our Children*, p. 60.

26. Ibid.

27. Ibid., p. 67.

28. U.S. Congress, Office of Technology Assessment, *Technology*, ch. 13, "Alternative Paths for the American Economy."

29. ABC News, "Surveillance on the Job" (transcript, June 23, 1987).

30. Hans-Georg Gadamer, *Truth and Method* (New York: The Crossroad Publishing Co., 1986), p. xxv.

31. U.S. Congress, Office of Technology Assessment, *Technology*, chap. 13.

32. Ibid., pp. 247–50.

33. Ibid., p. 240.

34. See "Apple Classroom of Tomorrow" (Apple Computer, Inc., Cupertino, Calif. 95014).

35. Freedman, Jackson, and Boles, *Effort of Teaching*, pp. 3–4.

36. Meier, "Good School," p. 549.

37. Michael Harrington, *The Politics at God's Funeral* (New York: Holt, Rinehart & Winston, 1983), p. 218.

84

Multicultural Education as a Form of Resistance to Oppression

Christine E. Sleeter

Multicultural education is a relatively new field that has faced a constant struggle for legitimacy, even though the issues it addresses regarding race relations and the form education should take in a pluralistic society are as old as the United States. Conservative educators dismiss it as radical and misdirected. Harry Broudy (1975), for example, believes that the stress on cultural diversity is divisive, and will lock minority groups out of the system by failing to teach them "to participate not only in the culture of this country but also in the intellectual and artistic achievements of the human race" (p. 175). More recently, E. D. Hirsch, Jr. (1988) has argued that in their attempts to teach children about diverse groups, schools have produced culturally illiterate Americans who have little sense of a shared culture. Such criticisms are hardly surprising: since multicultural education challenges the conservative position, one would not expect it to garner much conservative support.

Of greater concern is its dismissal by many radical educators, since they also mount a challenge to oppression in society and schooling. Many critical theorists locate the main source of oppressive social relationships in the economy and relations of production, and rarely or never address issues of racial and gender oppression. Philip Wexler (1982), for example, in reviewing contributions by sociologists of school knowledge, repeatedly emphasizes social class only:

> School knowledge reflects class interest. . . . School knowledge is the unequal representation of the experience and culture of social classes. . . . School knowledge is an organizational representation of different class languages. . . . School knowledge develops as cultural representation in response to the system needs of capitalism. (p. 278)

Source: *Journal of Education*, 171(3) (1989): 51–71.

Such theorists simply ignore multicultural education, partly because it typically has offered a much stronger critique of race relations than of social class relations.

Growing numbers of other radical educators occasionally string together the words "race, class, and gender," recognizing that there are multiple forms of social oppression. However social class and class theorists still receive most of their attention, and they also have given little attention to multicultural education.

Some radical theorists in the United States are beginning to criticize the field of multicultural education in print (McCarthy, 1988; Olneck, 1990). Radical theorists have also criticized it in other countries, but since the history of and thought within the field differs somewhat in different countries, this article will concern itself with criticisms originating in the United States; reasons why will be developed below. Radical theorists criticize multicultural education on the grounds that it is part of the liberal, but not the radical, tradition. Their criticisms are important to attend to because, whether others voice them in print or not, they represent grounds for failing to take multicultural education seriously. They also illustrate problems in how the field is often interpreted today, which suggests directions it should take in its development.

I will argue that radical criticisms or tacit dismissals of multicultural education represent some lack of understanding of its intent, as well as a fragmenting of leftist educational advocates and practitioners. This can only weaken attempts in this conservative era to challenge oppressive social relationships through schooling. I will suggest that radical educators can constructively understand multicultural education as a form of resistance to dominant modes of schooling. I will review its history as well as changes in its social context over the past 25 years, and suggest five tasks for the future development of the field that will strengthen its political intent.

Criticisms of Multicultural Education in the United States

Multicultural education has been a target of radical criticism in England, Canada, and Australia (e.g., Bullivant, 1986; Cole, 1986; Troyna, 1987). Recently two criticisms of the field in the U.S. have been produced. Cameron McCarthy (1988) described multicultural education as "a body of thought which originates in the liberal pluralist approaches to education and society," and which is "a curricular truce, the fallout of a political project to deluge and neutralize Black rejection of the conformist and assimilationist curriculum models solidly in place in the 1960's" (p. 267). He went on to say that multicultural education attempts to "absorb Black radical demands for the restructuring of school knowledge and pedagogical practices," focusing instead on "sensitizing White teachers and school administrators to minority 'differences'" (p. 268). As such, it advocates a "benign pluralism ('We are all the same because we are different')" (p. 276). He leveled two main criticisms at the field. First, he argued that it attempts to move racial minority young people into better jobs by promoting academic achievement through raising their self-concepts; this is a naive approach to the job market because it ignores institutional racist practices in the economic structure (p. 269). Second, he noted that, "By focusing on sensitivity training and on individual differences, multicultural proponents typically skirt the very problem which multicultural education seeks to address: WHITE RACISM" (p. 269).

Michael Olneck (1990) made fairly similar charges against the field. Unlike McCarthy, he recognized that it originated in protests during the 1960s by Americans of color to subordination by Whites, and that it asserts the value and importance of the experiences of Americans of color. However, he agreed with McCarthy that multicultural education concerns itself mainly with individual differences and the primacy of the individual over the collective, and that it depoliticizes race relations by focusing on expressions of culture rather than sociopolitical relations among groups. In describing multicultural education as emphasizing the development of positive attitudes and intergroup harmony, Olneck argued that it serves as a vehicle for social control more than for social change. He summarized his arguments as follows:

> Like intercultural education, dominant versions of multicultural education delimit a sanitized cultural sphere divorced from sociopolitical interests, in which culture is reified, fragmented, and homogenized, and they depict ethnic conflict as predominantly the consequence of negative attitudes and ignorance about manifestations of difference, which they seek to remedy by cultivating empathy, appreciation, and understanding.

Both McCarthy and Olneck have oversimplified the field of multicultural education, enabling them to characterize it as misdirected. They provide good examples of grounds on which leftist educators tend to dismiss multicultural education. I will argue that it is more productive to identify ways in which the field works to challenge oppression, and to amplify and develop those dimensions of thought and practice. I will first provide an overview of the field's complexity that its critics tend to gloss over.

Complexities within the Field of Multicultural Education

Critics, as well as advocates, of multicultural education often assume that it is a fairly homogeneous set of practices, and that all advocates subscribe to the same ends and the same models of social change. As a result, critics often condemn practices that many multicultural education advocates also criticize, or condemn the field for not addressing issues some of its theorists do address. The field is often treated as static and homogeneous rather than as dynamic and growing, with its own internal debates. This is important to recognize, because there is much within the field that radical educators should be working *with* rather than *against*.

First, the diversity across national borders must be recognized. While there is considerable dialogue among advocates in the United States, Canada, England, and Australia, the histories of race relations in these countries are sufficiently different that debates in one country cannot simply be transplanted to another country. The United States has struggled with race relations on its home territory since its inception, in addition to sharing with England, Canada, and Australia increasing diversification of its population due to recent waves of immigrants of color. Not only did Whites in the U.S. subjugate aboriginal people, as did Whites in Australia and Canada; Whites in the U.S. also imported large numbers of African slaves, whose descendants have lived here for about four centuries. The United States also colonized Puerto Rico and half of Mexico, absorbing Hispanics into its borders while continuing to live next to sovereign Hispanic nations. This history, which has helped shape relations among racial and ethnic groups in the United States, as well as dialogue about racial and ethnic relations, differs from that of other English-speaking countries. Only since World War II has Britain experienced a significant influx of people of color, while it historically had dominated people of color outside its borders, through colonialism. Australia shares with the U.S. a history of Whites subjugating aboriginal people, but only very small numbers of other groups of color have been permitted to immigrate there until recently. Neither Canada nor Australia shares the U.S. experience of enslaving large numbers of Black people, or of conquering and absorbing other nonwhite nations. Unlike the United States, however, Canada has a history of struggle between two strong White language and ethnic groups.

As a result of these different histories and cultural contexts, multicultural education in the United States today has a longer history and a more varied body of thought than the field has in other English-speaking countries, and race (as opposed to White ethnicity) has longer been at its core. In addition, there is a difference among countries in who is involved in the debates about multicultural education. In the United States educators of color have always been at the forefront of the development of multicultural education, along with some Whites; in England and Australia, debates are carried on mainly by Whites, and people of color are largely excluded. In the U.S., the federal government is not a participant in debates about multicultural education; in Britain, Canada, and Australia, the national governments have appropriated the term "multicultural education" to refer to recommended interventions that many argue are too weak and assimilationist (e.g., Green, 1982). These different cultural contexts have produced somewhat different alignments of educators who use the term "multicultural education." In Britain, for example, a lively debate is being waged between proponents of multicultural education and proponents of antiracist teaching. In the U.S., many proponents of multicultural education, such as Bob Suzuki (1984), *agree* with proponents of antiracist teaching, but do so under the umbrella of multicultural education. Both McCarthy and Olneck apply to the U.S. criticisms leveled in other countries toward multicultural education in those countries, although Olneck is more careful to show that the ideas being criticized also apply to the U.S.

Second, within the United States, one can distinguish between five quite different approaches to multicultural education. These have been described and reviewed elsewhere (Sleeter & Grant, 1987, 1988), but will be summarized briefly here. One approach, Teaching the Culturally Different, attempts to raise the achievement of students of color, although more through designing culturally compatible education programs than through simply raising student self concept (e.g., Jordan, 1985; Ramirez & Castaneda, 1974; Shade, 1982). Partly because this approach does not address structural barriers to economic access, it is not the approach most advocates of multicultural education prefer. The second approach, Human Relations, aims toward sensitivity training, and teaching that "We are all the same because we are different" (Colangelo, Foxley, & Dustin, 1979; Tiedt & Tiedt, 1986). This approach does not address institutional racism; its intent is to improve the school experience itself more than to restructure society, and it occurs mainly at the primary level of education. The third approach, which we call Single Group Studies, includes such programs as Black Studies, Chicano Studies, and Women's Studies. This approach explicitly teaches students about the history of the group's oppression and how oppression works today, as well as the culture the group developed within oppressive circumstances (e.g., Blassingame, 1971; Spender, 1981). Its major limitation is its focus on only one form of oppression and ignoring of others (such as gender and class). The fourth approach is most commonly subscribed to by American multicultural education advocates (e.g., Baker, 1983; Banks, 1981; Gay, 1983; Gollnick, 1980). Its processes involve redesigning schooling to make it model the ideal pluralistic and equal society. Finally, the fifth approach, Education that is Multicultural and Social Reconstructionist, teaches directly about political and economic oppression and discrimination, and prepares young people in social action skills (e.g., Grant & Sleeter, 1986a; Suzuki, 1984).

Advocates of different approaches debate with and sometimes criticize each other. It is important for those outside the field to identify which approach or approaches are actually being discussed, rather than assuming that all approaches are alike. Both McCarthy and Olneck, for example, describe and cite mainly Human Relations ideas and sources. Neither mentions ideas associated with Single Group Studies or Education that is Multicultural and Social Reconstructionist, approaches *within* the field with which they and other radical educators might sympathize.

Third, one must distinguish between an approach as formulated by its main theorists, and superficial application of it that one often finds in schools as well as in the literature. As James Banks (1984) has pointed out, quite often "the critics have chosen some of the worst practices that are masquerading as multicultural education and defined these practices as multicultural education" (p. 60). For example, the Single Group Studies approach as envisioned by its theorists includes examining a group's historic and contemporary oppression, and also includes mobilizing its members as well as sympathetic out-group members for social action. In schools this approach sometimes takes the form of superficial study of the food, music, and dances of a group. Rather than condemning Single Group Studies, or the entire field of multicultural education, for how an approach is often carried out in classrooms, it would be more productive to develop ways to strengthen its application and use.

Fourth, one can differentiate among advocates who address only race and ethnicity; race, ethnicity, and gender; race, ethnicity, and language; and multiple forms of diversity. Some theorists treat these as multiple layers of individual difference, while others treat them as multiple forms of oppression. This is an important distinction. While the Human Relations approach stresses acceptance of a wide variety of manifestations of uniqueness, Education that is Multicultural and Social Reconstructionist searches for ways to build coalitions to combat oppression in its various forms.

Fifth, advocates often articulate their agendas for school reform using language that recognizes the resistance multicultural education typically encounters. Therefore, one cannot assume that advocates of multicultural education spell out their entire agenda in print, and that one can infer all they are thinking or doing by reading the multicultural education literature. Multicultural education has been a highly political change strategy; many of its writings can be understood as attempts to mobilize particular changes in schooling, on the part of individuals who often would resist those changes. A large proportion of active advocates of the last three approaches are educators of color who have experienced a lifetime of White racism and know fully well that this is a major issue that needs to be addressed. But schools, as well as the colleges and job markets they serve, are controlled mainly by Whites, and substantive reforms must have White support. Thus, advocates have had to address White educators in order to gain space within the curriculum to teach about the experiences of Americans of color, and to reduce the obvious hostility schools often display toward children of color. Having had considerable experience with White educators, advocates have known that Whites do not usually listen to educators of color, and particularly when they show emotion (Delpit, 1988). Thus, the politics of bringing about change has necessitated frequently couching arguments for school reform in language that White educators would attend to. Many advocates deliberately have chosen terms such as "human relations" because nobody opposes good human relations, while the term "multicultural" signals a red flag to many people, and the term "race" literally scares many more away.

The strategy of appealing to Whites through relatively benign language has been more effective than many recognize. For example, in its state regulations for teacher education, Wisconsin includes a set of Human Relations requirements, specifying that teacher education programs require content such as:

> study in the values, lifestyles, learning styles, contributions, and heritage-history of women and various racial, cultural, and economic groups . . . study of the psychological and social implications of the forces of discrimination, especially racism and sexism, and their broader impact on relationships among members of various groups in American society . . . [and] experiences for students to systematically evaluate the impact of the forces of discrimination, especially racism and sexism, on [several specific aspects of schooling].

This requirement can be dealt with weakly or strongly; several institutions have indeed treated it very weakly. However, in order to comply with state regulations, several teacher education programs have hired faculty who now teach courses about oppression based on race, class, and gender. Attendance at Human Relations conferences in Wisconsin finds educators discussing not sensitivity training, individual differences, and stereotyping, but political and economic oppression based on race, language, gender, sexual orientation, social class, and disability. Similarly, in Minnesota under the state's term "Human Relations," Bob Terry developed a curriculum called "Foundations of Oppression" which is used by many teacher education programs. St. Cloud State in particular has been able to develop a very strong campus-wide program in the study of oppression based on race, gender, social class, and sexual orientation. While no Human Relations educator in Wisconsin or Minnesota would argue that this work sufficiently resolves institutional discrimination in either state's education system – indeed it only begins to address it – the requirement has created considerable space in teacher education programs for addressing oppression and institutional racism. And this has been accomplished by appealing to White educators and legislators in language they would listen to. Had this requirement been articulated within the language of anti-racist education, it probably would not have become institutionalized. Paradoxically, while terms such as "Human Relations" can be criticized for depoliticizing race relations, use of such terms can be politically quite effective.

This is not to say that all advocates of multicultural education are radicals using benign language for political purposes. Many do indeed subscribe to limited visions of or naive theories about social change. But many are activists who are working to make changes in education, and work with whatever points of entree they can gain in whatever fashion is acceptable to others with whom they work. In order to understand what any advocate really thinks or believes, one should interact personally with him or her.

Earlier I noted that criticisms of multicultural education by the left fracture it (often along racial lines) in a way that weakens it. It could be of great mutual benefit for those interested primarily in class, in race, and in gender oppression to work together as much as possible. The remainder of this essay will argue that multicultural education can be understood by critical theorists as a form of resistance to racial oppression. As such, it offers some help in formulating educational practices that challenge oppression. But it also needs further development at both the theoretical and practical levels, partly due to changes in the social context in which multicultural education has been articulated.

Multicultural Education as a Form of Resistance

Over the last few years, critical theorists have found themselves plagued by overly deterministic models of structural and cultural reproduction (e.g., Bourdieu & Passeron, 1977; Bowles & Gintis, 1976), and have been exploring the implications of contradiction and resistance as a means of agency for social change. For example, Michael Apple (1982) argues:

> Functionalist accounts of the hidden curriculum – accounts that sought to demonstrate both that students, like workers, were effectively socialized and that the power of technical/administrative forms used by capital was unchallenged – were part of the very process of ideological reproduction I wanted to struggle against. (p. 24)

He goes on to say:

> Clearly, then, workers resist in subtle and important ways, I believe. They often contradict and partly transform modes of control into opportunities for resistance and maintaining their own informal norms which guide the labor process. (p. 25)

Henry Giroux, among others, has explored the concept of resistance in some detail. He defines resistance as "a personal 'space,' in which the logic and force of domination is contested by the power of subjective agency to subvert the process of socialization" (1988, p. 162). Resistance can take many forms, ranging from "an unreflective and defeatist refusal to acquiesce to different forms of domination" to "a cynical, arrogant, or even naive rejection of oppressive forms of moral and political regulation" (1988, p. 162). The power of resistance is its celebration "not of what is but what could be" (1983, p. 242), and the energy it mobilizes for social change. Resistance provides an entree into education for social change; Giroux has argued the need "to develop strategies in schools in which oppositional cultures might provide the basis for a viable political force" (1983, p. 101).

Apple (1982) also emphasizes the need to attend seriously to forms of resistance that occur.

> They provide significant points of reference for demonstrating what can be done now in the way of concrete work. Yet these successful struggles are not as helpful as they might be if they are not communicated. If we are to overcome apathy and cynicism, as well as the workings of the selective tradition, the non-reformist reforms that people throughout society are putting in place can be put on the agenda only if others are aware of them. (pp. 173–174)

Multicultural education can be viewed as a form of resistance to oppressive social relationships. It represents resistance on the part of educators to White dominance of racial minority groups through education, and also (to many) to male dominance. Multicultural education developed out of the ferment of the 1960s and early 1970s, receiving its major impetus from the rejection of racial minority groups to racial oppression; it subsequently was joined to some extent by feminist groups rejecting sexual oppression. It was grounded in a vision of equality and served as a mobilizing site for struggle within education. However, I will argue that, due to changes over the past 15 years in the social and political context of multicultural education, its meaning is heard and interpreted today quite differently than it was two decades ago. The field needs to speak to oppression and struggle today much more explicitly than it did in its inception.

Geneva Gay, one of the field's major proponents and developers, has provided a useful discussion of the history of the field. She notes that it

> originated in a socio-political milieu and is to some extent a product of its times. Concerns about the treatment of ethnic groups in school curricula and instructional materials directly reflected concerns about their social, political, and economic plight in the society at large. (1983, p. 560)

She goes on to point out connections between the civil rights movement and the inception of multicultural education. In the mid-1960s, "The ideological and strategic focus of the [civil rights] movement shifted from passivity and perseverance in the face of adversity to aggression, self-determination, cultural consciousness, and political power" (p. 560). Racial minority groups actively proclaimed and developed consciousness of their own histories and identities. On college campuses this ferment took the form of demands for ethnic studies courses and elimination of stereotypic and derogatory treatment. Some of this energy was directed toward the public school curricula and to the "ethnic distortions, stereotypes, omissions, and misinformation" in textbooks (p. 561). At the same time, the movement was aided by social science research that undermined cultural deprivation theories and suggested that "the academic failure of minority youths was due more to the conflicting expectations of school and home and to the schools' devaluation of minority group cultures" (p. 561).

Gay describes the 1970s as "prime times for multiethnic education. This was an era of growth and expansion both quantitative and qualitative" (p. 562). During the 1970s "an avalanche of revisionist materials – including pedagogies, psychologies, ethnographies, histories, and sociologies" – were created in the forms of "a wide variety of ethnic books, films and filmstrips, recordings, audio-visual packets, course outlines, and study guides" (p. 562). Conferences, workshops, and policies such as the Ethnic Heritage Act and the NCATE standards for accreditation supported this activity. The activity of the 1970s can best be thought of as a good beginning. Gay cautions that, while "theory was advancing, emerging, and evolving with apparent continuity," at the same time "multiethnic practice remained largely fragmentary, sporadic, unarticulated, and unsystematic" (p. 562).

In its inception, multicultural education was clearly connected with and attempting to contribute to a much larger social and political racial struggle. According to Banks (1984),

> A major goal of most ethnic revival movements is to attain equality for the excluded ethnic group. . . . Since the school is viewed by ethnic reformers as an important institution in their oppression, they attempt to reform it because they believe that it can be a pivotal vehicle in their liberation. (p. 58)

One task of the social movements of the 1960s was, as Michael Omi and Howard Winant (1986) put it, to create "collective identity by offering their adherents a different view of themselves and their world; different, that is, from the worldview and self-concepts offered by the established social order" (p. 93). Multicultural education's attempts to instill in children pride in their own facial heritage were a part of this larger task of creating new collective identities that emphasize strength and pride.

The social movements were directed toward equalizing power and legal status among racial and gender groups. Omi and Winant point out that "The modern civil rights movement sought not to survive racial oppression, but to overthrow it" (p. 94). Multicultural education's emphasis on cultural pluralism was an articulation of this vision of equality in power and rights among racial groups without resorting to separatism. Multicultural education's attempts to incorporate groups of color into curricula were part of larger attempts to make social institutions more accessible to and inclusive of Americans of color; the Brown decision and the Civil Rights Act of 1964 had opened the doors of White schools to children of color, but the histories and cultures of groups of color were still excluded.

Multicultural education workshops for teachers during the late 1960s and early 1970s conveyed the militancy of the broader social movements by dealing directly with White racism and trying to have teachers own and admit their own participation in and benefits from a racist system. Needless to say, such workshops often were not very popular among White teachers.

In the late 1970s and 1980s the political climate shifted. Omi and Winant describe the shift: "For the first time in a sustained and programmatic way, setbacks in the domestic economy and U.S. reversals on the international level were 'explained' by attacking the liberal interventionist state" (p. 110). The civil rights movement had succeeded in placing race on the national political agenda and in attaining popular support for the idea (or at least the phrase) of racial equality. However, the right, which had suffered ideological losses during the 1960s, quickly began to rearticulate the nation's racial ideology. Omi and Winant describe this rearticulated vision: "With the exception of some on the far right, the racial reaction which has developed in the last two decades claims to favor racial equality. Its vision is that of a 'colorblind' society where racial considerations are never entertained" (p. 114). Its vision is also that of an individualistic society; "Racial discrimination and racial equality – in the neoconservative model – are problems to be confronted ONLY at an individual level, once legal systems of discrimination such as DE JURE segregation have been eliminated" (Omi & Winant, 1986, p. 129).

The left has lost considerable visibility and momentum, and some segments of the left have shifted strategies toward working within the system. Carlos Munoz (1987), for example, describes the shift in Chicano politics "that took place during the 1970s from a politics of militant protest to a politics focused on the electoral process and the two-party system" (p. 43). Manning Marable (1987) describes rifts within the Black community, concluding that, "The absence of a coherent Black left program and strategy, and the contradictory and sometimes antagonistic relationship between Black elected officials and their constituents, has created a political vacuum within Black America" (pp. 11–12).

To White America, the absence of mass protest, the presence of a small number of Black, Hispanic, and Asian women and men as well as White women in new positions (e.g., administrative jobs), and passage of civil rights laws all suggest that inequalities of the past have been remedied. This is quite false, of course; the persistence of poverty and discrimination among historically disenfranchised groups is well documented. However, mainstream White America today is well versed in the right's rearticulation of a racial ideology, and is fairly ignorant of or indifferent to limitations to gains made by racial minority groups and women during the past 25 years.

Within this context, many who are relatively new to multicultural education do not see it as directly connected with political struggle. Rather, like McCarthy and Olneck, they tend to see it as a means of reducing prejudice and stereotyping among individuals – as an attempt to learn to overlook differences in an effort to allow Americans of color to "progress" in the historic manner of White ethnic groups. This is not what multicultural education has meant to most of its developers and activists, but it is nevertheless a common interpretation. It reflects the fact that the language and recommendations in multicultural education have not changed to take account of changes in the political context.

When Carl Grant and I reviewed literature in the field of multicultural education (see Grant & Sleeter, 1985; Grant, Sleeter, & Anderson, 1986;

Sleeter & Grant, 1987), we expected to find an evolution from less radical to more radical approaches. Instead, we found all five approaches to exist side by side since the early 1970s, with theorists writing most frequently about the Multicultural Education approach and published teaching guides most frequently employing the Human Relations approach. The field as a whole demands changes in race relations today that are no less radical than demands of the 1960s.

What has changed is the manner in which the field is presented to teachers, and especially White teachers. Presentations that exposed teachers to racial anger have given way to more upbeat, practice-oriented approaches. To try to help White teachers understand multicultural concepts and to convince them to implement multicultural education, many educators begin with the concept of ethnicity and ethnic culture, having White teachers examine their own ethnic cultures (e.g., Bennett, 1986). The assumption is that White teachers will see that the needs, feelings, and experiences of racial minority groups are not so very different from their own; this may, however, suggest to them that race is not different from White ethnicity. Teachers are taught to analyze textbooks for bias and to develop curricula that incorporate people of color and women. Teachers are taught TESA (Teacher Expectations and Student Achievement) strategies and increasingly cooperative learning to ensure that all their students are involved in whole-class instruction. Harold Hodgkinson's (1985) analysis of changing demographics is often used to convince teachers of the need to multiculturalize their teaching. What teachers are taking away from such workshops is a set of piecemeal strategies they can add occasionally to what they already do (Sleeter, in press).

State support of multicultural education is another recent change. Increasingly it is becoming a state requirement for teacher certification, at the same time the teaching profession is becoming increasingly White and student populations increasingly of color and of poverty backgrounds. Omi and Winant (1986) point out that "In response to political pressure, state institutions adopt policies of absorption and insulation" (p. 81). Multicultural education is gaining state legitimacy as a part of the preparation of White teachers for culturally diverse classrooms. However, in the process it often becomes rearticulated and depoliticized. White teachers today commonly share McCarthy's and Olneck's perception of multicultural education. They interpret it as a form of individualism, a way of teaching "at-risk" children, and an extension of the ethnicity paradigm which suggests that "though hard work, patience, delayed gratification, etc., blacks [and other groups of color] could carve out their own rightful place in American society" (Omi & Winant, 1986, p. 20).

As we enter the 1990s, the field must develop in ways that are consonant with its original mission: to challenge oppression, and to use schooling as much as possible to help shape a future America that is more equal, democratic, and just, and that does not demand conformity to one cultural norm.

And it must reaffirm its radical and political nature. The following section will outline some directions for developing theory and practice which build on this mission.

Developing Political Resistance through Education

A first task for multicultural education theorists is to articulate more clearly what social changes are desired, and to clarify the relative importance of addressing individual prejudice and stereotyping versus inequality among groups. To what extent do prejudice and stereotyping *cause* inequality, and to what extent are they *manifestations and rationales* for it? There is merit to the criticism that the field focuses too much on stereotyping and individual prejudice and not enough on disparities in the distribution of wealth and power among groups. Most White teachers do not see themselves as oppressed, at least not on the basis of race, and do not think in terms of racial oppression. White educators who equate ethnicity with race miss the profound impact of racism. Their personal response to race is discomfort, which leads them to believe that interpersonal comfort is the main goal of multicultural education. Cultural pluralism becomes harmonious integration in which color is rendered unimportant (Sleeter, in press).

Structuralist theory, on the other hand, provides guidance in putting attitudes into perspective. Structuralist theory holds that attitudes and stereotypes are part of a group's culture, which is created within a context of social and economic relationships. Structural inequalities help to generate attitudes and stereotypes, enabling people to explain the world as they experience it. Lois Weis (1985) explains that:

> Insights are thus deprived of their independence in two ways: (1) existing social and economic structures act partially to shape them; and (2) they are bound back finally into the very structures they are uncovering. . . . While the cultural level is never totally determined by existing economic and social arrangements, it is also never independent from such arrangements. (p. 130)

One cannot change attitudes and perceptions at the cultural level on a large scale, without also changing the structural context in which given attitudes and stereotypes make sense. The field of multicultural education needs to articulate clearly that its goal is equality in the distribution of social resources, rather than simply elimination of stereotyping and prejudice, which structuralist theory holds could not be done anyway without social structural changes.

Attitudes and stereotypes should not simply be disregarded, however, because at the individual level they cause behavior that can reinforce inequality, and to some extent can be changed. For example, research on teacher expectations demonstrates that many teachers treat students somewhat differently on the basis of what they believe about the students, and that differential treatment can create or exacerbate differences in student achievement. One can effect changes in student achievement by teaching teachers specific teaching behaviors that are associated with high teacher expectations (e.g., Anderson, Evertson, & Brophy, 1979). One can make school a more hospitable environment for children by reducing or eliminating name-calling and other expressions of prejudice. But if ultimately multicultural education aims toward redistribution of power and other social resources, then more effort should go into developing strategies for social and institutional change, rather than dwelling on attitude change.

Literature in the social and political sciences provides some guidance for how social changes are brought about. Dennis Wrong (1979), for example, describes characteristics of effective political groups. They have solidarity "based on an awareness by the members of their collective identity as a group and their common commitment to a goal, interest or set of values" (p. 148). Members are aware of their collective conflict with another group; and the group has developed a "social organization specifically designed to promulgate and promote" its interests (p. 149). Those who wield power most successfully learn to develop and use a variety of power bases. David Kipnis (1976) elaborates, drawing on the five power bases described by John French and Bertram Raven (1959): reward power, coercive power, legitimate power, expert power, and referent power. He argues that those who feel powerless tend to use coercive power only, and often violently: this is not necessarily the most effective power base. Power can be mobilized by expanding an individual's or group's power bases, and by learning to judge more effectively when to use which base.

Four additional tasks follow from these theorists which should direct future development of multicultural education. After the first task of articulating more clearly the relationship between social structural changes and attitudes, a second task is delineating exactly who is struggling against whom over what, and developing strategies to promote solidarity and a clear sense of an agenda for social action. Struggles that are racial place members of racial minority groups in opposition with Whites, in general. This raises several problems with which multicultural educators need to grapple more explicitly.

One problem is how (or whether) to develop a collective racial identity among children from a variety of racial and ethnic groups. Identity development has been a problem for individual racial groups because of their own internal diversity. For example, writing about Chicanos, Munoz (1987) observes: "The multicultural, multiracial, regional, generational, and class character of the Chicano people has contributed to the uneven development of political consciousness. Chicano identity has therefore been a central problem in political organizing" (p. 40). It is even much more complex to attempt to bring diverse racial groups together within a common identity, but the result can be a much more powerful collective. Marable (1987) argues that,

> Only with the recognition among the Black left that their political future lies across racial and ethnic boundaries can the level of resistance now evident in the ghettoes hold out any promise for authentic social revolution. Continuing the isolation among different ethnic groups that has characterized the political activism among people of color up to the present will only serve to sustain the hegemony of the rulers whose divide and conquer strategy has effectively isolated Blacks from Hispanics and Asians. (p. 33)

Simplistically we can advocate that we are all part of a rainbow, but exactly what that means needs to be constructed within the context of racial and ethnic identity development today. As Omi and Winant (1986) point out, this is essential for a successful political movement: "Racially based movements have as their most fundamental task the creation of new identities, new racial meanings, new collective subjectivity" (pp. 85–86). Very real ethnic diversities among American groups of color cannot simply be ignored or downplayed, but celebrating differences without attending to the task of coalition-building will not help to mobilize an effective challenge to institutional racism.

An overly simplistic solution that teachers often adopt is to promote a common identity as Americans. However, this obscures the fact that some Americans are struggling against other American people and institutions for emancipation. This leads to the problem of what to do with Whites. Are educators to regard Whites as part of the collective involved in challenging racial oppression, or as the oppressors? This issue rarely is addressed in the literature on multicultural education, and virtually never in the practice of multicultural education. Being White myself, I would suggest that Whites can become involved in a rainbow coalition, but special attention must be directed toward preparing Whites to work with people of color against racism. The usual inclination of Whites is to take charge, and then to redefine the agenda so that it does not threaten their position in society. How to involve or work with White educators and White children is an issue that must be addressed much more explicitly.

The issue of identity and who is struggling against whom over what becomes even more complex when we consider other forms of oppression, such as sexism and classism. As noted above, the term "multicultural education" is usually associated with race and ethnicity, although many educators address additional forms of diversity and oppression. Educators tend to take a stand either to stick with racism only, or to include additional "isms," but the issue itself has not been discussed much in the multicultural education literature, although it is discussed widely in the social science literature. At issue is the extent to which attending to multiple forms of oppression maximizes power or fragments it. As noted above, successfully organized groups have clearly defined membership, a sense of solidarity, and a clearly articulated agenda of concerns.

Some educators argue that multicultural education's assault on racism will be weakened considerably if it attempts to deal simultaneously with additional forms of discrimination. Gay (1983), for example, emphasizes the importance of Black Americans siding with each other against White racism; introducing other forms of oppression such as sexism can only fragment Blacks, as well as other groups of color, and weaken opposition to racism. Julianne Malveaux (1987) points out, "Some Blacks view efforts to place the 'feminization of poverty' in the forefront as an attempt to shift attention from the plight of the Black community. Others view with suspicion the attempts by white women to become spokespersons for the poor" (p. 59). Furthermore, issues are often different for different groups and are sometimes contradictory, which Emily Hicks (1981) terms "nonsynchrony." Failing to discuss these issues in some depth has led many multicultural education practitioners to string "isms" together in an overly simplistic fashion. It is not uncommon, for example, to find White feminist teachers promoting the idea of women aspiring to careers, not considering the fact that women of color have worked for centuries and are struggling for the luxury of staying home.

On the other hand, all people are members simultaneously of at least one racial group and language group, a gender group, a social class group, and other groups based on age, religion, and so forth. To address only one form of diversity forces many people artificially to separate out other loyalties and interests. Johnnella Butler (1989), for example, describes the particular difficulty in which she feels this places many women of color, for whom the "struggle against sexism and racism [and classism] is waged simultaneously" (p. 151). In addition, failure to address more than one form of oppression can fracture a power group, according to some theorists. Marable (1987) argues that Blacks need to deal with class issues as well as racial issues: "The more pervasive problem in contemporary Black politics [as opposed to developing Black capitalism] is that there remains no formation with a working-class base which is capable of articulating a more advanced public policy program in economics, domestic and international politics" (p. 16). Malveaux (1987) argues that it is in White women's interest to become involved in racial issues: 'The political conditions some white women hope to build will be weak and narrow, not strong and empowering, because these women cannot sit down at the negotiating table and say 'I represent women,' since they manifestly do not speak for women of color" (p. 69).

Therefore, some advocate building coalitions to address multiple forms of oppression simultaneously, focusing on oppression broadly rather than the oppression of one group (Grant & Sleeter, 1986b; Schniedewind & Davidson, 1983). The issue then becomes determining which instances of oppression are most worth challenging collectively, how to build coalitions that will work together for common ends, and how to develop group consciousness on the part of members without asking groups composing the coalition to give up their own identities or agendas. Lucius Outlaw (1987) asks "whether there is sufficient commonality in our sufferings and our hopes, in the modes and sources of our oppressions and in the requirements for a social order that would eliminate them, to allow our coming together and forging a concrete universal, a unity in diversity" (p. 121).

A third task is continuing to develop organizational structures that articulate and promote the goals of multicultural education and social movements with which it is connected. Various organizational structures exist within multicultural education, but they tend to be underfunded and loosely organized, in addition, multiple structures exist side by side in many states and communities, separately organizing teacher educators, teachers, and university professors in social sciences. More efforts to communicate among organizations and, where feasible, to coalesce organizational structures would help strengthen grass-roots efforts.

In addition, multicultural education organizational structures need to join with other organizations that are based in social movements. Geoff Whitty (1985) has argued that radical scholarship alone is politically ineffective, and that "interventions within education can be regarded as effectively radical *only when* they have the potential to be linked with similar struggles elsewhere to produce transformative effects" (p. 168, emphasis mine). An example of an organization with which multicultural education organizations could join is the Rainbow Coalition that developed around Jesse Jackson's campaign. Founded in 1986, the Coalition has stated that it is "a new political movement dedicated to healing the nation by implementing a program of human priorities at home and peace and human rights abroad, seeking to achieve social, political and economic justice" (Marable, 1987, p. 9). As it has operated, the movement has embodied the interests of Blacks more than any other group. But it has the potential of being a strong social movement that works on behalf of many oppressed groups. Omi and Winant (1986) write that Jackson's campaign

> sought to weld together groups traditionally marginalized in electoral politics (such as racial minorities, the poor, women, environmentalists, and even the organized left) to consolidate a new political bloc. Thus the Rainbow Coalition recognized that any politics which aspires to majoritarian status in the current period needs to move beyond a purely racially based agenda. (p. 143)

Educators should consider joining with such a national social movement to ensure that our efforts actually connect with and reinforce political work outside education. This is especially important during a time when the connections between multicultural education and other social movements are not obvious to many educators, who then miss its political intent.

A fourth task is to study the politics of social change and translate this into teaching approaches for classroom use. For example, Robert Jiobu (1988) compares the experiences of different ethnic and racial groups in California in order to determine why Japanese Americans there succeeded economically more than other racial and ethnic groups. Based on his study, he rejects common explanations, such as discrimination-prejudice factors, cultural factors (e.g., strong families, stress on education), and human capital factors (years of education). He shows how Japanese Americans in California gained hegemony over an economic arena in agriculture, both horizontally and vertically, which provided a base from which they then were able to deal with White society from a position of strength. This provides a very useful case study from which one can learn how a group can build a power base. What other case studies illustrate principles of successful power-building? What implications do these have for education?

Finally, a fifth task is to systematize insights into educational organizational structures, curriculum, and instruction in a developmental fashion. Teaching guides in multicultural education currently show mainly isolated lessons and occasionally units (Grant, Sleeter, & Anderson, 1986). They rarely address how to work with children over a period of time in order to develop their understanding of oppression. A good exception is *Open Minds to Equality* (Schniedewind & Davidson, 1983), a series of lessons to be used in sequence. Lessons first develop communication and trust among students in the classroom; then cooperative learning lessons build a sense of the collective and skills in teamwork. After that, lessons on institutional discrimination teach children about inequalities and the structures that perpetuate them. Subsequent lessons involve children in examining their school and neighborhood environment for evidence of discrimination. Finally, the last set of lessons help children envision a better society and explore steps they can take collectively to combat discrimination. Multicultural education needs to develop more teaching strategies and materials like this, that are planned to forge the kind of political coalition necessary for social change, with the understanding and sense of a political agenda that is needed.

Plans for schools also need to move beyond the individual classroom. Structures in schools such as tracking, which stratifies children unequally, need to be replaced with different structures. Multicultural educators should define organizational alternatives for schools.

Conclusions

Multicultural education in the United States has many insights and theorists needed to strengthen and lead radical challenges to racism through education. Rather than ignoring or dismissing the field, educators on the left should be working with it. At the same time, multicultural educators need to recognize the impact which its social context has on how the field is understood and interpreted. The social movements of the 1960s have receded; educators and students today who did not participate in them do not necessarily connect multicultural education with social movement. We have today, however, a growing body of scholarship in the social and political sciences that can be used to develop multicultural education. I have outlined here five tasks that would help to strengthen the field. I hope that these tasks are undertaken cooperatively by multicultural education advocates along with other radical educators.

Acknowledgements

I would like to express my appreciation to James Banks, Carl Grant, Kent Koppelman, and Evelyn Reid for their thoughtful and helpful comments on an earlier draft of this paper.

References

Anderson, L. M., Evertson, C. M., & Brophy, J. E. (1979). First-grade Reading Study. *Elementary School Journal, 79,* 193–233.

Apple, M. W. (1982). *Education and Power.* Boston: Ark Paperbacks.

Baker, G. C. (1983). *Planning and Organizing for Multicultural Instruction.* Reading, MA: Addison-Wesley.

Banks, J. A. (1981). *Multiethnic Education: Theory and Practice.* Boston: Allyn & Bacon.

Banks, J. A. (1984). Multicultural Education and its Critics: Britain and the United States. *The New Era, 65,* 58–65.

Bennett, C. I. (1986). *Comprehensive Multicultural Education.* Boston: Allyn & Bacon.

Blassingame, J. E. (Ed.). (1971). *New Perspectives on Black Studies.* Urbana: University of Illinois Press.

Bourdieu, P., & Passeron, J. C. (1977). *Reproduction in Education, Society, and Culture.* Beverly Hills: Sage.

Bowles, S., & Gintis, H. (1976). *Schooling in Capitalist America.* New York: Basic Books.

Broudy, H. S. (1975). Cultural Pluralism: New Wine in Old Bottles. *Educational Leadership, 33,* 173–175.

Bullivant, B. (1986). Towards Radical Multiculturalism: Resolving Tensions in Curriculum and Educational Planning. In S. Modgil et al. (Eds.), *Multicultural education: The interminable debate* (pp. 33–47). London: Falmer Press.

Butler, J. E. (1989). Transforming the Curriculum: Teaching about Women of Color. In J. A. Banks & C.A.M. Banks (Eds.), *Multicultural Education: Issues and Perspectives* (pp. 145–164). Boston Allyn & Bacon.

Colangelo, N., Foxley, C. H., & Dustin, D. (Eds.). (1979). *Multicultural Nonsexist Education: A Human Relations Approach.* Dubuque: Kendall Hunt.

Cole, M. (1986). Teaching and Learning about Racism: A Critique of Multicultural Education in Britain. In S. Modgil et al. (Eds.), *Multicultural Education: The Interminable Debate* (pp. 123–148). London: Falmer Press.

Delpit, L. D. (1988). The Silenced Dialogue: Power and Pedagogy in educating Other People's Children. *Harvard Educational Review, 38,* 280–298.

French, J. R. P., Jr., & Raven, B. (1959). The Bases of Social Power. In D. Cartwright (Ed.), *Studies in Social Power* (pp. 150–167). Ann Arbor: University of Michigan Institute for Social Research.

Gay, G. (1983). Multiethnic Education: Historical Developments and Future Prospects. *Phi Delta Kappan, 64,* 560–563.

Giroux, H. A. (1983). *Theory and Resistance in Education.* South Hadley, MA: Bergin & Garvey.

Giroux H. A. (1988). *Teachers as Intellectuals.* South Hadley, MA: Bergin & Garvey.

Gollnick, D. M. (1980). Multicultural Education. *Viewpoints in Teaching and Learning, 56,* 1–17.

Grant, C. A., & Sleeter, C. E. (1985). The Literature on Multicultural Education: Review and Analysis. *Educational Review, 37*, 97–118.

Grant, C. A., & Sleeter, C. E. (1986a). Educational Equity, Education that is Multicultural and Social Reconstructionist. *Journal of Educational Equity and Leadership, 6*, 105–118.

Grant, C. A., & Sleeter, C. E. (1986b). Race, Class and Gender: An Argument for Integrative Analysis. *Review of Educational Research, 56*, 195–211.

Grant, C. A., Sleeter, C. E., & Anderson, J. E. (1986). The Literature on Multicultural Education: Review and Analysis, Part II. *Educational Studies, 12*, 47–71.

Green, A. (1982). In Defense of Anti-racist Teaching: A Reply to Recent Critiques of Multicultural Education. *Multiracial Education, 10*, 19–35.

Hicks, E. (1981). Cultural Marxism: Non-synchrony and Feminist Practice. In L. Sargent (Ed.), *Women and Revolution* (pp. 219–238). Boston: South End Press.

Hirsch, E. D., Jr. (1988). *Cultural Literacy: What every American Needs to Know*. New York: Random House, Vintage Books.

Hodgkinson, H. L. (1985). *All One System: Demographics of Education – Kindergarten through Graduate School*. Washington, DC: Institute for Educational Leadership.

Jiobu, R. M. (1988). *Ethnicity and Assimilation*. Albany: SUNY Press.

Jordan, C. (1985). Translating Culture: From Ethnographic Information to Educational Program. *Anthropology and Education Quarterly, 16*, 105–123.

Kipnis, D. (1976). *The Powerholders*. Chicago: University of Chicago Press.

Malveaux, J. (1987). The Political Economy of Black Women. In M. Davis, M. Marable, F. Pfeil, & M. Sprinker (Eds.), *The Year Left 2* (pp. 52–72). London: Verso.

Marable, M. (1987). The Contradictory Contours of Black Political Culture. In M. Davis, M. Marable, F. Pfeil, & M. Sprinker (Eds.), *The Year Left 2* (pp. 1–17). London: Verso.

McCarthy, C. (1988). Rethinking Liberal and Radical Perspectives on Racial Inequality in Schooling: Making the Case for Nonsynchrony. *Harvard Educational Review, 58*, 265–279.

Munoz, C., Jr. (1987). Chicano Politics: The Current Conjuncture. In M. Davis, M. Marable, F. Pfeil, & M. Sprinker (Eds.), *The Year left 2* (pp. 35–51). London: Verso.

Olneck, M. (1990). The Recurring Dream: Symbolism and Ideology in Intercultural and Multicultural Education. *American Journal of Education, 98*(2), 147–174.

Omi, M., & Winant, H. (1986). *Racial Formation in the United States*. New York: Routledge & Kegan Paul.

Outlaw, L. (1987). On Race and Class, or, on the Prospects of "Rainbow Socialism." In M. Davis, M. Marable, F. Pfeil, & M. Sprinker (Eds.), *The Year left 2* (pp. 106–121). London: Verso.

Ramirez, M., & Castaneda, A. (1974). *Cultural Democracy, Bicognitive Development, and Education*. New York: Academic Press.

Schniedewind, N., & Davidson, E. (1983). *Open Minds to Equality*. Englewood Cliffs, NJ: Prentice-Hall.

Shade, B. (1982). Afro-American Cognitive Style: A Variable in School Success? *Review of Educational Research, 52*, 219–244.

Sleeter, C. E. (in press). *Keepers of the American Dream*. Basingstoke, Britain: Falmer Press.

Sleeter, C. E., & Grant, C. A. (1987). An Analysis of Multicultural Education in the United States. *Harvard Educational Review, 57*, 421–444.

Sleeter, C. E., & Grant, C. A. (1988). *Making Choices for Multicultural Education*. Columbus: Merrill.

Spender, D. (Ed.). (1981). *Men's Studies Modified: The Impact of Feminism on the Academic Disciplines*. New York: Pergamon Press.

Suzuki, B. H. (1984). Curriculum Transformation for Multicultural Education. *Education and Urban Society, 16*, 294–322.

Tiedt, P., & Teidt, I. (1986). *Multicultural Teaching: A Handbook of Activities, Information and Resources*. Boston: Allyn & Bacon.

Troyna, B. (Ed.). (1987). *Racial Inequality in Education*. London: Tavistock.

Trueba, H. (1988). Culturally based Explanations of Minority Students Academic Achievement. *Anthropology and Education Quarterly, 19*, 270–281.

Weis, L. (1985). *Between Two Worlds*. Boston: Routledge & Kegan Paul.

Wexler, P. (1982). Structure, Text, and Subject: A Critical Sociology of School Knowledge. In M. W. Apple (Ed.), *Cultural and Economic Reproduction in Education: Essays on Class, Ideology and the State* (pp. 275–303). Boston: Routledge & Kegan Paul.

Whitty, G. (1985). *Sociology and School Knowledge*. London: Methuen.

Wrong, D. H. (1979). *Power: Its Forms, Bases and Uses*. South Hampton, Britain: Basil Blackwell.

85

Why Doesn't This Feel Empowering? Working through the Repressive Myths of Critical Pedagogy

Elizabeth Ellsworth

In the spring of 1988, the University of Wisconsin-Madison was the focal point of a community-wide crisis provoked by the increased visibility of racist acts and structures on campus and within the Madison community. During the preceding year, the FIJI fraternity had been suspended for portraying racially demeaning stereotypes at a "Fiji Island party," including a 15-foot-high cutout of a "Fiji native," a dark-skinned caricature with a bone through its nose. On December 1, 1987, the Minority Affairs Steering Committee released a report, initiated and researched by students, documenting the university's failure to address institutional racism and the experiences of marginalization of students of color on campus. The report called for the appointment of a person of color to the position of vice chancellor of ethnic minority affairs/affirmative action; effective strategies to recruit and retain students of color, faculty, and staff; establishment of a multicultural center; implementation of a mandatory six-credit ethnic studies requirement; revamping racial and sexual harassment grievance procedures; and initiation of a cultural and racial orientation program for all students. The release of the report and the university's responses to it and to additional incidents such as the FIJI fraternity party have become the focus of ongoing campus and community-wide debates, demonstrations, and organizing efforts.

In January, 1988, partly in response to this situation, I facilitated a special topics course at UW-Madison called "Media and Anti-Racist Pedagogies," Curriculum and Instruction 607, known as C&I 607. In this article, I will offer an interpretation of C&I 607's interventions against campus racism and traditional educational forms at the university. I will then use that interpretation to support a critique of current discourses on critical pedagogy".[1]

Source: *Harvard Educational Review*, 59(3) (1989): 297–324.

The literature on critical pedagogy represents attempts by educational researchers to theorize and operationalize pedagogical challenges to oppressive social formations. White the attempts I am concerned with here share fundamental assumptions and goals, their different emphases are reflected in the variety of labels given to them, such as "critical pedagogy," "pedagogy of critique and possibility," "pedagogy of student voice," "pedagogy of empowerment," "radical pedagogy," "pedagogy for radical democracy," and "pedagogy of possibility."[2]

I want to argue, on the basis of my interpretation of C&I 607, that key assumptions, goals, and pedagogical practices fundamental to the literature on critical pedagogy – namely, "empowerment," "student voice,," "dialogue," and even the term "critical" – are repressive myths that perpetuate relations of domination. By this I mean that when participants in our class attempted to put into practice prescriptions offered in the literature concerning empowerment, student voice, and dialogue, we produced results that were not only unhelpful, but actually exacerbated the very conditions we were trying to work against, including Eurocentrism, racism, sexism, classism, and "banking education." To the extent that our efforts to put discourses of critical pedagogy into practice led us to reproduce relations of domination in our classroom, these discourses were "working through" us in repressive ways, and had themselves become vehicles of repression. To the extent that we disengaged ourselves from those aspects and moved in another direction, we "worked through" and out of the literature's highly abstract language ("myths") of who we "should" be and what "should" be happening in our classroom, and into classroom practices that were context specific and seemed to be much more responsive to our own understandings of our social identities and situations.

This article concludes by addressing the implications of the classroom practices we constructed in response to racism in the university's curriculum, pedagogy, and everyday life. Specifically, it challenges educational scholars who situate themselves within the field of critical pedagogy to come to grips with the fundamental issues this work has raised – especially the question, What diversity do we silence in the name of "liberatory" pedagogy?

Pedagogy and Political Interventions on Campus

The nation-wide eruption in 1987–1988 of racist violence in communities and on campuses, including the University of Wisconsin-Madison, pervaded the context in which Curriculum and Instruction 607, "Media and Anti-Racist Pedagogies" was planned and facilitated. The increased visibility of racism in Madison was also partly due to the UW Minority Student Coalition's successful documentation of the UW system's resistance to and its failure to address monoculturalism in the curriculum, to recruit and retain students and professors of color, and to alleviate the campus culture's insensitivity or hostility to cultural and racial diversity.

At the time that I began to construct a description of C&I 607, students of color had documented the extent of their racial harassment and alienation on campus. Donna Shalala, the newly appointed, feminist chancellor of UW-Madison, had invited faculty and campus groups to take their own initiatives against racism on campus. I had just served on a university committee investigating an incident of racial harassment against one of my students, I wanted to design a course in media and pedagogy that would not only work to clarify the structures of institutional racism underlying university practices and its culture in spring 1988, but that would also use that understanding to plan and carry out a political intervention within that formation. This class would not debate whether or not racist structures and practices were operating at the university; rather, it would investigate *how* they operated, with what effects and contradictions – and where they were vulnerable to political opposition. The course concluded with public interventions on campus, which I will describe later. For my purposes here, the most important interruption of existing power relations within the university consisted of transforming business-as-usual – that is, prevailing social relations – in a university classroom.

Before the spring of 1988, I had used the language of critical pedagogy in course descriptions and with students. For example, syllabi in the video production for education courses stated that goals of the courses included the production of "socially responsible" videotapes, the fostering of "critical production" practices and "critical reception and analysis" of educational videotapes. Syllabi in the media criticism courses stated that we would focus on "critical media use and analysis in the classroom" and the potential of media in "critical education." Students often asked what was meant by critical – critical of what, from what position, to what end? – and I referred them to answers provided in the literature. For example, critical pedagogy supported classroom analysis and rejection of oppression, injustice, inequality, silencing of marginalized voices, and authoritarian social structures.[3] Its critique was launched from the position of the "radical" educator who recognizes and helps students to recognize and name injustice, who empowers students to act against their own and others' oppressions (including oppressive school structures), who criticizes and transforms her or his own understanding in response to the understandings of students.[4] The goal of critical pedagogy was a critical democracy, individual freedom, social justice, and social change – a revitalized public sphere characterized by citizens capable of confronting public issues critically through ongoing forms of public debate and social action.[5] Students would be empowered by social identities that affirmed their race, class, and gender positions, and provided the basis for moral deliberation and social action.[6]

The classroom practices of critical educators may in fact engage with actual, historically specific struggles, such as those between students of color and university administrators. But the overwhelming majority of academic articles appearing in major educational journals, although apparently based on actual practices, rarely locate theoretical constructs within them. In my review of the literature I found, instead, that educational researchers who invoke concepts of critical pedagogy consistently strip discussions of classroom practices of historical context and political position. What remains are the definitions cited above, which operate at a high level of abstraction. I found this language more appropriate (yet hardly more helpful) for philosophical debates about the highly problematic concepts of freedom, justice, democracy, and "universal" values than for thinking through and planning classroom practices to support the political agenda of C&I 607.

Given the explicit antiracist agenda of the course, I realized that even naming C&I 607 raised complex issues. To describe the course as, "Media and Critical Pedagogy," or "Media, Racism, and Critical Pedagogy," for example, would be to hide the politics of the course, making them invisible to the very students I was trying to attract and work with – namely, students committed or open to working against racism. I wanted to avoid colluding with many academic writers in the widespread use of code words such as "critical," which hide the actual political agendas I assume such writers share with me – namely, antiracism, antisexism, anti-elitism, anti-heterosexism, anti-ableism, anticlassism, and anti-neoconscrvatism.

I say "assume" because, white the literature on critical pedagogy charges the teacher with helping students to "identify and choose between sufficiently articulated and reasonably distinct moral positions,"[7] it offers only the most abstract, decontextualized criteria for choosing one position over others, criteria such as "reconstructive action"[8] or "radical democracy and social justice."[9] To reject the term "critical pedagogy" and name the course "Media and Anti-Racist Pedagogies" was to assert that students and faculty at UW-Madison in the spring of 1988 were faced with ethical dilemmas that called for political action. While a variety of "moral assessments" and political positions existed about the situation on campus, this course would attempt to construct a classroom practice that would act *on the side* of antiracism. I wanted to be accountable for naming the political agenda behind this particular course's critical pedagogy.

Thinking through the ways in which our class's activities could be understood as political was important, because white the literature states implicitly or explicitly that critical pedagogy is political, there have been no sustained research attempts to explore whether or how the practices it prescribes actually alter specific power relations outside or inside schools. Further, when educational researchers advocating critical pedagogy fail to provide a clear statement of their political agendas, the effect is to hide the fact that as critical pedagogues, they are in fact seeking to appropriate public resources (classrooms, school supplies, teacher/professor salaries, academic requirements and degrees) to further various "progressive" political agendas that they believe to be for the public good – and therefore deserving of public resources.

But however good the reasons for choosing the strategy of subverting repressive school structures from within, it has necessitated the use of code words such as "critical," "social change," "revitalized public sphere," and a posture of invisibility. As a result, the critical education "movement" has failed to develop a clear articulation of the need for its existence, its goals, priorities, risks, or potentials. As Liston and Zeichner argue, debate within the critical education movement itself over what constitutes a radical or critical pedagogy is sorely needed.[10]

By prescribing moral deliberation, engagement in the full range of views present, and critical reflection, the literature on critical pedagogy implies that students and teachers can and should engage each other in the classroom as fully rational subjects. According to Valerie Walkerdinc, schools have participated in producing "self-regulating" individuals by developing in students capacities for engaging in rational argument. Rational argument has operated in ways that set up as its opposite an irrational Other, which has been understood historically as the province of women and other exotic Others. In schools, rational deliberation, reflection, and consideration of all viewpoints has become a vehicle for regulating conflict and the power to speak, for transforming "conflict into rational argument by means of universalized capacities for language and reason."[11] But students and professor entered C&I 607 with investments of privilege and struggle already made in favor of some ethical and political positions concerning racism and against other positions. The context in which this course was developed high-lighted that fact. The demands that the Minority Student Coalition delivered to the administration were not written in the spirit of engaging in rationalist, analytical debates with those holding other positions. In a racist society and its institutions, such debate has not and cannot be "public" or "democratic" in the sense of including the voices of all affected parties and affording them equal weight and legitimacy. Nor can such debate be free of conscious and unconscious concealment of interests, or assertion of interests which some participants hold as non-negotiable no matter what arguments are presented.

As Barbara Christian has written, ". . . what I write and how I write is done in order to save my own life. And I mean that literally. For me literature is a way of knowing that I am not hallucinating, that whatever I feel/ know *is*."[12] Christian is an African-American woman writing about the literature of African-American women, but her words are relevant to the issues raised by the context of C&I 607. I understood the words written by the Minority Student Coalition and spoken by other students/professors of difference[13] on campus to have a similar function as a reality check for survival. It is inappropriate to respond to such words by subjecting them to rationalist debates about their validity. Words spoken for survival come already validated in a radically different arena of proof and carry no option or luxury of choice. (This is not to say, however, that the positions of students of color, or of any other group, were to be taken up unproblematically – an issue I will address below.)

I drafted a syllabus and circulated it for suggestions and revisions to students I knew to be involved in the Minority Student Coalition, and to colleagues who shared my concerns. The goal of "Media and Anti-Racist Pedagogies," as stated in the revised syllabus, was to define, organize, carry out, and analyze an educational initiative on campus that would win semiotic space for the marginalized discourses of students against racism. Campus activists were defining these discourses and making them available to other groups, including the class, through documents, demonstrations, discussions, and press conferences.

The syllabus also listed the following assumptions underlying the course:

1. Students who want to acquire knowledge of existing educational media theory and criticism for the purpose of guiding their own educational practice can best do so in a learning situation that interrelates theory with concrete attempts at using media for education.
2. Current situations of racial and sexual harassment and elitism on campus and in the curriculum demand meaningful responses from both students and faculty, and responses can be designed in a way that accomplishes both academic and political goals.
3. Often, the term "critical education" has been used to imply, but also to hide positions and goals of anti-racism, anti-classism, anti-sexism, and so forth. Defining this course as one that explores the possibility of using media to construct anti-racist pedagogies asserts that these are legitimate and imperative goals for educators.
4. What counts as an appropriate use of media for an anti-racist pedagogy cannot be specified outside of the contexts of actual educational situations; therefore student work on this issue should be connected to concrete initiatives in actual situations.
5. Any anti-racist pedagogy must be defined through an awareness of the ways in which oppressive structures are the result of *intersections* between racist, clas-sist, sexist, ableist, and other oppressive dynamics.
6. Everyone who has grown up in a racist culture has to work at unlearning racism – we will make mistakes in this class, but they will be made in the context of our struggle to come to grips with racism.

Naming the political agenda of the course, to the extent that I did, seemed relatively easy. I was in the fourth year of a tenure-track position in my department, and felt that I had "permission" from colleagues to pursue the line of research and practice but of which this course had clearly grown. The administration's response to the crisis on campus gave further "permission" for attempts to alleviate racism in the institution. However, the directions in which I should proceed became less clear once the class was underway. As I began to live out and interpret the consequences of how discourses of "critical reflection," "empowerment," "student voice," and "dialogue" had influenced my conceptualization of the goals of the course and my ability to make sense of my experiences in the class, I found myself struggling against (struggling to unlearn) key assumptions and assertions of current literature on critical pedagogy, and straining to recognize, name, and come to grips with crucial issues of classroom practice that critical pedagogy cannot or will not address.

From Critical Rationalism to the Politics of Partial Narratives

The students enrolled in "Media and Anti-Racist Pedagogies" included Asian American, Chicano/a, Jewish, Puerto Rican, and Anglo-European men and women from the United States; and Asian, African, Icelandic, and Canadian international students. It was evident after the first class meeting that all of us agreed, but with different understandings and agendas, that racism was a problem on campus that required political action. The effects of the diverse social positions and political ideologies of the students enrolled, my own position and experiences as a woman and a feminist, and the effects of the course's context on the form and content of our early class discussions quickly threw the rationalist assumptions underlying critical pedagogy into question.

These rationalist assumptions have led to the following goals: the teaching of analytic and critical skills for judging the truth and merit of propositions, and the interrogation and selective appropriation of potentially transformative moments in the dominant culture.[14] As long as educators define pedagogy against oppressive formations in these ways the role of the critical pedagogue will be to guarantee that the foundation for classroom interaction is reason. In other words, the critical pedagogue is one who enforces the rules of reason in the classroom – "a series of rules of thought that any ideal rational person might adopt if his/her purpose was to achieve propositions of universal validity."[15] Under these conditions, and given the coded nature of the political agenda of critical pedagogy, only one "political" gesture appears to be available to the critical pedagogue. S/he can ensure that students are given the chance to arrive logically at the "universally valid proposition" underlying the discourse of critical pedagogy – namely, that all people have a right to freedom from oppression guaranteed by the democratic social contract, and that in the classroom, this proposition be given equal time vis-à-vis other "sufficiently articulated and reasonably distinct moral positions."[16]

Yet educators who have constructed classroom practices dependent upon analytic critical judgment can no longer regard the enforcement of rationalism as a self-evident political act against relations of domination. Literary criticism, cultural studies, post-structuralism, feminist studies, comparative studies, and media studies have by now amassed overwhelming evidence of the extent to which the myths of the ideal rational person and the "universality" of propositions have been oppressive to those who are not European, White, male, middle class, Christian, able-bodied, thin, and heterosexual.[17]

Writings by many literary and cultural critics, both women of color and White women who are concerned with explaining the intersections and inter-actions among relations of racism, colonialism, sexism, and so forth, are now employing, either implicitly or explicitly, concepts and analytical methods that could be called feminist poststructuralism[18] While post-structuralism, like rationalism, is a tool that can be used to dominate, it has also facilitated a devastating critique of the violence of rationalism against its Others. It has demonstrated that as a discursive practice, rationalism's regulated and systematic use of elements of language constitutes rational competence "as a series of exclusions – of women, people of color, of nature as historical agent, of the true value of art."[19] In contrast, poststructuralist thought is not bound to reason, but "to discourse, literally narratives about the world that are admittedly *partial*. Indeed, one of the crucial features of discourse is the intimate tie between knowledge and interest, the latter being understood as a 'standpoint' from which to grasp 'reality.'"[20]

The literature on critical pedagogy implies that the claims made by docu-ments, demonstrations, press conferences, and classroom discussions of students of color and White students against racism could rightfully be taken up in the classroom and subjected to rational deliberation over their truth in light of competing claims. But this would force students to subject themselves to the logics of rationalism and scientism which have been predicated on and made possible through the exclusion of socially constructed irrational Others – women, people of color, nature, aesthetics. As Audre Lorde writes, "The master's tools will never dismantle the master's house,"[21] and to call on students of color to justify and explicate their claims in terms of the master's tools – tools such as rationalism, fashioned precisely to perpetuate their ex-clusion – colludes with the oppressor in keeping "the oppressed occupied with the master's concerns,"[22] As Barbara Christian describes it:

> the literature of people who are not in power has always been in danger of extinction or cooptation, not because we do not theorize, but because what we can even imagine, far less who we can reach, is constantly limited by societal structures. For me, literary criticism is promotion as well as understanding, a response to the writer to whom there is oflen no response, to folk who need the writing as much as they need anything. I know, from literary history, that writing disappears unless there is a response to it. Because I write about writers who are now writing, I hope to help ensure that their tradition has continuity and survives.[23]

In contrast to the enforcement of rational deliberation, but like Chris-tian's promotion and response, my role in C&I 607 would be to interrupt institutional limits on how much time and energy students of color, White students, and professors against racism could spend on elaborating their positions and playing them out to the point where internal contradictions and effects on the positions of other social groups could become evident and subject to self-analysis.

With Barbara Christian, I saw the necessity to take the voices of students and professors of difference at their word – as "valid" – but not without response,[24] Students' and my own narratives about experiences of racism, ableism, elitism, fat oppression, sexism, anti-Semitism, hcterosexism, and so on are partial – partial in the sense that they are unfinished, imperfect, limited; and partial in the sense that they project the interests of "one side" over others. Because those voices are partial and partisan, they must be made problematic, but not because they have broken the rules of thought of the ideal rational person by grounding their knowledge in immediate emotional, social, and psychic experiences of oppression,[25] or are somehow lacking or too narrowly circumscribed.[26] Rather, they must be critiqued because they hold implications for other social movements and their struggles for self-definition. This assertion carries important implications for the "goal" of classroom practices against oppressive formations, which I will address later.

Have We Got a Theory for You![27]

As educators who claim to be dedicated to ending oppression, critical pedagogues have acknowledged the socially constructed and legitimated authority that teachers/professors hold over students.[28] Yet theorists of critical pedagogy have failed to launch any meaningful analysis of or program for reformulating the institutionalized power imbalances between themselves and their students, or of the essentially paternalistic project of education itself. In the absence of such an analysis and program, their efforts are limited to trying to transform negative effects of power imbalances within the classroom into positive ones. Strategies such as student empowerment and dialogue give the illusion of equality white in fact leaving the authoritarian nature of the teacher/student relationship intact.

"Empowerment" is a key concept in this approach, which treats the symptoms but leaves the disease unnamed and untouched. Critical pedagogies employing this strategy prescribe various theoretical and practical means for sharing, giving, or redistributing power to students, For example, some authors challenge teachers to reject the vision of education as inculcation of students by the more powerful teacher. In its place, they urge teachers to accept the possibility of education through "reflective examination" of the plurality of moral positions before the presumably rational teacher and Students.[29] Here, the goal is to give students the analytical skills they need to make them as free, rational, and objective as teachers supposedly are to choose positions on their objective merits. I have already argued that in a classroom in which "empowerment" is made dependent on rationalism, those perspectives that would question the political interests (sexism, racism, colonialism, for example) expressed and guaranteed by rationalism would be rejected as "irrational" (biased, partial).'

A seeond strategy is to make the teacher more like the student by redefining the teacher as learner of the student's reality and knowledge. For example, in their discussion of the politics of dialogic teaching and epistcmology, Shor and Freire suggest that "the teacher selecting the objects of study knows them *better* than the students as the course begins, but the teacher *re-learns* the objects through studying them with their students."[30] The literature explores only one reason for expecting the teacher to "*re-learn*" an object of study through the student's less adequate understanding, and that is to enable the teacher to devise more effective strategies for bringing the student "up" to the teacher's level of understanding. Giroux, for example, argues for a pedagogy that "is attentive to the histories, dreams, and experiences that . . . students bring to school. It is only by beginning with these subjective forms that critical educators can develop a language and set of practices"[31] that can successfully mediate differences between student understandings and teacher understandings in "pedagogically progressive" ways.[32] In this example, Giroux leaves the implied superiority of the teacher's understanding and the undefined "progressiveness" of this type of pedagogy unproblematized and untheorized.

A third strategy is to acknowledge the "directiveness"[33] or "authoritarianism"[34] of education as inevitable, and judge particular power imbalances between teacher and student to be tolerable or intolerable depending upon "towards what and with whom [they are] directive,"[35] "Acceptable" imbalances are those in which authority serves "common human interests by sharing information, promoting open and informed discussion, and maintaining itself only through the respect and trust of those who grant the authority."[36] In such cases, authority becomes "emancipatory authority," a kind of teaching in which teachers would make explicit and available for rationalist debate "the political and moral referents for authority they assume in teaching particular forms of knowledge, in taking stands against forms of oppression, and in treating students as if they ought also to be concerned about social justice and political action."[37] Here, the question of "empowerment for what" becomes the final arbiter of a teacher's use or misuse of authority.

But critical pedagogues consistently answer the question of "empowerment for what?" in ahistorical and depoliticized abstractions. These include empowerment for "human betterment,"[38] for expanding "the range of possible social identities people may become,"[39] and "making one's self present as part of a moral and political project that links production of meaning to the possibility for human agency, democratic community, and transformative social action."[40] As a result, student empowerment has been defined in the broadest possible humanist terms, and becomes a "capacity to act effectively" in a way that fails to challenge any identifiable social or political position, institution, or group.

The contortions of logic and rhetoric that characterize these attempts to define "empowerment" testify to the failure of critical educators to come to terms with the essentially paternalistic project of traditional education.

"Emancipatory authority"[41] is one such contortion, for it implies the presence of or potential for an emancipated teacher. Indeed, it asserts that teachers "can link knowledge to power by bringing to light and teaching the subjugated histories, experiences, stories, and accounts of those who suffer and struggle."[42] Yet I cannot unproblematically bring subjugated knowledges to light when I am not free of my own learned racism, fat oppression, classism, ableism, or sexism. No teacher is free of these learned and internalized oppressions. Nor are accounts of one group's suffering and struggle immune from reproducing narratives oppressive to another's – the racism of the Women's Movement in the United States is one example.

As I argued above, "emancipatory authority" also implies, according to Shor and Freire, a teacher who knows the object of study "better" than do the students. Yet I did not understand racism better than my students did, especially those students of color coming into class after six months (or more) of campus activism and whole lives of experience and struggle against racism – nor could I ever hope to. My experiences with and access to multiple and sophisticated strategies for interpreting and interrupting sexism (in White middle-class contexts) do not provide me with a ready-made analysis of or language for understanding my own implications in racist structures. My understanding and experience of racism will always be constrained by my white skin and middle-class privilege. Indeed, it is impossible for anyone to be free from these oppressive formations at this historical moment. Furthermore, while I had the institutional power and authority in the classroom to enforce "reflective examination" of the plurality of moral and political positions before us in a way that supposedly gave my own assessments equal weight with those of students, in fact my institutional role as professor would always weight my statements differently from those of students.

Given my own history of white-skin, middle-class, able-bodied, thin privilege and my institutionally granted power, it made more sense to see my task as one of redefining "critical pedagogy" so that it did not need utopian moments of "democracy," "equality," "justice," or "emancipated" teachers – moments that are unattainable (and ultimately undesirable, because they are always predicated on the interests of those who are in the 'position to define utopian projects). A preferable goal seemed to be to become capable of a sustained encounter with currently oppressive formations and power relations that refuse to be theorized away or fully transcended in a utopian resolution – and to enter into the encounter in a way that owned up to my own implications in those formations and was capable of changing my own relation to and investments in those formations.

The Repressive Myth of the Silent Other

At first glance, the concept of "student voice" seemed to offer a pedagogical strategy in this direction. This concept has become highly visible and influential in current discussions of curriculum and teaching, as evidenced by its appearance in the titles of numerous presentations at the 1989 American Educational Research Association Convention. Within current discourses on teaching, it functions to efface the contradiction between the emancipatory project of critical pedagogy and the hierarchical relation between teachers and students. In other words, it is a strategy for negotiating between the directiveness of dominant educational relationships and the political commitment to make students autonomous of those relationships (how does a teacher "make" students autonomous without directing them?). The discourse on student voice sees the student as "empowered" when the teacher "helps" students to express their subjugated knowledges.[43] The targets of this strategy are students from disadvantaged and subordinated social class, racial, ethnic, and gender groups – or alienated middle-class students without access to skills of critical analysis, whose voices have been silenced or distorted by oppressive cultural and educational formations. By speaking, in their "authentic voices," students are seen to make themselves visible and define themselves as authors of their own world. Such self-definition presumably gives students an identity and political position from which to act as agents of social change,[44] Thus, while it is true that the teacher is directive, the student's own daily life experiences of oppression chart her/his path toward self-definition and agency. The task of the critical educator thus becomes "finding ways of working with students that enable the full expression of multiple 'voices' engaged in dialogic encounter,"[45] encouraging students of different race, class, and gender positions to speak in self-affirming ways about their experiences and how they have been mediated by their own social positions and those of others.

Within feminist discourses seeking to provide both a place and power for women to speak, "voice" and "speech" have become commonplace as metaphors for women's feminist self-definitions – but with meanings and effects quite different from those implied by discourses of critical pedagogy. Within feminist movements, women's voices and speech are conceptualized in terms of self-definitions that are oppositional to those definitions of women constructed by others, usually to serve interests and contexts that subordinate women to men. But white critical educators acknowledge the existence of unequal power relations in classrooms, they have made no systematic examination of the barriers that this imbalance throws up to the kind of student expression and dialogue they prescribe.

The concept of critical pedagogy assumes a commitment on the part of the professor/teacher toward ending the student's oppression. Yet the literature offers no sustained attempt to problematize this stance and confront the likelihood that the professor brings to social movements (including critical pedagogy) interests of her or his own race, class, ethnicity, gender, and other positions. S/he does not play the role of disinterested mediator on the side of the oppressed group.[46] As an Anglo, middle-class professor in C&I 607, I could not unproblematically "help" a student of color ia find her/his authentic voice as a student of color. I could not unproblematically "affiliate" with the social groups my students represent and interpret their experience to them. In fact, I brought to the classroom privileges and interests that were put at risk in fundamental ways by the demands and defiances of student voices. I brought a social subjectivity that has been constructed in such a way that I have not and can never participate unproblematically in the collective process of self-definition, naming of oppression, and struggles for visibility in the face of marginalization engaged in by students whose class, race, gender, and other positions I do not share. Critical pedagogues are always implicated in the very structures they are trying to change.

Although the literature recognizes that teachers have much to learn from their students' experiences, it does not address the ways in which there are things that I as professor could *never know* about the experiences, oppressions, and understandings of other participants in the class. This situation makes it impossible for any single voice in the classroom – including that of the professor – to assume the position of center or origin of knowledge or authority, of having privileged access to authentic experience or appropriate language. A recognition, contrary to all Western ways of knowing and speaking, that all knowings are partial, that there are fundamental things each of us cannot know – a situation alleviated only in part by the pooling of partial, socially constructed knowledges in classrooms – demands a fundamental retheorizing of "education" and "pedagogy," an issue I will begin to address below.

When educational researchers writing about critical pedagogy fail to examine the implications of the gendered, raced, and classed teacher and student for the theory of critical pedagogy, they reproduce, by default, the category of generic "critical teacher" – a specific form of the generic human that underlies classical liberal thought. Like the generic human, the generic critical teacher is not, of course, generic at all. Rather, the term defines a discursive category predicated on the current mythical norm, namely: young, White, Christian, middle-class, heterosexual, able-bodied, thin, rational man. Gender, race, class, and other differences become only variations on or additions to the generic human – "underneath, we are all the same."[47] But voices of students and professors of difference solicited by critical pedagogy are not additions to that norm, but oppositional challenges that require a dismantling of the mythical norm and its uses as well as alternatives to it. There has been no consideration of how voices of, for example. White women, students of color, disabled students, White men against masculinist culture, and fat students will necessarily be constructed in opposition to the teacher/ institution when they try to change the power imbalances they inhabit in their daily lives, including their lives in schools.

Critical pedagogues speak of student voices as "sharing" their experiences and understandings of oppression with other students and with the teacher in the interest of "expanding the possibilities of what it is to be human."[48] Yet White women, women of color, men of color, White men against masculinist culture, fat people, gay men and lesbians, people with disabilities, and Jews do not speak of the oppressive formations that condition their lives in the spirit of "sharing." Rather, the speech of oppositional groups is a "talking back," a "defiant speech"[49] that is constructed within communities of resistance and is a condition of survival.

In C&I 607, the defiant speech of students and professor of difference constituted fundamental challenges to and rejections of the voices of some classmates and often of the professor. For example, it became clear very quickly that in order to name her experience of racism, a Chicana student had to define her voice in part through opposition to – and rejection of – definitions of "Chicana" assumed or taken for granted by other student/ professor voices in the classroom. And in the context of protests by students of color against racism on campus, her voice had to be constructed in opposition to the institutional racism of the university's curriculum and policies – which were represented in part by my discourses and actions as Anglo-American, middle-class woman professor. Unless we found a way to respond to such challenges, our academic and political work against racism would be blocked. This alone is a reason for finding ways to express and engage with student voices, one that distances itself from the abstract, philosophical reasons implied by the literature on critical pedagogy when it fails to contextualize its projects. Furthermore, grounding the expression of and engagement with student voices in the need to construct contextualized political strategies rejects both the voyeuristic relation that the literature reproduces when the voice of the professor is not problematized, and the instrumental role critical pedagogy plays when student voice is used to inform more effective teaching strategies.

The lessons learned from feminist struggles to make a difference through defiant speech offer both useful critiques of the assumptions of critical pedagogy and starting points for moving beyond its repressive myths.[50] Within feminist movements, self-defining feminist voices have been understood as constructed collectively in the context of a larger feminist movement or women's marginalized subcultures. Feminist voices are made possible by the interactions among women within and across race, class, and other differences that divide them. These voices have never been solely or even primarily the result of a pedagogical interaction between an individual student and a teacher. Yet discourses of the pedagogy of empowerment consistently position students as individuals with only the most abstract of relations to concrete contexts of struggle. In their writing about critical pedagogy, educational researchers consistently place teachers/professors at the center of the consciousness-raising activity. For example, McLaren describes alienated middle-class youth in this way:

> . . .these students do not recognize their own self-representation and suppression by the dominant society, and in our vitiated learning environments they are not provided with the requisite theoretical constructs to help them understand why they feel as badly as they do. Because teachers lack a critical

pedagogy, these students are not provided with the ability to think critically, a skill that would enable them to better understand why their lives have been reduced to feelings of meaningless, randomness, and alienation. . . .[51]

In contrast, many students came into "Media and Anti-Racist Pedagogies" with oppositional voices already formulated within various antiracism and other movements. These movements had not necessarily relied on intellectuals/ teachers to interpret their goals and programs to themselves or to others.

Current writing by many feminists working from antiracism and feminist post-structuralist perspectives recognize that any individual woman's politicized voice will be partial, multiple, and contradictory.[52] The literature on critical pedagogy also recognizes the possibility that each student will be capable of identifying a multiplicity of authentic voices in her/himself. But it does not confront the ways in which any individual student's voice is already a "teeth gritting" and often contradictory intersection of voices constituted by gender, race, class, ability, ethnicity, sexual orientation, or ideology. Nor does it engage with the fact that the particularities of historical context, personal biography, and subjectivities split between the conscious and unconscious will necessarily render each expression of student voice partial and predicated on the absence and marginalization of alternative voices. It is impossible to speak from all voices at once, or from any one, without the traces of the others being present and interruptive. Thus the very term "student voice" is highly problematic. Pluralizing the concept as "voices" implies correction through addition. This loses sight of the contradictory and partial nature of all voices.

In C&I 607, for example, participants expressed much pain, confusion, and difficulty in speaking, because of the ways in which discussions called up their multiple and contradictory social positioning. Women found it difficult to prioritize expressions of racial privilege and oppression when such prioritizing threatened to perpetuate their gender oppression. Among international students, both those who were of color and those who were White found it difficult to join their voices with those of U.S. students of color when it meant a subordination of their oppressions as people living under U.S. imperialist policies and as students for whom English was a second language. Asian American women found it difficult to join their voices with other students of color when it meant subordinating their specific oppressions as Asian Americans. I found it difficult to speak as a White woman about gender oppression when I occupied positions of institutional power relative to all students in the class, men and women, but positions of gender oppression relative to students who were White men, and in different terms, relative to students who were men of color.

Finally, the argument that women's speech and voice have not been and should not be constructed primarily for the purpose of communicating women's experiences to men is commonplace within feminist movements. This position takes the purposes of such speech to be survival, expansion of women's own understandings of their oppression and strength, sharing common experiences among women, building solidarity among women, and political strategizing. Many feminists have pointed to the necessity for men to "do their own work" at unlearning sexism and male privilege, rather than looking to women for the answers. I am similarly suspicious of the desire by the mostly White, middle-class men who write the literature on critical pedagogy to elicit "full expression" of student voices. Such a relation between teacher/student becomes voyeuristic when the voice of the pedagogue himself goes unexamined.

Furthermore, the assumption present in the literature that silence in front of a teacher or professor indicates "lost voice," "voicelessness," or lack of social identity from which to act as a social agent betrays deep and unacceptable gender, race, and class biases. It is worth quoting bell hooks at length about the fiction of the silence of subordinated groups:

> Within feminist circles silence is often seen as the sexist defined "right speech of womanhood" – the sign of woman's submission to patriarchal authority. This emphasis on woman's silence may be an accurate remembering of what has taken place in the households of women from WASP backgrounds in the United States but in Black communities (and in other diverse ethnic communities) women have not been silent. Their voices can be heard. Certainly for Black women our struggle has not been to emerge from silence to speech but to change the nature and direction of our speech. To make a speech that compels listeners, one that is heard. . . . Dialogue, the sharing of speech and recognition, took place not between mother and child or mother and male authority figure, but with other Black women. I can remember watching, fascinated, as our mother talked with her mother, sisters, and women friends. The intimacy and intensity of their speech – the satisfaction they received from talking to one another, the pleasure, the joy. It was in this world of woman speech, loud talk, angry words, women with tongues sharp, tender sweet tongues, touching our world with their words, that I made speech my birthright – and the right to voice, to authorship, a privilege I would not be denied. It was in that world and because of it that I came to dream of writing, to write.[53]

White women, men and women of color, impoverished people, people with disabilities, gays and lesbians, are not silenced in the sense implied by the literature on critical pedagogy. They just are not talking in their authentic voices, or they are declining/refusing to talk at all, to critical educators who have been unable to acknowledge the presence of knowledges that are challenging and most likely inaccessible to their own social positions. What they/ we say, to whom, in what context, depending on the energy they/we have for the struggle on a particular day, is the result of conscious and unconscious assessments of the power relations and safety of the situation.

As I understand it at the moment, what got said – and how – in our class was the product of highly complex strategizing for the visibility that speech gives without giving up the safety of silence. More than that, it was a highly complex negotiation of the politics of knowing and being known. Things were left unsaid, or they were encoded, on the basis of speakers' conscious and unconscious assessments of the risks and costs of disclosing their understandings of themselves and of others. To what extent had students occupying socially constructed positions of privilege at a particular moment risked being known by students occupying socially constructed positions of subordination at the same moment? To what extent had students in those positions of privilege relinquished the security and privilege of being the knower?[54]

As long as the literature on critical pedagogy fails to come to grips with issues of trust, risk, and the operations of fear and desire around such issues of identity and politics in the classroom, their rationalistic tools will continue to fail to loosen deep-seated, self-interested investments in unjust relations of, for example, gender, ethnicity, and sexual orientation.[55] These investments are shared by both teachers and students, yet the literature on critical pedagogy has ignored its own implications for the young, White, Christian, middle-class, heterosexual, able-bodied man/pedagogue that it assumes. Against such ignoring Mohanty argues that to desire to ignore is not cognitive, but performative. It is the incapacity or refusal "to acknowledge one's own implication in the information."[56] "[Learning] involves a necessary implication in the radical alterity of the unknown, in the desire(s) not to know, in the process of this unresolvable dialectic."[57]

From Dialogue to Working Together across Differences

Because student voice has been defined as "the measures by which students and teacher participate in dialogue,"[58] the foregoing critique has serious consequences for the concept of "dialogue" as it has been articulated in the literature on critical pedagogy. Dialogue has been defined as a fundamental imperative of critical pedagogy and the basis of the democratic education that insures a democratic state. Through dialogue, a classroom can be made into a public sphere, a locus of citizenship in which:

> students and teachers can engage in a process of deliberation and discussion aimed at advancing the public welfare in accordance with fundamental moral judgments and principles. . . . School and classroom practices should, in some manner, be organized around forms of learning which serve to prepare students for responsible roles as transformative intellectuals, as community members, and as critically active citizens outside of schools.[59]

Dialogue is offered as a pedagogical strategy for constructing these learning conditions, and consists of ground rules for classroom interaction using language. These rules include the assumptions that all members have equal opportunity to speak, all members respect other members' rights to speak and feel safe to speak, and all ideas are tolerated and subjected to rational critical assessment against fundamental judgments and moral principles.

According to Henry Giroux, in order for dialogue to be possible, classroom participants must exhibit "trust, sharing, and commitment to improving the quality of human life."[60] White the specific form and means of social change and organization are open to debate, there must be agreement around the goals of dialogue: "all voices and their differences become unified both in their efforts to identify and recall moments of human suffering and in their attempts to overcome conditions that perpetuate such suffering."[61]

However, for the reasons outlined above – the students' and professor's asymmetrical positions of difference and privilege – dialogue in this sense was both impossible and undesirable in C&I 607. In fact, the unity of efforts and values unproblematically assumed by Giroux was not only impossible but potentially repressive as well. Giroux's formula for dialogue requires and assumes a classroom of participants unified on the side of the subordinated against the subordinators, sharing and trusting in an "us-ness" against "them-ness." This formula fails to confront dynamics of subordination present among classroom participants and within classroom participants in the form of multiple and contradictory subject positions. Such a conception of dialogue invokes the "all too easy polemic that opposes victims to perpetrators," in which a condition for collective purpose among "victims" is the desire for home, for synchrony, for sameness.[62] Biddy Martin and Chandra Mohanty call for creating new forms of collective struggle that do not depend upon the repressions and violence needed by "dialogue" based on and enforcing a harmony of interests. They envision collective stuggle that starts from an acknowledgement that "unity" – interpersonal, personal, and political – is necessarily fragmentary, unstable, not given, but chosen and struggled for – but not on the basis of "sameness."[63]

But despite early rejections of fundamental tenets of dialogue, including the usually unquestioned emancipatory potentials of rational deliberation and "unity," we remained in the grip of other repressive fictions of classroom dialogue for most of the semester. I expected that we would be able to ensure all members a safe place to speak, equal opportunity to speak, and equal power in influencing decisionmaking – and as a result, it would become clear what had to be done and why. It was only at the end of the semester that I and the students recognized that we had given this myth the power to divert-our attention and classroom practices away from what we needed to be doing. Acting as if our classroom were a safe space in which democratic dialogue was possible and happening did not make it so. If we were to re-spond to our context and the social identities of the people in our classroom in ways that did not reproduce the oppressive formations we were trying to work against, we needed classroom practices that confronted the power dynamics inside and outside of our classroom that made democratic dialogue impossible. During the last two weeks of the semester, we reflected in class on our group's process – how we spoke to and/or silenced each other across our differences, how we divided labor, made decisions, and treated each other as visible and/or invisible. As students had been doing with each other all along,

I began to have informal conversations with one or two students at a time who were extremely committed on personal, political, and academic levels to breaking through the barriers we had encountered and understanding what had happened during the semester. These reflections and discussions led me to the following conclusions.

Our classroom was not in fact a safe space for students to speak out or talk back about their experiences of oppression both inside and outside of the classroom. In our class, these included experiences of being gay, lesbian, fat, women of color working with men of color, White women working with men of color, men of color working with White women and men.[64] Things were not being said for a number of reasons. These included fear of being misunderstood and/or disclosing too much and becoming too vulnerable; memories of bad experiences in other contexts of speaking out; resentment that other oppressions (sexism, heterosexism, fat oppression, classism, anti-Semitism) were being marginalized in the name of addressing racism – and guilt for feeling such resentment; confusion about levels of trust and commitment surrounding those who were allies to another group's struggles; resentment by some students of color for feeling that they were expected to disclose "more" and once again take the burden of doing the pedagogic work of educating White students/professor about the consequences of White middle-class privilege; and resentment by White students for feeling that they had to prove they were not the enemy.

Dialogue in its conventional sense is impossible in the culture at large because at this historical moment, power relations between raced, classed, and gendered students and teachers are unjust. The injustice of these rela-tions and the way in which those injustices distort communication cannot be overcome in a classroom, no matter how committed the teacher and students are to "overcoming conditions that perpetuate suffering." Conventional no-tions of dialogue and democracy assume rationalized, individualized subjects capable of agreeing on universalizable "fundamental moral principles" and "quality of human life" that become self-evident when subjects cease to be self-interested and particularistic about group rights. Yet social agents are not capable of being fully rational and disinterested; and they are subjects split between the conscious and unconscious and among multiple social positionings. Fundamental moral and political principles are not absolute and universalizable, waiting to be discovered by the disinterested researcher/ teacher; they are "established intersubjectively by subjects capable of inter-pretation and reflection."[65] Educational researchers attempting to construct meaningful discourses about the politics of classroom practices must begin to theorize the consequences for education of the ways in which know-ledge, power, and desire are mutually implicated in each other's formations and deployments.

By the end of the semester, participants in the class agreed that commit-ment to rational discussion about racism in a classroom setting was not enough to make that setting a safe space for speaking out and talking back.

We agreed that a safer space required high levels of trust and personal commitment to individuals in the class, gained in part through social interactions outside of class – potlucks, field trips, participation in rallies and other gatherings. Opportunities to know the motivations, histories, and stakes of individuals in the class should have been planned early in the semester.[66] Furthermore, White students/professor should have shared the burden of educating themselves about the consequences of their White-skin privilege, and to facilitate this, the curriculum should have included significant amounts of literature, films, and videos by people of color and White people against racism – so that the students of color involved in the class would not always be looked to as "experts" in racism or the situation on the campus.

Because all voices within the classroom are not and cannot carry equal legitimacy, safety, and power in dialogue at this historical moment, there are times when the inequalities must be named and addressed by constructing alternative ground rules for communication. By the end of the semester, participants in C&I 607 began to recognize that some social groups represented in the class had had consistently more speaking time than others. Women, international students for whom English was a second language, and mixed groups sharing ideological and political languages and perspectives began to have very significant interactions outside of class. Informal, overlapping affinity groups formed and met unofficially for the purpose of articulating and refining positions based on shared oppressions, ideological analyses, or interests. They shared grievances about the dynamics of the larger group and performed reality checks for each other. Because they were "unofficial" groups constituted on the spot in response to specific needs or simply as a result of casual encounters outside of the classroom, alliances could be shaped and reshaped as strategies in context.

The fact that affinity groups did form within the larger group should not be seen as a failure to construct a unity of voices and goals – a possibility unproblematically assumed and worked for in critical pedagogy. Rather, affinity groups were necessary for working against the way current historical configurations of oppressions were reproduced in the class. They provided some participants with safer home bases from which they gained support, important understandings, and a language for entering the larger classroom interactions each week. Once we acknowledged the existence, necessity, and value of these affinity groups, we began to see our task not as one of building democratic dialogue between free and equal individuals, but of building a coalition among the multiple, shifting, intersecting, and sometimes contradictory groups carrying unequal weights of legitimacy within the culture and the classroom. Halfway through the semester, students renamed the class Coalition 607.

At the end of the semester, we began to suspect that it would have been appropriate for the large group to experiment with forms of communication other than dialogue. These could have brought the existence and results of affinity group interactions to bear more directly on the larger group's understandings and practices. For example, it seemed that we needed times when one affinity group (women of color, women and men of color, feminists, White men against masculinist culture, White women, gays, lesbians) could "speak out" and "talk back" about their experience of Coalition 607's group process or their experience of racial, gender, or other injustice on the campus, white the rest of the class listened without interruption. This would have acknowledged that we were not interacting in class dialogue solely as individuals, but as members of larger social groups, with whom we shared common and also differing experiences of oppression, a language for naming, fighting, and surviving that oppression, and a shared sensibility and style. The differences among the affinity groups that composed the class made communication within the class a form of cross-cultural or cross-subcultural exchange rather than the free, rational, democratic exchange between equal individuals implied in critical pedagogy literature.

But I want to emphasize that this does not mean that discourses of students of difference were taken up and supported unconditionally by themselves and their allies. There had been intense consciousness-raising on the UW-Madison campus between African American students, Asian American, students, Latino/a, Chicano/a students, Native American students, and men and women of color, about the different forms racism had taken across the campus, depending on ethnicity and gender – and how no single group's analysis could be adopted to cover all other students of color.

Early in the semester, it became clear to some in Coalition 607 that some of the anti-racism discourses heard on campus were structured by highly problematic 'gender politics, and White women and women of color could not adopt those discourses as their own without undercutting their own struggles agairist sexism on campus-and in their communities. We began to define coalition-building not only in terms of what we shared – a commitment to work against racism – but in terms of what we did not share – gender, sexual orientation, ethnicity, and other differences. These positions gave us different stakes in, experiences of, and perspectives on, racism. These differences meant that each strategy we considered for fighting racism on campus had to be interrogated for the implications it held for struggles against sexism, ableism, elitism, fat oppression, and so forth.

We agreed to a final arbiter of the acceptability of demands/narratives by students of color and our class's actions on campus. Proposals would be judged in light of our answers to this question: to what extent do our political strategics and alternative narratives about social difference succeed in alleviating campus racism white at the same time managing *not to undercut* the efforts of other social groups to win self-definition?

A Pedagogy of the Unknowable

Like the individual students themselves, each affinity group possessed only partial narratives of its oppressions – partial in that they were self-interested and predicated on the exclusion of the voices of others – and partial in the sense that the meaning of an individual's or group's experience is never self-evident or complete. No one affinity group could ever "know" the experiences and knowledges of other affinity groups or the social positions that were not their own. Nor can social subjects who are split between the conscious and unconscious, and cut across by multiple, interseeting, and contradictory subject positions, ever fully "know" their own experiences. As a whole, Coalition 607 could never know with certainty whether the actions it planned to take on campus would undercut the struggle of other social groups, or even that of its own affinity groups. But this situation was not a failure; it was not something to overcome. Realizing that there are partial narratives that some social groups or cultures have and others can never know, but that are necessary to human survival, is a condition to embrace and use as an opportunity to build a kind of social and educational interdependency that recognizes differences as "different strengths" and as "forces for change."[67] In the words of Audre Lordc, "Difference must be not merely tolerated, but seen as a fund of necessary polarities between which our creativity can spark like a dialectic. Only then does the necessity for interdependency become unthreatening."[68]

In the end. Coalition 607 participants made an initial gesture toward acting out the implications of the unknowable and the social, educational, and political interdependency that it necessitates. The educational interventions against racism that we carried out on campus were put forth as Coalition 607's statement about its members' provisional, partial understanding of racial oppression on the UW-Madison campus at the moment of its actions. These statements were not offered with the invitation for audiences to participate in dialogue, but as a speaking out from semiotic spaces temporarily and problematically controlled by Coalition 607's students. First, we took actions on campus by interrupting business-as-usual (that is, social relations of racism, sexism, classism, Eurocentrism as usual) in the public spaces of the library mall and administrative offices. (The mall is a frequent site for campus protests, rallies, and graffiti, and was chosen for this reason.) These interruptions consisted of three events.

At noon on April 28, 1988, a street theater performance on the library mall, "Meet on the Street," presented an ironic history of university attempts to coopt and defuse the demands of students of color from the 1950s through the 1980s. The affinity group that produced this event invited members of the university and Madison communities who were not in the class to participate. That night, after dark, "Serawl on the Mall" used overhead and movie projectors to project towering images, text, and spontaneously written "graffiti" on the white walls of the main campus library. Class members and passersby drew and wrote on transparencies for the purpose of deconstructing, defacing, and transforming racist discourses and giving voice to perspectives and demands of students of color and White students against racism. For example, students projected onto the library a page from the administration's official response to the Minority Student Coalition demands, and "edited" it to reveal how it failed to meet those demands. Throughout the semester, a third group of students interrupted business-as-usual in the offices of the student newspaper and university administrators by writing articles and holding interviews that challenged the university's and the newspaper's response to the demands by students of color.

These three events disrupted power relations, however temporarily, within the contexts in which they occurred. Students of color and White students against racism opened up semiotic space for discourses normally marginalized and silenced within the everyday uses of the library mall and administrators' offices. They appropriated means of discourse production – overhead projectors, microphones, language, images, newspaper articles – and controlled, however problematically, the terms in which students of color and racism on campus would be defined and represented within the specific times and spaces of the events. They made available to other members of the university community, with unpredictable and uncontrollable effects, discourses of antiracism that might otherwise have remained unavailable, distorted, more easily dismissed, or seemingly irrelevant. Thus students engaged in the political work of changing material conditions within a public space, allowing them to make visible and assert the legitimacy of their own definitions, in their own terms, of racism and anti-racism on the UW campus.

Each of the three actions was defined by different affinity groups according to differing priorities, languages of understanding and analysis, and levels of comfort with various kinds of public action. They were "unified" through their activity of mutual critique, support, and participation, as each group worked through, as much as possible, ways in which the others supported or undercut its own understandings and objectives. Each affinity group brought its proposal for action to the whole class to check out in what ways that action might affect the other groups' self-definitions, priorities, and plans for action. Each group asked the others for various types of labor and support to implement its proposed action. During these planning discussions, we concluded that the results of our interventions would be unpredictable and uncontrollable, and dependent upon the subject positions and changing historical contexts of our audiences on the mall and in administrative offices. Ultimately, our interventions and the process by which we arrived at them had to make sense – both rationally and emotionally – to *us*, however problematically we understand "making sense" to be a political action. Our actions had to make sense as interested interpretations and constant rewritings of ourselves in relation to shifting interpersonal and political contexts. Our interpretations had to be based on attention to history, to concrete experiences of oppression, and to subjugated knowledges.[69]

Conclusion

For me, what has become more frightening than the unknown or unknowable, are social, political, and educational projects that predicate and legitimate their actions on the kind of knowing that underlies current definitions of critical pedagogy. In this sense, current understandings and uses of "critical," "empowerment," "student voice," and "dialogue" are only surface manifest-ations of deeper contradictions involving pedagogies, both traditional and critical. The kind of knowing I am referring to is that in which objects, nature, and "Others" are seen to be known or ultimately knowable, in the sense of being "defined, delineated, captured, understood, explained, and diagnosed" at a level of determination never accorded to the "knower" herself or himself.[70]

The experience of Coalition 607 has left me wanting to think through the implications of confronting unknowability. What would it mean to recognize not only that a multiplicity of knowledges are present in the classroom as a result of the way difference has been used to structure social relations inside and outside the classroom, but that these knowledges are contradictory, partial, and irreducible? They cannot be made to "make sense" – they cannot be known, in terms of the single master discourse of an educational project's curriculum or theoretical framework, even that of critical pedagogy. What kinds of classroom practice are made possible and impossible when one af-finity group within the class has lived out and arrived at a currently useful "knowledge" about a particular oppressive formation on campus, but the professor and some of the other students can never know or understand that knowledge in the same way? What practice is called for when even the com-bination of all partial knowledges in a classroom results in yet another partial knowing, defined by structuring absences that mark the "terror and loathing of any difference?"[71] What kinds of interdependencies between groups and individuals inside and outside of the classroom would recognize that every social, political, or educational project the class takes up locally will already, at the moment of its definition, lack knowledges necessary to answer broader questions of human survival and social justice? What kind of educational project could redefine "knowing" so that it no longer describes the activities of those in power "who started to speak, to speak alone and for everyone else, on behalf of everyone else?"[72] What kind of educational project would redefine the silence of the unknowable, freeing it from "the male-defined con-text of Absence, Lack, and Fear," and make of that silence "a language of its own" that changes the nature and direction of speech itself?[73]

Whatever form it takes in the various, changing, locally specific instances of classroom practices, I understand a classroom practice of the unknowable right now to be one that would support students/professor in the never-ending "moving about" Trinh Minh-ha describes:

> After all, she is this Inappropriate/d Other who moves about with always at least two/four gestures: that of affirming "I am like you" white pointing insistently to the difference; and that of reminding "I am different" while unsettling every definition of otherness arrived at.[74]

In relation to education, I see this moving about as a strategy that affirms "you know me/I know you" while pointing insistently to the interested par-tialness of those knowings; and constantly reminding us that "you can't know me/I can't know you" while unsettling every definition of knowing arrived at. Classroom practices that facilitate such moving about would support the kind of contextually politically and historically situated identity politics called for by Alcoff, hooks, and others.[75] That is, one in which "identity" is seen as "nonessentialized and emergent from a historical experience"[76] as a necessary stage in a process, a starting point – not an ending point. Identity in this sense becomes a vehicle for multiplying and making more complex the subject positions possible, visible, and legitimate at any given historical moment, requiring disruptive changes in the way social technologies of gender, race, ability, and so on define "Otherness" and use it as a vehicle for subordination.

Gayatri Spivak calls the search for a coherent narrative "counterproductive" and asserts that what is needed is "persistent critique"[77] of received narratives and a priori lines of attack. Similarly, unlike post-liberal or post-Marxist movements predicated on repressive unities, Minh-ha's moving about refuses to reduce profoundly heterogeneous networks of power/desire/interest to any one a priori, coherent narrative. It refuses to know and resist oppression from any a priori line of attack, such as race, class, or gender solidarity.

But participants in Coalition 607 did not simply unsettle every definition of knowing, assert the absence of a priori solidarities, or replace political action (in the sense defined at the beginning of this article) with textual critique. Rather, we struggled, as S. P. Mohanty would have us do, to "develop a sense of the profound *contextuality* of meanings [and oppressive knowledges] in their play and their ideological effects."[78]

Our classroom was the site of dispersed, shifting, and contradictory contexts of knowing that coalesced differently in different moments of student/professor speech, action, and emotion. This situation meant that individuals and affinity groups constantly had to change strategies and priorities of resistance against oppressive ways of knowing and being known. The antagonist became power itself as it was deployed within our classroom – oppressive ways of knowing and oppressive knowledges.

This position, informed by post-structuralism and feminism, leaves no one off the hook, including critical pedagogues. We cannot act as if our membership in or alliance with an oppressed group exempts us from the need to confront the "grey areas which we all have in us."[79] As Minh-ha reminds us, "There are no social positions exempt from becoming oppressive to others . . . any group – any position – can move into the oppressor role,"[80] depending upon specific historical contexts and situations. Or as Mary Gentile puts it, "everyone is someone else's 'Other.'"[81]

Various groups struggling for self-definition in the United States have identified the mythical norm deployed for the purpose of setting the standard of hurnanness against which Others are defined and assigned privilege and limitations. At this moment in history, that norm is young, White, heterosexual, Christian, able-bodied, thin, middle-class, English-speaking, and male. Yet, as Gentile argues, no individual embodies, in the essentialist sense, this mythical norm.[82] Even individuals who most closely approximate it experience a dissonance. As someone who embodies some but not all of the current mythical norm's socially constructed characteristics, my colleague Albert Selvin wrote in response to the first draft of this article: "I too have to fight to differentiate myself from a position defined for me – whose terms are imposed on me – which limits and can destroy me – which does destroy many White men or turns them into helpless agents. . . . I as a White man/boy was not allowed – by my family, by society – to be anything *but* cut off from the earth and the body. That condition is not/was not an essential component or implication of my maleness."[83]

To assert multiple perspectives in this way is not to draw attention away from the distinctive realities and effects of the oppression of any particular group. It is not to excuse or relativize oppression by simply claiming, "we are all oppressed." Rather, it is to clarify oppression by preventing "oppressive simplifications,"[84] and insisting that it be understood and struggled against contextually. For example, the politics of appearance in relation to the mythical norm played a major role in our classroom. Upon first sight, group members tended to draw alliances and assume shared commitments because of the social positions sve presumed others to occupy (radical, heterosexual, anti-racist person of color, and so on). But not only were these assumptions often wrong, at times they denied ideological and personal commitments to various struggles by people who appeared outwardly to fit the mythical norm.

The terms in which I can and will assert and unsettle "difference" and unlearn my positions of privilege in future classroom practices are wholly dependent on the Others/others whose presence – with their concrete experiences of privileges and oppressions, and subjugated or oppressive knowledges – I am responding to and acting with in any given classroom. My moving about between the positions of privileged speaking subject and Inappropriate/d Other cannot be predicted, prescribed, or understood before-hand by any theoretical framework or methodological practice. It is in this sense that a practice grounded in the unknowable is profoundly contextual (historical) and interdependent (social). This reformulation of pedagogy and knowledge removes the critical pedagogue from two key discursive positions s/he has constructed for her/himself in the literature – namely, origin of what can be known and origin of what should be done. What remains for me is the challenge of constructing classroom practices that engage with the discursive and material spaces that such a removal opens up. I am trying to unsettle received definitions of pedagogy by multiplying the ways in which I am able to act on and in the university both as the Inappropriate/d Other and as the privileged speaking/making subject trying to unlearn that privilege.

This semester, in a follow-up to Coalition 607, Curriculum and Instruction 800 is planning, producing, and "making sense" of a day-long film and video event against oppressive knowledges and ways of knowing in the curriculum, pedagogy, and everyday life at UW-Madison. This time, we are not focusing on any one formation (race *or* class *or* gender *or* ableism). Rather, we are engaging with each other and working against oppressive social formations on campus in ways that try to "find a commonality in the experience of difference without compromising its distinctive realities and effects."[85]

Right now, the classroom practice that seems most capable of accomplishing this is one that facilitates a kind of communication across differences that is best represented by this statement: "If you can talk to me in ways that show you understand that your knowledge of me, the world, and 'the Right thing to do' will always be partial, interested, and potentially oppressive to others, and if I can do the same, then we can work together on shaping and reshaping alliances for constructing circumstances in which students of difference can thrive."

Notes

This article is a revised version of a paper presented at the Tenth Conference on Curriculum Theory and Classroom Practice, Bergamo Conference Center, Dayton, Ohio, October 26–29, 1988. It was part of a symposium entitled "Reframing the Empirical 'I/Eye': Feminist, Neo-Marxist, and Post-structuralist Challenges to Research in Education." I want to thank Mimi Orner, Ph.D. candidate and teaching assistant in the Department of Curriculum and Instruction, UW-Madison, for her insights and hours of conversations about the meanings of C&I 607. They have formed the backbone of this article.

1. By "critique" I do not mean a systematic analysis of the specific articles or individual authors' positions that make up this literature, for the purpose of articulating a "theory" of critical pedagogy capable of being evaluated for its internal consistency, elegance, powers of prediction, and so on. Rather, I have chosen to ground the following critique in my interpretation of my experiences in C&I 607. That is, I have attempted to place key discourses in the literature on critical pedagogy *in relation to* my interpretation of my experience in C&I 607 – by asking which interpretations and "sense making" do those discourses facilitate, which do they silence and marginalize, and what interests do they appear to serve?
2. By "the literature on critical pedagogy," I mean those articles in major educational journals and special editions devoted to critical pedagogy. For the purpose of this article, I systematically reviewed more than thirty articles appearing in journals such as *Harvard Educational Review, Curriculum Inquiry, Educational Theory, Teachers College Record, Journal of Curriculum Theorizing, and Journal of Curriculum Studies* between 1984 and 1988. The purpose of this review was to identify key and repeated claims, assumptions, goals, and pedagogical practices that currently set the terms of debate within this literature. "Critical pedagogy" should not be confused with "feminist pedagogy," which constitutes a separate body of literature with its own goals and assumptions.
3. Some of the more representative writing on this point can be found in Michelle Fine. "Silencing in the Public Schools," *Language Arts, 64* (1987), 157–174; Henry A. Giroux, "Radical Pedagogy and the Politics of Student Voice," *Interchange, 17* (1986), 48–69; and Roger Simon, "Empowerment as Pedagogy of Possibility," *Language Arts, 64* (1987), 370–382.
4. See Henry A. Giroux and Peter McLaren, "Teacher Education and the Politics of Engagement: The Case for Democratic Schooling," *Harvard Educational Review, 56* (1986), 213–238; and Ira Shor and Paulo Freire, "What is the 'Dialogical Method' of Teaching?" *Journal of Education, 169* (1987), 11–31.
5. Shor and Freire, "What is the 'Dialogical Method'?" and Henry A. Giroux, "Literacy and the Pedagogy of Voice and Political Empowerment," *Educational Theory, 38* (1988), 61–75.

6. Daniel P. Liston and Kenneth M. Zeichner, "Critical Pedagogy and Teacher Education," *Journal of Education, 169* (1987), 117–137.
7. Liston and Zeichner, "Critical Pedagogy," p. 120.
8. Liston and Zeichner, "Critical Pedagogy," p. 127.
9. Giroux, "Literacy and the Pedagogy of Voice," p. 75.
10. Liston and Zeichner, "Critical Pedagogy," p. 128.
11. Valerie Walkerdine, "On the Regulation of Speaking and Silence: Subjectivity, Class, and Gender in Contemporary Schooling," in *Language, Gender, and Childhood,* ed. Carolyn Steedman, Cathy Urwin, and Valerie Walkerdine (London: Routledge and Kegan Paul, 1985), p. 205.
12. Barbara Christian, "The Race for Theory." *Cultural Critique,* 6 (Spring, 1987), 51–63.
13. By the end of the semester, many of us began to understand ourselves as inhabiting inter-sections of multiple, contradictory, overlapping social positions not reducible either to race, or class, or gender, and so on. Depending upon the moment and the context, the degree to which any one of us "differs" from the mythical norm (see conclusion) varies along multi-ple axes, and so do the consequences. I began using the terms "students of difference," "professor of difference." to refer to social positionings in relation to the mythical norm (based on ability, size, color, sexual preference, gender, ethnicity, and so on). This reminded us of the necessity to reconstruct how, within specific situations, particular socially con-structed differences from the mythical norm (such as color) get taken up as vehicles for institutions such as the university to act out and legitimate oppressive formations of power. This enabled us to open up our analysis of racism on campus for the purpose of tracing its relations to institutional sexism, ableism, elitism, anti-Semitism, and other oppressive formations.
14. Giroux and McLaren, "Teacher Education and the Politics of Engagement," p. 229.
15. Stanley Aronowitz, "Postmodernism and Politics," *Social Text, 18* (Winter, 1987/88), 99–115.
16. Liston and Zeichner, "Critical Pedagogy," p. 120.
17. For an excellent theoretical discussion and demonstration of the explanatory power of this approach, see Julian Henriques, Wendy Hollway, Cathy Urwin, Couze Venn, and Valerie Walkerdine, *Changing the Subject: Psychology, Social Regulation, and Subjectivity* (New York: Methuen, 1984): Gloria Anzaldua, *Berderlands/La Frontera: The New Mestiza* (San Francisco: Spinsters/Aunt Lute, 1987); Theresa de Lauretis, ed., *Feminist Studies/ Critical Studies* (Bloomington: Indiana University Press, 1986); Hal Foster, ed., *Discussions in Contemporary Culture* (Seattle: Bay Press, 1987); Chris Weedon, *Feminist Practice and Poststructuralist Theory* (New York: Basil Blackwell, 1987).
18. Weedon, *Feminist Practice and Poststruturalist Theory.*
19. Aronowitz, "Postmodernism and Politics," p. 103.
20. Aronowitz, "Postmodernism and Politics," p. 103.
21. Audre Lorde, *Sister Outsider* (New York: The Crossing Press, 1984). p. 112.
22. Lorde, *Sister Outsider*, p. 112.
23. Christian, "The Race for Theory," p. 63.
24. For a discussion of the thesis of the "epistemic privilege of the oppressed," see Uma Narayan, "Working Together Across Difference: Some Considerations on Emotions and Political Practice," *Hypatia, 3* (Summer, 1988), 31–47.
25. For an excellent discussion of the relation of the concept of "experience" to feminism, essentialism, and political action, see Linda Alcoff, "Cultural Feminism versus Post-Structuralism: The Identity Crisis in Feminist Theory," *Signs, 13* (Spring, 1988), 405–437.
26. Narayan, "Working Together Across Difference," pp. 31–47.
27. This subtitle is borrowed from Maria C. Lugones and Elizabeth V. Spelman's critique of imperialistic, ethnocentric, and disrespectful tendencies in White feminists' theorizing about women's oppression, "Have We Got a Theory for You! Feminist Theory, Cultural Imperialism, and the Demand for 'The Woman's Voice,'" *Women's Studies International Forum* (1983), 573–581.

28. Nicholas C. Burbules. "A Theory of Power in Education," *Educational Theory, 36* (Spring, 1986), 95–114; Giroux and McLaren. "Teacher Education and the Politics of Engagement," pp. 224–227.

29. Liston and Zeichner, "Critical Pedagogy and Teacher Education," p. 120.

30. Shor and Freire, "What is the 'Dialogical Method' of Teaching?," p. 14.

31. Giroux, "Radical Pedagogy," p. 64.

32. Giroux, "Radical Pedagogy," p. 66.

33. Shor and Freire, "What is the 'Dialogical Method' of Teaching?," p. 22.

34. Burbules, "A Theory of Power in Education"; and Giroux and McLaren, 'Teacher Education and the Politics of Engagement," pp. 224–227.

35. Shor and Freire, "What is the 'Dialogical Method' of Teaching?," p. 23.

36. Burbules, "A Theory of Power in Education," p. 108.

37. Giroux and McLaren, "Teacher Education and the Politics of Engagement," p. 226.

38. Walter C. Parker, "Justice, Social Studies, and the Subjectivity/Structure Problem." *Theory and Research in Social Education, 14* (Fall, 1986), p. 227.

39. Simon, "Empowerment as a Pedagogy of Possibility," p. 372.

40. Giroux, "Literacy and the Pedagogy of Voice," pp. 68–69.

41. Giroux and McLaren, "Teacher Education and the Politics of Engagement," p. 225.

42. Giroux and McLaren, "Teacher Education and the Politics of Engagement," p. 227.

43. Shor and Freire, "What is the 'Dialogical Method' of Teaching?" p. 30; Liston and Zeichner, "Critical Pedagogy," p. 122.

44. Simon, "Empowerment as a Pedagogy of Possibility," p. 80.

45. Simon, "Empowerment as a Pedagogy of Possibility," p. 375.

46. Aronowitz, "Postmodernism and Politics," p. 111.

47. Acloff, "Cultural Feminism versus Post-Structuralism," p. 420.

48. Simon, "Empowerment as a Pedagogy of Possibility."

49. bell hooks, "Talking Back," *Discourse, 8* (Fall/Winter, 1986/87), 123–128.

50. bell hooks. *Talking Back: Thinking Black* (Boston: South End Press, 1989).

51. Peter McLaren, *Life in Schools* (New York: Longman, 1989).

52. Alcoff, "Cultural Feminism versus Post-Structuralism"; Anzaldua, *Borderlands/La Frantera:* de Lauretis, *Feminist Studies/Critical Studies*; hooks, *Talking Back*; Trihn T. Minh-ha, *Woman, Native, Other* (Bloomington: Indiana University Press, 1989); Weedon, *Feminist Practice and Poststructuralist Theory*.

53. hooks, "Talking Back," p. 124.

54. Susan Hardy Aiken, Karen Anderson, Myra Dincrstein. Judy Lensink, and Patricia MacCorquodale, "Trying Transformations: Curriculum Integration and the Problem of Resistance," *Signs, 12* (Winter, 1987), 225–275.

55. Aiken et al., "Trying Transformations," p. 263.

56. Shoshana Felman, "Psychoanalysis and Education: Teaching Terminable and Interminable," *Yale French Studies*, 63 (1982), 21–44.

57. S. P. Mohanty, "Radical Teaching, Radical Theory: The Ambiguous Politics of Meaning," in *Theory in the Classroom*, ed. Cary Nelson (Urbana: University of Illinois Press, 1986), p. 155.

58. Giroux and McLaren, "Teacher Education and the Politics of Engagement," p. 235.

59. Giroux and McLaren, "Teacher Education and the Politics of Engagement," p. 237.

60. Giroux, "Literacy and the Pedagogy of Voice," p. 72.

61. Giroux, "Literacy and the Pedagogy of Voice," p. 72.

62. Biddy Martin and Chandra Talpade Mohanty, "Feminist Politics: What's Home Got to Do with It?" in *Feminist Studies/Critical Studies*, ed. Theresa dc Lauretis (Bloomington: Indiana University Press, 1986), pp. 208–209.

63. Martin and Mohanty, "Feminist Politics," p. 208.

64. Discussions with students after the semester ended and comments from students and colleagues on the draft of this article have led me to realize the extent to which some international students and Jews in the class felt unable or not safe to speak about experiences

of oppression inside and outside of the class related to those identities. Anti-Semitism, economic and cultural imperialism, and the rituals of exclusion of international students on campus were rarely named and never fully elaborated in the class. The classroom practices that reproduced these particular oppressive silences in C&I 607 must be made the focus of sustained critique in the follow-up course, C&I 800, "Race, Class, Gender, and the Construction of Knowledge in Educational Media."

65. John W. Murphy, "Computerization, Postmodern Epistemology, and Reading in the Postmodern Era," *Educational Theory, 38* (Spring, 1988), 175–182.

66. Lugones and Spelman assert that the only acceptable motivation for following Others into their worlds is friendship. Self-interest is not enough, because "the task at hand for you is one of extraordinary difficulty. It requires that you be willing to devote a great part of your life to it and that you be willing to suffer alienation and self-disruption . . . whatever the benefits you may accrue from such a journey, they cannot be concrete enough for you at this time and they are not worth your while" ("Have We Got a Theory for You," p. 576). Theoretical or political "obligation" is inappropriate, because it puts Whites/Anglos "in a morally self-righteous position" and makes people of color vehicles of redemption for those in power (p. 581). Friendship, as an appropriate and acceptable "condition" under which people become allies in struggles that are not their own, names my own experience and has been met with enthusiasm by students.

67. Lorde. *Sister Outsider*, p. 112.

68. Lorde, *Sister Outsider*, p. 112.

69. Martin and Mohanty, "Feminist Politics," p. 210.

70. Alcoff, "Cultural Feminism versus Post-Structuralism," p. 406.

71. Lorde, *Sister Outsider*, p. 113.

72. Trinh T. Minh-ha, "Introduction," *Discourse, 8* (Fall/Winter, 1986/87), p. 7.

73. Minh-ha, "Introduction," p. 8.

74. Minh-ha, "Introduction," p. 9.

75. Alcoff, "Cultural Feminism versus Post-Structuralism"; bell hooks, "The Politics of Radical Black Subjectivity," *Zeta Magazine* (April, 1989), 52–55.

76. hooks, "The Politics of Radical Black Subjectivity," p. 54.

77. Gayatri Chakravorty Spivak, "Can the Subaltern Speak?" in *Marxism and the Interpretation of Culture*, ed. Cary Nelson and Lawrence Grossberg (Urbana: University of Illinois Press, 1988), p. 272.

78. S. P. Mohanty, "Radical Teaching, Radical Theory," p. 169.

79. Minh-ha, "Introduction," p. 6.

80. A. Selvin, Personal Correspondence (October 24, 1988).

81. Mary Gentile, *Film Feminisms: Theory and Practice* (Westport, CT: Greenwood Press, 1985), p. 7.

82. Gentile, *Film Feminisms*, p. 7.

83. A. Selvin, personal correspondence.

84. Gentile, *Film Feminisms*, p. 7.

85. Gentile, *Film Feminisms*, p. 7.

86

Democratic Education in Difficult Times

Amy Gutmann

These are difficult times because we are difficult people. There are undoubtedly other, less "personal" reasons that make these difficult times and also other, more "structural" reasons that help explain why we are difficult people, but I want to begin by focusing on the fact that we *are* – for whatever simple or complicated reasons – difficult people.

When I say we are difficult people, I have something very simple in mind. Most Americans value freedom of speech and also value protection from falsehood, deceit, and defamation. Yet it is impossible to provide complete freedom of speech and still prevent the widespread dissemination of falsehoods, deceits, and defamations. Most Americans value freedom of religion, and also want governments to shape the social environment so that people are predisposed to believe in "good" religions (or philosophies of life) rather than "bad" ones. Yet a society that grants complete freedom of religion cannot shape an environment resistant to repugnant religions.

Most Americans value living and working where we like, and also value stable, friendly, and familiar places in which to live and work. We value the freedom to choose our sexual partners and rechoose them, and we also place a high value on stable nuclear families. Most Americans want to use their market freedom to secure a standard of living that is staggeringly high by any historical perspective, yet we are also sensitive to the plight of other people's children, which threatens this expectation. Most Americans would like to see our freedoms extended to other people, but we fear that by opening our borders, we decrease the chances of our own (and our children's) educational and economic improvement.

The tension within each set of values – between individual freedom and civic virtue – poses a challenge for educating Americans. It is impossible to educate children to maximize both their freedom and their civic virtue. Yet Americans want both – although some people seem willing to settle for freedom for themselves and civic virtue for others. This formula obviously will

Source: *Teachers College Record*, 92(1) (1990): 7–20.

not work. Far from obvious, however, is how our educational institutions should come to terms with the tension between individual freedom and civic virtue. Should they try to reconcile these seemingly unreconcilable values? Or give priority to one value over the other? Or find the one, morally best way of coping with each of these tensions? Or should we continue to muddle through much as we have done in the past? Rarely do Americans turn to philosophy for help, except in those rare times when the consequences of muddling through seem unbearable. We then reconcile ourselves to philosophizing; we make a necessity out of a virtue.

While these times are undoubtedly difficult in many ways, philosophy is probably not necessary for getting us through them (and philosophy will certainly not be sufficient). Our nation's political ideals – liberty *and* justice *for all* – remain at risk, but the risks to economically and educationally advantaged Americans are not so great that we have no practical alternative to muddling through. Philosophizing still seems to be a practical luxury. Some of us may be able to withstand the practical risks of politics and education as usual. But, as a society we would do better, both morally and practically, to be more philosophically guided in our educational politics.

By what philosophy should we be guided? The several philosophies that compete for our allegiance suggest radically different ways of dealing with the tensions that make us difficult people. Despite their differences, they all try to *dissolve* the tension between individual freedom and civic virtue in a potent philosophical solution, and thereby avoid the political problems that flow from the tension. Perhaps the most distinctive feature of a democratic theory of education is its simultaneous refusal to dissolve these tensions philosophically and its insistence on finding a principled, rather than simply a pragmatic, way of living with the tensions. Living with the tensions will never be easy, but the alternatives to democratic education that promise to make us easier people are far worse. One of the strongest arguments for democratic education – as for democracy itself – is that the alternatives are worse. So let us consider the two most philosophically potent and politically influential alternatives to a democratic state of education: a Platonic family state and a liberal state of individuals.

The Family State and the Liberal State

One of the greatest treatises on education ever written, Plato's *Republic*, offers a way of dissolving the tensions between individual freedom and civic virtue: Subsume all that is valuable with regard to individual freedom into civic virtue. The means of subsumption is education: Teach children that they cannot realize their own good except by contributing to the social good. Not just any social good will do: Children must be taught the true good, the one that rightly orders their souls, the one consonant with their varying natures. Unless children learn to associate their own good with the social good, a peaceful and prosperous society will be impossible. Unless the social good that they are taught is consonant with their nature and worthy of their pursuit, they will grow to be unfulfilled and dissatisfied with the society that miseducated them. All education that is not guided by *the* social good and the *truth* in human nature is miseducation. All such societies will degenerate because of internal disharmony.

Peculiarly enough, the Platonic family state provides the philosophical underpinnings of an ongoing American search for "the one best system." The system tries to dissolve the tensions between individual freedom and civic virtue by educating all children to identify their interests with the social good. In practice, the moral costs of dissolving the tension are great: Catholic children were once whipped for refusing to read the ("right") King James version of the Bible; college students today are ridiculed (or dismissed as uneducable) for reading Plato's *Phaedrus* in the wrong way. (So Allan Bloom asks rhetorically: "How does a youngster who sees sublimation where Plato saw divination learn from Plato, let alone think Plato can speak to him?")[1]

Repression of reasonable points of view is half the problem of the family state. The other half is political tyranny justified in the name of educational enlightenment. In the *Republic*, Socrates tells Glaucon that "it's better for all to be ruled by what is divine and prudent, especially when one has it as his own within himself; but, if not, *set over one from outside*, so that insofar as possible all will be alike and friends, piloted by the same thing."[2] Children must not be set free until the right regime – the "divine and prudent" one – is established within their souls.

Who holds the key to the right regime? Not the Socrates who boasts of being the only Athenian wise enough to know his own ignorance. Socrates imagines that there may be someone wiser even than he, someone who has left the cave, and seen the light, someone who therefore knows the right regime for all souls. To create a family state, that philosopher must return to the cave, become "king," and wipe the social slate clean by exiling "all those in the city who happen to be older than ten: and taking over their children . . . rear them – far away from those dispositions they now have from their parents."[3] This is not a small price to pay for dissolving the tensions with which we now live. Socrates himself recoils from the idea on behalf of his imaginary philosopher king, suggesting that he "won't be willing to mind the political things . . . unless some divine chance coincidentally comes to pass."[4]

This problem with the family state is not a purely practical one – pointing to the impossibility of finding someone wiser than Socrates who could educate well-ordered souls in a poorly ordered society. Even if there were someone wiser than Socrates in our midst, he or she still could not claim the right to order the souls of all citizens. A good life must be one that a person recognizes as such, lived from the inside, according to one's own best lights. The neo-Platonic quest for the one best system, which subsumes individual freedom into the social good, denies this insight of individualism. Even if Plato were right about the objectively good life, we would still have to look past the *Republic* for a politically legitimate way of associating individual freedom and civic virtue, through governing.

Radically opposed to the family state is what I call the state of individuals, or the liberal state as it is commonly but misleadingly called. The state of individuals overcomes the tensions between freedom and virtue in a way precisely the opposite of that in the family state: It actively supports only those institutions instrumental to individual freedom of choice. The principled neutrality of the state of individuals aims to maximize the freedom of individuals to pursue their diverse conceptions of the private good. If the Platonic family state strives for the unity of a traditional family, the state of individuals strives for the diversity of a modern shopping mall. To paraphrase John Stuart Mill: All attempts by the state to bias the conclusions of its citizens, including its children, on disputed subjects are evil, as are all unnecessary restrictions on their choices. This is the contemporary liberal credo of neutrality for the sake of opportunity and choice.

Just as the family state provides the philosophical underpinnings for "the one best system," the state of individuals provides philosophical inspiration for "child-centered" education. Of course, proponents of the state of individuals recognize that all educators must limit children's choices, but only for the sake of developing their capacity for rational choice or for the sake of cultural coherence. American schoolchildren are taught English rather than Bengali or Spanish, not by choice but by cultural determination. This culturally determined curriculum, contemporary liberals like Bruce Ackerman tell us, legitimately limits the range of their future choices insofar as such limitation is necessary for cultural coherence. Other limits on children's choices – whether for the sake of moral development or the shaping of democratic character – are unjustified, for these would be based on what Ackerman calls "adult pretensions to moral superiority."[5]

The horticultural imagery so prevalent in Plato – pruning and weeding children's desires, shaping their character – has no place in the state of individuals: "We have no right to look upon future citizens as if we were master gardeners who can tell the difference between a pernicious weed and a beautiful flower."[6] We do have a right, according to Ackerman, perhaps even a duty, to shape the character and bias the choices of children for the sake of cultural coherence. Education in the state of individuals builds on our cultural but not our moral biases. We educate children to be Americans who are free to choose but we do not bias their choices (or shape their character) for the sake of moral goodness. We educate rational shoppers but not good people or virtuous citizens.

Why say that parents and teachers should be free to guide children's choices for the sake of cultural coherence but not for the sake of cultivating good character or choosing a morally good life? After all, sometimes the claim on the part of parents and teachers that they know the difference between morally good and bad, or better and worse, is not a *pretension* to moral superiority, but a reflection of their greater moral understanding. Honesty is better than deceitfulness, industriousness better than sloth, insight better than insensitivity, kindness better than cruelty – and not just because honest, industrious, insightful, and kind people have more freedom of choice. They may have less freedom of choice precisely because they are constrained by these virtues. We nonetheless value these virtues because there is more to a good life and to a good society than freedom; that is one good reason why we are likely to remain difficult people, torn between freedom and other virtues that are not mere means to or byproducts of freedom.

The "neutrality" premise (no authority has a right to act on a belief that one conception of the good life is better than any other) simplifies life for some contemporary liberals, allowing them to defend freedom of choice single-mindedly, but the lameness of the defense is particularly evident in American education. Consumer choice is a reasonable guiding principle for designing a shopping mall, but it is an irresponsible and incomplete principle for designing a high school. Educators must limit students' freedom of choice on some ground; otherwise education simply ceases. Cultural prejudice may seem like the politically safest guide to limiting choice, but it is not a satisfactory substitute for moral principle. Nor is it politically safe: Teaching cultural prejudices is no less politically controversial than teaching moral principles, as recent battles over bilingualism and the content of core curricula indicate.

The family state and the state of individuals offer us the following choice: Either we must educate children so that they are free to choose among the widest range of lives because freedom of choice is the paramount good, or we must educate children so that they will choose *the* life that is best because a rightly ordered soul is the paramount good. Let children define their own identity or define it for them. Give children liberty or give them virtue. This is a morally false choice. Cultivating character and intellect through education constrains children's future choices, but it does not uniquely determine them. There need be nothing illegitimate about such constraints, although some constraints surely are illegitimate. The question we must therefore ask is not whether to maximize freedom or to inculcate virtue, but how to combine freedom with virtue. This creates a new question: which freedoms and what virtues? We must focus not just on the future freedom of children but also the present freedom of parents, not just on the virtues necessary for a good life but also those necessary for a just society.

This reformulation does not resolve but at least it comprehends the problem of associating individual freedom and civic virtue that Americans face today: Citizens of a religiously and ethnically diverse society disagree on the relative value of freedom and virtue; we disagree on the nature of a good life and good character. No political philosophy can authoritatively resolve all our disagreements – not only because no one is smart enough to comprehend a comprehensive good, but because no mortal, no matter how wise, can legitimately impose a good life on people who cannot live that life from the inside. Nor can anyone legitimately impose liberal neutrality on people who value virtue as well as freedom. We stand at a philosophical and political impasse unless we can defend another alternative.

A Democratic Alternative: Public Debate

The alternative I want to defend is democratic in several significant respects. First, it does not tyrannize over common sense, either by subsuming individual freedom into the common social good or by collapsing civic virtue (or social justice) into individual freedom. Second, a democratic theory of education provides principled criticism of all educational authorities (including parents) who tyrannize children in any way, whether by depriving them of an education adequate to citizenship or by repressing reasonable challenges to popular ideas. Third, a democratic theory supports educational institutions that are conducive to democratic deliberation, institutions that make a democratic virtue out of our inevitable disagreements over educational problems. The virtue, too simply stated, is that we can publicly debate educational problems in a way much more likely to increase our understanding of education and each other than if we were to leave the management of schools, as Kant suggested, "to depend entirely upon the judgment of the most enlightened experts."[7] The policies that result from our democratic deliberations will not always be the right ones, but they will be more enlightened – by the values and concerns of the many communities that constitute a democracy – than those that would have been made by unaccountable experts.

This understanding of democratic education is, however, incomplete. The threat of repression and discrimination remains. Democratic processes can be used to destroy democratic education. They can be used to undermine the intellectual foundations of future democratic deliberations by repressing unpopular ways of thinking or excluding some future citizens from an education adequate for participating in democratic politics. A democratic society must not be constrained to legislate what the wisest parent or philosopher wants for his or her child, but it must be constrained not to legislate policies that render democracy repressive or discriminatory. A democratic theory of education recognizes the importance of empowering citizens to make educational policy and also of constraining their choices to a broad range of policies that are nonrepressive and nondiscriminatory, so as to preserve the intellectual and social foundations of democracy. Democracy must be understood not merely (or primarily) as a *process* of majority rule, but rather as an *ideal* of a society whose adults members are, and continue to be, equipped by their education and authorized by political structures to share in ruling. A democratic society must educate all educable children to be capable of participating in collectively shaping their society.

Democracy makes no claim to being an uncontroversial standard. Not all societies or all citizens in our society are committed to democracy (although all, according to this argument, should be). Those who are not committed to democracy are stuck at the impasse I characterized earlier: They assert their commitment to civic virtue or to individual freedom always at the expense of denying the legitimacy of the other value. The practical consequence of this thinking is that basic freedoms are sacrificed to communal virtue or freedom is expanded so far as to forgo the virtues essential to a just society. The legitimating claim of democracy is therefore not that it will be accepted by all citizens (let alone all philosophers) – no political philosophy can sensibly claim such a Panglossian future. Its legitimating claim is one of political morality: A state of democratic education is minimally objectionable insofar as it leaves maximum moral room for citizens deliberately to shape their society, not in their own image, but in an image that they can legitimately identify with their informed, moral choices.

You cannot govern unless you have first been governed. You must govern after you have been governed. These twin maxims, not Platonic but Aristotelian in origin, are at the root of a democratic understanding of both politics and education: being governed and governing in turn, where governing includes the nurturing of children by parents, their formal instruction by professionals, the structuring of public instruction by public officials accountable to citizens, and the shaping of culture by both private and public authorities – constrained or ideally informed by the principles of nonrepression and nondiscrimination.

There are many ways that this democratic understanding (were it more fully elaborated) could make a difference in the way we think about education and practice it. I offer here one small but significant example.

Evolution or Creationism: A Test Case

In October 1986, a federal district court ruled that the public schools of Hawkins County, Tennessee, must exempt the children of a group of fundamentalist Christian parents from basic reading classes. Those classes assigned Holt, Rinehart, & Winston texts, texts that had been unanimously approved by the Hawkins County Board of Education on recommendation of their textbook selection committee. The content of the Holt, Rinehart series offended the religious views of these parents, who had joined together as Citizens Organized for Better Schools (COBS) and unsuccessfully petitioned the school board to have their children taught from unoffensive texts. The parents objected to, among other things: a story depicting a young boy having fun while cooking on grounds that the story "denigrates the differences between the sexes" that the Bible endorses; a story entitled "A Visit to Mars" on grounds that it encourages children to use their imaginations in ways incompatible with fundamentalist faith; a story entitled "Hunchback Madonna," which describes the religious and social practices of an Indian settlement in New Mexico, on grounds that the story teaches Catholicism; and an excerpt from Anne Frank's *Diary of a Young Girl* on grounds that it suggests that nonorthodox belief in God is better than no belief at all. The principal and school board both refused to exempt the children from using the Holt, Rinehart readers. The parents took the Hawkins County Public School District to court.

District Court Judge Thomas Hull found nothing wrong with the Holt, Rinehart series, and said so. Yet he concluded that the children must be exempted from reading the series and therefore from their reading classes because, in his words,

> plaintiffs [the parents of the children] sincerely believe that the affirmation of these philosophical viewpoints is repulsive to their Christian faith, so repulsive that they must not allow their children to be exposed to the Holt series. This is their religious belief. They have drawn a line, and it is not for us to say that the line they drew was an unreasonable one.[8]

Why is it not for us to say?

> Not because the parents of those children should have ultimate authority over their education. If that were the case, it would not be for us (or Judge Hull) to say that they must be educated at all. Yet Judge Hull ruled that the children take standardized tests in reading rather than read standardized texts. If standardized tests are justified, then there must be something that all children should learn independently of what their parents want them to learn.
>
> Not because democratic education is compatible with the fundamentalist view that forbids exposure to knowledge about religions, cultures, and convictions that differ from their own, on grounds that such knowledge corrupts the soul. The parents in this case claimed that their children would be corrupted by exposure to beliefs and values that contradict their own religious views unless it was explained that the other views are incorrect and that their views are the correct ones. Democratic education is surely incompatible with this fundamentalist view of knowledge and morality.
>
> Not because democratic education rests on a conception of the good society that threatens the fundamentalist view of a good life and must defer to fundamentalism for the sake of neutrality. Any defensible political understanding of education depends on some conception of a good society, and every conception worth defending threatens some way of life.
>
> It is a sad fact of democracy in the United States that some citizens still hold religious beliefs that reject teaching children the democratic values of mutual respect for reasonable differences of opinion and rational deliberation among differing ways of life. A rejection of democratic values does not, however, constitute a criticism of democracy any more than the rejection by a committed misogynist of the rights of women constitutes a critique of feminism. Both the parents and the misogynists of course have a right to voice their opinions, but in neither case do they have a right to insist that a democratic state teach or sanction their opinions.

Another argument sometimes offered in defense of the claims of fundamentalist parents is that democratic education consists solely of teaching certain facts, not certain values or virtues, to future citizens. This position is superficially similar to John Stuart Mill's conclusion that the state limit its educational authority to public examinations "confined to facts and positive science exclusively."[9] If this is what we should say about public education, it cannot be because knowing facts is more crucial to a good life or good citizenship than being virtuous. Nor can it be because facts are neutral, while values are not. Might it be because citizens can more easily agree on a body of facts than on a set of values or virtues to be taught to all children? Perhaps this argument was soundly prudential when Mill made it, but its premise is surely very shaky today. The political controversies that have raged in recent years over the biases of testing and the claims of creationism against evolution amply demonstrate how controversial the teaching and testing of facts can be. This is no more or less controversial, however, than the teaching (or not teaching) of civic virtue. If it is political controversy that we wish the state above all else to avoid, our only alternative is to advocate repression, in its most thoroughgoing and insidious form.

Neither Discrimination nor Repression

There is no defensible political understanding of education that is not tied to some conception of a good society, and there is no conception that is not controversial. Which conception should we therefore defend? Judge Hull hinted at a conception of liberal neutrality: Secular texts must not be imposed on fundamentalist children because they are not neutral among all competing conceptions of the good life. The Holt, Rinehart readers surely are not neutral between fundamentalist Christianity and secular humanism. Nor, as Judge Hull recognized, could any readers be neutral between deference to God's will as literally revealed in the Bible or authoritatively interpreted by a fundamentalist church, and critical inquiry or mutual respect among persons. Liberal individualists think of themselves as committed only to the latter set of virtues – critical inquiry and mutual respect – but the logic of liberal neutrality does not support their commitment in politics, except as a morally lame expression of personal opinion. This expression is insufficient to justify any form of public schooling. The content of public schooling cannot be neutral among competing conceptions of the good life, and if it could, we would not and should not care to support it.

It is not for us to deny fundamentalist parents the right to draw the wrong line for their children in their homes and churches. Parental freedom entails this limited right.[10] It *is* for us to say that parents do not have a right to veto a line drawn by public schools unless that line is repressive or discriminatory. If parents, judges, or philosopher-kings are allowed to veto lines drawn by public schools when those lines are neither repressive nor discriminatory, then democratic institutions are denied their legitimate role in shaping the character of citizens.

Is democracy not also repressive if it denies the teaching of Christian fundamentalist convictions within public schools, or, what amounts to the same thing, if it requires the teaching of views inimical to fundamentalist convictions?

This challenge to democratic education rests on a serious misunderstanding: that a policy is repressive simply because it requires publicly funded or subsidized schools to teach views that are inimical to the sincerely held beliefs of some parents. Nonrepression requires the prevention of repressive practices, that is, practices that stifle rational understanding and inquiry. It is a reductio ad absurdum to claim that preventing such prevention itself constitutes repression.

To defend public schools against the charge of repression by fundamentalist parents does not, however, entail defending the status quo in American public education – far from it. We must criticize schools that fall short of the democratic ideal by, for example, being overly centralized and bureaucratized, and therefore unconducive to the exercise of both democratic deliberation by citizens and democratic professionalism by teachers. (Simply summarized, democratic professionalism authorizes teachers, at the same time that it obligates them, to uphold the principle of nonrepression, for example, by cultivating in future citizens the capacity for critical reflection on their culture. The ideal of democratic professionalism also obligates public officials to create the working conditions that make possible the exercise of democratic professionalism.) These comments can only begin to touch on the problems that plague our schools, judged from the perspective of a democratic ideal of education.

A democratic society cedes to citizens, parents, teachers, and public officials authority over education, but that authority is limited by the very democratic ideal that supports it. Not even an overwhelming majority has the authority to maintain separate schools for blacks, to ban sex education from schools, to teach creationism as science, or to ban politically unpopular books from school libraries. The first two practices are discriminatory, the second two are repressive. The defense of these judgments concerning our educational practices requires interpretation and application of the democratic standards of nonrepression and nondiscrimination. Because the standards are not merely formal, there is no way of mechanically applying them to cases. We cannot, for example, simply ask whether teaching evolution (or creationism) conflicts with some parents' convictions and if it does, conclude that the practice is repressive. The test of nonrepression and nondiscrimination is not popularity among citizens, parents, teachers, or public officials. Repression entails restriction of rational inquiry, not conflict with personal beliefs, however deeply held those beliefs. For every educational practice or institution, we must therefore ask whether the practice or institution in its actual context restricts (or impedes) rational inquiry and therefore is repressive, or whether it excludes some children from educational goods for reasons unrelated to the legitimate social purposes of those goods and therefore is discriminatory.

Some judgments will be relatively easy: Forcing teachers to teach creationism instead of evolution restricts rational inquiry for the sake of furthering sectarian religion and therefore is repressive. Other judgments require more extended argument: Is it repressive to teach evolution but to require equal time for creationism? If equal time for creationism entails teaching that it is as reasonable to believe that the world with all its creatures was created in seven days as it is to believe that it took *much* longer, then the demand for equal time is indirectly repressive: It undermines the secular standards of reasoning that make democratic education possible in this country. If public schools are permitted to teach the reasonableness of creationism, then the same principle will allow them to teach the reasonableness of divine punishment for the sins of non-Christians or any other minority that happens not to control the school curriculum. On the other hand, if teachers may subject creationist ideas to the same standards of reasoning to which other views presented in their classrooms are subjected, then the demand for equal time may be benign – or even conducive to democratic education. Of course, this is not the interpretation of equal time that proponents of creationism have in mind.

Education and Politics

Democratic standards often do not yield either simple or single answers to questions – such as how much money schools should allocate for educating the handicapped, the gifted, and the average student. That democratic standards do not yield simple answers is a necessity, given the complexity of our collective life; that they do not yield single answers is a virtue, which underscores the democratic critique of "the one best system." Democracy is valuable for far more than its capacity to achieve correct outcomes. It is also valuable for enabling societies to govern themselves, rather than to be governed by an intelligence unrelated to their nature. If democratic societies are to be self-governing, they must remain free to make mistakes in educating children, so long as those mistakes do not discriminate against some children or prevent others from governing themselves freely in the future. The promise of a democratic education is to support self-government without sanctioning majority tyranny or sacrificing future self-government.

It is not for me to say whether my theoretical understanding of democratic education fulfills this promise, but I am sure that the practical promise of any decent theory of democratic education is far from fulfilled in the United States today. I believe that the burden of a democratic theory of education is to show how, with the proper will, we could restructure American society to approach the democratic ideal, even if we never realize it entirely. As a democrat, the most I can consistently offer is criticism of our dominant educational ideas and institutions, and constructive suggestions for democratic directions of change. The possibility of constructive change depends on the will of those who wield political and economic power in this country. In a better society, that will would be more democratic.

These are therefore difficult times for democratic education not only because we are difficult people who must find a principled way of accommodating both individual freedom and civic virtue, but also (and as importantly) because our political and economic institutions are so far from being democratic that they discriminate against the very people who would benefit most directly from a more democratic education and therefore would be most likely to support it. Democratic education is unlikely to succeed if these institutions remain significantly undemocratic. We cannot conclude from this that political or economic reform must precede educational reform. Our choices are not so stark, nor so easy. To improve significantly the working conditions, the political opportunities, or the schooling of poor Americans requires political pressure from the poor themselves, yet they are the citizens most likely to have been educated in highly authoritarian schools (and families) and least likely to participate in politics (or to be effective when they do).

To realize democratic education in this country, political and economic institutions must become more democratic. For these institutions to become more democratic, education must be democratized. It would be foolish to focus solely on a single sphere, whether politics, economics, or education: first, because the prospects of success in any sphere are limited, and second, because the spheres are interdependent. Small but significant changes in one often bring small but significant changes in the others.

Democratic education does not simplify our outlook on education, but it reorients it away from conventional goals (such as educating every child for the appropriate occupation or for choice among the widest range of occupations) toward a more political understanding of educational ends. The cultivation of the virtues, knowledge, and skills necessary for democratic deliberation should have primacy over other ends of public education in a democratic society because such political education prepares citizens to share as equals in *consciously* reproducing (not replicating) their own society, rather than being subject to external forces of reproduction beyond their collective control. Conscious social reproduction is the ideal not only of democratic education but of democratic politics as well.

At the level of primary schooling, the primacy of political education supplies a principled argument against tracking, sexist education, racial segregation, and narrowly vocational education. Even when these practices improve the academic achievement of students, they neglect the virtues of citizenship, cultivated by a common education characterized by respect for racial, religious, intellectual, and sexual differences among students. The moral primacy of political education also supports a presumption in favor of more participatory and deliberative over more disciplinary methods of teaching. Even when student participation threatens to produce some degree of disorder within schools, it may be defended on democratic grounds for cultivating political skills and social commitments. Conversely, even when a principal succeeds in bringing order to an unruly student body, as has

Joe Clark of Eastside High School in Paterson, New Jersey, he may be criticized on democratic grounds for intimidating students rather than reasoning with them, for not tolerating peaceful dissent among teachers, and for expelling problem students in unprecedented numbers (over a three-year period, more than 1,900 students dropped out of Eastside High, many of them expelled by Clark).

Democratic education aims at the empowerment of free and equal citizens, people who are willing and able to share together in shaping their own society. Democratic education therefore constrains public policies by the principles of nonrepression and nondiscrimination for the sake of securing democratic self-government. Within these constraints, democratic education makes a virtue out of the disagreements that inevitably flow from ethnic, religious, sexual, and intellectual diversity.

Above all, democratic education accepts the fact that we are difficult people. Whereas the Platonic family state denies this fact by subsuming individual freedom into civic virtue and the state of individuals denies it by elevating freedom above virtue, democratic education empowers citizens to make their own decisions on how to combine freedom with virtue. Democratic education thereby authorizes people to direct their individual and collective destinies. Fully recognizing that the aims of democratic education may never be fully realized, difficult people should demand no more of our political and educational institutions, and should settle for no less.

Notes

1. Allan Bloom, *The Closing of the American Mind* (New York: Simon & Schuster, 1987), p. 238.
2. Socrates, *Republic of Plato*, trans. Allan Bloom (New York: Basic Books, 1968), p. 273 (590D).
3. Ibid., p. 220 (541A).
4. Ibid., p. 274 (592A).
5. Bruce Ackerman, *Social Justice in the Liberal State* (New Haven: Yale University Press, 1980), p. 148.
6. Ibid., p. 139.
7. Immanuel Kant, *Kant on Education*, trans. Annette Churton (Boston: D.C. Heath, 1900), p. 17.
8. *Bob Mozart et al. v. Hawkins County Public Schools et al.*, U.S. District Court for the Eastern District of Tennessee, Northeastern Division, No. CIV-2-83-401 (October 24, 1986), p. 12. The United States Court of Appeals (Sixth Circuit) reversed the decision of the district court and remanded with directions to dismiss the complaint (827 F. 2d. 1058 [6th Cir. 1987]).
9. John Stuart Mill, "On Liberty," in *Utilitarianism, On Liberty, Essays on Bentham* (New York: New American Library, 1962), p. 241 (chap. 5, paragraph 14).
10. The right is limited not by virtue of being weak, but by virtue of leaving room for other educational authorities.

87

Post-Critical Pedagogies: A Feminist Reading

Patti Lather

Pedagogy must itself be a text. (Ulmer, 1985, p. 52)

. . . teaching is a question of strategy. That is perhaps the only place where we actually get any experience in strategy, although we talk a lot about it. (Spivak, 1989, p. 146)

This paper foregrounds the conflicts between the emancipatory projects and Reconstruction by attempting a constructive displacement of the emancipatory impulse at work in the discourses of "critical pedagogy". Understanding what I mean by such a statement entails some sense of my working definitions of at least three terms: deconstruction, critical and pedagogy.

I frame *deconstruction* as "not a method", but a disclosure of how a text functions as desire (Derrida, in Kearney, 1984, p. 124). Rather than an exposure of error, deconstruction is "a way of thinking . . . about the danger of what is powerful and useful. . . . You deconstructively critique something which is so useful to you that you cannot speak another way" (Spivak, 1989, pp. 135, 151).[1] The goal of deconstruction is neither unitary wholeness nor dialectical resolution. The goal of deconstruction is to keep things in process, to disrupt, to keep the system in play, to set up procedures to continuously demystify the realities we create, and to fight the tendency for our categories to congeal (Caputo, 1987, p. 236). Deconstruction foregrounds the lack of innocence in any discourse by looking at the textual staging of knowledge, the constitutive effects of our uses of language. As the postmodern equivalent of the dialectic, deconstruction provides a corrective moment, a safeguard against dogmatism, a continual displacement.

As noted by Spivak, such a strategy cannot ground a politics (Harasym, 1988). This raises many concerns regarding the politics of postmodernism/poststructuralism,[2] especially its undercutting of the claims to truth and

---

Source: *Education and Society*, 9(1–2) (1991): 100–111.

justice that undergird emancipatory efforts (e.g., Habermas, 1987; Haraway, 1988; Hartsock, 1987; West, 1987). In a time marked by the dissolution of authoritative foundations of knowledge, the possibilities of liberatory praxis grow increasingly problematic. Lyotard, for example, writes that "oppositional thinking . . . is out of step with the most vital modes of postmodern knowledge" (quoted in Schrift, 1990, p. 2). Additionally, the "interpretive praxis" that is deconstruction includes the development of a Foucauldian awareness of the oppressive role of ostensibly liberatory forms of discourse (Atkins and Johnson, 1985, p. 2). In a move to "salvage praxis" (Foucault, 1984), reflexive, practice is strategically privileged as a site for learning the possibilities and limits of turning critical thought into emancipatory action: "In periods when fields are without secure foundations, practice becomes the engine of innovation" (Marcus and Fischer, 1986, p. 166). This entails a reflexivity that attends to the politics of what is and is not done at a practical level in order to learn "to 'read out' the epistemologies in our various practices" (Hartsock, 1987, p. 206). Exploring whether such a salvaging of praxis is possible in a post-foundational era is a major focus of this paper.

Within the context of Frankfurt School critical theory, *critical* reason was used as the interlocutor of *instrumental* reason, the driving force behind modernism. In Poster's words, "critical theory springs from an assumption that we live amid a world of pain, that much can be done to alleviate that pain, and that theory has a crucial role to play in that process" (1989, p. 3). The various feminisms, neomarxisms and the "postmodernisms of resistance" (Hutcheon, 1988, 1989), then, become kinds of critical theories which are informed by identification with and interest in "oppositional" social movements.[3] While in practice not unknown to have *instrumental* moments, critical theories are positioned in relation to counter-hegemonic social movements and take as their charge "the self-clarification of the struggles and wishes of the age" (Marx, quoted in Fraser, 1987, p. 31). As critical practices derive their forms and meanings in relation to their changing historical conditions, positions of resistance can never be established once and for all. They must, instead, be perpetually refashioned to address adequately the shifting conditions and circumstances that ground them (Solomon-Godeau, 1988, p. 208).

I take *pedagogy* to mean that which addresses "the transformation of consciousness that takes place in the intersection of three agencies – the teacher, the learner and the knowledge they together produce" (Lusted, 1986, p. 3). According to Lusted's oft-quoted definition, pedagogy refuses to instrumentalize these relations, diminish their interactivity, or value one over another. It, furthermore, denies the teacher as neutral transmitter, the student as passive, and knowledge as immutable material to impart. Instead, the concept of pedagogy focuses attention on the conditions and means through which knowledge is produced. All pedagogies are situated – specific and contingent to the cultural fields within which they operate. Lusted sees the disattention, the "desperately undertheorized" (p. 3) nature of pedagogy as at the root of the failure of emancipatory objectives. Such a claim constructs the interactive productivity, as opposed to the merely transmissive nature of what happens in the pedagogical act, as a central issue in the struggle for a more just world.[4]

Within my definitional web, *critical pedagogy* is positioned as that which attends to practices of teaching/learning intended to interrupt particular historical, situated systems of oppression. Such pedagogies go by many names: Freirean, feminist, anti-racist, radical, empowering, liberation theology. With both overlaps and specificities within and between, each is constructed out of a combination of Frankfurt School critical theory, Gramscian counter-hegemonic practice and Freirean conscientization (Luke, this volume). It is the central claim of this paper that, too often, such pedagogies have failed to probe the degree to which "empowerment" becomes something done "by" liberated pedagogies "to" or "for" the as-yet-unliberated, the "Other", the object upon which is directed the "emancipatory" actions (Ellsworth, this volume). It is precisely this question that postmodernism frames: How do our very efforts to liberate perpetuate the relations of dominance? What follows explores that question by looking first at the discourses of emancipatory education and then at what I am presently calling "post-critical pedagogies".

The Discourses of Emancipatory Education

> If intellectuals have to talk to one another in specialized terms, so be it. The question becomes "Does that get translated at some level into the classroom?" And if it *does*, then the barn door is open. Once you get into the undergraduate classroom successfully, then you're outside the ivory tower. You're into the culture (Lentricchia, quoted in DeCurtis, 1989, p. 8.)

Lentricchia's pedagogical strategy uses deconstruction to help students create subject positions such as "a kind of new person who's not going to be satisfied with the usual canonical things" (ibid., p. 148). In this section, I explore the problematic intersection between the emancipatory projects and deconstruction via a tracing of its inscription in the discourses of emancipatory education. With Lentricchia's argument for pedagogical intervention in mind, I first construct a necessarily partial "review of the literature" to provide an overview of that intersection. I then position it as a site of struggle by juxtaposing multiple, conflicting readings of Ellsworth's (this volume) essay, "Why Doesn't This Feel Empowering? Working Through the Repressive Myths of Critical Pedagogy."

At one level, the problematic of postmodernism is to "make of our disorders new knowledge" (Hassan, 1987, p. 81). What this might mean within the context of educational thought and practice is captured by

Johnson's (1987) argument that the politics of undecidability, the unavoidable openendedness and inherent perspectivity of knowledge, "become an access route to a whole rethinking of the educational enterprise" (p. 44). Some of this work is beginning regarding pedagogy. Much of the "deconstructivist pedagogy" literature comes from the area of literary criticism and cultural studies, but work located in educational studies is emerging.[5] Ellsworth's situated problematizing of the abstract prescriptions of critical pedagogies, which I will address later, is a highly visible example, given its publication in a major educational journal and its targeting for commentary by some of the chief architects of "critical pedagogy" (Giroux, 1988; McLaren, 1988).

In terms of the ways that postmodernism is being inscribed in the discourses of emancipatory education, Britzman's (1991) exploration of a poststructural account of teacher identity brings issues of subjectivity, language and power to bear on teacher education. The postmodern focus on what makes our knowledge both possible and problematic underscores the projects of Cherryholmes (1988), Wexler (1987), and Whitson (1988). Cherryholmes' book, the first in education to have "poststructural" in the title, is especially valuable in its effort to work at an introductory level. Arguing that "much of the unfamiliarity and strangeness of poststructuralism recedes when applied to everyday life" (p. 142), Cherryholmes describes educational reform as one structural invasion after another by looking at Bloom's toxonomy, Tyler's rationale, Schwab's "The Practical 4", the relationship between textbooks, standardized tests and teaching, empirical research, and critical "emancipatory" practice.[6]

First in Britain and now globally, Stuart Hall and the cultural studies groups probe popular culture as a means to understand the formation of subjects in relations of power. A growing body of such work is developing (e.g., Roman, Christian-Smith and Ellsworth, 1988). Schooling is one of many sites looked at in the development of a non-dualistic theory of subjectivity that privileges neither the romanticized individual nor social, linguistic and cultural structures as determinants (Henriques et al., 1984). A more complex understanding of identity and citizenship is constructed via a discursive focus on networks of practices which constitute subjects in shifting, multiple, contradictory sites. Hence, identity is positioned as an effect of subjectification, rather than as a natural right or an essence which the discourses of emancipation can unfurl (Donald, 1985). As such, poststructural perspectives problematize received wisdom in social theory regarding identity, subjectivity and agency. Context and meaning in everyday life are posited as co-constructions, multiple, complex, open and changing, neither pre-given nor explainable by large-scale causal theories. They are, rather, made and re-made across a multiplicity of minor scattered practices. Agency is reconceptualized within the context of a fluid, changeable social setting, in motion via the interaction of a plurality of multiply sited, diffused agents who create "always there and always fragile systems" (Bauman, 1989, p. 51). Walkerdine has amassed a considerable body of work in this area:

a deconstruction of Piaget and theories of developmental psychology (1984), the effects on girls of their contradictory positioning in primary classrooms in both dominant/subordinate and power/resistance discourse/practices (1985), and the discursive positioning of females as teachers and students in schools (1981, 1986).

A focus on the reception by students of curricular interventions done in the name of liberation is exemplified in Davies' (1989) work on pre-school student responses to feminist fairy tales. By foregrounding the ambiguities of how texts make meaning, such a focus has great implications for curriculum. Other efforts to rethink curricular issues are Doll (1989), Stephen Ball's (1990) edited collection, *Foucault and Education*, and such work as Bowers (1988), and Murphy (1988), on computers and the move away from text-based pedagogy. Henry Giroux has edited a 1988 special issue of the *Journal of Education*, "Schooling in the Postmodern Age," and co-authored, with Stanley Aronowitz, *Postmodern Education: Politics, Culture and Social Criticism* (1990). Finally, the pages of *Educational Theory, Educational Foundations and Qualitative Studies in Education* increasingly attend to the implications of postmodernism for education.

Why Doesn't This Feel Empowering?

To explore the problems and possibilities that this emerging body of work raises for emancipatory education, I turn to Ellsworth's implosion of the canons of critical pedagogy. She places the key discourses in the literature of critical pedagogy in relation to her interpretation of her experience of teaching a university-level anti-racism course, and then examines the discourses within which critical pedagogues are caught up. Problematizing the concepts of empowerment, student voice, dialogue and the term "critical" itself, she asks which interpretations and 'sense making' these discourses facilitate, which do they silence and marginalize, and what interests do they serve?

Rooted in her own experience of the limits of the prescriptions of critical pedagogy, she suggests a movement from "dialogue" to "working together across differences" (p. 106), from a concept of an eventually unified dialogue to the construction of "strategies in context" (p. 109) for dealing with the unsaid and unsayable present within classrooms. There "all voices . . . are not and cannot carry equal legitimacy, safety, and power" given present social structures. As she notes, this problematizes the concept of "voice" so evident in liberatory discourse in education.[7] "Pluralizing the concept as 'voices' implies correction through addition. Such unproblematic pluralizing loses sight of the contradictory and partial nature of all voices" (p. 104):

> Conventional notions of dialogue and democracy assume rationalized, individualized subjects capable of agreeing on universalizable "fundamental moral principles" and "quality of human life" that become self-evident when

subjects cease to be self-interested and particularistic about group rights. Yet social agents are not capable of being fully rational and disinterested; and they are subjects split between the conscious and unconscious and among multiple social positionings. (p. 108)

Ellsworth is especially interested in what she calls "the violence of rationalism against its Others" (p. 96). She shifts the focus from the effort to create a dialogical community to an effort toward "sustained encounter with currently oppressive formations and power relations." This encounter "owned up to my own implications in those formations and was capable of changing my own relation to and investments in those formations" (p. 100). Unsettling received definitions, multiplying subject positions, unlearning our own privileges, "profoundly contextual (historical) and interdependent (social)" (p. 115), such a pedagogy has no prescriptions. Moving out of the position of "master of truth and justice" (Foucault, 1977, p. 12), Ellsworth conceptualizes her task as "the challenge of constructing classroom practices that engage with the discursive and material spaces that such a removal opens up" (p. 115).

In terms of exploring the intersection of postmodernism and the emancipatory projects, Ellsworth's essay and reactions to it evoke a keen sense of the complexities of doing praxis-oriented intellectual work in a post-foundational context. By positioning modernist assumptions of truth, objectivity and "correct readings" as ensnared in phallocentric and logocentric rationalities, can postmodernism begin to clear the ground and challenge the plethora of concepts that appear as givens in our debates about the possibilities and limits of emancipatory education? How can such self-reflexivity both render our basic assumptions problematic and provisional and yet still propel us to take a stand?

In raising such issues, postmodernism positions emancipatory reason as vulnerable to interrogation. It traces the collusion of oppositional intellectuals with the very cultural dominants they are opposing via the intersection of liberatory intentions and the "will to power" that underscores the privileged positions of knowing and changing. Hence, the discourses of emancipation are located as much within Foucault's "regimes of truth" as not. Additionally, rather than separating the "true" from the "false", postmodernism destabilizes assumptions of interpretive validity and shifts emphasis to the contexts in which meanings are produced.

Any exploration of the conditions of receptivity within which an intervention such as Ellsworth's is situated grows out of the postmodern assumption that audiences are fragmented and multiple in their production of any meanings that a text might have. Given congested and conflicted semiotic environments and different positionalities in the "difference crisis" that repositions centers and margins in leftist discursive practices, multiple and contradictory readings are to be expected. As an example, I will read McLaren (1988) and Giroux's (1988) readings of Ellsworth's text against time.

McLaren, admittedly ambivalent about postmodernism, frames Ellsworth in a "post-critical" position of

> . . . political inertia and moral cowardice where educators remain frozen in the zone of "dead" practice in which it is assumed that all voices are those which silence or which contain the "other" by a higher act of violence, and all passionate ethical stances are those built upon the edifices of some form of tyranny or another. Unable to speak with any certainty, or with an absolute assurance that his or her pedagogy is untainted by any form of domination, the 'post-critical' educator refuses to speak at all. (pp. 71–72)

According to McLaren, her essay is, furthermore, an attempt to "discredit" selected critical educators via the assumedly inadequate "proof" of her account of her own teaching and the use of "decontextualized quotes" to represent theorists' positions, thereby "setting up critical pedagogy to fail from the very beginning." This "woeful misreading of the tradition she so cavalierly indicts" is full of "distortions, mystifications, and despair" based on her "self-professed lack of pedagogical success" and "her inability to move beyond her own self-doubt", thereby "hold[ing] her voice hostage" and "using theory as a scapegoat for failed practice" (p. 72).

Giroux positions Ellsworth's piece as "a liberal call to harmonize and resolve differences" (p. 170). Conversely, her view of differences as "merely antagonistic" results in "separatism [a]s the only valid political option for any kind of pedagogical and political action . . . a crippling form of political disengagement" (p. 177). An "attempt to delegitimate the work of other critical educators" (p. 177), he positions her as

> . . . claiming rather self-righteously the primacy and singularity of her own ideological reading of what constitutes a political project . . . degrad[ing] the rich complexity of theoretical and pedagogical processes that characterize the diverse discourses in the field of critical pedagogy. In doing so, she suc-cumbs to the familiar academic strategy of dismissing others through the use of straw-man tactics and excessive simplifications which undermine not only the strengths of her own work, but also the very nature of social criticism itself. This is "theorizing" as a form of "bad faith," a discourse imbued with the type of careerism that has become all too characteristic of many left academics, (p. 178)

Across McLaren and Giroux's readings, I present two of my own readings of Ellsworth. The first focuses on the textual practices that she uses to locate her intervention. The second reading offers a construction of both how she evokes ways to work with rather than be paralyzed by the loss of Cartesian stability and unity (Weedon, 1987), and what the material consequences of her project might be. Foregrounding the reductiveness of the interpretive act, I propose my readings across these complex, shifting and polyvalent fields as neither "correct" nor final. Like Lanser (1989) in her reading of the political unconscious inscribed in white academic feminist readings of Gilman's "The Yellow Wallpaper," I call on Adrienne Rich in order to frame my readings as evocations to look beyond old critical premises and toward continuing revision:

> How can I fail to love
>   your clarity and fury
> How can I give you
>   all your due
>   take courage from your courage
> honor your exact
>   legacy as it is
> recognizing
>   as well
>   that it is not enough?
>   (Rich, in Lanser, 1989, p. 436)

In terms of textual performativity in her essay, Ellsworth's move is to clear a space from which to articulate her own difference within a field of competing discourses. Using self-reflexive experience as a basis for knowing, she operates out of what Hutcheon (1989) calls "a very feminist awareness of the value of experience and the importance of its representation in the form of 'life-writing' – however difficult or even falsifying that process might turn out to be" (p. 167). Self-consciously positioning herself as an alternative to the presumed dominant, she sets herself both within and against the political terrain where Enlightenment discourses function and have their effectivity. Inserting herself into a largely unexplicated but privileged field of feminist pedagogy, she does battle with other texts according to her own ground rules, texts which precede and surround the "intertextual arena" that she creates (Collins, 1989). Intensifying differences as a way to clear such a space, she tends to "a counter-cultural Salvation Army beating its moral drum about the wickedness of the dominant" (Collins, p. 122). Her seizing of a moral high ground and her demonizing of critical pedagogy's "repressive myths" per-petuate monolithic categories of dominant/dominated, thereby intensifying the conflictive nature of the semiotic environment. A way out of this might have been to foreground how her construction of herself as a privileged alternative inscribes as well as subverts, in essence deconstructing her own strategies of self-legitimation. Such a move would have added another textual dimension to the Foucauldian suspicion of every operation that seeks to center a subject who is in a position to know, a suspicion that is at the heart of her project.

Shifting from textual practices to her positioning of the realms of pedagogy as a powerful site for liberatory intervention, Ellsworth's work displaces the totalizing desire to establish foundations with a move toward self-critique. This move is premised on her acknowledgment of the profound challenge that poststructural theories of language and subjectivity offer to our capacity to know the "real" via the mediations of critical pedagogy. Primary in this move is her decentering of the "transformative intellectual" (Aronowitz and Giroux, 1985) as the origin of what can be known and done. To multiply the ways in which we can interrupt the relations of dominance requires deconstructing such vanguardism. Britzman's (1989) questions evoke this reflexive process: "What kinds of practices are possible once vulnerability, ambiguity, and doubt are admitted? What kinds of power and authority are taken up and not admitted?" (p. 17). Deconstructing vanguardism means asking ourselves hard questions about how our interventionary moves render people passive, "positioned as potential recipients of predefined services rather than as agents involved in interpreting their needs and shaping their life-conditions" (Fraser, 1989, p. 174).

Rather than attacking the work of others, Ellsworth's project can be read as an example of how deconstruction can serve to problematize critical pedagogy in ways that *resituate* our emancipatory work as opposed to destroy it. Making the workings of pedagogy more apparent, her project demonstrates how deconstructing our own practices can animals and expand our sense of the structure of possibilities in regards to change-oriented practices. Ellsworth also begins to give a feel for the political possibilities of the multiply-sited subject of poststructuralist theory, a subject characterized by heterogeneity, irreducible particularities, and incalculable differences. Her focus on different differences or Derrida's différance, the condition of differences *and* identity (Grosz, 1989, p. 31), is radically other than the separatism of which Giroux accuses her. Rather than speaking to Ellsworth's intervention as "a crippling form of political disengagement" (p. 177), I read his accusation as saying more about his own continued investments in the liberal struggle for equality and identity politics via the mediations of critical pedagogy.

Against the inertia and moral cowardice that McLaren speaks of, I position Ellsworth's intervention as an act of courage in taking on such dominant architects of critical pedagogy. This seems especially so given the vitriol she has evoked, e.g., McLaren's reading of Ellsworth's openness and uncertainties regarding her pedagogical strategies as "a scapegoat for failed practice." Instead of "dead" or "failed" practice, I read her as positioning herself "always in the position of beginning again" (Foucault, 1984, p. 47) within the context of both the foregrounding of limits that is postmodernism and the embodied reflexivity that characterizes feminist pedagogy. In regards to Giroux's pronouncements about the effects of her self-reflexive decentering, I read his statements about "careerism" and the undermining of "the very nature of social criticism itself" (p. 178) as ironically repositioning himself and the other (largely male) architects of critical pedagogy at the center of her discourse. She is reduced to the "Young Turk", the "daughter" out to displace her fathers. Disrupting any notion of a privileged, unproblematic position from which to speak, she seems to have unleashed "the virulence and the power invested in logocentric thought" (Grosz, 1989, p. 34).

McLaren and Giroux worry much about the nihilism assumed to undergird postmodernism's suspicion of claims to truth, the will to knowledge and the primacy of reason. I share Derrida's suspicion of the nihilism charge often levelled against postmodernism as "not just a simplification; it is symptomatic of certain political and instrumental interests" (in Kearney, 1984, p. 124). Ellsworth's project belies the spectre of such nihilism. Like most of the work mentioned in this section, her project demonstrates how postmodernism has much to offer those of us who do our work in the name of emancipation, constructing the material for struggle present in the stuff of our daily lives to which we all have access.

Such a reading of the incursion of postmodernism into the discourses of liberatory education foregrounds my position that there is nothing in post-modernism that makes it intrinsically reactionary. The postmodern moment is an open-ended construction that is contested, incessantly perspectival and multiply-sited. Framing reactions to Ellsworth as disparate, full of un-resolvable tensions, and necessarily partial, I have used what Collins (1989) terms "juxtaposition as interrogation" (p. 140) in order to foreground what is at stake in our interpretive practices. Such deconstructive textual strategy embodies how postmodernism imposes a severe reexamination of the thought of the Enlightenment. It also enacts how it is being inscribed by those who want to critically preserve the emancipatory impulse within a framework sympathetic to postmodernism's resituating of that impulse (Peters, 1989). I now turn to the difficulties of a position that seeks to use postmodernism to both problematize and advance emancipatory pedagogy. My focus in this final section is on the relationship of the self-proclaimed discourses of feminist and critical pedagogies.

Post-Critical Pedagogies

It is the early 1970's. Picture a room of male marxists around a table, debating the role of feminism in the struggle, deciding that it is, in fact, important. They go to the door, having decided to invite in the feminists. In the meantime, the feminists break through the window and shit on the table (Paraphrase of a story told by Stuart Hall at the Cultural Studies. Now and in the Future Conference, University of Illinois, April, 1990).

The relationship between feminist pedagogy and the largely male in-scribed liberation models of critical pedagogy is generally unexamined. Until very recently, what small attention there had been often called for feminism as the practice, Marxism as the theory (e.g., Lather, 1984). Rather than such a "handmaiden" positioning of Marxism and feminism, much more likely today are calls for serious skepticism of and critical attention to those contemporary education narratives that claim to be emancipatory. Luke, for example, positions radical pedagogy as an "exemplary text" of masculinist epistemology (this volume p. 45). Ellsworth (this volume) brings a feminist suspicion to the largely male discourses of "critical pedagogy". And Gore (this volume) follows the counter-canonical Foucauldian tenet that "nothing is innocent", as she places feminist as well as critical pedagogies under suspicion.

Rather than positioning liberatory pedagogies as logical unfoldings toward a desired goal, such work explores their contradictions and contingencies, their tensions, and internal resistances to their own "forward" movement. Foregrounded are the exclusions, limitations and constraints placed on practice, including the inevitable collusion of liberatory pedagogues with that to which they are opposed. In my own work, for example, I have tried to turn the gaze upon myself as well as others, as I look at the sins of imposition that we commit in the name of liberation (Lather, 1988a, 1991).

One reading of Hall's story is that the object of the noxious waste left by feminists is the male movement of inclusion into the site of "critical pedagogy", a site men have constructed to serve themselves. Refusing the invitation, feminists left to create the discourses of feminist pedagogy, thereby contributing to the "difference crisis" which challenges the status of Marxism as the center of leftist discursive practices and forms of cultural struggle that hope to make a difference. Now, spurred on by deconstruction, feminists return to the site of "critical pedagogy" in order to reconfigure the relationship between feminist and masculinist discourses of liberatory pedagogy.

The relationship of feminism and Marxism so pungently evoked in Hall's story is reconfigured in postmodernism as Other to dutiful wife/daughter/handmaid. Kroker and Cook, in my favorite example of this reconfiguration, have termed feminism "*the quantum physics of postmodernism*" (1986, p. 22, original emphasis). I have thought much about what this might mean. I shall only briefly rehearse here a line of argument more fully developed elsewhere (Lather, 1991). This argument, of course, is deeply inscribed with my own investments of privilege and struggle.

Feminism displaces the articulation of postmodernism from the site of the fathers and opens up the possibility of a heteroglot articulation premised on multiplicities and particularities. Full of contestatory and contradictory theories and practices "while still producing solidarity and concerted action" (Smith, 1988, p. 155), feminism is, at this particular historical juncture in western academic culture, "the paradigmatic political discourse of postmodernism" (Kipnis, 1988, p. 60). Such a claim can be advanced on three grounds: feminism's tendency toward practice-based theorizing that interrupts the "theoreticism" of Marxism, its relegation of practice to an object of theory (Reiss, 3988); feminism's disruption of the "death of the subject" postulated by poststructuralism (Hartsock, 1987); and, finally, feminism's long-running practices of self-reflexivity which both render basic assumptions partial and provisional and yet, never the less, act in and on the world, refusing the political surrender, the Nietzschean anger assumed by so many, in some interestingly gendered ways, to be attendant upon "the postmodern turn" (Hassan, 1987; Riley, 1988).

While both feminist and Marxist thought share aspirations to be theories in the service of a politics, my argument for foregrounding feminist thought and practice in the inscribing of postmodernism displaces the hegemony of Marxism over Left discourse/practices. In doing so, it is important to not set up a false and problematic "male" system beneath which is a true "female" essence recuperable via "correct" practices. In developing counter-practices, the multiplicity of minor scattered practices that make up the fabric of our lives, feminism is no more "the angel in the house of critical theory" (Scholes, quoted in Fuss, 1989, p. 80) than are male practices. Feminism is, however, doubly positioned both within and against the discourses of the fathers, inscribed in logocentrism, patriarchal rationality and imperialistic practices even as it struggles to transform such practices. A stunning example is Lanser's (1988) deconstruction of the layers of racial politics in white feminist readings of Gilman's "The Yellow Wallpaper." Positioning herself both within and against the standard feminist readings of the story, Lanser demonstrates how our readings are both transformative and limiting, inevitably fixed and reductive of possibilities. Most impressive to me, she does so in a way that is respectful of the difficulties of such work, that loves the "clarity" and "fury" and "courage" of such work, but pushes against it from within as she demonstrates "that it is not enough" (p. 436). As such, feminism has much to offer in the development of practices of self-interrogation and critique, practice-based theorizing and more situated and embodied discourses about pedagogy.

If deconstruction is about probing the limits of what we cannot think without, deconstructing "critical" is as necessary to critical pedagogies as deconstructing "woman" is to any "forwarding" movement of feminism (Riley, 1988). In the "difference crisis" that repositions centers and margins in leftist discursive practices, what might the sign of "post-critical" mean?

McLaren's fixing of the term as political quietude and "dead" practice (1988, pp. 1–71) is symptomatic of the tenuous relationship of many leftist intellectuals with deconstruction. Much more comfortable with practices of ideology critique, with its binary logic which demonizes some "Other" and positions itself as innocent, many find unnerving the "new canon" (Rajchman, 1985) of deconstructive self-reflexivity: "'There are no social positions exempt from becoming oppressive to others. . . . any group – any position – can move into the oppressor role' . . . 'everyone is someone else's 'Other'" (Minh-ha and Gentile, respectively, quoted in Ellsworth, this volume, p. 114).

Perhaps the need to look beyond old critical premises and toward continuing revision might be more palatable if displayed under the sign of (post)critical – a textual display of the continued centrality of critical reason, as defined at the beginning of this essay. Practices of pedagogy that work against systems of oppression are more, not less, needed in a world marked by growing global maldistribution of power and resources. In translating critical theory into a pedagogical agenda, (post)critical foregrounds movement beyond the sedimented discursive configurations of essentialized, romanticized subjects with authentic needs and real identities, who require generalized emancipation from generalized social oppression via the mediations of liberatory pedagogues capable of exposing the "real" to those caught up in the distorting meaning systems of late capitalism.

Within (post)critical practices of pedagogy, emancipatory space is problematized via deconstruction of the Enlightenment equation of knowing, naming and emancipation. Especially placed under suspicion are the philosophies of presence, which assume the historical role of self-conscious human agency and the vanguard role of critical intellectuals. Addressing the impasse between idealist voluntarism and structuralist fatalism, theories of the irreducibly necessary subject are reinscribed in postmodern discourses via a problematizing of "a metaphysics of human agency . . . an inflated conception of the powers of human reason and will" (Fay, 1987, pp. 26,9). In an especially important move, feminist postmodernism refuses both Althusser's "process without a subject" and post-structuralism's fractured, fragmented subject. Neither the romanticized individual nor the pawn of social determinants, the subject of contemporary feminism is theorized in ways that offer hope for sustained contestation and resistance (for more on identity politics, consciousness and agency, see Lather, 1989). I conclude with some thoughts on the possibilities for post-critical intellectuals.

To abandon crusading rhetoric, and begin to think outside of a framework which sees the "other" as the problem for which they are the solution, is to shift the role of critical intellectuals. This shift entails a move away from positions of either universalizing spokespeople for the disenfranchised, or cultural workers who struggle against the barriers which prevent people from speaking for themselves. This postmodern re-positioning of critical intellectuals has to do with struggling to decolonize the space of academic discourse that is accessed by our privilege, to open that space up in a way that contributes to the production of a politics of difference. Such a politics recognizes the paradox, complexity and complicity at work in our efforts to understand and change the world. Hence, perhaps the subtext of what Foucault (1980) and Lyotard (1984) are saying about the end of the great metanarratives of emancipation and enlightenment is that *who speaks* is more important than *what is said* (Said, 1986, p. 153, original emphasis). Their pronouncements may have more to do with the end of some speaking for others than the end of liberatory struggle.

Conclusion

Rather than epistemologically constituted domains of norms, I have positioned both feminist and critical pedagogies as historically produced and situated sites from which to ask questions about the relationship of feminism and marxism in a post-foundational context. From my own marked position of feminism, I have tried to construct a non-agonistic narrative which proceeds otherwise than by thinking via oppositions (de Lauretis, 1989). In a place where there is no innocent discourse of liberation, my hope has been to use both our internal contradictions and our differences across one another to refigure community, to include ways of disagreeing productively among ourselves, as we struggle to use postmodernism to both problematize and advance emancipatory pedagogy.

Notes

This paper is reprinted with permission from James Nicholas Publishers and originally appeared in *Education and Society*, 9(2), 1991, pp. 100–111, and in Peter McLaren (Ed.), *Postmodernity and Pedagogy*, James Nicholas Publishers, Albert Park, Australia, in press.

1. While impossible to freeze conceptually, deconstruction can be broken down into three steps: 1) identify the binaries, the oppositions that structure an argument; 2) reverse/displace the dependent term from its negative position to a place that locates it as the very condition of the positive term; and 3) create a more fluid and less coercive conceptual organization of terms which transcends a binary logic by simultaneously being both and neither of the binary terms (Grosz, 1989, p. xv).

   This somewhat linear definition is deliberately placed in the endnotes in order to displace the desire to domesticate deconstruction as it moves across the many sites of its occurrence, e.g., the academy, architecture, and the arts.

2. While suspicious of the desire for definitions which analytically "fix" complex, contradictory and relational constructs, I generally use the term *postmodern* to mean the shift in material conditions of advanced monopoly capitalism brought on by the micro-electronic revolution in information technology, the growth of multinational capitalism and the global uprising of the marginalized. This conjunction includes movements in art, architecture, and the practices of everyday life. I generally use *poststructural* to mean the working out of cultural theory within that context, but I also sometimes use the terms interchangeably. For a more extensive wrestling with these definitions, see Lather, 1991.

3. "Oppositional" is a problematic term on many levels, subscribing as it does to a binary logic of opposites. Nancy Fraser, however, has come up with a relational definition rather than a definition statically grounded in binaries. She defines oppositional as "forms of needs talk, which arise when needs are politicized 'from below'" (1989, p. 171).

   Another problematic term in this sentence is "postmodernisms of resistance". Calinescu (1987) warns that the tendency to construct "a bad reactionary" postmodernism" and "a good, resistant, anticapitalist variety" reproduces the very binaries to which postmodernism is purportedly other than (p. 292).

4. The centrality of pedagogy in postmodern discursive practices can be explored by contrasting the title of a 1987 conference, "Postmodernism: Text, Politics, Instruction" (sponsored by the University of Kansas and the International Association for Philosophy and Literature), with the complete lack of attention to issues of teaching and learning in the conference program. A recent "turn to pedagogy" in cultural studies is evident in such work as Henricksen and Morgan (1990), Morton and Zavarzadeh (1991), and a special issue of *Strategies: A Journal of Theory, Culture and Politics* on "Pedagogical Theories/Educational Practices" (2, 1989).

5. For examples of poststructuralist discourse on pedagogy, in addition to note #4, from literary criticism and cultural studies: Atkins and Johnson, 1985; Zavarzadeh and Morton, 1986–87;

Naidus, 1987; Nelson, 1986. From educational studies: Orner and Brennan, 1989; Giroux, 1988; McLaren, 1988; Maher and Tetreault, 1989; Brodkey, 1987; Lewis, 1990; Miller, 1990; Berlak, 1990; Bromley, 1989; Lather, 1990.

6. Cherryholmes' book ignores what Newton, 1988, terms "the mother roots" of post-structuralism. For a review, sec Lather, 1988b.

7. The concept of "voice" is also problematized in Morton and Zavarzadeh, 1988–89 and, especially, London, 1990, who draws on feminist theory, cultural criticism, cultural ethnography and narrative theory to challenge traditional assumptions about voice as a reliable marker of individuality, originality and self-identity.

References

Aronowitz, Stanley and Giroux, Henry (1985) Radical Education and Transformative Intellectuals. *Canadian Journal of Political and Social Theory*, 9(3), 48–63.

Aronowitz, Stanley and Giroux, Henry (1990) *Postmodern Education: Politics, Culture and Social Criticism*. Minneapolis: University of Minnesota Press.

Atkins, G. Douglas and Johnson, Michael L. (1985) *Writing and Reading Differently: Deconstruction and the Teaching of Composition and Literature*. Lawrence, Kansas: University of Kansas Press.

Ball, Stephen (Ed.) (1990) *Foucault and Education*. London: Routledge.

Bauman, Zygmunt (1989) Sociological Responses to Post-modernity. *Thesis Eleven, 23*, 35–63.

Berlak, Ann (April, 1990) Experiencing Teaching: Viewing and Re-viewing Education 429. Paper Presented at the Annual Meeting of the American Educational Research Association, Boston.

Bowers, C. A. (1988) *The Cultural Dimensions of Educational Computing: Understanding the Non-neutrality of Technology*. New York: Teacher's College Press.

Britzman, Deborah (Feb, 1989) The Terrible Problem of "Knowing Thyself": Toward a Poststructural Account of Teacher Identity. Paper presented at the Ethnography and Education Research Forum, University of PA.

Britzman, Deborah (1991) *Practice makes Practice: A Critical Study of Learning to Teach*. Albany: State University of New York Press.

Brodkey, Linda (1987) Postmodern Pedagogy for Progressive Educators: An Essay Review. *Journal of Education, 196*(3), 138–143.

Bromley, Hank (1989) Identity Politics and Critical Pedagogy. *Educational Theory, 39*(3), 207–223.

Calinescu, Matei (1987) *Five Faces of Modernity: Modernism, Avant-garde, Decadence, Kitsch and Postmodernism*. Durham, N.C.: Duke University Press.

Caputo, John (1987) *Radical Hermeneutics: Repetition, Reconstruction, and the Hermeneutic Project*. Bloomington, Indiana: University of Indiana Press.

Cherryholmes, Cleo (1988) *Power and Criticism: Poststructural Investigations in Education*. New York: Teacher's College Press.

Collins, Jim (1989) *Uncommon Cultures: Popular Culture and Post-modernism*. New York: Routledge.

Davies, Bronwyn (1989) *Frogs and Snails and Feminist Tales*. Sydney: George Allen and Unwin.

DeCurtis, Anthony (March 23, 1989) Postmodern Romance: What the Kids who Really Read are Really Reading. *Rolling Stone, 146*, 5–6.

de Lauretis, Teresa (1989) The Essence of the Triangle or, Taking the Risk of Essentialism Seriously: Feminist Theory in Italy, the U.S., and Britain. *Differences, 1*(2), 3–37.

Doll, William E. Jr. (1989) Foundations for a Post-modern Curriculum. *Journal of Curriculum Studies, 21*(3), 243–253.

Donald, James (1985) Beacons of the Future: Schooling, Subjection and Subjectification. In Veronica Beechey and James Donald (Eds.), *Subjectivity and Social Relations*. Milton Keynes: Open University Press, 214–249.

Fay, Brian (1987) *Critical Social Science*. Ithaca, N.Y.: Cornell University Press.

Foucault, Michel (1977) The Political Function of the Intellectual. *Radical Philosophy*, 17, 12–14.

Foucault, Michel (1980) *Power/Knowledge: Selected Interviews and Other Writings, 1972–1977*. Colin Gordon (Ed.) and Gordon et al. (Trans.). New York: Pantheon.

Foucault, Michel (1984) What is Enlightenment? In Paul Rabinow (Ed.) *The Foucault Reader*. New York: Pantheon, 32–50.

Fraser, Nancy (1987) What's Critical about Critical Theory? The Case of Habermas and Gender. In Seyla Benhabib and D. Cornell (Eds.) *Feminism as Critique*. Minneapolis: University of Minnesota Press, 31–55.

Fraser, Nancy (1989) *Unruly Practices: Power, Discourse and Gender in Contemporary Social Theory*. Minneapolis: University of Minnesota Press.

Fuss, Diana (1989) Reading like a Feminist. *Differences, 1*(2), 7–92.

Giroux, Henry (1988) Border Pedagogy in the Age of Postmodernism. *Journal of Education, 170*(3), 162–181.

Gore, Jennifer (April, 1990) The Struggle for Pedagogies: Critical and Feminist Discourses as "Regimes of Truth". Paper Presented at the annual meeting of the American Educational Research Association, Boston.

Grosz, Elizabeth (1989) *Sexual Subversions: Three French Feminists*. Sydney: Allen and Unwin.

Habermas, Jurgen (1987) *The Philosophical Discourse of Modernism*. Cambridge: Mass., M.I.T. Press.

Harasym, Sarah (1988) Practical Politics of the Open End: An Interview with Gayatri Spivak. *Canadian Journal of Political and Social Theory*, 12(1–2), 51–69.

Haraway, Donna (1988) Situated Knowledges: The Science Question in Feminism and the Privilege of Partial Perspective. *Feminist Studies, 14*(3), 575–599.

Hartsock, Nancy (1987) Rethinking Modernism: Minority vs. Majority Theories. *Cultural Critique, 7*, 187–206.

Hassan, Ihab (1987) *The Postmodern Turn: Essays in Postmodern Theory and Culture*. Columbus, Ohio: The Ohio State University Press.

Henricksen, Bruce and Morgan, Thais (Eds.) (1990) *Reorientations: Critical Theories and Pedagogies*. Urbana: University of Illinois Press.

Henriques, Julian, Holloway, Wendy, Unwin, Cathy, Venn, Couze, and Walkerdine, Valerie (Eds.) (1984) *Changing the Subject: Psychology, Social Regulation and Subjectivity*. London: Methuen.

Hutcheon, Linda (1988) A Postmodern Problematics. In Robert Merrill (Ed.), *Ethics/Aesthetics: Postmodern Positions*. Washington, D.C.: Maisonneuve Press, 1–10.

Hutcheon, Linda (1989) *The Politics of Postmodernism*. London: Routledge.

Johnson, Barbara (1987) *A World of Difference*. Baltimore: Johns Hopkins University Press.

Kearney, Richard (1984) *Dialogues with Contemporary Continental Thinkers: The Phenomenological Heritage*. Manchester: Manchester University Press.

Kipnis, Laura (1988) Feminism: The Political Conscience of Postmodernism? In Andrew Ross (Ed.), *Universal Abandon: The Politics of Postmodernism*. Minneapolis, University of Minnesota Press, 149–166.

Kroker, Arthur and Cook, David (1986) *The Postmodern Scene: Excremental Culture and Hyper-aesthetics*. New York: St. Martin's Press.

Lather, Patti (1984) Critical Theory, Curricular Transformation and Feminist Mainstreaming. *Journal of Education*, 66(1), 49–62.

Lather, Patti (1988a) Feminist Perspectives on Empowering Research Methodologies. *Women's Studies International Forum, 11*(6), 569–581.

Lather, Patti (1988b) Pretext: Unmasking the Politics of Educational Thought and Practice. *Review of Power and Criticism: Poststructural Investigations in Education* by Cleo Cherryholmes, *Journal of Curriculum Theorizing, 8*(4), 127–134.

Lather, Patti (1989) Postmodernism and the Politics of Enlightenment. *Educational Foundations,* 3(3), 7–28.

Lather, Patti (April, 1990) Staying Dumb? Student Resistance to Liberatory Curriculum. Paper Presented at the Annual Meeting of the American Educational Research Association, Boston.

Lather, Patti (1991) *Getting Smart: Feminist Research and Pedagogy with/in the Postmodern.* New York: Routledge.

Lanser, Susan S. (1989) Feminist Criticism, "The Yellow Wallpaper," and the Politics of Color in America. *Feminist Studies, 15*(3), 415–441.

Lewis, Magda (April, 1990) Framing: Women and Silence: Disrupting the Hierarchy of Discursive Practices. Paper presented at the Annual Meeting of the American Educational Research Association, Boston.

London, Bette (1990) *The Appropriated Voice: Narrative Authority in Conrad, Forster, and Woolf.* Ann Arbor: University of Michigan Press.

Lusted, David (1986) Why Pedagogy? *Screen, 27*(5), 2–14.

Lyotard, Jean-Francois (1984) *The Postmodern Conditions: A Report on Knowledge.* Translated by Geoff Bennington and Brian Massumi. Minneapolis: University of Minnesota Press.

Maher, Frinde and Tetreault, Mary Kay (March, 1989) Feminist Teaching: Issues of Mastery, Voice, Authority and Positionality. Paper Presented at the Annual Meeting of the American Educational Research Association, San Francisco.

Marcus, George and Fischer, Richard (1986) *Anthropology as Cultural Critique.* Chicago: University of Chicago Press.

McLaren, Peter (1988) Schooling the Postmodern Body: Critical Pedagogy and the Politics of enfleshment. *Journal of Education, 170*(3), 53–83.

Miller, Janet (1990) *Creating Spaces and Finding Voices: Teachers collaborating for Empowerment.* New York: State University of New York Press.

Morton, Donald and Zavarzadeh, Mas'ud (1988–89) The Cultural Politics of the Fiction Workshop. *Cultural Critique, 11,* 155–173.

Morton, Donald and Zavarzadeh, Mas'ud (Eds.) (1991) *Texts for Change: Theory/Pedagogy/ Politics.* Urbana: University of Illinois Press.

Murphy, John W. (1988) Computerization, Postmodern Epistemology, and Reading in the Postmodern Era, *Educational Theory, 38*(2), 175–182.

Naidus, Beverly (1987) The Artist/Teacher as Decoder and Catalyst. *Radical Teacher* (Sept.), 17–20.

Nelson, Cary (Ed.) (1986) *Theory in the Classroom.* Urbana: University of Illinois Press.

Newton, Judith (1988) History as Usual? Feminism as the "New Historicism". *Cultural Critique,* 9, 87–121.

Orner, Mimi and Brennan, Marie (March, 1989) Producing Collectively: Power, Identity and Teaching. Paper Presented at the Annual Meeting of the American Educational Research Association, San Francisco.

Peters, Michael (1989) Techno-science, Rationality, and the University: Lyotard on the "Postmodern Condition". *Educational Theory, 39*(2), 93–105.

Poster, Marc (1989) *Critical Theory and Poststructuralism: In Search of a Context.* Ithaca: Cornell University Press.

Rajchman, John (1985) *Michel Foucault: The Freedom of Philosophy.* New York: Columbia University Press.

Reiss, Timothy J. (1988) *The Uncertainty of Analysis: Problems of Truth, Meaning and Culture.* Ithaca: Cornell University Press.

Riley, Denise (1988) *"Am I that Name?" Feminism and the Category of 'women' in History.* Minneapolis: University of Minnesota Press.

Roman, Leslie, Christian-Smith, Linda and Ellsworth, Elizabeth (Eds.) (1988) *Becoming Feminine: The Politics of Popular Culture.* London: The Falmer Press.

Said, Edward (1986) Orientalism Reconsidered. In Francis Barker, Peter Hulme, Margaret Iversen, and Diana Loxley (Eds.), *Literature, Politics and Theory.* London: Methuen, 210–229.

Schrift, Alan D. (1990) The Becoming-Postmodern of Philosophy. In Gary Shapiro (Ed.), *After the Failure: Postmodern Times and Places*. Albany: State University of New York Press, 99–114.

Smith, Paul (1988) *Discerning the Subject*. Minneapolis: University of Minnesota Press.

Solomon-Godeau, Abigail (1988) Living with Contradictions: Critical Practices in the Age of Supplyside Aesthetics. In Andrew Ross (Ed.), *Universal Abandon: The Politics of Postmodernism*. Minneapolis: University of Minnesota Press, 191–213.

Spivak, Gayatri, with Rooney, Ellen (1989) In a Word. Interview. *Differences, 1*(2), 124–156.

Ulmer, Gregory (1985) *Applied Grammatology: Post(e)-pedagogy from Jacques Derrida to Joseph Beuys*. Baltimore: Johns Hopkins University Press.

Walkerdine, Valerie (1981) Sex, Power and Pedagogy. *Screen Education, 38*, 14–24.

Walkerdine, Valerie (1984) Developmental Psychology and Child-centered Pedagogy. In Julian Henriques, W. Holloway, C. Unwin, C. Venn and V. Walkerdine (Eds.), *Changing the Subject*. London: Methuen, 153–202.

Walkerdine, Valerie (1985) On the Regulation of Speaking and Science: Sexuality, Class and Gender in Contemporary Schooling. In Carolyn Steedman, C. Urwin and V. Walkerdine (Eds.), *Language, Gender and Childhood*. London: Routledge and Kegan Paul, 203–242.

Walkerdine, Valerie (1986) Post-Structuralist Theory and Everyday Social Practices: The Family and the School. In Sue Wilkinson (Ed.), *Feminist Social Psychology: Developing Theory and Practice*. Milton Keynes: Open University Press, 57–76.

Weedon, Chris (1987) *Feminist Practice and Poststructuralist Theory*. Oxford: Basil Blackwell.

West, Cornel (1987) Postmodernism and Black America. *Zeta Magazine, 1*(6), 27–29.

Wexler, Philip (1987) *Social Analysis of Education: After the New Sociology*. New York: Routledge and Kegan Paul.

Whitson, Tony (1988) The Politics of "Non-political" Curriculum: Heteroglossia and the Discourse of "Choice" and "Effectiveness." In William Pinar (Ed.), *Contemporary Curriculum Discourses*. Scottsdale, Arizona: Gorsuch Scarisbrick, 279–330.

Zavarzadeh, Mas'ud and Morton, Donald (1986–87) Theory Pedagogy Politics: The Crisis of "the Subject" in the Humanities. *Boundary 2, 15*(1–2).

88

Radical Pedagogy as Cultural Politics: Beyond the Discourse of Critique and Anti-Utopianism

Henry A. Giroux and Peter L. McLaren

Within the last fifteen years a radical theory of education has emerged in the United States. Broadly defined as "the new sociology of education" or "a critical theory of education," a critical pedagogy developed within this discourse attempts to examine schools both in their historical context and as part of the social and political relations that characterize the dominant society. While hardly constituting a unified discourse, critical pedagogy nevertheless has managed to pose an important counter-logic to the positivistic, ahistorical, depoliticized discourse that often informs modes of analysis employed by liberal and conservative critics of schooling, modes all too readily visible in most colleges of education. Taking as one of its fundamental concerns the need to reemphasize the centrality of politics and power in understanding how schools function within the larger society, critical pedagogy has catalyzed a great deal of work on the political economy of schooling, the state and education, the politics of representation, discourse analysis, and the construction of student subjectivity.

Critical pedagogy has provided a radical theory and analysis of schooling, annexing new discourses from various strands of critical social theory and developing at the same time new categories of inquiry and new methodologies. It is not physically housed in any one school or university department, nor does it constitute a homogeneous set of ideas. Critical educational theorists are united in their attempts to empower the powerless and to transform social inequalities and injustices. Constituting a small minority of the academic profession and of public schoolteachers, the critical pedagogical movement nevertheless is substantial enough to present a challenging presence within the teaching profession.[1]

Source: Donald Morton and Mas'ud Zavarzadeh (eds), *Texts for Change: Theory/Pedagogy/Politics* (Urbana, Illinois: University of Illinois Press, 1991), pp. 152–186.

One major task of critical pedagogy has been to disclose and challenge the school's privileged ideological terrain in our political and cultural life. Especially within the last decade, educational theorists have increasingly come to view schooling as a resolutely political and cultural enterprise. Recent advances in the sociology of knowledge, the history of consciousness, the critical study of colonial discourse, cultural Marxism, continental social theory, and feminist theory have provoked a conceptual recasting of schools as more than simply instructional sites. They may instead be considered as cultural arenas where heterogeneous ideological, discursive, and social forms collide in an unremitting struggle for dominance. Within this context, schools have generally been analyzed as sorting mechanisms for human capital, in which groups of students are privileged on the basis of race, class, and gender; and less frequently as agencies for self- and social empowerment.

'This new perspective has ushered in a view of the school as a terrain of contestation. Groups from dominant and subordinate cultures negotiate on symbolic terms; students and teachers engage, accept, and sometimes resist how school experiences and practices are named and legitimated. The traditional view of classroom instruction – of learning as a neutral or transparent process antiseptically removed from the concepts of power, politics, history, and context – can no longer be credibly endorsed. In fact, researchers within the critical tradition have given primacy to the categories of the social, cultural, political, and economic, in order to better understand the workings of contemporary schooling.

Theorists within the critical tradition examine schooling as a form of *cultural politics*. From this perspective, schooling always represents forms of social life and is always implicated in relations of power, social practices, and the privileging of forms of knowledge that support a specific vision of past, present, and future. In general, critical educational theorists maintain that the cultural politics of the schools historically and currently inculcate a meritocratic-professional ideology, rationalizing the knowledge industry into class-divided tiers; reproduce inequality, racism, and sexism; and fragment democratic social relations through an emphasis on competitiveness, androcentrism, logocentrism and cultural ethnocentrism.

While remaining indebted to specialized frameworks appropriated from European intellectual traditions, critical pedagogy also draws upon a uniquely American tradition. That tradition extends from the mainstream progressive movement of John Dewey, William H. Kilpatrick, and others, to the more radical efforts of the social reconstructionists of the 1920s, such as George Counts and John Childs, to the work of Theodore Brameld, and finally to the more current theoretical contributions of revisionist educators.[2]

Fundamental to the principles that inform critical pedagogy is the conviction that schooling for self- and social empowerment *is ethically prior to questions of epistemology or to a mastery of technical or social skills* that are primarily tied to the logic of the marketplace. Concern over education's atrophied ethical dimension has provoked leftist scholars to undertake a socially critical reconstruction of what it means to "be schooled." Their efforts stress that any genuine pedagogical practice demands a commitment to social transformation in solidarity with subordinated and marginalized groups. In its broadest possible sense, this entails a preferential option for the poor and the elimination of conditions that promote human suffering. Such theorists are critical of liberal democracy's emphasis on individualism and autonomy, questioning the assumption that individuals are ontologically independent or that they are the autonomous, rational, and self-motivating social agents that liberal humanism has constructed. The theoretically and historically unsituated analyses of schooling, promulgated by liberal and conservative critics alike, represent different ideological aspects of the dominant society; each perspective privileges the interests of the dominant culture with equal facility. The liberal perspective especially has been shown to be reappropriated by the very logic it purports to criticize. By contrast, the radical perspective involves a critical reinscription of liberalism in a concerted attempt to displace its Eurocentric, patriarchal, and logocentric assumptions. Employing theoretical strategies that allow the unstated and submerged grammar of schooling to be more insistently critiqued and transformed, radical educators work to reveal the social and material conditions of schooling's production and reception.

Challenging the dominant assumption that schools currently function as a major mechanism for the development of the democratic and egalitarian social order, radical educational theorists have argued that schools do not provide opportunities for self- and social empowerment. It has also challenged the dominant assumption that schools currently constitute major sites of social and economic mobility, arguing instead that American schooling has defaulted on its promise of egalitarian reform. In this view, the economic, social, and political returns from schooling are far greater for the economically affluent than for the disadvantaged. Curriculum becomes both a "selective tradition" and a duplicitous practice that provides students with particular forms of knowledge, coded in ways similar to the goods and services that have been subjected to the logic of commodification.[3]

In their efforts to explode the popular belief that schools are fundamentally democratic institutions, radical critics have attempted to demonstrate how curricula, knowledge, and policy depend on the corporate marketplace and the fortunes of the economy. They warn against being deluded into thinking that either conservatives or liberals occupy a truly progressive platform from which educational decisions can be made on the basis of transparent and disinterested standards. Furthermore, their critique has revealed that the application of rigorous standards is never innocent of social, economic, and institutional contexts. In this view, schooling must always be analyzed as a cultural and historical process in which select groups are positioned within asymmetrical relations of power. Radical scholars refuse to accept the task capitalism assigns them as intellectuals, teachers, and social theorists:

to service the existing ideological and institutional arrangements of the public schools, while simultaneously disconfirming the values and abilities of minority groups. In short, educators within the critical tradition regard mainstream schooling as supporting the transmission and reproduction of what Paulo Freire terms "the culture of silence."

Central in their attempt to reform public education has been a critical rejection of the worst aspects of the modern Enlightenment project, defined in terms of a debilitating positivism, instrumental reason, and bureaucratic control, which have been tacitly lodged in models of curriculum planning and dominant approaches to educational theory and practice. Bolstered by certain strands of feminist theory and postmodernist social theory, critical pedagogy continues to challenge the often uncontested relationship between school and society, effectively unmasking mainstream pedagogy's development as a purveyor of equal opportunity and its claim to access such virtues as egalitarian democracy and critical thinking. Rejecting the conservative claim that schooling is a politically opaque and value-neutral process, critical pedagogy has attempted to empower teachers and researchers with more critical means of understanding the school's role within a race-, class-, and gender-divided society. Radical pedagogy has generated categories crucial for interrogating the production of student experiences, texts, teacher ideologies, and aspects of school policy that conservative and liberal analyses too often leave untouched. In effect, critical pedagogy has sharply etched the political dimensions of schooling, arguing that schools operate mainly to reproduce the discourses, values, and privileges of existing elites. Critical pedagogy commits itself *to forms of learning and action that are undertaken in solidarity with subordinated and marginalized groups.* In addition to interrogating what is taken for granted or seemingly self-evident or inevitable regarding the relationship between schools and the social order, critical pedagogy is dedicated to self-empowerment and social transformation.

At the same time, many current trends in critical pedagogy are embedded in the endemic weaknesses of a theoretical project overly concerned with developing a language of critique. Critical pedagogy is steeped in a posture of moral indignation toward the injustices reproduced in American public schools. Unfortunately, this one-sided emphasis on critique is matched by the lack of ethical and pragmatic discourse upon which to ground its own vision of society and schooling and to shape the direction of a critical praxis.

How does one redefine the purpose of public schooling and rethink the role of teaching and learning in emancipatory terms? More orthodox radical educational theorists have been unable to move from a posture of criticism to one of substantive vision, from a language of critique to a language of possibility. Drawing inspiration from the traditional perspectives of Marxism and socialism, of liberalism and democratic theory, critical educators have constructed a powerful critique of the culture and knowledge industries; yet they have been unable to conceive of pedagogical and curricular reform outside of the most debilitating metaphysical assumptions of the Enlightenment. At the same time they have failed to achieve the most ennobling goals of modernity, which are to link reason to values and ethical reflection to the project of individual emancipation and social justice. These critics have been unable either to adequately mobilize key public constituencies or to challenge the current conservative attack on the schools[4] and the philistinism of the federal bureaucrats at the U.S. Department of Education. This theoretical and political impasse appears to mark a fin-de-siècle frustration with political economy models of educational reform and a failure of liberal progressivism. To a great extent their work remains fettered by a mode of analysis that hovers over, rather than directly engaging, the contradictions of the social order that their efforts seek to transform.

Generally speaking, critical educators have been unable to develop a critical discourse that provides the theoretical basis for alternative approaches to school organization, curricula, classroom pedagogy, and social relations.[5] Nor have attempts been made to redefine the individual social actor – whether teacher or student – as constituting multiply organized subjectivities that are both gendered and discursively embedded in complex and contradictory ways. The programmatic impetus of much radical educational reform remains fettered by the limited emancipatory goal of making the everyday problematic. But while calling into question the ideological dimensions of classroom transactions – i.e., the structural positioning of thought in relation to the larger social totality – is certainly commendable as a starting point, it cannot further the project of democratizing our classrooms unless united with the larger goal of reconstituting schools as counterpublic spheres.[6] The language of critique that informs much radical theorizing is overly individualistic, Eurocentric, androcentric, and reproductive; radical educators fail to acknowledge that the struggle for democracy, in the larger sense of transforming schools into democratic public spheres, takes political and ethical precedence over making teachers more adept at deconstructive "double readings." That is, this language's programmatic suggestions are locked into the limited posture of reproduction and resistance theories.[7] In general, critical pedagogy can be accused of purveying either a mechanical and deterministic view of the social order or a liberal, humanist, and Cartesian view of human agency. Its emphasis on individual student subjectivity constructed within particular discursive alignments and power/knowledge configurations has deflected attention from the concept of collective struggle. While we recognize, along with feminist theorists and others, that we must challenge the claims of a unitary female experience and universal experiences based on race or class, we remain optimistic that critical pedagogy will be able to address these issues while at the same time discovering new ways of establishing itself as a collective countervailing force with the power to inscribe a condition of radical possibility, what Laclau and Mouffe refer to as the construction of a "radical imaginary."[8]

Critical Pedagogy as a Form of Cultural Politics

Despite the advances of critical pedagogy over the last decade, there remains the problem of how cultural politics is to be defined and developed. The problem results from the one-sidedness of the critical tradition's analysis. Critical pedagogy has failed to articulate a vision for self-empowerment and social transformation; consequently, the term "critical pedagogy" needs to have its meaning specified in more precise terms.

"Pedagogy" refers to the process by which teachers and students negotiate and produce meaning. This, in turn, takes into consideration how teachers and students are positioned within discursive practices and power/knowledge relations. "Pedagogy" also refers to how we represent ourselves, others, and the communities in which we choose to live. The term "critical pedagogy," by distinction, underscores the partisan nature of learning and struggle; it provides a starting point for linking knowledge to power and a commitment to developing forms of community life that take seriously the struggle for democracy and social justice. Critical pedagogy always presupposes a particular vision of society. As Roger Simon reminds us, a critical pedagogy is based on a project of empowerment. Without a vision of the future – without asking, "Empowerment for what?" – critical pedagogy becomes reduced to a method for participation that takes democracy as an end, not a means. In Simon's terms, critical pedagogy must be distinguished from teaching:

> To me "pedagogy" is a more complex and extensive term than "teaching," referring to the integration in practice of particular curriculum content and design, classroom strategies and techniques, and evaluation, purpose and methods. All of these aspects of educational practice come together in the realities of what happens in classrooms. Together they organize a view of how a teacher's work within an institutional context specifies a particular version of what knowledge is of most worth, what it means to know something, and how we might construct representations of ourselves, others, and our physical and social environment. In other words, talk about pedagogy is simultaneously talk about the details of what students and others might do together *and* the cultural politics such practices support. In this perspective, we cannot talk about teaching practice without talking about politics.[9]

Unfortunately, the New Right has naturalized the term "critical" by repeated and imprecise usage, removing its political and cultural dimensions and its analytic potency to mean "thinking skills." Teaching is thus reduced to "transmitting" basic skills and information and sanctifying the canons of the dominant cultural tradition. The moral vision that grounds such a view encourages students to succeed in the world of existing social forms. Critical pedagogy, as we are using the term, refers to a form of cultural politics aimed at enhancing and transforming the social imagination. Our task here is to outline what such a conceptualization might mean for education.

Critical pedagogy as a form of cultural politics attempts to redress the ideological shortcomings of current analyses of schooling and mainstream discussions of pedagogy, particularly as found in teacher education programs. For instance, student teachers are often introduced to a one-dimensional conception of schooling. Rather than viewing the classroom as cultural terrain where heterogeneous discourses collide in a struggle for dominance, student teachers often encounter schooling as a set of rules and regulative practices that have been laundered of ambiguity, contradiction, paradox, and resistance. Schools are presented as free of all ideological contestation and struggle. Educators usually think of struggle in schools as "behavioral struggle" – attempts to delegitimate certain forms of unruly behavior – a perception enforced by myths of the "culture of poverty" or the naturalness of cultural or racial "deficiencies," which we read as a perception of students' "lack of whiteness" on the part of many teachers from the dominant white culture. Classroom reality is rarely presented as socially constructed, historically determined, and mediated through institutionalized relationships of class, gender, race, and power. This dominant conception of schooling vastly contradicts the economies of power, privilege, and subject-formation in which student teachers are actually located during the practicum, especially in a working-class school. Student teachers are often taught to view their own cultural capital and lived experiences as constituting a meaningless subjective referent; what counts most, in the dominant view, is not the fragility or importance of one's own voice and beliefs, but the "force" and imperatives of a technocratic logic that unifies subjectivity in a masculinist regime of power and authority. In mainstream schools of education, teaching practices and methods are often linked to a menu of learning models employed in stipulated conditions – conditions where questions of culture and power are completely annulled or else shunted to the margins, in favor of questions having to do with procedural proprieties, learning strategies, developmental theories, and behavioral outcomes.[10]

In effect, critical pedagogy as a form of cultural politics speaks to a form of curriculum theory and application that stresses the historical, cultural, and discursive in relation to classroom materials and teaching practices. As such, it speaks to a fundamental intersection between social and curriculum theorizing. It also seeks to render problematic the experiences and needs of students as the basis for exploring the interface between their immediate lives and the constraints and possibilities of the wider society. Critical pedagogy as a form of cultural politics attempts to provide educators with an opportunity to examine, dismantle, analyze, bracket, de- and reconstruct pedagogical practices. How is meaning produced? How is power constructed and reinforced in classroom and school life? Deconstructive strategies from postmodern social theory are instrumental tools for answering such questions through radical critique. Central to such a perspective is not simply the critical appropriation of semiotic, hermeneutic, or Marxian strategies, but also a commitment to hope and emancipation and a desire to link educational practice to the public good. Underscoring this commitment is an understanding of curriculum as an expression of struggle and an acknowledgment that curriculum constitutes a primary agent for introducing, preparing, and legitimizing forms of social life.

Critical pedagogy as a form of cultural politics is also concerned with constructing a language that empowers teachers to take seriously the role of schooling in joining knowledge and power. Teachers need critical categories that probe the factual status of white, Western, androcentric epistemologies that will enable schools to be interrogated as sites engaged in producing and transmitting social practices that reproduce the linear, profit-motivated imperatives of the dominant culture, with its attendant institutional dehumanization. By conceptualizing radical pedagogy as a form of cultural politics, we are underscoring the idea that *school culture is not neutral, but ideological*. It consists of stipulated social practices and diffuse configurations of power, as well as historically mediated ideas and worldviews that often work to sustain the interests of dominant groups. In this view, schooling does not reflect the dominant ideology but constitutes it. That is, schooling is an integral (though mediated) aspect of the dominant ideology and provides the social practices and material constraints necessary for ideology to do its work. Part of this work consists of a disciplining of consciousness by selective languages of analysis and the reproduction of specific social and cultural forms in which pedagogy occurs; it also consists of constructing relations of race, class, and gender dependency and generating feelings of self-negation and defeat, all of which are underwritten by a victim-blaming psychologization of school failure that rests on a conception of the masculinized and privatized Cartesian ego. This position highlights the need for educators to explore how the experiences of students are produced, contested, and legitimated at school; in addition, it points to the need for educators to remake schools into sites for greater social probity and equity and deeper challenges to dominant definitions of truth and structures of power.

Curriculum as a Form of Cultural Politics

To conceive of critical pedagogy as a form of cultural politics is to underscore the importance of understanding schooling and pedagogy as an expression of radical social theory.[11] In recent years, leftist educational theorists have employed critical social theory to increase our understanding of schooling as essentially a political enterprise, as a way of reproducing or privileging particular discourses, along with the knowledge and power they carry. As a result, many educators have come to recognize schooling as both determinate and determining, constraining and enabling. The conceptual core of radical scholarship over the last decade has been strongly influenced by the rediscovery of Marx and has involved unpacking the submerged connections between schooling and the economic sphere of capitalist production. We are certainly sympathetic with this position, especially with Ernest Mandel's argument that we are now entering a form of corporate capitalism in which capital has expanded into hitherto uncommodified areas.[12] We also agree that forms of power and control have become more difficult to uncover because they now are disguised within circuits of electronically produced signs and meanings that saturate almost every aspect of public and private life.[13] But this position has failed to escape the economic reductionism that it attempts to press beyond. Such reductionism, in its more sophisticated forms, is evident in the continuing work of radical educational theorists who overemphasize the relationship between schools and the economic sphere, even as they neglect to interrogate the role of signs, symbols, rituals, narratives, and cultural formations in naming and constructing student subjectivities and voices.[14] State capitalism is much more than a series of economic determinations, and the economic process is not always causally related to the appearance of new symbolic and cultural discourses that sustain as well as disrupt and decenter important dimensions of modern social life.

While economic forces and the intervention of the state are important determinants of school policy, they require reexamination in light of theoretical considerations that stress the mutually constitutive roles played by language, culture, and power in affecting how teachers and students impose, negotiate, and resist meaning in the classroom. Questions about how students make meanings and create their cultural histories cannot be answered with sole recourse to discussions of social class and economic determinism; rather, we must analyze how the discursive mediations of culture and experience intersect to constitute powerfully determining aspects of human agency and struggle.

A curriculum as a form of cultural politics stresses the importance of making social, cultural, political, and economic issues the primary categories for understanding contemporary schooling.[15] Within this context, school life is to be conceptualized not as a monolithic and iron-clad system of rules and relations, but from the perspective of a theory of culture that insinuates elements of discontinuity and indeterminacy into what is usually perceived by educational researchers as uniform and determinate. School life can best be seen as a turbulent arena of conflicting discourses and struggles, a terrain where classroom and streetcorner cultures collide and where teachers, students, and administrators negotiate, accept, and sometimes resist how school experiences and practices are named and accomplished. To conceptualize curriculum as a form of cultural politics is to acknowledge the overriding goal of education as the creation of conditions for social transformation, through the constitution of students as political subjects who recognize their historical, racial, class, and gender situatedness and the forces that shape their lives and are politically and ethically motivated to struggle in the interest of greater human freedom and emancipation.

The project of "doing" a curriculum of cultural politics consists of linking radical social theory to a language of critique and possibility through which teachers can dismantle and interrogate preferred and officially sanctioned educational discourses. Our concern here is not just with developing a language of critique and demystification; we are more concerned with developing a language of possibility that can create alternative teaching practices capable of shattering the syntax of dominant systems of intelligibility and representation, both within and outside schools. We are committed to articulating a language that can examine public schooling as a new public sphere, one that seeks to recapture the idea of critical democracy and build alliances with progressive social movements.

Schools are historical and structural embodiments of ideological forms reproduced through uneven discursive alignments that privilege certain groups, and asymmetrical relations of power that sustain such privilege. They signify reality in unitary ways that fail to acknowledge the heterogeneous, multilayered, and often contradictory process of subject formation. Schools in this sense are ideological and political terrains out of which the dominant culture, in part, produces its hegemonic "certainties" and popular assurances of received orthodoxies; they are also places where dominant and subordinate groups define and constrain each other through an ongoing battle and exchange in response to socio-historical conditions. Schools are not ideologically innocent, nor do they simply reproduce dominant social relations and interests. At the same time, schools do produce forms of political and moral regulation intimately connected with technologies of power, which in turn "produce asymmetries in the abilities of individuals and groups to define and realize their needs."[17] More specifically, schools establish the conditions under which some individuals and groups define the terms by which others live, resist, affirm, and participate in the construction of their own identities and subjectivities. Roger Simon illuminates some of the important theoretical considerations that must be addressed within a radical pedagogy:

> Our concern as educators is to develop a way of thinking about the construction and definition of subjectivity within the concrete social forms of our everyday existence in a way that grasps schooling as a cultural and political site that embodies a project of regulation and transformation. As educators we are required to take a position on the acceptability of such forms. We also recognize that while schooling is productive it is not so in isolation, but in complex relations with other forms organized in other sites. . . . [Moreover,] in working to reconstruct aspects of schooling [educators should attempt] to understand how it becomes implicated in the production of subjectivities . . . [and] recognize that existing social forms legitimate and produce real inequities which serve the interest of some over others and that a transformative pedagogy is oppositional in intent and is threatening to some in its practice.[18]

Simon rightly argues that schools are sites of contestation and struggle; as sites of cultural production, they embody representations and practices that construct as well as constrain the possibilities for social agency among students.

Developing a radical pedagogy consistent with the view of cultural politics involves rethinking the very nature of curriculum discourse. At the outset, this demands understanding curriculum as representing a set of underlying interests that structure how a particular "story" is presented, represented, and legitimated. In this respect, curriculum itself represents a narrative or voice, one that is multilayered and often contradictory but also situated within forms of representation and relations of power that in the majority of traditional institutions favor white, male, middle-class, English-speaking students. We can discuss the classroom as a site of discursive production and reception, and we can learn from the deconstructive and textual strategies now finding their way into the critical educational tradition. Curriculum discourse and pedagogic practice are now viewed as orderings and transformations of time, text, and space that position both teachers and students within particular renderings of authority and experience but do not automatically reproduce the messages they carry and legitimate. Curriculum and pedagogical practice are thus considered as offering the possibility of contestation and resistance. Without overlooking the degree of struggle and resistance possible among both teachers and students, it is important to extend the practice of post-structuralist critique to the development of narratives and reconstituted histories, values and representations that also point to new visions of social life.

To speak of curriculum as a form of cultural politics is to assert that curriculum cannot be understood outside a theory of interest. Such a conceptualization of curriculum is only possible if it can justify both its particular assumptions and the presuppositions that constitute its analytic framework. First, since all knowledge and social practice become intelligible only within the ideologies and systems of representation they produce and legitimate, it is essential to analyze curricula in relation to the interests that structure the questions they raise, the version of the past and present they legitimate, and the social relations they either affirm or marginalize. Second, since curriculum implies a picture of how to live, it cannot be understood outside a theory of experience. Curriculum is deeply implicated in the production and organization of student experiences within historically produced social forms such as language usage, the organization of knowledge into high- and low-status categories, and the affirmation of particular teaching strategies and tactics. Third, as a form of cultural politics, curriculum not only represents a configuration of particular interests and experiences; it also represents a site of battle over whose versions of authority, history, the present, and the future will prevail in schools. Finally, critical curriculum theorists want to restore to educational theorizing a public language that interrogates the ways in which the voices of teachers and subordinate groups are produced and legitimated.

Curriculum as a form of cultural politics must attend to the contradictory nature of student experience and voice and therefore must establish the grounds whereby such experiences can be interrogated and analyzed. This often means refusing the very frames of reference that split off the marginalized from the dominators and creating new vocabularies of resistance that do not separate curriculum from gender politics, values from aesthetics, pedagogy from power. The concept of "voice" in this case not only provides a theoretical framework for recognizing the cultural logic that produces, contains, and enables learning; it also provides a referent for criticizing the kind of romantic celebration of student experience that characterized much of the radical pedagogy of the 1960s and the culturalism of the 1970s. At issue here is linking the pedagogy of student voice to a project of possibility: students affirming and celebrating the interplay of different voices and experiences, while at the same time recognizing that such voices must always be interrogated for their metaphysical, epistemological, ethical, and political interests. Voice becomes a pedagogical site for asserting and interrogating spoken/unspoken interests. As a form of historical, textual, political, and gender production, student voice must be rooted in a pedagogy that allows students to speak, to appreciate, and to practice the emancipatory politics of difference. Such difference is more than a function of democratic tolerance; it is also a fundamental condition for critical dialogue and the development of forms of solidarity rooted in the principles of trust, sharing, and a commitment to improving the quality of human freedom. While we recognize that a pedagogy of voice is in itself fraught with difficulties, we believe such a pedagogy allows students to believe that to be critical is to be present in history, to make a difference with respect to the future. This type of curriculum must be developed around a politics of difference and community that is not rooted simply in a celebration of liberal pluralism. Rather, such a pedagogy must be grounded in a particular form and vision of human community in which a politics of difference becomes dignified.[19] Such a vision means acknowledging the different ways in which the generative themes that suture and codify the materiality of our experiences are produced, affirmed, and disconfirmed according to ruling discourses. This is not to suggest that community must be constructed mainly out of supportive discourses or actions at the expense of oppositional ones. Rather, a language of possibility must provide a version of community that offers serious consideration of political and pedagogical alternatives under nonrevolutionary as well as revolutionary circumstances.

Critical Pedagogy and the Politics of Experience

Critical pedagogy as a form of cultural politics takes as one of its most fundamental aims an understanding of how the socially constructed and often contradictory experiences and needs of students might be made problematic. Such experiences can then provide the basis for exploring the interface between their own lives and the constraints and possibilities within the wider social order. Traditionally, radical educators have emphasized the ideological nature of knowledge (either as a form of ideology critique, or as ideologically correct content to convey to students) as the primary focus for critical educational works. Central to this perspective is a view of knowledge that suggests that it is produced in the head of the educator or teacher/theorist and not in interaction. In short, knowledge is theoretically abstracted from its own production as part of a pedagogical encounter. The notion that knowledge cannot be constructed outside a pedagogical encounter is lost in the misconceived assumption that the propositional logic or "truth content" of knowledge is the most essential issue to be addressed in one's teaching. In this way, the relevance of the notion of pedagogy as part of a critical theory of education is either undertheorized or merely "forgotten." This view has often brought about the following division of labor: theorists who produce knowledge are limited to the university, those who merely reproduce it are seen as public schoolteachers, and those who passively receive it at all levels are students.

We propose a critical pedagogy as a form of cultural politics that is fundamentally concerned with student experience in a threefold sense. First, a post-structuralist concept of student experience allows subjectivity to be analyzed outside the exigencies of humanist psychology. In this perspective, experience and subjectivity do not collapse into the humanist notion of the integrated ego as the source of all actions and behavior. If student experience is viewed as constituted out of and by difference and rooted in contradictory discursive and nondiscursive practices, then the experience that students bring to schools, as well as the cultural forms out of which those experiences are produced, operate within tensions that are never closed or unassailable. The concept of the nomadic and post-colonial subject that emerges from our view of student experience as a terrain of struggle is articulated by Larry Grossberg:

> This "post-humanistic" subject does not exist with a unified identity (even understood as an articulated hierarchical structure of its various subject-positionings) that somehow manifests itself in every practice. Rather, it is a subject that is constantly remade, reshaped as a mobilely situated set of relations in a fluid context. The nomadic subject is amoeba-like, struggling to win some space for itself in its local situation. The subject itself has become a site of struggle, an ongoing site of articulation with its own history, determinations and effects.[20]

We are suggesting that one way of opposing and transforming the unified, singular, monolithic subject of patriarchy is to formulate a concept of subject formation that stresses negotiation among discourses, and subject positions as social practices that are both determined and determining. Second, a pedagogy of student experience encourages a critique of dominant forms of knowledge and cultural mediation that collectively shape student experiences. Such a pedagogy emphasizes the link between experience and the issues of language and representation. Third, it attempts to provide students with the critical means to examine their own lived experiences, deep memories, and subordinate knowledge forms. This means helping students analyze their own experiences outside of frames of reference produced in the "master's house" so as to illuminate the processes by which they are produced, legitimated, or disconfirmed. Student experience, as the fundamental medium of culture, agency, and identity formation, must be given preeminence in an emancipatory curriculum; therefore critical educators must learn how to understand, affirm, and analyze such experience. This means not only understanding the cultural and social forms through which students as embattled subjects learn to define themselves, but also learning how to engage student experience within a pedagogy that is both affirmative and critical.

Knowledge must be made meaningful to students before it can be made critical. School knowledge never speaks for itself; rather, it is constantly filtered through the experiences, critical vernacular, and mutual knowledge that students bring to the classroom. Unfortunately, most approaches to teaching and learning fail to consider the critical justification for local knowledges and belief-claims that students use to give relevance and meaning to their experiences. Nor do teachers often invite students to consider the ideological ramifications of their commonly held beliefs and routine social practices. David Lusted is worth quoting on this issue:

> Knowledge is not produced in the intentions of those who believe they hold it, whether in the pen or in the voice. It is produced in the process of interaction, between writer and reader at the moment of reading, and between teacher and learner at the moment of classroom engagement. Knowledge is not the matter that is offered so much as the matter that is understood. To think of fields or bodies of knowledge as if they are the property of academics and teachers is wrong. It denies an equality in the relations at moments of interaction and falsely privileges one side of the exchange, and what that side "knows," over the other. Moreover, for critical cultural producers to hold this view of knowledge carries its own pedagogy, an autocratic and elite pedagogy. It's not just that it denies the value of what learners know, which it does, but that it misrecognizes the conditions necessary for the kind of learning – critical, engaged, personal, social – called for by the knowledge itself.[21]

This position is exemplified by teachers who define the success of their teaching exclusively through *the ideological correctness* of the subject matter they teach. Sharon Welch speaks directly to this issue by arguing against using theory as a form of social control. She points out that the most important concern in teaching is *to support the process of theorizing and not the mere exposure to correct ideas*. Welch is all too aware of the trap that theory-building often creates, the use of theory to silence the voices of others:

> I find it difficult, yet essential, to avoid the trap of more traditional educational methods, the use of theory as a form of social control. This takes several forms, all ways of containing and eventually destroying the boldness of students. One obvious strategy is the smug reminder that a student's ideas – whether critical or constructive – are not new, and giving the long list of all

those who have already formulated a similar notion with, of course, greater sophistication and rhetorical power. Another way of preventing boldness is encapsulated in the aversion to "reinventing the wheel." Theories are taught in their final form, and the complex process of engendering them, moving through the requisite understanding of particular forms of oppression, particular visions of liberation, is ignored. I think we would do well to take as a model for our work one that is used in some elementary education. Students are actively encouraged to reinvent the wheel – they are given the problems that lend to creating a formula for finding the area of a rectangle, the volume of a box. By creating the formulas themselves they understand the mathematical theory more thoroughly, and as a not so incidental side-effect – gain confidence, boldness if you will, as thinkers. The fact that the formulas they derive are not new, the fact that others have reached the same conclusions, can be presented after the fact as confirmation of the students' work, as an affirmative that they are not alone or crazy, outside the bounds of communal discourse.[22]

Teachers are often apprehensive and defensive about letting students tell their own stories. Teachers must be careful not to silence students unwittingly through the unacknowledged play of discourses in their own pedagogical practices.

To have a voice means knowing when to express and assert it. In this respect, students should be encouraged to listen as well as to speak, especially if their voices tend to dominate and control others. But teachers should *never tell students that their stories don't count*. Michelle Fine provides an excellent example of one teacher who unwittingly silences a student during an attempt to establish a lively debate on an issue relevant to the lives of her students:

In early Spring, a social studies teacher structured an in-class debate on Bernard Goetz – New York City's "subway vigilante." She invited "those students who agree with Goetz to sit on one side of the room, and those who think he was wrong to sit on the other side." To the large residual group who remained mid-room the teacher remarked, "Don't be lazy. You have to make a decision. Like at work, you can't be passive." A few wandered over to the "pro-Goetz" side. About six remained in the center. Somewhat angry, the teacher continued: "OK, first we'll hear the pro-Goetz side and then the anti-Goetz side. Those of you who have no opinions, who haven't even thought about the issue, you won't get to talk unless we have time."

Deidre, a black senior, bright and always quick to raise contradictions otherwise obscured, advocated the legitimacy of the middle group. "It's not that I have no opinions. I don't like Goetz shootin' up people who look like my brother, but I don't like feeling unsafe in the projects or in my neighborhood either. I got lots of opinions. I ain't bein 'quiet' cause I can't decide if he's right or wrong. I'm talking." Deidre's comment legitimized for herself and others the right to hold complex, perhaps even contradictory positions on a complex situation. Such legitimacy was rarely granted by faculty – with clear and important exceptions including activist faculty and paraprofessionals who lived in central Harlem with the kids, understood and respected much about their lives.[23]

The social studies teacher in Fine's anecdote has unreflectively privileged her own ideological position; consequently, she has undermined and delegitimized Deidre's refusal to oversimplify what she considers a complex issue. Student experience frequently becomes unintentionally devalued despite the best political and ethical intentions; as a consequence, any sense of equality in the exchange between teacher and students is lost. A teacher's own pedagogy can thus become unknowingly elitist and autocratic.

Critical Pedagogy and the Politics of the Body

Any critical pedagogy as a form of cultural politics must take seriously the premise that learning occurs relationally. Knowledge as a form of ideology cannot be reduced to social practices that simply mirror, follow from, or obey cognitive operations. As important as it is to link learning to the production and legitimation of particular discursive positions, it is equally important to understand learning as taking place within historically situated practices involving political regimes of the body. Ideology needs to be understood as lived experience constructed as common sense, and hegemony as the process whereby students not only unwittingly consent to domination but sometimes find pleasurable the form and content through which such domination is manifested. Knowledge cannot be theorized in terms of rationality, nor can ignorance be relegated to the status of inadequate or inappropriate information or to distorted communication. Such a view denies that ideology is fundamentally related to the politics of pleasure, the typography of the body, and the production of desire.[24] To say that ideology is related to the domain of the affective is to assert that ideology must be understood as operating within a politics of feeling – structures of desire that both enable and constrain emancipatory struggle. As Larry Grossberg writes,

> Affective struggles cannot be conceptualized within the terms of theories of resistance, for their oppositional quality is constituted, not in a negative dialectics, but by a project of or struggle over empowerment, an empowerment which energizes and connects specific social moments, practices and subject positions. Thus, if we want to understand particular cultural practices, we need to ask how they empower their audiences and how the audiences empower the practices; that is, how the very materiality (including ideological) of cultural practices functions within an affective economy of everyday life.[25]

For instance, McLaren's recent ethnographic study of Portuguese Catholic students in Toronto attempts to draw attention to the importance of the body as an organ of mediation in the construction of student resistance to the authoritative pedagogy of the school.[26] McLaren observes that while engaging in the life and language of the streets, students acquire and react to information viscerally; that is, *students make affective investments in certain kinds of knowledge.*[27] Knowledge, in this instance, is not something to be "understood"; it is always, understood or not, felt and responded to somatically, that is, in its corporeal materiality.

Streetcorner knowledge is epistemologically different from traditional conceptions of school knowledge. It is a type of mimesis or visceral/erotic identification. For the Italian and Portuguese students in McLaren's study, knowledge acquired in the streets was "lived" and mediated through discursive alignments and affective ideological investments not found in school. In the streets, what mattered was always somehow "felt," whereas classroom knowledge was often sullied by an inflated rationalism and logocentrism. In the streets, students made use of more affective engagement with symbols marked by the emotive rather than the rational, and the inchoate rather than the homogeneous. Classroom knowledge was more formally differentiated, but because such knowledge was not a lived engagement it remained distant, isolated, abstract. Students chose not to invest affectively in this kind of knowledge. It was knowledge that had become safely insulated from the "tainted" production of desire, a knowledge that had been congruent with the discourse of the Other, one whose elaborated code speaks *for* the students but one to which they have little access without relinquishing the ritual codes that affirm their dignity and streetcorner status. Students whose subjectivities were "decentered" or displaced in school – in the sense of having their voices disconfirmed and delegitimized – could reclaim their sense of subjective continuity and social and cultural agency through affective investment in the popular realism of street life. Students battled daily to reconcile the disjunction between the lived meaning of the streets and the ideological boundaries and fixed lines of desire produced through the pedagogical and social practices of classroom life. In school, inordinate emphasis was placed on knowledge *about*, on the digital dimension of learning (univocality, precision, logic) as opposed to knowledge *of*, or the analogic dimension (equivocation, ambiguity, description) experienced by students in the street. Classroom instruction constituted what Robert Everhart calls "reified knowledge" – knowledge that is given, linear, relatively unproblematic, and that places the student in the role of passive recipient.[28] Resistance to this type of knowledge in the classroom mirrored student behavior in the street, and constituted a ritualized attempt to bring the hybridized and transgressive discourses of the street into the school. In Everhart's terminology, the knowledge gathered through such resistance becomes a form of "regenerative knowledge" that attempts to assert creative control over the knowledge-production process.[29] This type of knowledge, "ritual knowledge," is essentially interpretive and provisional and does not draw upon assumed categories. Furthermore, it is established to resist the role that students occupy in the labor process of the school.[30]

We are suggesting that classroom instruction must be understood within a reformulated theory of ideology that problematizes the classroom as a gathering point for the construction of Otherness in which racial, class, and gender determinations are tightly woven. Power structures and mediates the pedagogical relation between teachers and students, the politics of knowledge production, the availability of critical discourses, and the social and cultural forms in which student subject positions are made available. Furthermore, power must be seen in relation to the production of affective investment – i.e., on the production of knowledge as the objects of desire. This demands a critical attentiveness to the sentience of human subject formation and the process by which meaning is transcoded through the body – a process we refer to as "enfleshment." Enfleshment refers to the mutually constitutive (enfolding) of social structure and desire; that is, the dialectical relationship between the material organization of interiority and the cultural forms and modes of materiality we inhabit subjectively. This is similar to the process that de Certeau refers to as "intextuation" in *The Practice of Everyday Life* (1984) or the transformation of bodies into signifiers of state power and law. We are suggesting, however, that power is not simply oppressive but works relationally and that schooling promotes and provokes relations of power that are both normalizing and resistant.

Schools serve as sites for locating students in subject positions that do not contest the discursive assumptions, dispositions, and dimensions of the dominant culture. Yet the classroom can also become a site of resistance, where students combine the countervailing and transgressive possibilities found in streetcorner culture; that is, where discourses laden with concreteness exist as possibilities, where self-negation, despair, and denial do not become the primary referents for the construction of racial, gender, and class identities. Rather, the sensuous body becomes the primary referent for the politics of knowledge construction. The students in McLaren's study reacted against the eros-denying quality of school life, where they became fetishized objects of surveillance and control. Intellectual labor had little affective currency for the students because it served to displace the sensuous body as a prime signifier for the organization and investment of meaning. This brings us to the important idea that ideological hegemony is not inscribed solely in the sphere of rationality, but through the fusion of politics and ethics at the level of the body.

Throughout classroom life, student gestures become reified into corporeal manifestations of hegemony. The cramped, defensive posturing of students and the brusque, authoritative gestures of teachers reveal the relations of power that have been grafted on to the medium of living flesh. Student bodies became tablets upon which teachers encoded a belief in their own class and cultural superiority.

Every body carries its own history of oppression, residues of domination preserved in breathing tissue. The bodies of the students in McLaren's study were ideologically swollen with surplus, polyvalent meaning. Accordingly, their bodies became sites of struggle. Resistance became a way of gaining power, celebrating pleasure through the shattering of sanctified codes, and fighting oppression in the lived moment and in the concrete and social materiality of the classroom. To resist meant to fight the monitoring of passion and desire and the capitalist symbolization of the flesh. Student resistance constituted a rejection of the historical subject reformulated as a docile object compliant with the grammar of capitalist domination. It was a reaction against the purging of the body's opportunity to invest in the pleasure of transgression and illicit knowledge in favor of a disembodied ideal of what constitutes "proper" modes of desire and patterns of conduct demanded by civil society. Resistance constituted a willingness of students to struggle against the prospect that their indigenous constructions of gender, sexuality, and identity would become rewritten and demonized by the subjectively defined tropes of Anglo male authorities and through narratives defined by the division between the high-status knowledge and culture of the middle class and the degraded knowledge and cultural Otherness of the subaltern.

We must pay more attention to the affective power invested in particular ideologies, cultural formations, and social practices and the body's sensuous relationship to the popular and everyday. Lawrence Grossberg recognizes that fields of discourse are organized both ideologically and affectively: "In order to understand the relation of this totalized subject to reality it is necessary to recognize that the world is affectively as well as semantically structured. I am using the term *affect* to refer to the intensity or desire with which we invest the world and our relations to it . . . this process of affective investment (through which the body is inserted into its physical and social environment) results in the very possibility of a totalized sense of reality."[31]

A reformulation of ideology that accommodates a political economy of affective investment is in order if educators are to better understand knowledge as more than a semantic construct. Ideology is fundamentally related both to the production of discourse and to the domain of bodily investment – that is, to the politics of pleasure.

Students' inability to be "literate" may constitute less an act of "ignorance" than an act of resistance. That is, members of the working class and other oppressed groups may consciously or unconsciously refuse to learn the cultural codes and competencies legitimated by the dominant culture. In this respect, it is important to view student behavior not as a measure of learned helplessness but as a form of moral and political indignation. Students resist what the school has to offer, including subtextual contours of instruction – what is now commonly referred to as "the hidden curriculum" – in order to survive with a modicum of dignity the vagaries of class and cultural servitude. Such resistance should be seen less as an unqualified act of conscious political refusal than as an opportunity to investigate the political and cultural conditions that warrant such resistance. The interests that inform such acts never speak for themselves; they must be analyzed within a framework that links the wider context of schooling with the interpretation students bring to the act of refusal. The "refusal" to learn may provide the pedagogical basis for engaging in a critical dialogue with those whose traditions and cultures are often the object of a massive assault by the dominant culture.

To help create and guide a liberating praxis, critical pedagogy must seize a concept of resistance that will allow teachers to construct pedagogical practices that resonate with their students' experiences without romanticizing them or affirming what might constitute racist, sexist, or otherwise oppressive ideologies and practices. Teachers would do well to tap the hidden utopian desire in those resistances. Within the current dominant forms of pedagogy, teacher and student produce oppositional discourses within unequal power relations. In a critical pedagogy, as we envision it, teacher-student dialogue cannot be framed within such stark binary oppositional discourses. On the contrary, as the work of Paulo Freire and others has made dramatically clear, a critical pedagogical encounter will represent the interplay, modification, and mutual exchange of teacher-student discourses set against structuring principles that promote human capacities which acknowledge a multiplicity of positionalities along the axes of gender, race, class, and sexual orientation and social forms compatible with a reconstituted democratic imaginary and public life.

Conclusion: Beyond the Discourse of Anti-Utopianism

While leftist educators and social theorists have constructed detailed and sophisticated forms and methods of ideological critique, they have, for the most part, failed to develop a radical notion of hope and possibility. Some radical educators have, in fact, argued that the notion of hope as the basis of a language of possibility is really nothing more than a "trick of counter-hegemony," and that hope is employed for ideological effect rather than for sound theoretical reasons. In other words, hope as a vision of possibility contains no immanent political project and as such has to be sacrificed on the altar of empirical reality. Ironically, this position makes the very notion of counterhegemony untenable, since all struggle implicitly signifies an element of utopian possibility.[32] In this case, the concept of hope is used to actually disclaim political action. Such a theoretical and political dead-end is the antithesis of what it means to speak the language of possibility while engaging in radical practice. It runs counter to the idea of challenging oppression while simultaneously struggling for a new kind of subjectivity and alternative forms of community.[33] These new kinds of subjectivities and alternative forms of community must recognize the multiplicity, contradictoriness, mutually informing and historically discontinuous character of discourses and social practices. This suggests, for us, the self-conscious production of post-colonial modes of subjectivity and multiple communities of solidarity and resistance which actively contest oppression both as a conscious subjective act and as forms of collective political praxis as part of an ongoing effort to rethink the social world from the perspective of the omnipresence of oppression. There is always the danger that critical modes of subjectivity may become reterritorialized by Eurocentric discourse, and that social practices may become recolonized by phallic desire, technocratic rationality, bourgeois instrumentalism, and the logic of fascism. There is also the danger of considering race, class, and gender relations independently or assuming that they produce effects equal in their oppressiveness, rather than examining such relations in their interlocking relatedness, contextual specificity, and within particular historical circumstances. Critics of schooling must examine how race, class, and gender intersect in specific contexts and in complex ways to create – such as in the case of workingclass black females – forms of triple oppression.

The exercise of hope and possibility that we are advocating as part of a critical pedagogical praxis bears a significant comparison with, and indebtedness to, new developments in liberation theology, political theology, and feminist theology. Arguing that both Protestant and Roman Catholic theologies have too often overlooked the biblical theme of oppression/liberation and the politically empowering message of the messianic mission of the Gospel, liberation theologians claim that such an oversight has functioned as an "unconscious hermeneutical option which served the political and material interests of the institutions both of established Christendom and of the rising middle class, and which today serves the interests of the American capitalist empire."[34]

Protestants such as Miguez Bonino, Roman Catholics such as Juan Luis Segundo, and other "theologians of the periphery" including Sharon Welch, Rebecca Chopp, Mary Daly, Cornel West, Elisabeth Schüsser Fiorenza, Jürgen Moltmann, Rubem A. Alves, Leonardo Boff, Clodovis Boff, Gustavo Gutiérrez, Enrique D. Dussel, Hugo Assmann, Severino Croatto, and Luis Metz (many of whom are Third World Roman Catholic pastoral theologians) articulate their theological positions not from the ahistorical, decontextualized, and putatively value-free commitment of the Gospel – that is, from the sovereign or authoritative Enlightenment perspective of a fixed reading of scriptural truth – but from a post-Enlightenment understanding of history, class struggle, and patriarchy, and from the point of view of the oppressed and the struggle for liberation. This position is at once a "hermeneutical wager" affirming "God's bias" for the poor, the disenfranchised, the marginalized, and the oppressed. From the perspective of critical pedagogy, liberation theology is more than an ecclesiastic addendum; it is fundamentally a contestatory ethical stance which, in its fundamental challenge to systematic theology, has transformed itself into a concrete pedagogical and political praxis. It follows Paulo Freire in striving for a *conscientization* of the masses – a process that invites learners to engage the world and others critically. The recent history of Latin America and South Africa has witnessed priests and laity alongside the downtrodden in solidarity and revolutionary struggle. For instance, in South Africa the black church has embraced the spirit and praxis of liberation theology in an attempt to repossess the symbols of the Gospel "that have been employed by successive rulers in southern Africa to divert the unquestionable right of the oppressed to be free."[35]

Liberation theology has much to offer critical educational theory. It confronts those forces that hold history captive and challenges the reactionary and patriarchal image of a God often championed by the forces of the New Right, a God "whose providence justifies passivity and resignation . . . a God enshrined in devotions and sacraments that lead to semi-fatalism."[36] It is, in effect, an attempt to "break with anything and everything that hinders real and effective solidarity with those who are suffering from a situation of injustice and spoliation."[37]

Liberation theology offers critical educational theory a way of reconceiving hope without falling prey to either cheery optimism or righteous certainty. Invoking a "theology of hope," Rubem A. Alves and Jürgen Moltmann argue that history must not be understood as "immanent process" but rather "as the creation of the word."[38] Hope, in this critical sense, is not created simply out of an act of negation or the language of critique, but out of a utopian conception of the future. This utopian form of hope can be conceived metaphysically as well as historically.

Richard Bernstein decries the "abstract skepticism" of much postmodernist social criticism, which takes aim at metaphysics in its attack on certainty, totality, the reconciliation of differences, and unquestioned ethical-ontological distinctions; Bernstein claims such attacks are based on a caricature of the metaphysical tradition, ignoring its spirit of critique, and especially its "commitment to critical encounter and dialogue, and its openness to what is different and other, a willingness to risk one's prejudgments seeking for common ground without any guarantees that it will be found."[39] Bernstein posits the important notion of "engaged pluralism" against other kinds of pluralism often (rightly) attacked by post-structuralist critics. What he calls "flabby pluralism" involves a simple acceptance of the existence of a variety of perspectives and paradigms, all regarded as virtually incommensurable, and a "decentered anarchistic pluralism" that can "take a despairing or celebratory form" – propelled in both cases by a recognition that we "live in a decentered, polycentric world in which there is no possibility of a unifying interpretation."[40] An engaged pluralism, on the other hand, accepts a lack of convergence of metaphysical speculation, even as it rejects the quest for certainty and absolutes; it does so while embracing a "critical encounter with what is different and other."[41] Such an engaged pluralism recognizes that metaphysical assumptions are always contextually and historically situated and informed by modes of theorizing and interpretation that are themselves structured social and historical practices.

The spirit of such a perspective highlights the major thrust of Ernst Bloch's writings on the theme of utopianism. Writing in the 1930s, Bloch attempted to counter the nineteenth-century perspective that dismissed the concept of utopia because it could not be legitimated through reason and grounded in empirical reality. Bloch's argued that utopia was a form of "cultural surplus" in the world, but not of it: "it contains the spark that reaches out beyond the surrounding emptiness."[42] Bloch struggled to keep alive a redemptive and radically utopian spirit at a time of grave cynicism, when the Enlightenment tradition was being absorbed by the logic of fascism. Yet Bloch refused to abandon the referent of "natural law" in which "the real is never exhausted by the immediacy of the present, but is always infected by possibility."[43]

Bloch, of course, denied the ontological, regional, and psychological claims of the standard critique of utopia and argued that utopian thinking is fundamental to understanding both our humanity and the humanization of the world.[44] As Bloch himself writes, "Utopia extends so far and imparts itself so powerfully to all human activities that every account of man and the world must essentially contain it. *There is no realism, worthy of the name, which abstracts from this strongest element in reality as something which is unfinished.*"[45]

Bloch's position has profound implications for radical educators: it represents the conviction that a Left unable to assert a utopian project consigns itself to political impotence, historical amnesia, and moral inertia. Such has been the case with many of the anti-foundationalist critiques of contemporary cultural and social formations, critiques that are marked by an apolitical aestheticism, polemics of skepticism, fetishism of the sign, and retreat into the Imaginary and into a negative metaphysics, all of which ignore the agony and smother the screams of the oppressed. Bloch reminds us that a utopian project not only uncovers the submerged longings inherent in all ideological distortions, but also attempts to reclaim those longings in ways based on both alternative and oppositional visions. Bloch's utopian project, as we have appropriated it for the construction of a pedagogy of postcolonial cultural politics, speaks to the elimination of forms of oppression and injustice. It demands educators' and students' recognition of the discursive and ideological underpinnings of the hidden curriculum and the manufacture of dreams and the mobilization of desire through the state's bureaucratic formations, institutional practices, and attendant culture industries, and through modes of subjectivity informed by the discourses and social practices of everyday life.

Bloch's work provides a basis for radical educators to consider how social institutions may be understood and developed as part of a wider political and educational struggle. Moreover, his work is instructive for those who perceive the benefit of combining a language of critique with a language of possibility, in an effort to broaden the social and political contexts in which pedagogical activity can function as part of a counterhegemonic strategy.

Whereas Bloch links power to the collective struggle for unrealized emancipatory potential, Michel Foucault links truth with the most fundamental workings of power and knowledge. In doing so, he provides an important conceptualization of the role of the intellectual and of intellectual practice.

In Foucault's terms, truth cannot be viewed as existing outside power. Nor is it product and reward of those intellectuals who have freed themselves from ignorance. On the contrary, truth is part of a political economy of power:

> Truth is a thing of this world: it is produced only by virtue of multiple forms of constraint. And it induces regular effects of power. Each society has its regime of truth, its "general politics" of truth: that is, the types of discourse which

it accepts and makes function as true; the mechanisms and instances which enable one to distinguish true and false statements, the means by which each is sanctioned; the techniques and procedures accorded value in the acquisition of truth; the status of those who are charged with saying what counts as true. . . . It seems to me that what must now be taken into account in the intellectual is not the "bearer of universal values." Rather, it's the person occupying a specific position, but whose specificity is linked, in a society like ours, to the general functioning of an apparatus of truth.[46]

Foucault's analysis of the political economy of truth and his study of how "regimes of truth" are organized and legitimated provides us with a theoretical basis, consonant with Bloch's, from which to develop the concept of pedagogical practice as a form of cultural politics. Teachers as intellectuals must be seen in terms of their social and political function within particular "regimes of truth." That is, they can no longer deceive themselves into believing they are intellectuals serving truth, when in fact they are deeply involved in battles "about the status of truth and the economic and political role it plays."[47]

If intellectual practice is to be tied to creating an alternative and emancipatory politics of truth, it must be grounded in forms of moral and ethical discourse and action that address the suffering and struggles of the oppressed. Such a practice must be attentive to the role of power in generating forms of knowledge that structure and legitimate particular forms of social and cultural life, that resonate with popular desires and everyday needs and that construct particular ways of naming and understanding experience. Following Foucault's important insight, the knowledge/power relation produces dangerous "positive" effects as it creates particular needs, desires, and truths. Here Foucault's analysis can provide educators with the basis for reconstructing a radical social theory that links pedagogy to forms of critique and possibility. By illuminating the productive effects of power, it becomes possible for teachers as intellectuals to develop practices that take seriously how subjectivities are constructed within particular "regimes of truth"; it also highlights the importance of developing a theory of experience as a central aspect of radical pedagogy. This also points to the role that educators can play as bearers of dangerous memory.[48] Educators can serve as transformative intellectuals engaged in the task of excavating historical consciousness and "repressed" knowledge that points to experiences of suffering, conflict, and collective struggle. In this sense, teachers as intellectuals can begin to link the notion of historical understanding to strategies of social critique and transformation.

Finally, the construction of a radical pedagogy as a form of cultural politics means that radical educators need to engage in counterhegemonic struggles, transforming their classrooms into social laboratories where new cultural spaces open up. Such zones of possibility not only destabilize alliances among passivity, helplessness, dependency, and despair, but also invite teachers and students to form partnerships dedicated to reconstructing subjectivity and redirecting the paths of human desire.[49] They must think not in terms of civility, professionalism, and tenure promotions, but must redefine their role within political, economic, and cultural sites where "regimes of truth" are produced, legitimated, and distributed. Within such contexts intellectuals can confront the microphysics of power and work, building oppositional public spheres connected to the production of everyday life and to wider institutional spheres of power.

The utopian project we envision is not an a priori universal scheme for schools and society in general, masterminded by an elite cadre of radical intellectuals. Nor do we suppose that an idealized radical ethics can simply be mapped onto the social order and magically transform it. Rather, such a vision of hope involves constructing a radical public philosophy that rank-and-file teachers and popular alliances can engage critically, appropriate dialectically, and mediate concretely in communities and classrooms. This construction of a provisional morality necessary for emancipatory social change can be accomplished only by understanding both the productive and the debilitating roles that power plays in producing school subject areas and student subjectivities.

The language of possibility constitutes a powerful countervailing discourse set within a praxis-grounded politics of culture, one that eschews the formulation of a grandiose blueprint for change. Such a language of hope mitigates the relativistic implications of a universal curriculum by conceiving critical pedagogy so that fundamental principles and foundational referents of a socialist democracy can ultimately emerge within a praxis of the particular and the specific. Educational theory and historical struggle may be woven together so that just as theory is served and dialectically informed by practice, theory can also place itself at the service of pressing political goals within the public sphere of everyday human struggle. In this way the language of hope and possibility may avoid excessive indebtedness to preestablished standards and self-generating theoretical formulations that exist outside the crucible of concrete human struggle and historical inquiry. Such a language must acknowledge its role in the construction of subjectivity. In so doing, the language of hope must de-authorize and challenge the master narratives of liberal, post-industrial democracy and the humanist, individual, and patriarchal discourses that underwrite it, while at the same time undermining and reconstructing the idealized and romantic conception of the subject, a conception shaped by Eurocentric and androcentric discursive practices. Such language of hope refuses the class subjugation of the proletarian body through its sterile aestheticization by bourgeois categories of the flesh. It also refuses the inscription of patriarchy upon the female body and the enfleshment of masculinist ideologies. Students must be provided with a language of critique and possibility that sets out to challenge and transform the violent repressiveness of modern bureaucracy, the barbarisms spawned by the technologies of androcracy, the systematic consolidation of class hierarchy by ruling elites, the logic of colonialism, and the demonization of racial minorities and the poor.

Finally, we emphasize that critical educators must function as more than mere agents of social critique. They must attempt to fashion a language of hope that points to new forms of social and material relations. Critical discourse then becomes more than a form of cultural dissonance, of deconstructive "double readings," more than a siphoning away of the potency of dominant meanings and social relations; it becomes, rather, part of an ongoing struggle for counterpublic spheres where the language of public association and a commitment to social transformation emerge as concrete social movements for change. Within this perspective, and rooted in a dialectical logic that makes critique and transformation central, creative and critical teaching takes on an anticipatory character of possibility and hope. We support pedagogy whose standards of achievement are determined in relation to the goals of critique and the enhancement of social imagination, pedagogy that links teaching and learning to the goal of educating students to take risks within ongoing relations of power and to envision a world that does not yet exist in order to alter the race-, class-, and gender-constituted grounds upon which life is lived.

Radical hope is always particular and specific. Without it, it becomes difficult to produce the conditions for human struggle and social transformation. Devoid of hope, we wither as social actors and merely echo the faint rustling of histories of resistance. Each act of hope is simultaneously an act of doubt; yet, in the case of radical hope, doubt refuses the totalizing logic that leads to a paralyzing despair. Radical hope – hope forged on the anvil of the particular and the specific – even when woven into the postmodern tapestry of pastiche, irony, and decentered and multiply organized subjectivities, deprivileges the will to cynical power in favor of a will to dream and to act upon such dreams. As postmodern dreamers, it has become our burden as well as our responsibility to transform our despair into compassion and commitment, to challenge our feelings of disorientation and hopelessness with an ethics of risk and refusal. A refusal of the totalizing logic of master narratives and a focus on specificity and particularity that a radical hope offers is not the same thing as rejecting the discourse of totality outright. While there may be a number of public and private spheres from which to wage an oppositional politics, and while a critical post-structuralism offers us the possibility of constructing new articulations of a deeper and more radical and indeterminate democracy,[50] the educational left still needs to profit from a collective vision to which education reform aspires. As Jameson remarks, "Local struggles . . . are effective only so long as they remain figures of allegories for some larger systematic transformation. Politics has to operate on the micro- and the macro-levels simultaneously; a modest restriction to local reforms within the system seems reasonable, but often proves politically demoralizing."[51]

Lipsitz underscores this idea, arguing that while totality can potentially do violence to the specificity of events, a rejection of all totality would likely "obscure real connections, causes, and relationships – atomizing common experience into accidents and endlessly repeated play . . . [and that] only by recognizing the collected legacy of accumulated human actions and ideas can we judge the claims to truth and justice of any one story."[52]

Without a shared vision of democratic community we risk endorsing struggles in which the politics of difference collapses into new forms of separatism. As Steve Best notes, post-structuralists rightly deconstruct essentialist and repressive wholes, yet in so doing they often fail to see how repressive and crippling the valorizing of difference, plurality, fragmentation, and agonistics can be. He writes, "The flip side of the tyranny of the whole is the dictatorship of the fragment . . . [and] . . . without some positive and normative concept of totality to counter-balance the poststructuralist/postmodern emphasis on difference and discontinuity, we are abandoned to the serialily of pluralist individualism and the supremacy of competitive values over communal life."[53] What needs to be abandoned are reductive uses of totality, and not the concept of totality itself. Otherwise we risk undermining the very concept of the democratic public sphere.

To reject the language of possibility as idealistic abstractions or impractical utopian longings is to fail to comprehend it as expressing those elements of a critical praxis that have not yet been realized but that must be dialectically appropriated and grounded in a critical theory of culture and politics of representation. In this context, schooling as a form of cultural politics is not an absolute category, but one that is critically provisional, concretely utopian, and historically and culturally specific. A pedagogy of liberation is one that is necessarily partial and incomplete, one that has no final answers. It is always in the making, part of an ongoing struggle for critical understanding, emancipatory forms of solidarity, and the reconstitution of democratic public life.

Notes

1. See Stanley Aronowitz and Henry A. Giroux, *Education under Siege: The Conservative, Liberal and Radical Debate over Schooling* (South Hadley, Mass.: Bergin and Garvey, 1985), 69–114 for a review and critical analysis of this literature. See also Henry A. Giroux, *Teachers as Intellectuals: Towards a Critical Pedagogy of Learning* (South Hadley, Mass.: Bergin and Garvey, 1988).
2. For a critical treatment of the social reconstructionists, see Henry A. Giroux, *Schooling and the Struggle for Public Life; Critical Pedagogy in the Modern Age* (Minneapolis: University of Minnesota Press, 1988). A version of this discussion of the critical pedagogical tradition appears in Peter McLaren, *Life in School: An Introduction to Critical Pedagogy in the Social Foundations of Education* (New York: Longman, 1989).
3. The relationship between curriculum and the logic and process of commodification and capital accumulation has been emphasized in the writings of Michael W. Apple. See especially *Ideology and Curriculum* (London and Boston: Routledge and Kegan Paul, 1979), *Education and Power* (London and Boston: Routledge and Kegan Paul, 1982), and *Teachers and Texts: A Political Economy of Class and Gender Relations in Education* (London and New York: Routledge and Kegan Paul, 1987).
4. See Henry A. Giroux and Peter McLaren, "Teacher Education and the Politics of Democratic Life: Beyond the Reagan Agenda in the Era of 'Good Times,'" in *Schools as Conduits:*

Educational Policymaking during the Reagan Years, ed. Carol Camp Yeakey and Gladys Styles Johnson (New York: Praeger Press, in press.).

5. See Henry A. Giroux and Peter McLaren, "Teacher Education as a Counterpublic Sphere: Notes towards a Redefinition," in *Critical Studies in Teacher Education: Its Folklore, Theory and Practice*, ed. Thomas S. Popkewitz (New York and London: Falmer Press, 1987), 266–97.

6. See Henry A. Giroux and Peter McLaren, "Teacher Education and the Politics of Engagement: The Case for Democratic Schooling," *Harvard Educational Review* 56. 3 (Aug. 1986): 213–38.

7. See Henry A. Giroux and Peter McLaren, "Critical Pedagogy and Rethinking Teacher Education," *Ontario Public School Teachers Federation News*, 1 Feb. 1986.

8. E. Laclau and C. Mouffe, *Hegemony and Socialist Strategy* (London: Verso Books, 1985), 190.

9. Roger Simon, "Empowerment as a Pedagogy of Possibility," *Language Arts* 64. 4 (Apr. 1987): 370.

10. We have discussed this issue extensively in Giroux and McLaren, "Teacher Education and the Politics of Engagement."

11. Versions of this section appear in Giroux and McLaren, "Teacher Education as a Counterpublic Sphere"; "Teacher Education and the Politics of Democratic Life"; and "Teacher Education as a Counter Sphere: Radical Pedagogy as a Form of Cultural Politics," *Philosophy and Social Criticism* 12. 1 (1987): 51–69.

12. E. Mandel, *Late Capitalism* (London: New Left Books, 1975).

13. See John Brenkman, "Mass Media: From Collective Experience to the Culture of Privatization," *Social Text* 1 (Winter 1979): 94–109. See also Stanley Aronowitz, *The Crisis in Historical Materialism: Class, Politics, and Culture in Marxist Theory* (New York: J.F. Bergin, 1981).

14. A critique of this position can be found in Peter McLaren, *Schooling as a Ritual Performance: Towards a Political Economy of Educational Symbols and Gestures* (London and New York: Routledge and Kegan Paul, 1986).

15. Henry A. Giroux and Roger Simon, "Curriculum Study and Cultural Politics," *Boston University Journal of Education* 166. 3 (1984): 226–38.

16. See Joshua Cohen and Jcel Rogers, *On Democracy: Toward a Transformation of American Society* (New York: Penguin Books, 1983).

17. Richard Johnson, "What Is Cultural Studies Anyway?" *Anglistica* 26. 1–2 (1983): 7–81.

18. Roger Simon, "Work Experience and the Production of Subjectivity," in *Critical Pedagogy and Cultural Power*, ed. David Livingstone (South Hadley, Mass.: Bergin and Garvey, 1986), 176–77.

19. See Iris Marion Young, "The Ideal of Community and the Politics of Difference," *Social Theory and Practice* 12. 1 (Spring 1986): 1–26.

20. Larry Grossberg, "History, Politics and Postmodernism: Stuart Hall and Cultural Studies," *Journal of Communication Inquiry* 10. 2 (Summer 1985): 72.

21. David Lusted, "Why Pedagogy?" *Screen* 27. 5 (Sept.–Oct. 1986): 4–5.

22. Sharon Welch, *A Feminist Ethic of Risk* (New York: Fortress Press, 1990).

23. Michelle Fine, "Silencing and Nurturing Voice in an Improbable Context: Urban Adolescents in Public Schools," in *Critical Pedagogy, the State and Cultural Struggle*, ed. Henry A. Giroux and Peter McLaren (Albany: State University of New York Press, 1990), 152–73.

24. Versions of this section appear in Peter McLaren, "On Ideology and Education: Critical Pedagogy and the Politics of Education," *Social Text* 19/20 (Fall 1988): 153–85; and McLaren, "On Ideology and Education: Critical Pedagogy and the Cultural Politics of Resistance," in *Critical Pedagogy, the State, and Cultural Struggle*, ed. Giroux and McLaren.

25. Grossberg, "History, Politics and Postmodernism," 73.

26. Not all resistance is linked to a politics of emancipation. See Henry A. Giroux, *Theory and Resistance in Education* (South Hadley, Mass.: Bergin and Garvey, 1983); also Peter McLaren, *Schooling as a Ritual Performance* (New York and London: Routledge and Kegan Paul, 1986).

27. On the question of affective investment, see Lawrence Grossberg, "Teaching the Popular," in *Theory in the Classroom*, ed. Cary Nelson (Urbana: University of Illinois Press, 1986), 177–200. See also Lawrence Grossberg, "The In-Difference of Television," *Screen* 28. 2 (Spring 1987): 28–45.

28. Robert Everhart, *Reading Writing and Resistance: Adolescence and Labor in a Junior High School* (London and Boston: Routledge and Kegan Paul, 1983).

29. Ibid.

30. Ibid.

31. Grossberg, "Teaching the Popular," 185.

32. See Daniel P. Liston, *Capitalist Schools: Explanation and Ethics in Radical Studies of Schooling* (New York: Routledge, Chapman and Hall, 1988). Liston's vision of education is driven by a collapse into a dystopian form of scientism. This form of dystopianism represents, in the words of Constance Penley, "the true atrophy of the utopian imagination [in which] we *can* imagine the future but we *cannot* conceive the kind of collective political strategies necessary to change or ensure that future." See Constance Penley, *The Future of an Illusion: Film, Feminism, and Psychoanalysis* (Minneapolis: University of Minnesota Press, 1989), 122.

33. Wayne Hudson has summarized the standard critique of utopian thinking as follows: "The standard critique of utopia rests on the ontological claim that the nature of things is given, on the regional claim that utopia is not grounded in the world at hand, and on the psychological claim that men depart from reality when they dream of perfection beyond the limitations which the reality at hand imposes. It maintains that utopia is not only unrealistic and impractical, but potentially dangerous, since it encourages men to give vent to totalistic, adolescent psychological states, and provides an illusory basis for human action. According to this critique, utopia is a form of unbridled subjectivism which ignores the fact that man cannot reshape the objective world in his own image, make it conform to abstract plans and schemata, or base his practical activities on maximally preferred values. It is *irrational* in its refusal to acknowledge the authority of objective reality, *immature* in its inability to realize the limited nature of the possible, and *irresponsible* in its failure to understand the role of fallibilism in the realization of the good. The standard critique, summed up in the smart phrase 'That's rather utopian,' recognizes that there are different kinds of utopians and that utopianism can adopt a scientific as well as Messianic guise; but it maintains that all utopians err in preferring the fulfillment of ideal representations to the more mundane improvements which are possible in their time" (Hudson, *The Marxist Philosophy of Ernst Bloch* [New York: St. Martin's Press, 1982], 50–51).

34. Harold Wells, "Political Theology in Conflict," *The Ecumenist* 22. 6 (Sept./Oct. 1984): 82. See also the response to Wells by Gregory Baum in the same issue.

35. Charles Villa-Vincencio, "South Africa: A Church within the Church," *Christianity and Crisis*, 9 Jan. 1989, 463.

36. Juan Luis Segundo, *Our Idea of God* (Dublin: Gill and Macmillan, 1980), 18.

37. Gustavo Gutiérrez, "Liberation Praxis and Christian Faith," in *Frontiers of Theology in Latin America*, ed. Rosino Gibellini (Maryknoll, N.Y.: Orbis Press, 1983), 9.

38. Rubem A. Alves, *A Theology of Human Hope* (St. Meinrad, Ind.: Abbey Press, 1975), 57.

39. Richard J. Bernstein, "Metaphysics, Critique, and Utopia," *Review of Metaphysics* 42. 2, issue no. 165 (Dec. 1988): 271. See also Leszek Kolakowski, "The Death of Utopia Reconsidered," *The Tanner Lectures on Human Values* (Salt Lake City: University of Utah Press, 1982), and Peter McLaren, "Review of Clodovis Boff's *Theology and Praxis: Epistemological Foundations*," *Small Press* 5. 4 (Apr. 1988): 64–65. See Peter McLaren